Rape and Representation

GENDER AND CULTURE
Carolyn G. Heilbrun and Nancy K. Miller, EDITORS

Edgar Degas, Interior (The Rape). Philadelphia Museum of Art: The Henry P. McIlhenny Collection in memory of Frances P. McIlhenny.

RAPE AND
REPRESENTATION

Edited by

LYNN A. HIGGINS

and

BRENDA R. SILVER

COLUMBIA UNIVERSITY PRESS   NEW YORK

Columbia University Press
New York   Oxford
Copyright © 1991 Columbia University Press
All rights reserved

The following essays have appeared in whole or in part elsewhere and are re-printed with the permission of the original publishers:

John J. Winkler, "The Education of Chloe: Erotic Protocols and Prior Violence": copyright © 1990, Routledge, Chapman and Hall, Inc. *Originally published as "The Education of Chloe: Hidden Injuries of Sex" in* The Constraints of Desire: The Anthropology of Sex and Gender in Ancient Greece *(Routledge: New York and London, 1990), pp. 101–126.*

Patricia Kliendienst Joplin, "The Voice of the Shuttle is Ours." Originally published in Stanford Literary Review *(1984) 1.1:25–53.*

Brenda R. Silver, "Periphrasis, Power, and Rape in A Passage to India*": copyright* NOVEL Corp. © 1989. *Originally published in* Novel: A Forum on Fiction *(Fall 1988), vol. 22, no. 1.*

"Ode on a Grecian Urn" reprinted by permission of the publishers from The Poems of John Keats, *edited by Jack Stillinger, Cambridge: The Belknap Press of Harvard University Press, copyright © 1978 by the President and Fellows of Harvard University.*

Library of Congress Cataloging-in-Publication Data

Rape and representation / edited by Lynn A. Higgins and Brenda R.
  Silver.
    p.   cm. — (Gender and Culture)
  Includes index.
  ISBN 0–231–07266–X
  1. Rape in literature.   2. Women in literature.   3. Women and
literature.   4. Sex in literature.   5. Sex crimes.   6. Rape.
I. Higgins, Lynn A.   II. Silver, Brenda R., 1942–   . III. Series.
PN56.R24R37   1991
809'.93355—dc20   90–19351
                                                CIP

Casebound editions of Columbia University Press books are Smyth-sewn
and printed on permanent and durable acid-free paper

Printed in the United States of America

c 10 9 8 7 6 5 4 3 2 1

CONTENTS

3. WRITING THE VICTIM

4. FRAMING INSTITUTIONS

5. UNTHINKING THE METAPHOR

ACKNOWLEDGMENTS

All books are collaborative: a collective effort of authors, editors, evaluators, production and marketing staffs, colleagues, secretaries, and families. Feminist anthologies (which have by now become a genre of their own) have transformed this implicit collectivity into a self-consciously dialogic mode of thinking and work. We want therefore and above all to acknowledge the crucial role each contributor played in the production of this volume, not only through their individual essays, but also by engaging us in debate about them in ways that enriched the complexity of our joint project.

In addition, we wish to thank the following:

Nancy J. Vickers organized, with Brenda Silver, the 1984 MLA panel on "Silence and the Rhetoric of Rape" that became the impetus for this work.

Nancy K. Miller (the moderator of the original panel) and Carolyn G. Heilbrun—the editors of this series on Gender and Culture—not only encouraged us to undertake the transition from papers to book but continued to encourage us throughout the process of collection and revision. Their astute comments on the various versions of the manuscript provided invaluable guidance and perspective.

Christina Crosby and the Women's Studies Program at Wesleyan University offered us an ideal audience for thinking about our introduction by inviting us to speak during Rape Awareness Week, 1988.

Jennifer Crewe, Executive Editor at Columbia University Press, gave generous assistance and exemplary commitment that more than once kept us from abandoning the project. As Managing Editor, Joan McQuary patiently and lightheartedly steered the manuscript through the labyrinth of production.

The two (anonymous) readers asked pertinent questions and supplied detailed criticism that helped us shape both the volume as a whole and our introduction. We hope they recognize their impact and accept our thanks.

Dartmouth College, through its research funds, has made possible the endless photocopying and the research assistance associated with such a project.

Our respective families—Roland Higgins, Julian Higgins, and Paul Tobias—volunteered just enough scepticism (about whether the book would ever be done) as well as unmeasurable comic and human relief.

We want to offer special tribute to one particular contributor: John J. (Jack) Winkler, whose death during the final stages of work on the volume was an enormous loss to the entire academic and feminist community. As his colleagues David M. Halperin and Susan A. Stephens have written, "his work revolutionized several fields of classical studies and promoted a variety of feminist, anthropological, narratological, and theoretical approaches to the study of Greek and Latin texts" ("In Memoriam," *APA Newsletter*, June 1990). It also serves as a model for revisionary rereading useful to scholars in all fields of cultural studies. We are proud to include his essay in this collection, and we will miss him.

Finally, with full understanding of the complexities of metaphor not only in discussions of rape but in feminist thought in general, we wish to dedicate this book to our sisters: our literal sisters, Janice L. Anthony, Lois Keates, and Carol Starrels, and then to all those women who share, unfortunately, a form of sisterhood in sharing the threat and reality of rape, with the hope that this book may play a role in the struggle to ensure that one day we will no longer live in a rape culture.

Rape and Representation

Introduction: Rereading Rape

LYNN A. HIGGINS AND
BRENDA R. SILVER

"What does it matter who is speaking?" For feminist literary critics confronting the entanglement of rape with representation, Beckett's question, so central to debates about the status of the subject in Western (post)modernism, demands the answer: who is speaking may be *all* that matters. Whether in the courts or the media, whether in art or criticism, who gets to tell the story and whose story counts as "truth" determine the definition of what rape *is*. Focusing on the tales told (or not told) by voices within texts, by authors, and by critics, the contributors to this collection chart the complex intersections of rape and representation, revealing their inseparability from questions of subjectivity, authority, meaning, power, and voice. The added recognition that the term *representation* cuts across boundaries of juridical, diplomatic, political, and literary discourses sustains the assumption underlying this book: that the politics and aesthetics of rape are one.

The urgency of this project derives from the fact that rape and the threat of rape are a major force in the subjugation of women. In "rape cultures" such as the United States, the danger, the frequency, and the acceptance of sexual violence all contribute to shaping behavior and identity, in women and men alike. Within this culture, as in others, the nature and degree of oppression will vary with the historical moment and, within that, the permutations of racial, class, gender, and institutional relations of power. Nevertheless, in this volume, analyses of specific texts, when read through and against each other, illustrate a number of profoundly disturbing patterns. Not the least of these is an obsessive inscription—and an obsessive erasure—of sexual violence against women (and against those placed by society in the position of "woman"). The striking repetition of inscription and erasure raises the question not only of why this trope recurs, but even more, of what it means and who benefits. How is it that in spite (or perhaps because) of their erasure, rape and sexual violence have been so ingrained and so rationalized through their representations as to appear "natural" and inevitable, to women as to men? Feminist modes of "reading" rape and its cultural inscriptions help identify and demystify the multiple manifestations, displacements, and transformations of what amounts to an insidious cultural myth. In the process, they show how feminist critique can challenge the representations that continue to hurt women both in the courts and on the streets.

One of the feminist strategies evident in this collection is to show how art and criticism share the well-documented bias of rape law, where representations of rape after the event are almost always framed by a masculine perspective premised on men's fantasies about female sexuality and their fears of false accusation, as well as their codified access to and possession of women's bodies. Even after recent reforms meant to correct this bias, women, particularly in cases where they know their assailants, are still often put on trial and still carry the burden of proving their innocence (e.g., by demonstrating their "resistance"; men's intentions and sexual history are usually not part of the record). Whether in legal or literary criticism, unmasking the privilege accorded masculine points of view reveals how patriarchal perspectives have prevented courts as well as texts, authors, and critics from asking who is speaking, who is hearing, and in what circumstances. In the courts, the split reality that often characterizes rape cases—the recognition that such cases may well involve an event experienced as rape by the woman but not perceived as rape by the man—falls prey to the need to have a single "truth." The question then becomes how undecidability, at least in the courts, may lead to the disappearance of rape from the social text. What remains is a conspicuous absence: a configuration where sexual violence against women is an origin of social relations and narratives in which the event itself is subsequently elided.

Over and over in the texts explored here, rape exists as an absence or gap that is both product and source of textual anxiety, contradiction, or censorship. The simultaneous presence and disappearance of rape as constantly deferred origin of both plot and social relations is repeated so often as to suggest a basic conceptual principle in the articulation of both social and artistic representations. Even when the rape does not disappear, the naturalization of patriarchal thinking, institutions, and plots has profound effects: just as victims of rape often end up blaming themselves, the texts explored below present women telling stories that echo or ventriloquize definitions of rape that obliterate what might have been radically different perceptions. The prevalence of masculine perspectives in stories told by women leads Coppélia Kahn, in her essay, to ask "who or what speaks in the character we call Lucrece?" and us to ask where, or how, critics can hear and validate another subjectivity and voice.

The stakes involved in finding answers to these questions are high: for literary and artistic representations not only depict (or fail to depict) instances of rape after or as if they have occurred; they also contribute to the social positioning of women and men and shape the cognitive systems that make rape thinkable. The essays suggest that rape and rapability are central to the very construction of gender identity and that our subjectivity and sense of ourselves as sexual beings are inextricably enmeshed in representations. Viewed from this angle, rape exists as a context independent of its occurrence as discrete event.

The process of unraveling the cultural texts that have obsessively made rape both so pervasive and so invisible a theme—made it "unreadable"—is multilayered. It involves listening not only to who speaks and in what circumstances, but who does *not* speak and why. It requires that we listen for those stories that differ from the master('s) story; that we recuperate what has too often been left out: the physical violation and the women who find ways to speak it. It also means reassessing the master('s) story itself for what it reveals about the construction of masculinity. When viewed through a feminist lens, even (or especially) the most canonical of texts—and their canonical interpretations—can, as Susan Winnett points out below, "divulge cultural secrets."

In the process of rereading rape, one crucial step taken by feminist literary critics, like feminist legal scholars, has been to trace the ways in which women (artists or characters) "represent" themselves, whether in law, in political systems, in speech. This entails discerning where or how they break through the discourses that have circumscribed their perceptions of the causes and nature of sexual violation and contributed to what amounts to a cultural cover-up. (The insistence that "no" means "no" and not a modest feminine "yes" provides one clear example.) Here the question of who speaks and who does not leads in a different direction. Where, textually, can we find these breakthroughs and begin to locate another point of view? What are the rhetorical strategies whereby rape gets represented in spite of (or through) its suppression? Equally important, what happens to women who go public about their violation? If they escape the dominant fate of silencing and erasure, what price do they pay? Will their speech, their protest, be reinscribed in the patriarchal economy as figures of a female violence even worse than that perpetrated against them?

But the act of rereading rape involves more than listening to silences; it requires restoring rape to the literal, to the body: restoring, that is, the violence—the physical, sexual violation. The insistence on taking rape literally often necessitates a conscious critical act of reading the violence and the sexuality back into texts where it has been deflected, either by the text itself or by the critics: where it has been turned into a metaphor or a symbol or represented rhetorically as titillation, persuasion, ravishment, seduction, or desire (poetic, narrative, courtly, military). Here, the recurrent motif of disfiguration becomes significant: disfiguration both in its rhetorical and physical senses (and ways in which the first hides the second), as both textual and corporeal deformation or mutilation. In reading the violence back into texts, then, the essays in this collection reclaim the physical, material bodies of women from their status as "figures" and reveal the ways in which violence marks the female subject both physically and psychologically.

Where, if anywhere, do literary texts offer possibilities of resistance? Is there, as Carla Freccero asks below, a "feminine difference" in texts about rape authored by women, and if so, where and how is it inscribed? Do women who write of rape—and until recently, especially among white women in the Anglo-American tradition, these have been few in number—find a way out of the representational double binds confronting those women who attempt to escape their entrapment in the patriarchal story? Do women of color within the United States or "third world" women, who have addressed the taboo subject more often and more openly, offer subversive perspectives? It is also necessary to recognize the disturbing fault lines that appear within men's texts and to ask what role male authors play in uncovering the structures that brutalize women's bodies and erase their subjectivity. Do these texts reveal traces of masculine sexual anxiety or guilt? And are even male authors who recognize their complicity in the violence of the gender system ultimately caught in its powerful meshes?

Each of the five sections in this book foregrounds a different aspect of the challenge collectively posed by these questions. The two essays in part 1, Prior Violence, highlight ways in which some of the earliest stories in the Western tradition have established precedents and left legacies that continue to animate our cultural (self-) representations. More important, both set out to confront the naturalization of "prior" erotic violence and rape in these founding tales: to reveal them as myths that simultaneously articulate and hide the socially constructed story of male and female sexuality, difference, and power that makes women "essentially" vulnerable and mute. The obsessive narrative that recurs in the volume as a whole begins with the glimpse, provided by John Winkler, of the layers of cultural work enacted by forms such as song, dance, games, and poetry in obscuring the violence they nonetheless transmit. Patricia Joplin's essay, which helped launch this entire field of inquiry, urges critics to reclaim both the hidden cultural plot and the women who tell it. The violation Joplin exposes is not just the double violation of Philomela—her rape by her brother-in-law, who then cuts out her tongue—but the subsequent appropriation of her story and her art by writers, anthropologists, and literary critics alike.

But the paradigm of rape and silencing presented in these two essays also contains the seeds of its own undoing, for the "prior violence," continually reiterated and erased, is neither lost nor left behind. Instead, it remains variously as a stain or bruise, as a gap or absence, a failed attempt at repression that ensures the violence will return. That trace or sign of imperfect erasure can have many meanings, however, and in the tension between attempt and failure to reveal violation, the story that often gets told is that of an inability to tell the story.

The essays in part 2, The Rhetoric of Elision, focus on how rape can be read in its absence. The texts here are among the most widely read white male fictions of rape—*The Marquise of O, Tess of the d'Urbervilles,* and *A Passage to India*—and the essays (by Susan Winnett, Ellen Rooney, and Brenda Silver) foreground the most striking recurrent motif in the collection: the elision of the scene of violence in male texts about rape that, ironically, both emphasizes the origins of the violence and suggests the possibility of making it visible again. In addition, these texts reveal, however unconsciously, the ambivalence of the male author caught up in representations of masculinity and subjectivity that he may question, but that he ultimately leaves in place—except for the subversive presence of the O, the gap, that for the critics, if not for the authors, provides a space to speak of women's violation and subjectivity. The term *elision* in the title of this section, deriving from the Latin *laedere*, to hurt or damage, and relating to *lesion*, suggests once again the secret ways in which representation is linked to the physical, and damaged stories can represent damaged bodies.

What, then, becomes of the woman's story? The essays in part 3, Writing the Victim—to borrow a phrase from Marta Peixoto's essay —focus more explicitly on the ways in which literary or critical strategies contribute to the social and narrative acts of victimization they wish to expose. In Coppélia Kahn's essay on Shakespeare's *Lucrece*, the complicity belongs to the author, whose embodiment of one of Western culture's urtexts of rape firmly reinstates its tormented victim within the patriarchal tale. In Eileen Julien's essay, the critic's own response to sexual violence in two postcolonial West African novels, Yambo Ouologuem's *Le Devoir de violence* and Soni Labou Tansi's *La Vie et demie*, allows her to differentiate between radically different representations of rape as it is connected to the power of the state. In Peixoto's essay on Clarice Lispector, we are presented with an author, a woman, who writes the issue of complicity into her text, allowing no distance between author, narrator, and reader: all are implicated in different ways. Nevertheless, Peixoto also notes that Lispector "refuses to naturalize the oppression of one class or gender or race by another or, for that matter, to see human life in heroic terms," leading us to ask whether this refusal is an example of a "feminine difference" and whether it suggests a high level of racial and class self-consciousness in Brazilian society.

Part 4, Framing Institutions, shifts the emphasis from writing the victim to the institutional discourses in which rape occurs. Medieval legal codes and juridical practice (Kathryn Gravdal); Renaissance political structures and the heroic ethos of courtly love (Carla Freccero); slavery and its legacy—racism—including their enactment in lynching (Nellie McKay): each of these discourses provides a context for reading literary representations of rape, and each one is shown to "frame" the rape victim by rationalizing violence against women and other oppressed groups as necessary to the patriarchal status quo. The shared concerns of these essays clarify the intersecting political and aesthetic meanings of "representation." Not surprisingly, what is at issue once again is who has the power to represent whom, in institutions as in texts, and the problematic position of those groups that are excluded from representation. One of the controlling institutions confronted in these essays is "history," particularly as it appears in literary interpretation: all three challenge not only accepted understandings of rape in past centuries, but the limited definitions used by historians for what constitutes rape and where its representations can be found. Equally notable, all three essays suggest how literature resembles other discourses in its figuring and disfiguring strategies of rape, illustrating how literature itself is one of the "framing" institutions.

In the concluding section of the volume, part 5, Unthinking the Metaphor, the discourses held up to scrutiny are aesthetic categories themselves. If in the previous section gender oppression was inseparable from other forms of oppression and was inherently political, in this section, as Froma Zeitlin notes, it is "poetics and the politics of gender [that] cannot be dissociated." For Nancy Jones and Zeitlin, the conventions at issue are no less than the Western lyric tradition and the quest for beauty, truth, and knowledge associated with the "Grecian spirit" in Western philosophy and art. For Lynn Higgins, the seductively multiple narratives and interpretive strategies of postmodernism become yet another formal way of mystifying rape by transforming it into another story. "Unthinking the metaphor" that naturalizes and elides rape—the act that Winkler, in the opening essay, argues might provide the premise of a different story— becomes here the unraveling of the dynamics, the mechanisms, by which aesthetic conventions and critical traditions continue to inscribe and displace rape as a founding event of art.

The juxtaposition, in the last two sections, of social and literary institutions suggests the dual movement at work in almost all the essays in the volume: outward to an analysis of contexts—historical, theoretical—and back to a close reading that brings social and textual/critical practices together. Anything less would leave in place the boundaries between art and politics, theory and practice, representation and power that this project intends to unsettle. Recognizing as well that feminist modes of demystification must include the critical act itself, the scholars here write into their texts the problem of who speaks, the positioning of their own subjectivity between academic privilege and the violent, embodied reality of rape. This often means writing against the fear and pain that surround the topic; it also means acknowledging the anger. By actively confronting rape at the level of literary texts these essays become a force for resistance and change.

BIBLIOGRAPHIC NOTE

The references in this note correspond to the topics addressed in the Introduction. We have included those works we found particularly helpful in conceptualizing our own project, rather than attempting to list all the sociological and literary studies that have appeared since the speak-outs on rape in the late 1960s and Susan Brownmiller's influential manifesto, *Against Our Will: Men, Women and Rape* (New York: Simon & Schuster, 1975).

Beckett's question appears in *Texts for Nothing*, trans. Beckett (London: Calder & Boyers, 1974), p. 16. It "supplies a direction" for Michel Foucault's "What is an Author?" in Josué V. Harari, ed., *Textual Strategies: Perspectives in Post-Structuralist Criticism*, pp. 141–160 (Ithaca: Cornell University Press, 1979), and it echoes in Roland Barthes' desire to keep the question "Who is speaking?" from ever being answered: *S/Z* (New York: Hill and Wang, 1974), p. 140. Andreas Huyssen evokes the question in his critique of the poststructuralist call for "the death of the subject," positing instead the development of "alternative and different notions of subjectivity" that would challenge "the *ideology of the subject* (as male, white, and middle-class)": "Mapping the Postmodern," *After the Great Divide: Modernism, Mass Culture, Postmodernism* (Bloomington and Indianapolis: Indiana University Press, 1986), pp. 212–213. Nancy K. Miller directly addresses the problematic nature of "the death of the (speaking/writing) subject" for women/women writers in "Arachnologies: The Woman, the Text, and the Critic" and "Changing the Subject: Authorship, Writing, and the Reader" in *Subject to Change: Reading Feminist Writing* (New York: Columbia University Press, 1988); and Alice Jardine's "concern with women as speaking and writing subjects" became the basis for her theory of gynesis, "the putting into discourse of 'woman' ": *Gynesis: Configurations of Woman and Modernity* (Ithaca and London: Cornell University Press, 1985). Beckett's question is also implicit in the wide-ranging discussion of the status of the colonial and postcolonial subject signified by the phrase "can the subaltern speak?"; see Gayatri Chakravorty Spivak's essay with that title in Cary Nelson and Lawrence Grossberg, eds., *Marxism and the Interpretation of Culture*, pp. 271–313 (Urbana: University of Illinois Press, 1988).

Our need to raise this question yet again signifies its only too material ramifications for women who attempt to voice their experience of rape, whether in the police station, the courtroom, the novel, or the critical essay. Who is speaking has a great deal to do with whether or not the victim, most commonly but not always a woman, is believed and whether a case will be made against the assailant. The nature of the "who" evoked here includes more than gender: race, class, the sexual history of the victim, the relationship of the victim to the perpetrator (e.g., whether he was a stranger or an acquaintance), all play a role in whether a "rape" is perceived to have occurred.

On the legal definitions of rape ("what rape *is*") and their implications for the victim, see Susan Estrich, *Real Rape* (Cambridge: Harvard University Press, 1987); Catharine A. MacKinnon, "Feminism, Marxism and the State: Toward Feminist Jurisprudence," *Signs: Journal of Women in Culture and Society* (1983), 8:635–658; Carol Smart, *Feminism and the Power of Law* (London and New York: Routledge, 1989); Monique Plaza, "Our Damages and Their Compensation. Rape: The Will Not to Know of Michel Foucault," *Feminist Issues* (1981), 1(3):23–35. Frances Ferguson links contradictory legal definitions of rape to questions of truth, fiction, and literary forms in "Rape and the Rise of the Novel," *Representations* (1987), 20: 88–112. Eve Kosofsky Sedgwick, using *Gone with the Wind* as her example, explores how "rape" means or signifies different things when brought into contact with the racial discourse of the South: *Between Men: English Literature and Male Homosocial Desire* (New York: Columbia University Press, 1985), pp. 9–10.

Two works that address the intersections of representation with other forms of violence are Teresa de Lauretis, "The Violence of Rhetoric: Considerations on Representation and Gender," *Technologies and Gender: Essays on Theory, Film, and Fiction* (Bloomington and Indianapolis: Indiana University Press, 1987), pp. 31–50; and Susanne Kappeler, *The Pornography of Representation* (Minneapolis: University of Minnesota Press, 1986).

De Lauretis' essay has subsequently been reprinted in a work that came to our attention after our own was completed: *The Violence of Representation: Literature and the History of Violence,* Nancy Armstrong and Leonard Tennenhouse, eds. (New York: Routledge, 1989). Sharing our assumption that politics and poetics are inseparable, it focuses on "the development of sophisticated technologies of the individual and its Others" that, along with imperialism, "have turned the violence of representation into [a] ubiquitious form of power" (p. 9) in the West.

For a theoretical discussion of the rape culture in the United States, see Dianne Herman, "The Rape Culture," in Jo Freeman, ed., *Women: A Feminist Perspective* (Palo Alto, Calif.: Mayfield, 1984). Timothy Beneke explores contemporary American men's attitudes toward rape and the cultural factors, including language, that shape them: *Men on Rape: What They Have to Say about Sexual Violence* (New York: St. Martin's Press, 1982). Anthropologist Peggy Reeves Sanday analyzes the idea of a "rape-prone" culture in two cross-cultural studies: "The Socio-Cultural Context of Rape," *Journal of Social Issues* (1981), 37:5–27; and "Rape and the Silencing of the Feminine," in Sylvana Tomaselli and Roy Porter, eds., *Rape,* pp. 84–101 (Oxford: Basil Blackwell, 1986). Hazel Carby emphasizes the importance of understanding rape in its specific historical context when she writes: "Rape itself should not be regarded as a transhistorical mechanism of women's oppression but as one that acquires specific political or economic meanings at different moments in history": *Reconstructing Womanhood: The Emergence of the Afro-American Woman Novelist* (New York, Oxford: Oxford University Press, 1987), p. 18.

For a multidisciplinary "reading" of rape, see Tomaselli and Porter, *Rape.* Tomaselli argues in her introduction that it would be a mistake to dismiss any of the various discourses that claim to define rape, for "each usage of the term seems to capture some relevant aspect of the problem even if none encompasses them all" (p. 10). The question of the violence done to "a woman reader of a literary tradition that inscribes violence against women" and woman writers' responses to it animates Christine Froula's "The Daughter's Seduction: Sexual Violence and Literary History," *Signs: Journal of Women in Culture and Society* (1986), 11:621–644. The importance of conflicting perspectives and "whose meaning wins" for both rape victims and literary critics reading rape informs Tania Modleski's "Rape versus Mans/laughter: *Blackmail*," in *The Women Who Knew Too Much: Hitchcock and Feminist Theory* (New York: Methuen, 1988). For an example of the stakes involved in feminist readings of rape, and the resistance to it, see Terry Castle's *Clarissa's Ciphers: Meaning and Disruption in Richardson's "Clarissa"* (Ithaca: Cornell University Press, 1982), in particular the "Bibliographic Postscript," and William Beatty Warner's response, "Reading Rape: Marxist-Feminist Figurations of the Literal," *Diacritics* (1983): 13–32.

On the bias of rape law and the recent reforms, see Estrich, *Real Rape.* On the concept of a split reality and the legal need for a single truth, see MacKinnon, "Feminism Marxism and the State," pp. 651–655. Both Estrich and MacKinnon ask what would happen if sexuality, violence, and rape were defined from women's perspectives; see also MacKinnon's *Feminism Unmodified: Discourses on Life and Law* (Cambridge: Harvard University Press, 1987), in particular, "A Rally Against Rape" and "Sex and Violence: A Perspective."

For "subversive perspectives" on rape in Afro-American literature, see Missy Dehn Kubitschek, "Subjugated Knowledge: Toward a Feminist Exploration of Rape in Afro-American Fiction," in Joe Weixlmann and Houston A. Baker, Jr., eds., *Studies in Black American Literature*, 3:43–56. (Greenwood, Florida: Penkevill, 1988). Three of the works explored in our collection— Hardy's *Tess of the D'Urbervilles,* Forster's *Passage to India,* and Shakespeare's *Rape of Lucrece*—are cited by Kubitschek as paradigmatic examples of the generally "oblique and symbolic" treatment, or "displacement," of rape in Euro-American literature by white men. In contrast to this tradition, Kubitschek argues, the depiction of rape in texts by African-American writers is more explicit and more realistic, including offering options for the victims other than madness or death. Deborah E. McDowell makes a similar point about works on slavery written by black women: "Negotiating between Tenses: Witnessing Slavery after Freedom—*Dessa Rose*," in McDowell and Arnold Rampersad, eds., *Slavery and the Literary Imagination*, p. 146 (Baltimore and London: Johns Hopkins University Press, 1989).

On the recurrence of rape scenes in contemporary Chicana literature and their statement about the "engendering" of Mexican-American women, see Maria Herrera-Sobek, "The Politics of Rape: Sexual Transgression in Chicana Fiction," *Americas Review* (1987), 15:171–181.

On "reading the violence back into texts" and on the connections between physical violation and language (or silence), see Elaine Scarry, *The Body in Pain: The Making and Unmaking of the World* (New York: Oxford University Press, 1985).

1
PRIOR VIOLENCE

1

The Education of Chloe: Erotic Protocols and Prior Violence

JOHN J. WINKLER

The Egyptian pharaoh Psammetichos (as Herodotos tells the tale, *Histories* 2.2) wanted to confirm the common opinion, at least among Egyptians, that they were the oldest people on the face of the earth. Historical records not being available, he devised the following test: He placed two newborn babies, chosen at random, in the care of a shepherd with instructions to keep them isolated in a remote hut and see to it that they heard no human speech at all. They were to be fed directly from nanny goats, perhaps because a wet nurse could not be trusted not to croon to them in her arms. The purpose was to determine what articulate and identifiable words babies so raised would first utter. After two years of this nurturance, if that is the word for it, the shepherd entered the hut one day and both infants reached out their little hands and said, "Bekos." Since, upon inquiry, it was learned that this is the Phrygian word for "bread," Psammetichos announced that the Phrygians must be the oldest people in the world; he remained confident without further testing that the Egyptians still held at least second place.

It is customary to think of Longus' *Pastorals of Daphnis and*

Chloe as a pastoral romance, a sport among the several dozen an-cient novels,[1] both the first of its kind and the last until Boccaccio's *Ameto* (1341) and the spate of sixteenth-century imitations. But the practice of reading backward in literary history, from later works in a tradition to earlier ones, can produce a dyslexic perception of the distinctive characteristics of the earlier ones, not written to be the founding instances of a "tradition."[2] In Longus' case what is often missed is that Daphnis and Chloe, the two exposed infants who grow up on the island of Lesbos to be suspiciously handsome teen-agers ("a beauty more than rustic," 1.7),[3] are not raised from child-hood as goatherd and shepherdess. On the contrary, their foster parents, who are subsistence farmers of slave status, have given them an education and a nurturance above the usual level of peasant life, banking on the foundlings' beauty and expensive recognition tokens. If Dryas and Lamon had their way, the children would serve as an economic step up for their households, either through their intrinsic value in the bartering process of arranged marriages or (less likely) through a reunion with their natural, and evidently wealthy, parents.[4]

Erôs has other ideas. He appears simultaneously to the two fathers in a dream and directs them to send Daphnis and Chloe, now fifteen and thirteen years old respectively,[5] out into the fields to tend the goats and sheep.

> On seeing this dream they were upset at the prospect that their children would be shepherds and goatherds, for their swaddling clothes and tokens had given hopes of a better lot. For that reason they had been rearing them with more delicate food and care, and had been teaching them letters and providing them with every good thing that was available in a rural environ-ment. But they decided that they had to obey the gods. . . , so they sent them out as pastors with the herds and taught them the routine—how to graze their flocks before noon and to rest them when the heat was oppressive, when to lead them to water and when back to sleep, in which cases to use the crook and in which the voice alone. (1.8)

This unexpected event decisively shapes the plot by reshaping the paternal intentions.[6] The playful and powerful godlet Erôs is in effect conducting a pastoral experiment. What will happen when two ado-lescents are set apart from the enculturating influences not only of city society in Mitylene but of the ambitious foster parents who want to rear them to a higher station than that of rural peasantry?

Their education in letters cut short, what will they learn in the open fields?

The short, abstract answer is that Erôs' experiment will display in turn the relative contributions of nature, culture, and happenstance to the erotic education of two attractive teenagers. Some readers dwell on the charm of *D&C*,[7] others on its rustic comedy[8] or its "aesthetic cogency of plot and symbol"[9] or its place in the bucolic tradition.[10] Calling it a pastoral experiment is my attempt to do justice both to its artifice and to what I perceive as its serious intellectual play with social reality. Longus and Erôs, designing authors both, have fashioned episodes as theorems to test (as it were) the interplay of instinct and learning, of nature and convention.[11] At some points they seem to suggest the possibility that without certain forms of schooling human beings might not succeed in being sexually active at all but would sit in helpless frustration like Daphnis at 3.14. After lying with Chloe in a naked embrace and then vainly imitating the sheep's position for copulation, "Daphnis sat down and cried to think that he was more ignorant [literally, more uninstructed, *amathesteros*] than the rams in the works of *erôs* [desire]."

D&C is not about the natural growth of erotic instinct but about the inadequacy of instinct to realize itself and about the many kinds of knowledge, education, and training required both to formulate the very meaning of spontaneous feelings and then to act on them.[12] Longus' tentative and exploratory fiction is, we might say, more about culture than about nature, and at times it seems to lead us in the direction of the thesis that sex itself is in no recoverable sense a natural fact but is through and through, on every conscious and preconscious level, a socially constructed reality. Insofar as that is true, we must wonder why the mythos of Chloe is a tale specifically of rape repeatedly escaped and yet continually and disturbingly resurfacing.[13]

My central topic here will be the inherent violence of the cultural system discovered by Daphnis and Chloe and the unequal impact of that violence. As will appear below, the novel contains a serious and repeated inspection of the forms of rape to which Chloe—and to a certain extent Daphnis—is subject and also a determined but ultimately unsuccessful effort to distinguish Daphnis as "good" suitor from the bad rapist-suitors. The sweetness of its overall tone cannot hide, perhaps does not try to, the pain of the experience. In some ways I would compare it to the experience of noticing a bruise on one's body and not being able to recall the moment of actual injury. (This happens to me a lot.) There may be good reasons to explain how one can discover an *already inflicted wound:* sometimes the shock of a collision focuses us on the persons or objects involved rather than on the actual physical pain, particularly in minor scrapes and embarrassing bumps. But the notion that female sexuality is constituted as a kind of vulnerability is more troubling by a quantum leap. The notion itself, discovered in the course of Chloe's education (which is conducted largely in terms of Daphnis' more explicit education, Chloe remaining a problematically mute pupil), feels like a deep, discolored bruise whose moment and manner of infliction have been erased. Longus' controlled experiment, placing the youngsters in an artificially "natural" environment, inevitably suggests the question, Was there a time before the wound was inflicted, either in the individual's consciousness or in the history of our culture? The present consciousness of the bruise or identity wound seems somehow to contain a memory or retrojected image of prior wholeness, for the concept is made to seem fundamentally arbitrary and the wound itself almost a metaphor that might be unthought, like a bruise that turns out to be an ink spot and the pain a psychosomatic reaction to the *thought* of a bruise.

Allusion, Ellipsis, and Displaced Authority

Before analyzing the recurring shadow of rape in Chloe's education, the larger issues of interpreting this allusive and elliptical fiction and its relation to social ideology must be briefly addressed. Second Sophistic is the (to us, rather misleading) name assigned by its first historian, Philostratos, to that brilliant period of Hellenic literary renaissance under the Roman empire, centering on the second century c.e.[14] Its stellar figures—Lucian, Herodes Atticus, Pausanias, Achilles Tatius, and many others—employed various styles and produced literary projects of great originality, but all acknowledged the authority of a by then classicized tradition of Greek letters.[15] For instance, when Daphnis, after being granted Chloe's hand in marriage, climbs up an almost bare fruit tree to pick the single apple remaining "highest on its high branches" (3.33) and gives it to Chloe, he is enacting a simile found in a three-line fragment of a wedding song by Sappho (fr. 105a Lobel-Page): "like the sweetapple ripening to red on the topmost branch, / on the very tip of the topmost branch, and the apple-pickers have overlooked it—/ no, they haven't overlooked it but they could not reach it." It is as if Longus' characters, living as they do on the island of Lesbos, now and again come across the same scenes that Sappho saw. The location (Lesbos), the occasion (hymeneal), and the language *(akrois akrotaton/akron ep' akrotatôi)* make the allusion certain, though the loss of Sappho's context makes it difficult to assess the tenor of the allusion.[16] It is not farfetched to maintain that if we had more than our meager extant flotsam of earlier Greek literature concerning the socialization of *erôs*, especially lyric poetry and New Comedy, we would be much better able to appreciate that stratum of Longus' fiction that is a deft collage of earlier treatments.

The same deftness and allusiveness are also characteristic of other sophisticated writers of rustic texts,[17] which helps us date Longus to the late second, early third century C.E. But such brevity, understatement, and appeal to a common fund of high literate tradition also causes deep problems of interpretation. There is no real doubt nowadays that Longus has fashioned and faceted his novel like a careful gem-cutter and that its mirroring of multiple poetic traditions is in some measure to be taken "seriously," in contrast perhaps to the more rhinestone quality of Aelian's and Alkiphron's *Rustic Letters.* But its rich and (for us) often nonspecific suggestiveness has led some modern readers to see more than is there, fancying that it alludes to religious mysteries, to initiatory scenarios of Dionysos, even to precise though otherwise unattested rituals of Erôs.[18] Longus' allusion and ellipsis make the temptation particularly strong to supply *D&C* with a framework and interpretative perspective not explicitly vouched for in the text. The temptation is real—and it is not simply to be resisted, for Longus wants us to supply a good deal of information not there, such as our knowledge of Sappho's hymeneal song and indeed of the large body of New Comedy, forensic rhetoric,[19] pastoral poetry, and earlier love novels. This means that in tracing the thematics of violence in Chloe's education and socialization we ought on the one hand to be cautious not to fill in those deliberate gaps with fantasies of our own making (a well-worn warning) and on the other we must be alert to the possible significance of the almost said, the discretely understated, the meaningful gestures left incomplete.

The narrator (who is unnamed and not automatically to be identified with the author, Longus) complicates the hermeneutic issue by sidestepping responsibility for his story. His compact proem posits a doubly displaced origin for the ensuing narrative.

While hunting game on Lesbos I saw in a grove of Nymphs the most beautiful vision I ever saw—an image inscribed, a narrative of desire. . . . As I watched and wondered a yearning seized me to counterscribe the painting;[20] I searched out an exegete of the icon and I carefully crafted four books, an offering to Eros and Nymphs and Pan, a joyous possession for all human beings, which will heal anyone who is sick with desire and will console anyone who is sorrowing, will remind anyone who has loved and will educate in advance anyone who has not loved. For it is a universal truth that no one has escaped or will escape Erôs (Desire) as long as there be beauty and eyes to see. And may god grant us soundness of mind as we write the experiences of others.

Note the gaps: The narrator, unnamed, almost says that the following tale is a record of what the local tour guide[21] told him in explanation of the figures in the painting. He certainly implies that the literary elaboration of it is his own *(exeponêsamên)*, a claim borne out by the text's sophisticated techniques—clausular rhythms, isocola, avoidance of hiatus.[22] But the material itself, he seems to say, is not his creation; rather it is a narrative already laid out in its essential lines in the painting and explained in more detail by a local authority. Both the painting and the exegete are assigned a prior responsibility for the shape and content of the narrative, designated as *ta tôn allôn*, the [things] of others.

This is surely the author's fiction about his fiction, one that we may come to recognize as a characteristic irony (in its original sense of false modesty) on the author's part. The narrator adopts an attitude of innocence about the fundamentals, as if he could bear no responsibility for the hard data, the basic facts made beautiful in the painting and even more beautiful in his text. But the *narrator's* irresponsibility in the proem and elsewhere should be recognized as a fiction and should not be misread as the *author's*. This is to say that the construction of events, the delicate and allusive style, the saying more by saying less, belong to Longus and are intentional, however little the narrator's voice calls attention to them. These premises are important for our assessment of the forms of social violence portrayed in *D&C* as "facts of life," deliberately chosen for a certain kind of inspection.

Not a Pretty Picture

For rural Greeks the facts of life *are* fairly harsh, and they themselves have regularly said so, in ancient literature as in modern times.

Anthropologists who have lived in the countryside of Greece describe a scarcity economy in which predation, calculation, and suspicion are paramount features.[23] Many reactions and behaviors in *D&C* are recognizably drawn from the ordinary dangers and difficulties of that culture—or from prior literary treatments of those dangers.[24] A piece of rope is hard to find in Longus' landscape (1.12), and when a hawser is left unguarded it may be stolen (2.13). Property and person are always at risk from marauders coming from the other cities of one's own island, whether they are high-class rowdy youths (2.12) or low-class bandits (1.28, the Pyrrhaian pirates[25]). The possessions of even well-off peasants are cheese and wine and bread (1.16.4). Chloe is valuable to her future in-laws' household as an extra hand "for the chores" (3.31.2).[26]

Though these families must save and scrimp, they are most reluctant to appear dependent. Favors may be accepted, but always with some kind of repayment or gratuity given (1.2.5). The unwritten accounting system of family status constantly monitors speech and behavior, looking for signs of defect, treachery, or concealed goods.[27] The classic scene of such canny tact in action is that the interview between Lamon and Dryas about the possible marriage of their children: both appear friendly, both are trying to maximize their profit on the transaction, and both are lying through their teeth (3.30.2ff.). Lying and detecting lies are carefully practiced arts (3.6.4; 4.11.3)—we might call them the native equivalents of the hermeneutic demanded by the book itself, insofar as its deliberate program of understatement calls for judicious supplement.

I stress this component because the greatest myth still made of this text is that it is too pretty, a picture perfect account of dreamy adolescence budding and ripening. There is great sweetness in the style, to be sure, but that is the narrator's cosmetic contribution (carefully wrought, as he says in the proem) to a plot whose structure has been designed by Erôs as a pastoral experiment. Analyzing a few episodes, or theorems, from that plot will suggest that Erôs' (and Longus') master plan is to display the fundamental terms that inform the conscious articulation and then the socialization of desire. I will refer to these as "protocols" because the naive promptings of desire in Daphnis and Chloe are shown being thwarted until they are integrated into the competitive and hostile economy of adult Greek culture. Protocols are the conventions and principles of precedence laid down to facilitate the interaction of opposing parties. Literally, they are the first *(prôto-)* sheet of writing glued *(col-)* to a scroll, the primary agreements laying down the terms on which enemy parties will negotiate or which contain fundamental concessions. So far from being about innocent hormonal energy, *D&C* is about the painful confrontation of unsocialized youth with real life.

"Real life," however, is itself made to seem problematic in this novel. What is uncovered as fundamental probably appeared universal and beyond question to some Greek readers of the second century c.e., but there is a more critical perspective implied in Longus' structure. The "prior violence" of my title refers to the experience of discovering that sexual violence is not merely an unhappy accident that might be avoided, but is a destiny written into the very premises of socially constructed reality. Daphnis experiences some of this, but Longus has made Chloe the silent center of the plot: it is she of whom Erôs wants to make a mythos (2.27), and it is she whose sexuality is discovered to be "essentially" (that is, conventionally) vulnerable, woundable. The lesson Chloe is taught is that nature itself (which is just a glorified name for those cultural imparities that are usually regarded as unquestionable) seems to endorse the painful conventions of male-prominent, phallocentric society. That lesson is a shock apparently unfelt by the narrator, but the designer of the experiment has arranged his text in ways that seem to call forth more knowledge than the narrator expresses.

Erotic Protocols

In ascending order of significance I will treat five passages in which versions of rape are crucial and problematic to the education of Daphnis and Chloe. In each case the author sets out certain paradoxes of nature and culture, conundrums suggesting perhaps that nature is simply the inscrutable mask that hides a part of culture usually left unscrutinized.

2.32–38: At an impromptu celebration of Chloe's rescue from enemy soldiers, all the traditional forms of a Greek festival are displayed— feasting, an all-night stay in the fields, religious songs and sacrificial offerings, stories of the old days, tales of the gods, musical competition, imitative dancing. The last three form a complex triad in which the younger generation (Daphnis and Chloe) absorb and adopt from the local patriarchs some of the accepted social meanings of *erôs*. Lamon tells the myth of Pan and Syrinx, in which Syrinx is a maiden singing, playing, tending her flock of goats, whom the goat-god approaches. When she rejects his advances, Pan pursues her to do violence *(es bian)*, that is, rape: "Syrinx tried to escape both from Pan and from his violence *[bian]*" (2.34). When she is transformed into reeds, he cuts them down in anger, trying to find her. Finally he binds together reeds of unequal length, symbolizing that "their *erôs* was unequal." "She who was then a beautiful maiden is now the musical syrinx [pan pipes]."

This tale is closely integrated into the immediately ensuing action. Philetas' son returns carrying an enormous syrinx, so much larger than the ordinary panpipes of shepherds that "one would think this was that very one which Pan first constructed" (2.35). On this syrinx Philetas plays many melodies, including a Dionysiac song to accompany the harvest and pressing of grapes while Dryas mimes the actions of the vintage in a dance. Then Daphnis and Chloe also perform a mimetic dance: the narrative they enact is that of Pan and Syrinx. But the sinister and essential elements of force, so vivid in the mythos as just related by Longus, are missing in the young lovers' imitation. Daphnis pleads, Chloe smiles her indifference; his pursuit is described by focusing on the charming detail of his tiptoe imitation of goats' hooves. What happened to the rape? Chloe feigns to be tired of the race; she does not pretend that she is terrified of the rapist. Daphnis then takes Philetas' great syrinx and plays three kinds of love melody—sad longing, persuasion, and invitation to return—none of them violent.

So excellently does Daphnis perform on that old man's syrinx that he is given it as a present, for he is a sort of successor to Philetas and is directed to pass it on to the next worthy successor. Longus thus notices the continuity from generation to generation of the cultural forms that enshrine erotic violence and at the same time hide it. The role of sheer force is unmistakably essential—no other erotic threat or tension could replace rape in such a myth—and it is just as essentially erased from the present-time enactment in mimetic dance. The whole occasion is a celebration of Chloe's rescue from violent men by the saving god Pan: Pan had personally terrified the sailors who had carried her off, and he had forced her release. Yet the festival of this saving now features a story of the savior as archenemy of the pastoral woman, Syrinx. The pupils are not forced or cajoled into imitating the myth but spontaneously volunteer, and in their performance they unthinkingly do what we have just been told is an act of violence, do it playfully and cheerfully.

The entire scene then is structured around the initial positing of a point of view (Syrinx's pastoral happiness before the irruption of

Pan) and the gradual effacement of all traces of her consciousness. All that remains are, so to speak, the rough marks on the page where the eraser has scraped the surface of the paper. Syrinx is eliminated from the world by a process both narrative (the tale) and imitative (the dance), which both repeats and forgets her suffering. Like children saying a word without knowing what it means, Daphnis and Chloe play at rape without taking it seriously. Their imitation on tippy-toe is very pretty; their obliviousness is potentially more serious.

1.11–21: The contrast of playful and serious began as a scheme of Erôs. "While Daphnis and Chloe were thus playing [paizontôn], Erôs devised the following serious event [spoudên]" (1.11). In the pastoral world of protected experiment, there exists an element of dangerous violence intruding from the wild that is imitated by the boy next door. The external threat is a mother wolf hunting sheep to feed her young; the internal threat is the attempt of Chloe's other would-be lover, Dorkôn, disguised in a wolfskin, to rape her.[28] Her predation is made to seem natural (a mother feeding her young), while his imitative predation is by contrast a cultural contrivance. The contrast with the wolf-predator is further signaled by his name, which means "gazelle," as the similarity is underlined by his disguise ("thus turning himself into a beast," hiding in the thickets where "a true wolf" might hide, 1.20). The wolf's intelligence outsmarts human craft, spotting the traps dug to catch her: she sees that they are artful imitations (1.11). Dorkôn by contrast is trapped by his own device: the herd dogs surround him and bite him before he can leap out of his hiding place in the brush and terrify Chloe into submission.

Yet this "serious" intrusion is again easily—and significantly—forgotten: "Because they had no experience of erotic assaults, they thought his donning the wolf-skin was a shepherd's joke [paidian, childish playfulness]" (1.21.5). Their misperception of his attempted rape is just that—a misperception due to their lack of education. Chloe knows that men are dangerous; she walks the fields less briskly than Daphnis because she is female (hôs korê), and she is keeping a watchful eye out for macho shepherds (phobôi tôn agerô-chôn poimenôn, 1.28). But she does not know what sexual violence is. The children's ignorance should not be taken as a model for the reader, which is in effect what those critics recommend who see the various kinds of violence in D&C as a simple rejected alternative to the blissful harmony that is Daphnis' and Chloe's birthright.[29]

4.2–9: Book 4 opens with a scene of gardening. In preparation for the arrival of the lord from the city, Lamon tends the lush garden of trees, shrubs, and flowers. It is designed according to the satisfying model of a proper household: the fruit-bearing plants are in the center, stockaded and defended by the nonbearing plants (4.2). The sensuous artistry of nature and the gardener work in perfect cooperation with each other, though in the center of it all is a frozen image of violence. A temple of Dionysos there is painted with some of his famous myths, each of which recalls death, mutilation, or loss of self —Semele's giving birth, Ariadne abandoned, Lykourgos in bondage, Pentheus in pieces, the defeated armies of India, and the Tyrrhenian sailors who tried to kidnap Dionysos. The garden is a microcosm of the pastoral world[30]—protected, fertile, flowering, with a structure of recollected violence in the center. Within the protected sphere memories of danger and force hover like ghosts and leave a slight chill in the very experience of safety and love. Thus Chloe, worried about the implications of the master's arrival, kisses Daphnis often, "but the kisses were fearful and their embraces anxious" (4.6).

There is a rapist here, too. A rejected suitor named Lampis plans to make the lord upset with his tenants so that perhaps he will not approve their plans for Daphnis and Chloe to marry. Knowing that the master cherishes this garden, Lampis decides to ravage it. It would be too noisy to chop down the trees, "so he concentrated his attention on the flowers. . . . Some he rooted up, some he twisted and broke, some he trambled on like a boar" (4.7). The devastation is obviously wanton and produces long laments from Daphnis and Lamon when they discover it, since their bodies will feel the master's blows. Over against the violent intruder there is a figure of nurturance and good tending: "There was a spring, which Daphnis discovered for the flowers; the spring was used exclusively for the flowers, and it was called Daphnis' Spring" (4.4). The gentle waterer, the male who found and opened the natural source of water for the flowers, is Daphnis.

Longus makes a symbolic contrast between the rejected suitor, who crushes tender blossoms, and the accepted suitor, who permanently and gently waters them. Daphnis is further placed on the side of gentleness and goodness by the threat of physical punishment to his own body. In this theorem of his longer calculus the author displays one familiar tactic for interpreting sexual violence: bad men do it; good men do not. But this proposition itself is called into question by the next two passages.

3.15–20: As Chloe was the object of a predator in wolf's clothing, so
Daphnis is watched by a rather more benign predator named Lykainion, "Little She-wolf." Like Dorkôn she lies in wait in the thickets
for her prey to pass by. Yet she appears not as an apparition of strange
horror and violence, but as a messenger from the gods. She is able to
divine (katamanteuomenê) Daphnis' love for Chloe by watching his
behavior. She then puts her own desire to acquire him as a lover into
action by telling a series of unscrupulous and wholly charming lies.
Her first lie is to her aged husband, that she must go off to help a
neighbor in labor; her second is to Daphnis, that she needs his help
in rescuing one of her geese from an eagle; her third lie is that the
Nymphs have appeared to her in a dream and have bid her be Daphnis'
teacher, saving him from his frustration by teaching him the works
of erôs. Her motivation is distinctly sympathetic as well as erotic:
when she had spied on them and seen their difficulty "she felt with
them in their sorrow and thought that the time was doubly right—
for their salvation and for her desire" (3.15.5).

Where Gazelle had appeared as a wild wolf, Little She-wolf appears as a sweet, saving teacher sent by the benign goddesses. "Give
yourself to me as a pupil," she offers, "and as a favor to those
Nymphs I will teach you" (3.17.3). Daphnis' response is piously
enthusiastic: "Daphnis could not hold out against his pleasure but
as one might expect of a country boy, a goatherd, a lover, a youth, he
threw himself at her feet and supplicated Lykainion to teach him as
quickly as possible the art [technê] whereby he could do what he
wanted with Chloe, and just as if he were about to be taught something important and truly god-sent he promised to give her a weaned
kid and soft cheeses from the first milking and the nanny herself"
(3.18).

This scene of epiphany reaches its apparent conclusion when
Lykainion shows Daphnis that the secret of sex is penetration. But
the real lesson is to follow. Daphnis wants to run quickly back to
Chloe to practice what he has just learned, lest he forget. But she
holds him back to add a footnote to this "erotic education" (erôtikês
paidagôgias):

> "You must learn this also, Daphnis. Since I am a gynê [wife/
> woman-not-maiden] I did not suffer now. Long ago another
> man educated me, taking my virginity as his payment. But
> when Chloe wrestles with you in a bout like this, she will
> scream and she will cry and she will lie in a large pool of blood
> as if slain.[31] You should not fear the blood, but at the time

when you persuade her to offer herself to you, bring her to this place, so that even if she cries aloud, no one will hear, and even if she weeps tears, no one will see, and even if she is bloodied, she may wash herself in the spring. And remember that it was I who have made you an *anêr* [husband/man-not-boy] before Chloe" (1.19).

This graphic image of a slain victim, crying with pain and bleeding profusely, is all the more striking in its context, and its three elements are repeated as if in a chant first by Lykainion and immediately thereafter by Daphnis. In a novel so careful about patterns this stands out as a thrice-stated tricolon: "But Daphnis began thinking about what Lykainion had said and therefore tempered his former zeal, reluctant to trouble Chloe beyond kisses and embraces, not wishing her to shout aloud as against an enemy nor to weep tears of pain nor to be covered with blood as if butchered" (3.20). Is it inevitable that even the protecting and tender male fall inevitably into this category of enemy *(polemios)*? The unexamined though ever more problematic protocols of male initiative, phallocentrism, and the invasive penetration seem to require it. This troubling thought governs the behavior of Daphnis for the rest of the novel: his fear of her blood/wounding/pain is what keeps the plot from being consummated then and there (3.24.3). But it is his secret. Lykainion's revelation with its dreadful addendum is not imparted to the intended victim, and Daphnis and Chloe continue their relation as more and more distinctly unequal partners, like Abraham and Isaac journeying up the mountain.

4.40: My final passage for comment is the closing paragraph of the novel, a description of the wedding night of Daphnis and Chloe. All the living characters in the novel reappear at the bridal feast, and all are forgiven their transgressions. Lykainion too is there, but the trauma that she foretold and that shaped the course of the action from 3.20 on both is and is not there. Lykainion had said, *"Remember* that it was I who made you a man before Chloe." May we presume that Daphnis and the reader have not forgotten that, nor Lykainion's careful description of defloration as trauma—the screams, the tears, the pool of blood? "Daphnis and Chloe lay down together naked, embracing each other and kissing, awake during that night more than owls; and Daphnis did some of what Lykainion had taught him; and then Chloe for the first time learned that the things which had taken place in the woods were only the playful games of children" (4.40).

If it were not for the mention of Lykainion and her instruction in the center of that sentence, we could take the image of Daphnis as Chloe's unwilling slayer to be truly forgotten. But there is yet more here to suggest that Chloe's education is presented not as a fact but as a problem:

(i)   The phrase "playful games of children" circles back to Erôs' original intervention, bringing something "serious" to their pastoral "play" at 1.11. "Serious" there referred to incursions by a predatory wolf and a wolf-clad rapist. The last sentence has a curiously elliptical quality, not saying what happened but only that it was *not* childish and that it was *not* play.

(ii) "Then as night fell everyone accompanied them to the bedroom, some playing on syrinxes, some on flutes, others holding aloft great torches. And when they were near the doors, they were singing *in a harsh and unpleasant voice, as if breaking up the earth with tridents, not singing a hymenaion.*" Again a negative, "not a hymenaion" (wedding song), but this time Longus gives us the positive. This amazing detail of attendant discord, unexplained roughness in the song, is mysterious and unexpected. The allusion to sowing fields is perfectly appropriate, since Greek marriage was conventionally said to be for the "sowing" of legitimate children, but the harsh unpleasantness and the explicit contrast to a wedding song are exceedingly odd in such a carefully controlled composition.

(iii) The structure of the entire plot is based on the series of scenes seen by the narrator in the Nymphs' grove in the proem. There too there was a missing element: "In the painting there were women giving birth and others wrapping the infants in swaddling clothes, babies exposed, herd animals nursing them, shepherds raking them up, youngsters coming together, an incursion of brigands, an attack of enemies, many other things and all to do with *erôs.*" The implied narrative is a familiar one in Greek story telling: infants exposed and nursed by animals are born from maidens raped. Pelopia raped by her father,

Aigisthos, Tyro raped by Poseidon, Auge raped by Herakles, Akakallis raped by Apollo. Even when animal-nannies are not part of the story, an exposed infant can often be assumed to be the unfortunate result of a maiden's rape or seduction. If the picture seen by the narrator is indeed a representation precisely of Daphnis and Chloe's story (a fact hinted at but not quite said), then the circle is complete. Or rather, its lines almost touch but just fail to do so, leaving a carefully designed gap just at the point where the unarguably harshest element of socially constructed sexuality falls on Chloe. This in turn lends an ominous tone to the last sentence of the novel, which focuses precisely on her and what she then experienced: "And Chloe learned. . . ."

(iv)   The divinities who preside over the book are arranged in a revelatory series. They are, by its own testimony, four in number: "He sacrificed to the gods who are in charge of things rustic—Demeter and Dionysos and Pan and the Nymphs" (4.13.3). The Nymphs are present from the beginning; Pan is introduced to the youngsters as a new object of veneration in book 2 (2.23.4); Dionysos is patron of the autumn vintage.[32] But though there are wheat fields on the estate (1.1.2) and the wedding guests sing what sounds like a song for the sowing of seed (which occurs in the fall, just as the winter rains are beginning[33]), Demeter seems to be invisible. Or rather, she was there all along in Chloe, whose name is a well-known cult title of the goddess whose daughter was seized by Hades and whose thesmophoric ceremonies were fundamental to the well-being of every Greek polis. The experiences of Demeter Chloe are allusively present, an absent presence placed at the crucial climax of the autumnal wedding night.

And what does it finally mean? I find it hard to say with unshakable conviction whether the well-concealed Longus had a fundamentally patriarchal attitude to Chloe—that she is to be simultaneously protected and made to undergo a painful rite of passage—or the more critical stance I have outlined here. The former reading is implied by most of the modern critics who have noticed the violence at all, such as Chalk.[34] A sophisticated version of the critical issue is proposed in a private letter by Helene Foley, who sees Longus as "taking

a very conscious and polemical stance towards the question of violence and sexuality," designing "a relationship in which this violence is deliberately minimized, though it can never be totally overcome and denied. . . . What seems to me remarkable about the story
is how relatively equal their development is," given the social protocols and literary precedents against which D&C is written.

The larger methodological issue is whether the author's meaning
should be the goal of our reading and thinking. Should we concede
that much authority to the writers we read?[35] If our critical faculties
are placed solely in the service of elucidating an author's meaning,
then we have already committed ourselves to the premises and
protocols of the past—past structures of cultural violence and their
descendants in the bedrooms and mean streets and school curricula
of the present. This above all we will not do. Recognizing the ambiguities and the probing of social convention in D&C at the very least
allows us to become resisting readers[36] in the complex guerrilla
fighting of cultural studies.

NOTES

A longer version of this essay, "The Education of Chloe: Hidden Injuries of
Sex," appears in my *Constraints of Desire: Essays in the Anthropology of
Sex and Gender in Ancient Greece* (New York: Routledge, 1989).

1. Only seven novels survive (five in Greek, two in Latin), and two of
those are seriously fractured (Petronius and Xenophon of Ephesos). Fragments of some two dozen other Greek novels are known from papyrus: see
S. A. Stephens and J. J. Winkler, *Ancient Greek Novels: The Fragments*
(Princeton: Princeton University Press, forthcoming). For a brief but powerful justification of the term *novel* in relation to Longus' text, see P. Turner,
"Novels, Ancient and Modern," *Novel* (1968), 2:15–24.

2. David M. Halperin shows how this backward reading has infected our
current readings of Theokritos in *Before Pastoral: Theocritus and the Ancient Tradition of Bucolic Poetry* (New Haven and London: Yale University
Press, 1983).

3. The text used in this essay is that of Michael Reeve (Leipzig: Tuebner,
1982); I have also consulted Georges Dalmeyda, *Longus, Pastorales [Daphnis
et Chloe]* (1934; reprint, Paris: Les Belles-Lettres, 1971); and O. Schönberger,
Longos: Hirtengeschichten von Daphnis und Chloe, in Greek and German,
2d ed. (Berlin: Akademie-Verlag, 1973). Most citations are given by book and
chapter only; occasionally for greater precision I have added the intracapitu-
lar number as well. Translations are my own; for the general reader that of
Paul Turner in the Penguin edition is recommended. The title is variously
given in the manuscripts—a normal uncertainty of ancient works. The two

principal manuscripts (F and V) call it *The Pastorals [Poimenika] of Daphnis and Chloe*, though the subscript of V calls it *Aipolika [Goatherd (Tales)]*. In my text I refer to the novel as *D&C*.

4. This aspect of their calculations is made clear at 3.25.3, 26.3, 30.5.

5. Since they were nursed by a sheep and a nanny goat who were also nursing their own kids, Daphnis and Chloe were born at about the same time that the herds drop their young—late winter, early spring (J. K. Campbell, *Honour, Family, and Patronage: A Study of Institutions and Moral Values in a Greek Mountain Community* [New York and Oxford: Clarendon, 1964], pp. 21–23). Eros' pastoral experiment begins in spring (1.9), so Daphnis and Chloe have just had their fifteenth and thirteenth birthdays.

6. There is a reminder of its significance at 2.8.4.

7. "It will by now be clear that I consider among the greatest attractions of *D&C* the very light touch with which Longus picks up and lets go all forms of literary and intellectual pretension and the skill with which this apparently simple tale seems to suggest layer after layer of meaning and resonance" (R. L. Hunter, *A Study of "Daphnis & Chloe"* [Cambridge, England: Cambridge University Press, 1983], 57).

8. G. Anderson, *Eros Sophistes: Ancient Novelists at Play*, vol. 9 of *American Classical Studies* (Chico, California: Scholars Press, 1982).

9. A. Heiserman, *The Novel Before the Novel* (Chicago: Chicago University Press, 1977), p. 140.

10. G. Rohde, "Longus und die Bukolik," *Rheinisches Museum* (1937), 86:23–49; W. E. McCulloh, *Longus* (New York: Twayne, 1970); L. R. Cresci, "Il romanzo di Longo Sofista e la tradizione bucolica," *Atene e Roma* (1981), n.w. 26:1–25; B. Effe, "Longos. Zur Funktionsgeschicte der Bukolik in der römischen Kaiserzeit," *Hermes* (1982), 110:65–84.

11. Froma I. Zeitlin, in a magisterial and wide-ranging essay, also regards *D&C* as a theorematic work, attending more to its implied systematization of the premises of the Greek literary genres that dealt with *erôs*—romance, pastoral, and New Comedy ("The Poetics of Desire: Nature, Art, and Imitation in Longos' *Daphnis and Chloe*," in D. M. Halperin, J. J. Winkler, and F. I. Zeitlin, eds., *Before Sexuality: The Construction of Erotic Experience in the Ancient Greek World* [Princetown: Princeton University Press, 1990]).

12. At 2.9 we find the Greek equivalent for *homework*—*nukterinon paideutêrion*, "nightly schooling."

13. On the Greek vocabulary for rape and the legal procedures for prosecuting it, see S. G. Cole, "Greek Sanctions Against Sexual Assault," *Classical Philology* (1984), 79:97–113.

14. Surveyed by B. P. Reardon, *Courants littéraires grecs des IIe et IIIe siècles après J.-C.* (Paris: Les Belles-Lettres, 1971); Philostratos' treatment is his *Lives of the Sophists*, available in English in the Loeb Classical Library edition, edited and translated by W. C. Wright (1921; reprint, 1968).

15. E. L. Bowie, "Greeks and Their Past in the Second Sophistic," *Past and Present* (1970), 46:3–41. One version of this past-centered literature restricted itself, more or less, to vocabulary used by classical Attic authors.

Longus' language appears to accommodate more of the postclassical (see G. Valley, *Über den Sprachgebrauch des Longus* [Uppsala: E. Berlings nya boktryckeri, 1926], pp. 45ff.), but one should also remember that Atticist scholars sometimes regarded rural folk as representative of the purest of cultural-linguistic traditions (see Philostratos on Aelian, in Wright, *Lives of the Sophists*, pp. 303 and 154).

16. In particular whether the bride compared to the unreached fruit remains unplucked in the rest of the wedding song: see J. J. Winkler, "Gardens of Nymphs: Public and Private in Sappho's Lyrics," in Helene P. Foley, ed., *Reflections of Women in Antiquity*, pp. 79–80 (New York: Gordon and Breach, 1981). The distinctive feature of Longus' scene is that Chloe is sad and angry at Daphnis' attempt to pluck the apple.

17. Alkiphron's *Letters*, of which book 2 is "Rustic Letters," and Aelian's *Rustic Letters*. Aelian's letter 2 is a paraphrase of Menander's *Georgos* 46–52; Letter 4 = Aristophanes, *Acharnians* 695–698; letter 6 is modeled on the farmers' dispute in Demosthenes 55, etc. Alkiphron is probably to be dated to not later than the first decade of the third century (B. Baldwin, "The Date of Alciphron," *Hermes* [1982], 110:253–254). Aelian, whose name, like Longus', is Latin and for whom Greek was a second language, flourished in the second half of the second century C.E. Other frail but cumulatively impressive arguments about Longus' date are surveyed by Schönberger, *Longos*, pp. 10–11, and Hunter, *A Study of "Daphnis & Chloe,"* pp. 1–15.

18. H. H. O. Chalk, "Eros and the Lesbian Pastorals of Longos," *Journal of Hellenic Studies* (1960), 80:32–51; R. Merkelbach, "Daphnis und Chloe: Roman und Mysterium," *Antaios* (1960), 1:47–60 and *Roman und Mysterium* (Munich: Beck, 1962. Refuted by M. Berti, "Sulla interpretazione mistica del romanzo di Longo," *Studi Classici e Orientali* (1967), 16:343–358, and A. Geyer, "Roman und Mysterienritual: Zum Problem eines Bezugs zum dionysischen Mysterienritual im Roman des Longos," *Würzberger Jahrbücher für die Altertumswissenschaft* (1977), n.f. 3:179–196. Mystery uncodings have also been claimed for Lollianos and Apuleius; these are answered by, among others, G. N. Sandy, "Notes on Lollianus' *Phoenicica*," *American Journal of Philology* (1979), 100:367–376; C. P. Jones, "Apuleius' *Metamorphoses* and Lollianus' *Phoinikika*," *Phoenix* (1980), 34:243–254; Winkler, "Gardens of Nymphs" and *Auctor & Actor: A Narratological Reading of Apuleius' "Golden Ass"* (Berkeley: University of California Press, 1985).

19. At 2.15–17 an altercation between some wealthy city boys and Daphnis is settled by speeches in the manner of a public court. The literary style of the urban disputants is described as "clear and curt since their judge was a cowherd," implying that the youths were capable of delivering more polished pleas in the manner of Demosthenes but chose a humble, sub-Lysian style.

20. *Antigrapsai têi graphêi*. The verb can refer both to duplication (to make an exact transcription) and to competition (to rival with an answering version).

21. On these exegetes at shrines, see Winkler, *Auctor & Actor*, pp. 233–238.

22. G. Valley, *Über den Sprachgebrauch des Longus;* and M. D. Reeve, "Hiatus in the Greek Novelists," *Classical Quarterly* n.s. 21 (1971):514–539. Reeve shows that most kinds of hiatus, "a serviceable measure of literary pretensions" (p. 537), are avoided by all the novelists, a testimony of their high rhetorical education and literary ambition and a refutation of the modern view that those works were either juvenile or unimportant.

23. A few representative works are E. Friedl, *Vasikila: A Village in Modern Greece* (New York: Holt, Rinehart & Winston, 1962); Campbell, *Honour, Family, and Patronage;* J. Du Boulay, *Portrait of a Greek Mountain Village* (Oxford: Clarendon, 1974); M.-E. Handman, *La violence et la ruse: Hommes et femmes dans un village grec* (Aix-en-Provence: Edisud, 1983); L. Danforth, ed., *Symbolic Aspects of Male/Female Relations in Greece,* in *Journal of Modern Greek Studies* (1983), 1:157–270; J. Dubisch, *Gender and Power in Rural Greece* (Princeton: Princeton University Press, 1986); and M. Herzfeld, *The Poetics of Manhood: Contest and Identity in a Cretan Mountain Village* (Princeton: Princeton University Press, 1986). P. Walcot, *Greek Peasants, Ancient and Modern: A Comparison of Social and Moral Values* (New York: Barnes and Noble, 1970), uses modern ethnographies to illuminate ancient literary texts.

24. A. M. Scarcella, "Realtà e letteratura nel paesaggio sociale ed economico del romanzo di Longo Sofista," *Maia* (1970), 22:103–131.

25. Earlier texts and translations speak here of Tyrian pirates; "Pyrrhaian," from the Lesbian city of Pyrrha, is Reeve's convincing correction, where the two principal manuscripts are divided between *Pyrrioi* and *Tyrioi.* They must be Greeks of some sort, not Tyrians, because they sail in a Karian vessel "so as to appear to be barbarians."

26. J. Du Boulay, "The Meaning of Dowry: Changing Values in Rural Greece," in Danforth, *Symbolic Aspects of Male/Female Relations,* pp. 243–270.

27. F. G. Bailey, *Gifts and Poison: The Politics of Reputation* (New York: Schocken, 1971); J. Du Boulay, "Lies, Mockery and Family Integrity," in J. G. Peristiany, ed., *Mediterranean Family Structures,* pp. 389–406 (Cambridge, England: Cambridge University Press, 1976); Walcot, *Greek Peasants.*

28. He had first tried to seduce her with gifts (1.15), then to seduce her father with gifts *(thelchtheis,* 1.19.3) to give her to him in marriage. Force, as a systematic alternative to persuasion, was in Dorkôn's mind from the beginning *(dôrois ê biai,* 1.15.1).

29. T. Pandiri, "Daphnis and Chloe: The Art of Pastoral Play," *Ramus* (1985), 14:116–141.

30. And of the novel: see Zeitlin, "The Poetics of Desire."

31. Reeve follows Castiglioni in deleting "as if slain," *kathaper pephoneumenê,* on the slim grounds that the phrase recurs at 3.20.1. But the two principal manuscripts have it, and it should be retained.

32. *D&C* is structured in two movements by the seasonal progression from spring to autumn of one year (books 1 and 2) and from winter to autumn of a second year (books 3 and 4). Dionysos' vintage is the backdrop of the whole of book 2, in which the ripening sexual attractiveness of both Daphnis and Chloe is recognized by the community at large: the women tease Daphnis; the men flirt with Chloe (2.2). It is also the backdrop of book 4, though by a typically deft sidestep Longus describes other Dionysan events, not the vintage itself. The cycle of two movements is demanded in part by the belief that females reach adolescence earlier than males: Chloe, at thirteen, is the first to feel desire and does so spontaneously, where Daphnis is prompted more by competition with a male rival (1.15.4). Sixteen is the age at which boys first reach *hêbê* (the bloom of youthful maturity) and are enrolled in the civic corporation. So it is only in the second year of the novel, when Daphnis has turned sixteen *(enhêbêsaw,* 3.13.4), that he "swells" with lust. At 3.30.4 the fathers acknowledge that their children have now reached the proper age for sleeping with each other.

33. Farming is given less prominence in the novel than pasturing, but it is decidedly there: e.g., 3.29.2, 3.30.3.

34. "For all his superficial *glukutês* [sweetness] Longos does not shrink from recognising as fundamental in life, and in Eros, the elements of violence, pain and contradiction," among which he includes rape: Chalk, "Eros and the Lesbian Pastorals of Longos," p. 46.

35. Many of the ancient novels, to be sure, are problem texts rather than authoritative texts, designed to provoke rather than to declare, so that the whole question of finding authoritative theses or perspectives may not arise: see Winkler, "The Mendacity of Kalasiris and the Narrative Strategy of Heliodoros' *Aithiopika,*" *Yale Classical Studies* (1982), 27:93–158 and *Auctor & Actor;* and S. Bartsch, *Decoding the Ancient Novel: The Role of Description in Heliodoros and Achilles Tatius* (Princeton: Princeton University Press, 1989).

36. J. Fetterley, *The Resisting Reader: A Feminist Approach to American Fiction* (Bloomington: Indiana University Press, 1978); E. A. Flynn and P. P. Schweickart, eds., *Gender and Reading: Essays on Readers, Texts, and Contexts* (Baltimore and London: Johns Hopkins University Press, 1986).

2

The Voice of the Shuttle Is Ours

PATRICIA KLINDIENST JOPLIN

For L. R. and J. F.

Aristotle, in the *Poetics* (16.4), records a striking phrase from a play by Sophocles, since lost, on the theme of Tereus and Philomela. As you know, Tereus, having raped Philomela, cut out her tongue to prevent discovery. But she weaves a tell-tale account of her violation into a tapestry (or robe) which Sophocles calls "the voice of the shuttle." If metaphors as well as plots or myths could be archetypal, I would nominate Sophocles' voice of the shuttle for that distinction.   Geoffrey Hartman

> Why do you [trouble] me, Pandion's
> daughter, swallow out of heaven?
>   Sappho

> I do not want them to turn
> my little girl into a swallow.
> She would fly far away into the sky
> and never fly again to my straw bed,
> or she would nest in the eaves
> where I could not comb her hair.
> I do not want them to turn
> my little girl into a swallow.
>   Gabriela Mistral
>   "Miedo" (Fear)

In returning to the ancient myths and opening them from within to the woman's body, the woman's mind, and the woman's voice, contemporary women have felt like thieves of language[1] staging a raid on the treasured icons of a tradition that has required woman's silence for centuries. When Geoffrey Hartman asks of Sophocles' metaphor "the voice of the shuttle": "What gives these words the power to speak to us even without the play?"[2] he celebrates Language and not the violated woman's emergence from silence. He celebrates Literature and the male poet's trope, not the woman's elevation of her safe, feminine, domestic craft—weaving—into art as a new means of resistance. The feminist receiving the story of Philomela via Sophocles' metaphor, preserved for us by Aristotle, asks the same question but arrives at a different answer. She begins further back, with Sappho, for whom Philomela, transformed into a wordless swallow, is the sign of what threatens the woman's voiced existence in culture.

When Hartman exuberantly analyzes the structure of the trope for voice, he makes an all too familiar elision of gender. When he addresses himself to the story or *context* that makes the metaphor for regained speech a powerful *text*, the story is no longer about the woman's silence or the male violence (rape and mutilation) that robs her of speech. Instead, it is about Fate. Hartman assumes the posture of a privileged "I" addressing a known "you" who shares his point of view: "You and I, who know the story, appreciate the cause winning through, and Philomela's 'voice' being restored but by itself the phrase simply disturbs our sense of causality and guides us, if it guides us at all, to a hint of supernatural rather than human agency" (p. 338). In the moment she reclaims a voice Philomela is said to partake of the divine; her utterance "skirts the oracular" (p. 347). Noting how Philomela's woven text becomes a link in the chain of violence, Hartman locates behind the woman weaver the figure of Fate, who "looms" like the dark figure of myth, spinning the threads from which the fabric of our lives is woven in intricate design. But if Hartman is right to locate the problem or mystery in the mechanism of revenge and right to suggest that Philomela's resistance has something of the oracular in it, he nonetheless misses his own part in the mystification of violence.

How curiously the critic remains unconscious of the implications of his own movement away from Philomela, the virgin raped, mutilated, and imprisoned by Tereus, and toward the mythical figure of Fate, the dangerous, mysterious, and enormously powerful "woman." Why is the figure of a depersonalized and distant Fate preferable for this critic? Perhaps because he cannot see in Philomela the violated woman musing over her loom until she discovers its hidden power. Perhaps because he cannot see the active, the empowered, the resistant in Philomela, he cannot see that the *woman* makes her loom do what she once hoped her voice/tongue could do. In book 6 of Ovid's

Metamorphoses, the most famous version of the tale, after Tereus rapes her, Philomela overcomes her training to submission and vows to tell her story to anyone who will listen:

> What punishment you will pay me, late or soon!
> Now that I have no shame, I will proclaim it.
> Given the chance, I will go where people are,
> Tell everybody; if you shut me here,
> I will move the very woods and rocks to pity.
> The air of Heaven will hear, and any god,
> If there is any god in Heaven, will hear me.[3]

For Philomela, rape initiates something like the "profound upheaval" Lévi-Strauss describes as the experience of "backward subjects" when they make "the sudden discovery of the function of language."[4] For Philomela, ordinary private speech is powerless. No matter how many times she says No, Tereus will not listen to her. Paradoxically, it is this *failure* of language that wakes in Philomela "the conception of the spoken word as communication, as power, as action" (p. 494). If this concept of speech as powerful action is one essential or "universal" aspect of human thought that both Lévi-Strauss and Hartman celebrate, neither addresses the conflictual nature of the discovery of language. No sooner do structure, difference, and language become visible in Lévi-Strauss' system than violence is present. No sooner does Philomela uncover the power of her own voice than Tereus cuts out her tongue.

But Tereus' plot is mysterious in its beginning and in its end. What initially motivates him to violate Philomela? And why, having raped and silenced her, does he preserve the evidence against himself by concealing rather than killing her? What is "the cause" that wins through when Philomela's tapestry is received and read, and why is her moment of triumph overcome by an act of revenge that only silences her more completely? To reconsider these questions is to reappropriate the metaphor of weaving and to redefine both the locus of its power and the crisis that gives rise to it. As Hartman suggests, the tension in the linguistic figure "the voice of the shuttle" is like "the tension of poetics" (p. 338). But for the feminist attending to the less obvious details of both text and context the story of Philomela's emergence from silence is filled with the tension of *feminist* poetics.

Prior Violence and Feminist Poetics: The Difference a Tale Makes

In *A Room of One's Own,* Virginia Woolf provides us with a comic metaphor for feminist poetics in the tailless Manx cat, unfortunate inhabitant of the Isle of Man. Woolf's narrator, moving to the window after luncheon at Oxbridge, suddenly sees a Manx cat crossing the lawn. She notes the cat's apparent "lack" but wonders if its condition is not primarily only a "difference" from cats with tails. Is the cat with no tail a freak of nature, a mutation? Or is it a product of culture, a survivor of some lost moment of amputation, mutilation? The cat, lacking its tail, of course cannot tell her. The figure is mute but pregnant with suggestion. While testifying to a real sense of difference, and a gender-specific one at that, the lost tail as *tale* craftily resists the violence inherent in Freud's reductive theory of women's castration as the explanation for our silence in culture. The narrator perceives a difference so radical that the tailless cat seems to "question the universe" and its Author, simply by being there.[5] This question echoes Woolf's rejection of Milton's bogey, his borrowing of religious authority to explain women's silence in terms of our original fall.[6] For Woolf, the lost tail signifies a present absence: X marks the spot where something apparently unrecoverable occurred; the extra letter signals a broken off story. It designates mystery; it designates violence.

The lost tail, made known by its stumpy remnant, not only represents our broken tradition, the buried or stolen tales of women who lie behind us in history. It also signifies the cut off voice or amputated tongue: what we still find it hard to recover and to say in ourselves. We are not castrated. We are not less, lack, loss. Yet we feel like thieves and criminals when we speak,[7] because we know that something originally ours has been stolen from us and that the force used to take it away still threatens us as we struggle to win it back. Woolf meets this threat with her own carefully fabricated tale. Employing old literary strategy to her new feminist ends, Woolf counters the violence implicit in Freud's and Milton's fictions with her own resisting, subversive fictions, which ask similar questions but refuse the old answers. Woolf's metaphor for muteness, the Manx cat, presses the ambiguities in Freud's and Milton's fictions that, like the myth of Philomela, conceal and reveal at once. For all posit an original moment in which an act of violence (the transgression of a boundary, the violation of a taboo) explains how difference became hierarchy, why women were forbidden to speak.[8]

In the myth of Philomela we can begin to recover the prior violence Woolf ironized in the punning metaphor of the tailless cat. Our muteness is our mutilation, not a natural loss but a cultural one, resisted as we move into language. Woolf has taught us to see the obstacles and to see that chief among them is internalization of the deadly images of women created in art. Any writer's desire to come into language is a burden. Why have so few women who have carried the burden before us been heard? Like men, women feel the keen anxiety of the writer's approach to the furthest reach of language, the limit or boundary where expression fails and we intimate the moment when death alone will "speak." But for the woman writer, coming into language, especially language about her body, has entailed the risk of a hidden but felt sexual anxiety, a premonition of violence. When Hartman ends his essay by noting: "There is always *something* that violates us, deprives our voice, and compels art toward an aesthetics of silence" (p. 353, my emphasis), the specific nature of the woman's double violation disappears behind the apparently genderless (but actually male) language of "us," the "I" and the "you" who agree to attest to that which violates, deprives, silences only as a mysterious unnamed "something." For the feminist unwilling to let Philomela become universal before she has been met as female this is the primary evasion. Our history teaches us that it is naive to trust that "the truth will out" without a struggle —including a struggle with those who claim to be telling us the truth. It may be that great art always carries within it an anxious memory of an original moment of rupture or violence in coming into being, but the woman writer, and with her the feminist critic, must also ask why art has been so particularly violent toward women, why the greatest of our writers, like Shakespeare, represent their own language anxiety in terms of sexual violation of the woman's body. It is the poet's struggle with words we hear speaking when Shakespeare, depicting the raped Lucrece pacing her bedchamber in grief and rage, says:

> And that deep torture may be called a hell,
> When more is felt than one has power to tell.[9]

What in the text "the voice of the shuttle" feels archetypal for the feminist? The image of the woman artist as a weaver. And what, in the context, feels archetypal? That behind the woman's silence is the incomplete plot of male dominance, which fails no matter how extreme it becomes. When Philomela imagines herself free to tell her own tale to anyone who will listen, Tereus realizes for the first time what would come to light, should the woman's voice become public. In private, force is sufficient. In public, however, Philomela's voice, if heard, would make them equal. Enforced silence and imprisonment are the means Tereus chooses to protect himself from discovery. But as the mythic tale, Tereus' plot, and Ovid's own text make clear, dominance can only contain, but never successfully destroy, the woman's voice.

Unraveling the Mythic Plot: Boundaries, Exchange, Sacrifice

> . . . but Athens was in trouble
> With war at her gates, barbarian invasion
> From over the seas, and could not send a mission—
> Who would believe it?—so great was her own sorrow.
> But Tereus, king of Thrace, had sent an army
> To bring the town relief, to lift the siege,
> And Tereus' name was famous, a great conquerer,
> And he was rich, and strong in men, descended
> From Mars, so Pandion, king of Athens
> Made him a son as well as ally, joining
> His daughter Procne to Tereus in Marriage.
> (Ovid *Metamorphoses* 6, lines 319–424)

> Terminus himself, at the meeting of the bounds,
> is sprinkled with the blood of a slaughtered lamb . . .
> The simple neighbors meet and hold a feast, and sing
> thy praises holy Terminus: thou dost set bounds
> to people and cities and vast kingdoms; without
> thee every field would be a root of wrangling.[10]

In most versions of the myth, including Ovid's, Tereus is said to be smitten with an immediate passion for the beautiful virgin Philomela, younger daughter of Athen's King Pandion.[11] What is usually not observed is that both Philomela and her sister Procne serve as objects of exchange between these two kings: Pandion of Athens and Tereus of Thrace, Greek and barbarian. For the old king to give his elder daughter to Tereus is for Greece to make an alliance with barbarism itself, for the myth takes as its unspoken pretext a proverbial distinction between "Hellenes, Greek speakers, and barbaroi, babblers."[12] In the myth, the political distinction between Athens and Thrace recedes. As the beginning of the mythic tale suggests, Athens was in trouble, but the invasion of the gates by barbarians that brings Tereus into alliance with the city initiates a new crisis of invasion, one that removes the violence from Athens' walls to the home of the barbarian himself: Thrace.

Philomela is the marriageable female Tereus seizes to challenge the primacy of Pandion and the power of Athens. His mythic passion is a cover story for the violent rivalry between the two kings. Apparently, the tragic sequence gets its start not from Tereus' desires, but from Procne's. After five years of married life in Thrace, she becomes lonely for her sister and asks Tereus to go to Pandion to ask that Philomela be allowed to visit her. When Tereus sees Philomela with Pandion, his desire becomes uncontrollable and he will brook no frustration of his plan to take her for himself.[13] First the political anxieties that fuel the myth are transformed into erotic conflicts; then the responsibility for Tereus' lust is displaced onto Philomela herself: as Ovid has it, the chaste woman's body is fatally seductive.[14] We are asked to believe that Philomela unwittingly and passively invites Tereus' desire by being what she is: pure. But if it is Philomela's purity that makes her so desirable, it is not because purity is beautiful. Tereus' desire is aroused not by beauty but by power: Pandion holds the right to offer Philomela to another man in a political bargain because Philomela is a virgin and therefore unexchanged. Tereus is a barbarian, and the giving of the first daughter as gift only incites him to steal the withheld daughter. But both barbarian and virgin daughter are proverbial figures of the Greek imagination. They are actors in a drama depicting the necessity for establishing and keeping secure the boundaries that protect the power of the key figure, Pandion, the sympathetic king who disappears from the tale as soon as he gives up both his daughters.[15] The exchange of women is the structure the myth conceals incompletely. What the myth reveals is how the political hierarchy built upon male sexual dominance requires the violent appropriation of the woman's power to speak.

This violence is implicit in Lévi-Strauss' idea that "marriage is the archetype of exchange" (p. 483) and that women are exchange objects, gifts, or "valuables *par excellence,*" whose transfer between groups of men "provides the means of binding men together" (pp. 481, 480). In Lévi-Strauss' view, women are not only objects. but also words: "The emergence of symbolic thought must have required that women, like words, should be things that were exchanged" (p. 496). But this discovery began with a connection between prohibitions against "*misuses* of language" and the incest taboo, which made Lévi-Strauss ask: "What does this mean except that women are treated as signs, which are *misused* when not put to the use reserved for signs, which is to be communicated?" (pp. 495–496, emphasis in original). In this light, Tereus' rape of Philomela constitutes a crisis in language—the barbarian refuses to use the women/ signs as they are offered him by the Greek; and a violation of the structure of exogamous exchange—the barbarian does not exchange; he steals and keeps all to himself. But nothing in Lévi-Strauss prepares us for the effects of this transgression upon the woman. Though he minimally recognizes that "a woman can never be merely a sign but must also be recognized as a generator of signs," Lévi-Strauss can still envision only women speaking in a "duet": monogamous marriage or right exchange (p. 496). Since marriage is the proper use of woman as sign, it is therefore *the* place where she has the power to speak. But is this pure description? Or does the modern anthropologist share a bias with his male informant, both satisfied that the male point of view constitutes culture? In effect, women are silenced partly by being envisioned as silent. The inability to question (on Lévi-Strauss' part), like the unwillingness to acknowledge (on the men's part) any articulated bonds between women, suggests how tenuous the bonds between men may be. That the bonding of men requires the silencing of women points to an unstated male dread: for women to define themselves as a group would mean the unraveling of established and recognized cultural bonds. Lévi-Strauss acknowledges the ambiguous status of women: woman is both sign (word) and value (person). That is, she is both spoken and speaker. However, he does not perceive either the violational or the potentially subversive aspects of women's position within the system of exchange.

Rather, for Lévi-Strauss the contradictory status of woman as both insider and outsider in culture provides for "that affective richness, that ardour and mystery" (p. 496) coloring relations between the sexes. Lévi-Strauss would preserve the "sacred mystery" (p. 489) marriage signifies, preferring the myth of passion to any serious investigation of the implications of the exchange of women for those cultures that practice it.

In the work of René Girard, who refuses to respect mythic passion, the origin of symbolic thought and language is linked not to the exchange of *women*, but to the exchange of *violence:* "The origin of symbolic thought lies in the mechanism of the surrogate victim."[16] For Girard, the mechanism by which the community expels its own violence by sacrificing a surrogate victim, someone marginal to the culture, is linked to the *arbitrary* nature of signs (p. 236). In Girard's revision of Lévi-Strauss we come closer to a view of exchange that sheds light on some of the paradoxes in the Greek myth: "The ritual violence that accompanies the exchange of women serves a sacrificial purpose for each group. In sum, the groups agree never to be completely at peace so that their members may find it easier to be at peace among themselves" (p. 249). For Girard, as for Mary Douglas, the aura of the sacred and the mysterious that envelops married sexual relations is a sign of the human need for clear boundaries to contain violence. But while both Douglas and Girard make extremely interesting connections between ritual pollution, violence, and the prohibitions focused on female sexuality in particular (especially on menstrual blood), neither presses these observations far enough.[17] Girard argues that "exchange ritualized into warfare and . . . warfare ritualized into exchange are both variants of the same sacrificial shift from the interior of the community to the exterior."[18] But Girard, too, tends to equate the male point of view with culture, so that he does not pause to see how the woman, in exchange, becomes the surrogate victim for the group. Her body represents the body politic.

When we address the question of the body of the king's daughter, we approach the structure Mary Douglas sees as a dialectical interaction of the "two bodies," the actual physical body and the socially defined body generated by metaphor: ". . . the human body is always treated as an image of society . . . Interest in apertures depends on the preoccupation with social exits and entrances, escape routes and invasions. If there is no concern to preserve social boundaries, I would not expect to find concern with bodily boundaries. The relation of head to feet, of brain and sexual organs, of mouth and anus are commonly treated so that they express *the relevant patterns of hierarchy*."[19]

The exchange of women articulates the culture's boundaries, the woman's hymen serving as the physical or sexual sign for the limen or wall defining the city's limits. Like the ground beneath the walls of Athens (or Rome),[20] the woman's chastity is surrounded by prohibitions and precautions. Both are protected by political and ritual sanctions; both are sacred. But female chastity is not sacred out of respect for the integrity of the woman as person; rather, it is sacred out of respect for violence. Because her sexual body is the ground of the culture's system of differences, the woman's hymen is also the ground of contention. The virgin's hymen must not be ruptured except in some manner that reflects and ensures the health of the existing political hierarchy. The father-king regulates both the literal and metaphorical "gates" to the city's power: the actual gates in the city's wall or the hymen as the gateway to his daughter's body. The first rupture of the hymen is always a transgression, but culture articulates the difference between the opened gate and the beseiged fortress:[21] Pandion will give Tereus free entry to Procne's body if he will agree not to use his force against Athens. Exchange of the king's daughter is nothing less than the articulation of his power and the reassertion of his city's sovereignty.

In the marriage rite the king's daughter is led to the altar as victim and offering, but instead of being killed, she is given in marriage to the rival king. War is averted. But in a crisis the woman can become identified with the very violence the exchange of her body was meant to hold in check.

The violence implicit in the exchange of women is central not only to Philomela's tale, but to one of Greek drama's great tragedies. The sacrificial nature of the exchange of women is terrifyingly clear in Euripides' *Iphigenia in Aulis,* in which the king's daughter is literally led to the altar as sacrifice under the ruse of wedding her to Achilles.[22] And as the play reveals, the king's daughter is finally a surrogate victim for the king himself: it is Agamemnon the mob of armed and restive Hellenes would kill, were Iphigenia not sacrificed.[23] The threat, as Achilles makes clear, is "stoning."[24] Like the myth of Philomela, the story of Iphigenia reaches back to Greek prehistory. (Pandion's boundary dispute was said to have been with Labdacus, of a generation before Laius, Oedipus' father.)[25] But both stories were retold in Athens during the years of the Peloponnesian War, when it became clear to the Greek dramatist's mind that the differences that give rise to human sacrifice were located within the city itself.[26]

In Euripides' tragedy it is peace (the stillness or quiet when the wind will not move the ships toward Troy) that makes discord among brother Greeks visible. Euripides interprets the current Greek crisis, imperial Athens' engagement in a protracted war, in terms of the distant past, Homer's tales of the Trojan War. Both are seen in antiheroic terms. The unmaking of Homeric heroes is also the unmasking of the cultural fictions that veil the sacrificial violence at the basis of political domination. As rivalry between brothers threatens to explode into internecine war instead of war against the com-

mon enemy, the culture represented by the amassed armies is reu-
nied under Agamemnon's authority only through a ritual sacrifice.
And Agamemnon knows that *he* weaves the plot that determines his
daughter's destiny.[27]

Two things must happen in order for Iphigenia to undergo her
startling transformation into a willing sacrificial victim who forbids
her mother from exacting revenge and absolves her father of all
responsibility for her death. First, Iphigenia must hear from Achilles
that the mob is calling for her and that even if she resists she will be
dragged by her hair, screaming, to the altar.[28] And second, Iphigenia
must begin to speak the language of the victim: she blames Helen,
she sees the Trojan War as an erotic conflict, and she echoes the men
who arranged her sacrifice by finally displacing responsibility for her
death onto the goddess Artemis.[29]

The myth of Philomela insists upon the difference between legitimate exchange (marriage) and the violent theft (rape). But this difference almost dissolves in Euripides' tragedy, not only in Iphigenia's
sacrifice, but in Clytemnestra's accusation against Agamemnon. It
seems he is guilty of the same crime as Paris; if he is different from
Paris, it is only because his later crime was worse:

CLYTEMNESTRA:
Hear me now—
For I shall give you open speech and no
Dark saying or parable any more.
And this reproach I first hurl in your teeth,
That I married you against my will, after
You murdered Tantalus, my first husband,
And dashed my living babe upon the earth,
Brutally tearing him from my breasts.
And then, the two sons of Zeus, my brothers,
On horseback came and in white armor made
War upon you. Till you got upon your knees
To my old father, Tyndareus, and he
Rescued you. So you kept me for your bed. (lines 1146–1158)

In the ambiguities of his final plays Euripides comes as close as
anyone to suggesting that Helen always was a pretext and that the
women who are violated (or, like Clytemnestra, who become violent) in exchanges between men are victims of the polis itself. In the
myth of Philomela the fact that both acts are performed by the same
man, Tereus, and that both daughters are taken from the same man,
Pandion, suggests that the difference between the generative rite

(marriage) and the dangerous transgression (rape) is collapsing within the Greek imagination. The myth records, but tries to efface, the political nature of the crisis of distinctions: the trouble at Athens' gates, or the fear that the most crucial distinction of all is about to give way, the identity of the city itself. The first exchange was meant to resolve the threat to Athens but instead brought on the invasion of the virginal daughter's body.

The relationship between the cure (marriage) and the cause (rape) of violence relies upon the assent of the males involved, who must agree to operate on the basis of a shared fiction. We can recover what the Greeks of fifth-century Athens feared by viewing barbarian invasion/rape as an unwilling recognition that fictions of difference are arbitrary, yet absolutely necessary. The effects of invasion we can see symbolized in Philomela's suffering once she is raped. The transgression of all bonds, oaths, and unstated but firmly believed rules initiates a radical loss of identity, a terrible confusion of roles:

> Were my father's orders
> Nothing to you, his tears, my sister's love,
> My own virginity, the bonds of marriage:
> Now it is all confused, mixed up; I am
> My sister's rival, a second-class wife, and you,
> For better and worse, the husband of two women,
> Procne my enemy now, at least she should be. (lines 533–539)

Philomela experiences rape as a form of contagious pollution because it is both adultery and incest, the two cardinal transgressions of the rule of exogamy. Should the rule collapse altogether, chaos would ensue. Then fathers (Pandion instead of Tereus) could have intercourse with daughters and brothers (Tereus as brother rather than brother-in-law) with sisters.

As the sign and currency of exchange, the invaded woman's body bears the full burden of ritual pollution. Philomela experiences *herself* as the source of dangerous contagion[30] because once violated she is both rival and monstrous double of her own sister. If marriage uses the woman's body as good money and unequivocal speech, rape transforms her into a counterfeit coin, a contradictory word that threatens the whole system. This paradox, the raped virgin as redundant or equivocal sign, is the dark side of Philomela's later, positive discovery about language: once she can no longer function as sign, she wrests free her own power to speak. To tell the tale of her rape is to hope for justice. But justice would endanger not only Tereus, but Pandion himself. For once raped, Philomela stands radically outside all boundaries: she is exiled to the realm of "nature" or what Girard calls undifferentiated violence; she is imprisoned in the woods. There she may see just how arbitrary cultural boundaries truly are; she may see what fictions prepared the way for her suffering. The rape of the king's daughter is like the sacrifice of Iphigenia. Both threaten to make fully visible the basis of structure by bringing to light the violence implicit in culture's inscription of its vulnerable exits and entries on the silenced woman's body.

Clytemnestra does not remind Agamemnon what the history of their own union is until the fiction of Iphigenia's marriage gives way to the reality of her sacrifice. This is precisely the paradoxical nature of domination: authority founded upon the suppression of knowledge and free speech relegates both the silenced people and the unsayable things to the interstices of culture. It is only a matter of time before all that has been driven from the center to the margins takes on a force of its own. Then the center is threatened with collapse. The system of differences the powerful had to create to define themselves as the center of culture or the top of the hierarchy turns against them. To the Greek imagination, this moment of transition was terrifying, and in both Euripides' drama and the mythic tale the dread of anarchic violence is obvious. As effectively and as ambiguously as Agamemnon in the act of sacrificing his own daughter, Greek culture uses the myth of Tereus' rape of Philomela on Thracian soil to avoid the knowledge that the violence originated within Athens, with the father-king himself. But like Agamemnon, who begins to see the truth only to turn his back on it, the myth preserves but transforms essential elements in the actual story.[31] The invasion of Athens/Philomela by Thrace/Tereus/barbarism collapses the sacrificial crisis into an isolated moment when the kinship system turns back upon itself. Memory of the chaos that follows unbridled rivalry between brothers is condensed into the moment when Philomela sees Procne as "the enemy." This confusion is part of the face-to-face confrontation with violence itself.

For Agamemnon to refuse to sacrifice his virgin daughter he would have to relinquish his authority. For Philomela to refuse her status as mute victim she must seize authority. When Philomela transforms her suffering, captivity, and silence into the occasion for art, the text she weaves is overburdened with a desire to tell. Her tapestry not only seeks to redress a private wrong, but should it become public (and she began to see the connection between the private and the political before her tongue was cut out), it threatens to retrieve from obscurity all that her culture defines as outside the bounds of allowable discourse, whether sexual, spiritual, or literary.

Art and Resistance: Listening for the Voice of the Shuttle

> Arachne also
> Worked in the gods, and their deceitful business
> With mortal girls . . . To them all Arachne
> Gave their own features and a proper background.
> Neither Minerva, no, nor even Envy
> Could find a flaw in the work; the fair-haired goddess
> Was angry now, indeed, and tore the web
> That showed the crimes of the gods, and with her shuttle
> Struck at Arachne's head, and kept on striking,
> Until the daughter of Idmon could not bear it,
> *Noosed her own neck, and hung herself.*
> (Ovid *Metamorphoses* 6, lines 79–84, my emphasis)

The explicit message of the myth can still be questioned and criticized from a standpoint that has never been tried and that should be the first to be tried since it is suggested by the myth itself . . . All we have to do to account for everything is to assume that *the lynching is represented from the standpoint of the lynchers themselves.*[32]

Once Procne receives Philomela's text, reads it, interprets it, and acts upon it by rescuing her, myth creates a dead end for both the production and the reception of the woman's text. The movement of violence is swift and sure: there is hardly any pause between Procne's hatching of a plot and its execution.[33] Nor is there any hesitation between Tereus' recognition that he has devoured his own child and his choice to rise up to kill the bloody sisters. The space most severely threatened with collapse is that between Tereus and the sisters themselves. Here the gods intervene: the three are turned into birds. But paradoxically, this change changes nothing. Metamorphosis preserves the distance necessary to the structure of dominance and submission: in the final tableau all movement is frozen. Tereus will never catch the sisters, but neither will the women ever cease their flight. Distance may neither collapse nor expand. In such stasis, both order and conflict are preserved, but there is no hope of change.

Metamorphosis and Ovid's *Metamorphoses* fix in eternity the pattern of violation-revenge-violation. Myth, like literature and ritual, abets structure by giving the tale a dead and deadly end. The women, in yielding to violence, become just like the man who first moved against them. The sisters are said to trade murder and dismemberment of the child for rape and mutilation of the woman. The sacrifice of the innocent victim, Itys, continues, without altering it, the motion of reciprocal violence. And as literary tradition shows, the end of the story overtakes all that preceded it; the women are remembered as *more* violent than the man.[34] This is done by suppressing a tale: the sacrifice of an actual woman, or the long history of scapegoating women. The social end toward which fictional closure reaches in this myth is the maintenance of structure. But narrative, like myth and ritual (like culture or consciousness), also preserves the contradictory middle. Because the end of the tale fixes itself against the middle so strenuously, we come to see it as false. It is the middle that we recover: the moment of the loom, the point of departure for the woman's story, which might have given rise to an unexpected ending.

Imprisoned in the plot, just as Philomela is imprisoned by Tereus, is the antiplot. Just as Philomela is not killed but only hidden away, the possibility of antistructure is never destroyed by structure; it is only contained or controlled until structure becomes deadened or extreme in its hierarchical rigidity by virtue of all that it has sought to expel from itself. Then antistructure, what Victor Turner calls *communitas*, may erupt. And it may be peaceful, or it may be violent.[35] The violence that ensues when Philomela is rescued and she brings back into culture the power she discovered in exile inheres not in her text, but in structure itself.[36] The end of the tale represents an attempt to forestall or foreclose a moment of radical transition when dominance and hierarchy might have begun to change or to give way. Culture hides from its own sacrificial violence. The Greek imagination uses the mythic end to expel its own violence and to avoid any knowledge of the process. Patriarchal culture feels, as Tereus does, that it is asked to incorporate something monstrous when the woman returns from exile to tell her own story.

But myth seeks to blame the women for the inability of the culture to allow the raped, mutilated, but newly resisting woman to return: the sisters must become force-feeders; they must turn out to be bloodthirsty. Supposedly, the sisters quickly forget their long delayed desire to be together in giving way to the wish for revenge. But the tale can reach this end only by leaving out the loom. There are, after all, two women, and peace (making) and violence (unmaking) are divided between them. Over against Procne's rending of her child and the cooking of the wrong thing that culminates in an inverted family meal—Tereus' cannibalism—myth preserves but effaces the hidden work of Philomela at her loom. Revenge, or dismembering, is quick. Art, or the resistance to violence and disorder inherent in the very process of weaving, is slow.

Philomela's weaving is the new, third term in what Greek culture often presents us as two models of the woman weaver, the false twins: virtuous Penelope, continually weaving and unraveling a shroud, and vicious Helen, weaving a tapestry depicting the heroics of the men engaged in the war they claim to fight over her body. But in either case the woman's weaving serves as sign for the male poet's prestigious activity of spinning his yarns, of weaving the text of the Trojan War. For their weaving to end, Homer's text/song must end. Both women weave because the structure of marriage is suspended. They will stop weaving when they are reunited with their proper spouses, when the war ends.

To this pair of weavers, Euripides and Aristophanes, writing when Athens was in extreme crisis, add metaphors of *un*weaving. In the *Bacchae,* the metaphor for violent antistructure is the bacchante, the woman *"driven* from loom and shuttle" by the god Dionysus. And the image Pentheus uses for the reimposition of structure is the bacchantes as women "sold as slaves or put to work at my looms," where they will be *silenced.*[37] But these are also false twins: both represent forms of violence between men worked through the "freeing" of Theban women from their looms (Dionysus' revenge) or the enslaving of the Asian Bacchae to the Theban loom (Pentheus' counterthreat).

In Aristophanes' *Lysistrata,* the crisis in Athens is not depicted as women fleeing to the hills to celebrate the rites of Dionysus, but as women moving to the center, occupying the Acropolis in an attempt to restore a true sense of differences among Greeks. To remind the men who their common enemy is will apparently stop their infighting. This requires the reassertion of gender as the primary difference, which makes marriage a comic replacement for war. In *Lysistrata,* the men try to lure their wives home by bringing them their babies and by telling them that the chickens have gotten into the work on their looms.[38] In both the tragic and comic representation of disorder as the abandonment of the loom, a return to order, or weaving, is a return to the gender status quo, to the rigid hierarchical roles that gave rise to the crisis at the beginning.

There is another kind of weaving: Arachne's tapestry at the opening of book 6 of the *Metamorphoses* and Philomela's at the close. For these two women weaving represents the unmasking of "sacred mystery" and the unmaking of the violence of rape. Before the angry goddess Athene (Minerva) tore Arachne's cloth, the mortal woman weaver told a very specific tale: women raped by gods metamorphosed into beasts. Before the advent of the jealous goddess, Arachne was the center of a community of women. Unsurpassed in her art, Arachne was so graceful that women everywhere came to watch her card, spin, thread her loom, and weave. Gathered around her were other women watching, talking, resting. Here the loom represents the occasion for communitas, or peace, a context in which it is possible for pleasure to be nonappropriative and nonviolent. In this Arachne suggests Sappho, who was also the center of a community of women and who also, in Ovid, meets a deadly end. Ovid codified the tradition of slander that followed Sappho's death and passed on in his own work the fiction that she died a suicide, killing herself out of desire for a man who did not want her.[39] Sappho's surviving work and the testimony of others enable scholars to reject Ovid's fictional end as false. But only by an act of interpretation can we suggest that Arachne, the woman artist, did not hang herself but was lynched. Suicide is substituted for murder. Arachne is destroyed by her own instrument in the hands of an angry goddess. But who is Athene? She is no real female but sprang, motherless, from her father's head, an enfleshed fantasy. She is the virgin daughter whose aegis is the head of that other woman victim, Medusa. Athene is like the murderous angel in Virginia Woolf's house, a male fantasy of what a woman ought to be, who strangles the real woman writer's voice.

Athene is the pseudowoman who tells the tale of right order. Central to her tapestry are the gods in all their glory. In the four corners, just inside the border of olive branches, Athene weaves a warning to the woman artist that resistance to hierarchy and authority is futile:

> The work has Victory's ultimatum in it,
> But that her challenger may have full warning
> What her reward will be for her daring rashness,
> In the four corners the goddess weaves four pictures,
> Bright in their color, each one saying *Danger!*
> In miniature design. (lines 81–86)

Arachne's daring rashness is only apparently her pride in her own artistry (which is justified: she wins the contest). In truth, she is in danger because she tells a threatening story. Among the women represented with "their own features and a proper background" in Arachne's tapestry is Medusa herself. To tell the tale of Poseidon's rape of Medusa is to suggest what the myth of the woman who turns men to stone conceals. The locus of that crime was an altar in the temple of Athene. The background of the crime was the city's need to choose what god to name itself for or what is usually represented as a rivalry between Poseidon and Athene for the honor.Was Medusa raped, or was she sacrificed on the altar to Athene? Was the woman "punished" by Athene, or was she killed during a crisis as an offering to the "angry" goddess by the city of Athens, much as Iphigenia was said to be sacrificed to a bloodthirsty Artemis?

Medusa does not become a beautiful human virgin in Greek myth until very late. Behind the decapitated woman's head Perseus uses to turn men to stone lies the ancient gorgon. The gorgon or Medusa head was also used as an apotropaic ritual mask and is sometimes found marking the chimney corners in Athenian homes.[40] The mythical Medusa may recall a real sacrificial victim. The violence is transformed into rape, but the locus of the act—the altar—is preserved, and responsibility for the crime is projected onto the gods. But even there, it must finally come to rest upon another "woman," Athene. Behind the victim's head that turns men to stone may lie the victim stoned to death by men. Perhaps it is the staring recognition of human responsibility for ritual murder that is symbolized in the gaze that turns us to stone. The story is eroticized to locate the violence between men and women, and Freud in his equation "decapitation = castration" continues the development of mythological and sacrificial thinking inherent in misogyny. If Medusa has become a central figure for the woman artist to struggle with, it is because, herself a silenced woman, she has been used to silence other women.[41]

For Arachne to tell the most famous tales of women raped by the gods is for her to begin to demystify the gods (the sacred) as the beasts (the violent). But it is also for Arachne to make Ovid's text unnecessary: he can spin his version of *Metamorphoses* only because the woman's version of the story has been torn to pieces and the woman weaver driven back into nature. Just as Freud, terrified of the woman-as-mother and the woman weaver, uses psychoanalysis to drive women's weaving back into nature, so myth uses Athene to transform Arachne into the repellent spider who can weave only literal webs, sticky, incomprehensible designs. Metamorphosis (like psychoanalysis in Freud's hands) reverses the direction of violence:

Medusa, like Arachne, threatens men. The spider traps and devours the males who mate with her. But Athene, who punished both Medusa and Arachne, does not threaten the male artist. The weaver's instrument, a shuttle, is used to silence her. But it is not used to silence the male artist who appropriates the woman's skill as a metaphor for his own artistry. As an instrument of violence, Athene is an extension of Zeus. However, revenge on the woman artist who uses her loom to tell stories we are never allowed to hear unless they are mediated by men is not the vengeance of the god, but of the culture itself.

When Philomela begins to weave over the long year of her imprisonment, it is not only her suffering but a specific motive that gives rise to her new use of the loom: to speak to and be heard by her sister. As an instrument that binds and connects, the loom, or its part, the shuttle, re-members or mends what violence tears apart: the bond between the sisters, the woman's power to speak, a form of community and communication. War and weaving are antithetical not because when women are weaving we are in our right place, but because all of the truly generative activities of human life are born of order and give rise to order. But just as Philomela can weave any number of patterns on her loom, culture need not retain one fixed structure.

The myth would have us think that after all her long patience and endurance, Philomela would be willing to turn from the labor of the loom to instant revenge. We are asked to believe that the weaver's supple and stubborn transformation of the prison into the workshop, the transfer of the old discipline of feminine domestic work into one year of struggle, would leave her unchanged, that Philomela's discovery would not have the power to change her sister or their situation. For the myth would also have us think that after grieving and mourning over her sister's grave for a year, Procne would make way for a rite not of reunion, but of murder. The one most important alternative suggested by Philomela's tapestry is the one never tried: the power of the text to teach the man to know himself. Is it the barbarian, Tereus, or the Greek male citizen who would respond to the woman's story with violence? Within the Greek tradition, the myth was used to teach women the danger of our capacity for revenge. But if the myth instructs, so does Philomela's tapestry, and we can choose to teach ourselves instead the power of art as a form of resistance. It is the attempt to deny that Philomela's weaving could have any end apart from revenge that makes the myth so dangerous, for myth persuades us that violence is inevitable and art is weak.

But the myth, like Ovid's text, testifies against its own ends, for if Arachne's and Philomela's art is truly weak it would not be repressed with such extreme violence. Why does "the voice of the shuttle" have the power to speak to us even without the *woman's* text? Because we have now begun to recover, to preserve, and to interpret our own tales. And our weaving has not unraveled culture, though we do seek to unravel many insidious cultural fictions. Women's texts of great vision, like Maxine Hong Kingston's *Woman Warrior*, ask us to remember against all odds what we have been required and trained to forget. Philomela and her loom speak to us because together they represent an assertion of the will to survive despite everything that threatens to silence us, including the male literary tradition and its critics who have preserved Philomela's "voice" without knowing what it says. Philomela speaks to us and speaks *in us* because, as the woman warrior knows when she puts down her sword and takes up her pen, her body was the original page on which a tale was written in blood. Kingston's tale, like Arachne's and Philomela's weaving, represents a moment of choice, the *refusal* to return violence for violence: "What we have in common are the words at our backs. The idioms for revenge are 'report a crime' and 'report to five families.' The reporting is the vengeance—not the beheading, not the gutting, but the words. And I have so many words —'chink' words and 'gook' words too—that they do not fit on my skin."[42] But the writer's act of renunciation and writing as the healing of what is torn in herself and in her community requires that she be *heard.*

The work of modern women writers speaks of the need for a communal, collective act of remembering. Like Gabriela Mistral, some women writers offer their words as food to feed other women. In "El Reparto" (Distribution), Mistral offers her poem not as a dismembered body, but as a sacramental text:

> If I am put beside
> the born blind,
> I will tell her softly, so softly,
> with my voice of dust,
> "Sister, take my eyes."
>
> . . . . .

Let another take my arms
if hers have been sundered
And others take my senses
with their thirst and hunger.[43]

For us, both the female sexual body and the female text must be rescued from oblivion. We rouse ourselves from culturally induced amnesia to resist the quiet but steady dismemberment of our tales by misogynist criticism. We remember and then hope to forget. Amnesia is repetition; it is being haunted by and continually reliving the pain and rage of each moment we have yielded to the pressure on us to not see, to not know, and to not name what is true for us.

If women have served as a scapegoat for male violence, if the silenced woman artist serves as a sacrificial offering to the male artistic imagination (Philomela as the nightingale leaning on her thorn—*choosing* it—to inspire the male poet who then translates her song into poetry), the woman writer and the feminist critic seek to remember the embodied, resisting woman. Each time we do, we resist our status as privileged victim; we interrupt the structure of reciprocal violence.

If the voice of the shuttle is oracular it tells us Fate never was a woman looming darkly over frightened men; she was a male fantasy of female reprisal. But in celebrating the voice of the shuttle as ours, we celebrate not Philomela the victim *or* Philomela waving Itys' bloody head at Tereus. Rather we celebrate Philomela weaving, the woman artist who in recovering her own voice uncovers not only its power, but its potential to transform revenge (violence) into resistance (peace). In freeing our own voices we need not silence anyone else's or remain trapped by the mythic end. In undoing the mythical plot that makes men and women brutally vindictive enemies we are refusing to let violence overtake the work of our looms again. We have that power. We have that choice.

NOTES

I wish to thank the following people for their generosity in reading and criticising various drafts of this essay: Jenny Franchot, John Freccero, Barbara Charlesworth Gelpi, L. Brown Kennedy, Catharine MacKinnon, Diane Middlebrook, David Wellbery, and John Winkler. Without the steady support of Michael Joplin and a Whiting Foundation Fellowship for 1983–1984, this research and writing would not have been possible.

The first epigraph is from Geoffrey Hartman, "The Voice of the Shuttle:

Language from the Point of View of Literature," in *Beyond Formalism, Literary Essays 1958–1970* (New Haven: Yale University Press, 1970), p. 337. Time and knowledge have changed how I would open this essay, were I to rewrite it now, having come to Yale and found, in Geoffrey Hartman, one of the few people with whom I can talk in earnest about violence, persecution, and the need to bear witness to the survivors of violation. The anger my reader hears in the opening of this essay I have chosen to leave unchanged; the words would never have come clear had anger not inspired them. But the anger has been relieved by dialogue and the discovery of common ground, and I wish to acknowledge this happy conclusion to an argument I had with a disembodied voice now that I know the person, the integrity, behind it.

The second epigraph is from Sappho, LP 135. See also Fragment # 197 in *Greek Lyric Poetry, Including the Complete Poetry of Sappho*, trans. Willis Barnstone (New York: Schocken, 1972), p. 83.

The third epigraph is from Gabriela Mistral, *Selected Poems*, trans. and ed. Doris Dana (Baltimore: Johns Hopkins University Press, 1961), p. 68.

1. The phrase is taken from the title of Claudine Harrmann's *Les Voleuses de langue* (Paris: des Femmes, 1979). Alicia Ostriker uses it as the title of her important essay about the ways American women poets have transformed received mythical images. See Ostriker, "The Thieves of Language: Women Poets and Revisionist Mythmaking," *Signs: Journal of Women in Culture in Society* (Autumn 1982), 8:69–80. My essay began as a commentary on Ostriker's paper delivered at the Stanford University Conference on Women Writing Poetry in America, April 1982.

2. Geoffrey Hartman, *Beyond Formalism*, p. 337. Further citations appear in text.

3. Ovid, *Metamorphoses*, trans. Rolfe Humphries (Bloomington: Indiana University Press, 1955), p. 147. Further citations will appear in text. The reader should note that Humphries' line count at the head of each page in his text is only an approximate guide to the number of each line.

4. Claude Lévi-Strauss, *The Elementary Structures of Kinship*, trans. James Harle Bell, John Richard von Sturmer, and Rodney Needham, ed. Rodney Needham, rev. ed. (Boston: Beacon, 1969), p. 494. Further citations will appear in text.

5. Virginia Woolf, *A Room of One's Own* (New York: Harcourt, Brace and World, 1929), pp. 11ff.

6. Hartman discusses the line "O Eve in evil hour . . ." (*Paradise Lost*, 9, line 1067) in "The Voice of the Shuttle" without discussing the "reader insult" or "language injury" Milton works here. (Please see epilogue.)

7. For Woolf's own account of her struggle not to be silenced or to feel that she should be punished for speaking/writing with authority, see "Professions for Women," *The Death of the Moth and Other Essays* (1942; reprint, New York: Harcourt Brace Jovanovich, 1970), pp. 235–242, and the earlier,

angrier version of the same essay, "Speech of January 21, 1931," in Mitchell A. Leaska, ed, *The Pargiters: The Novel-Essay Portion of The Years* (New York: Harcourt Brace Jovanovich, 1977), pp. xxvii–xliv.

8. For Milton, the prohibition is God-given and the transgression is the distance/difference between the mortal and the divine. Why this had to become the difference between male and female is, of course, the obvious question. For Freud, the problem of origins does not begin in relation to the sacred but in relation to violence; that which men most fear happening to themselves has always already happened to women: castration. But as his brooding and strange thoughts on "Medusa's Head" indicate, the prior violence he refuses to name as that which gives rise to Medusa's power to turn men to stone is rape. For his absurd but telling attempt to repress women's weaving back into Nature (our nature—they are the same), see also "The Psychology of Women," *New Introductory Lectures*, p. xxxiii. For the short piece on Medusa, see "Medusa's Head," in Philip Rieff, ed., *Sexuality and the Psychology of Love* (New York: Collier, 1963), pp. 212–213.

9. William Shakespeare, *The Rape of Lucrece,* lines 1287–1288. Philomela plays an important role as icon in the dramatic poem. By imitating not Philomela the weaver, but Philomela the nightingale leaning on a thorn, Lucrece is shown learning how to complete the cycle of violence by taking revenge on herself: she chooses a weapon like the sword Tarquin held to her throat and kills herself (see lines 1128–1148). This essay is part of a longer study of the iconography of rape, which includes Lucrece and her later Roman counterpart, Verginia, and others who were written about and painted in very different ways to varying ideological ends over the centuries. For my interpretation of the stories of Lucrece and Verginia see "Ritual Work on Human Flesh: Livy's Lucrece and the Rape of the Body Politic," *Helios* (Spring 1990); 17:1.

10. Ovid, *Fasti,* trans. Sir James George Frazer (1931; reprint, Cambridge: Harvard University Press, 1959), pp. 105, 107. There is no room to explore the connections here, but three entries in the *Fasti* that follow each other without commentary or transition first made me study rape as a crisis of boundaries and as sacrifice: the sacrifice to Terminus, the rape of Lucrece, and the perpetual flight of Procne from Tereus. Note that Roman tradition reverses the sisters, Procne becoming the swallow and Philomela the nightingale, taken up in the English tradition as the bird pressing her breast to a thorn to make herself sing.

11. Frazer, in his edition of Apollodorus' *Library,* which also records the myth of Philomela, notes that Sophocles' lost play *Tereus* is the text "from which most of the extant versions of the story are believed to be derived." See Apollodorus, *The Library,* trans. Sir James George Frazer (New York: Putnam's, 1921), 2:98. The myth was so well known in fifth-century Athens that Aristophanes could use it to make a lewd joke about the lust of women in his comic account of Athens in crisis, *Lysistrata,* trans. Douglass Parker (New York: New American Library, 1964), p. 74.

12. Page du Bois, *Centaurs and Amazons, Women and the Pre-History of the Great Chain of Being* (Ann Arbor: University of Michigan Press, 1982), p. 78. See also Herodotus' interesting description of Thrace and Thracians at the opening of book 6 of his *History.* In the Thracians the Greek historian imagines the inverse of the virtues most highly valued among Hellenes.

13.

> . . . And Tereus, watching,
> Sees beyond what he sees: she is in his arms,
> That is not her father whom her arms go around,
> Not her father she is kissing. Everything
> Is fuel to his fire. He would like to be
> Her father, at that moment; and if he were
> He would be as wicked a father as he is husband. (lines 478–484)

Ovid's choice to elaborate on the erotic theme of incest is not merely an element of his voyeurism; it is the sign of mimetic desire/rivalry: Tereus wants to become Pandion, not primarily to have full control over Philomela's body, but to control Athens. This is all, of course, seen from the point of view of the Greek imagination, first, then mediated by the Roman poets' perspective.

14. As Ovid does in his description of Tereus looking at Philomela, Shakespeare implicates himself in the very violence he is depicting in the curiously energetic verses about the sleeping Lucrece. The very bed she lies in is male and angry that she cheats it of a kiss. The chaste woman is a tease even in her sleep:

> Her lily hand her rosy cheeks lies under
> Coz'ning the pillow of a lawful kiss;
> Who, therefore angry, seems to part in sunder,
> Swelling on either side to want his bliss;
> Between whose hills her head entombed is;
>> Where like a virtuous monument she lies,
>> To be admired of lewd unhallowed eyes. (lines 386–392)

The poet's eyes are hardly less lewd than the rapist Tarquin's in the lines that follow (393–420). Implicit in Shakespeare's description of Lucrece asleep is the violence of the male eye. Here the woman does not turn the man to stone. Rather, the desiring gaze transforms her into a dead object: she is both "entombed" and as reified as a "monument."

15. Ovid, following others, briefly mentions Pandion at the close of the tale as having been ravaged by grief at the loss of both daughters, which shortened his reign (ll. 673–674). After his death, the exchange of women and violence between Athens and Thrace continues (lines 675–721).

16. René Girard, *Violence and the Sacred,* trans. Patrick Gregory (Baltimore: Johns Hopkins University Press, 1977), p. 235. Further citations will appear in text.

17. See ch. 9 in Mary Douglas, *Purity and Danger: An Analysis of the*

Concepts of Pollution and Taboo (1966; reprint, London: Routledge and Kegan Paul, 1980); also ch. 1 of Girard's *Violence and the Sacred*.

18. When Girard says: "For me, prohibitions come first. Positive exchanges are merely the reverse of avoidance taboos designed to ward off outbreaks of rivalry among males" (p. 239), he assumes a hierarchical structure within culture in which men vie with each other for possession of the dominated group, women. He does not address the question of how gender difference becomes hierarchy any more effectively than does Lévi-Strauss. Both treat hierarchy as a given; both also assume that the male point of view constitutes culture. They work with male texts and male informants, with almost no recognition that the other part of the story—the woman's point of view—is not there. When Girard speaks momentarily of "a father and son —that is, a family" (p. 217), he is representing the most important weakness in his own approach: the person necessary to the birth of the son is left out, the mother. There is no serious discussion of women or of the role of the mother in Girard. I have also found that the denial or erasure of the mother or any articulated community of women is a crucial aspect of the myths I am studying. Unlike Philomela, who has a sister, Lucrece and Verginia have neither mother, sister, nor daughter.

19. Mary Douglas, *Natural Symbols, Explorations in Cosmology* (1970; reprint, New York: Pantheon, 1982), p. 70. Douglas does not pursue the question in feminist terms when she argues: "There is a continual exchange of meanings between the two kinds of bodily experiences so that each reinforces the categories of the others" (p. 65). Feminist literary and art criticism demonstrates that this exchange of meanings becomes conflictual the moment the woman decides to reshape the reigning metaphors, whether in language or in the plastic arts. Then her art threatens the other "body" and does, indeed, represent a problem. By its implicit violence, literary criticism that resolves women's artworks back into known categories of bodily images helped give rise to feminist literary criticism: the recovery of a vocabulary to discuss the oppressive as well as the liberating dialectical exchange of meanings for the female body and the body politic.

For a brilliant discussion of one woman painter's use of a received image to represent her suffering when she was raped by her art teacher and then tortured with thumb screws during her suit against the rapist, see Mary Garrard's essay on Artemisia Gentileschi, "Artemisia and Susanna," in Norma Broude and Mary D. Garrard, eds., *Feminism and Art History: Questioning the Litany* pp. 147–172 (New York: Harper and Row, 1982). The raped woman artist who repaints *Susanna and the Elders* reproduces the sacrificial crisis from the point of view of the falsely accused woman. In doing so, Artemisia takes over the role of Daniel and for the first time the woman can speak and free herself—in art if not yet in law and the culture at large.

Ostriker (see note 1) has demonstrated how women poets first imitate, then deconstruct, and finally refashion the mythical images of their bodies.

20. See Thucydides, *The Peloponnesian War*, trans. Rex Warner (New York: Penguin, 1954), book 2, ch. 2, pp. 107–108. Thucydides notes that the

population had to crowd into Athens, within the Long Walls, so that some had to settle on what was believed to be the sacred ground abutting the wall itself. Some believed that this transgression brought war and plague to Athens. Though skeptical himself, Thucydides carefully records both the mythic interpretation of violence and his own reading of events: "It appears to me that the oracle came true in a way that was opposite to what people expected. It was not because of unlawful settlement in this place that misfortune came to Athens, but it was because of the war that the settlement had to be made. The war was not mentioned by the oracle, though it was foreseen that if this place was settled, it would be at a time when Athens was in difficulties." The echo of the phrase "Athens was in trouble" is noteworthy, as is Thucydides' description of the plague within Athens' walls following the settlement on sacred ground: it has all the elements of the sacrificial crisis—the collapse of all order and differences, legal and religious. See ch. 5 of *The Peloponnesian War*.

For a similar crisis in Rome that ends in rape and not war, see Livy's *Early History of Rome*, book 1. There he describes Servius' wall and the Tarquins' dangerous extension of both the city's wall and the monarch's power, which give rise to the rape of Lucrece. As Livy's *History* and Ovid's *Fasti* suggest, the rape of Lucrece is a crisis of boundaries. The unsuccessful siege of Ardea's walls by Romans gives way to an assault within Rome: or, as Shakespeare puts it, Lucrece becomes the "sweet city" the king's son takes instead (see *Lucrece*, line 469). In Rome, the women victims, Lucrece and Verginia, are not the daughters of kings, but of the leaders of the republican rebellions.

21. See Freud's essay "The Taboo of Virginity" (1918), in which he addresses the question of why so many cultures have generated rituals surrounding the first penetration of the hymen. Freud does not see the same implications that I argue for in this essay.

22. Agememnon tells the Old Man, "Not in fact but in name only / Is there a marriage with Achilles" (lines 127–128), and the Old Man replies, "To bring her here a victim then—a death offering—you promised her to the son of the goddess!" (lines 134–135).

23. Menelaus chides Agamemnon, "You are wrong / To fear the mob so desperately" (line 518).

24. See lines 1345–1350.

25. See Apollodorus, *The Library* 2:98: "But war having broken out with Labdacus on a question of boundaries, he [Pandion] called in the help of Tereus, son of Ares, from Thrace, and having with his help brought the war to a successful close, he gave Tereus his own daughter Procne in marriage."

26. "Difference is represented by Euripides as *internal* rather than external, omnipresent in the body of the Greeks. In the *Bacchae*, Euripides' greatest masterpiece, the tragedian collapses all boundaries, fuses male and female, human being and animal, Greek and barbarian . . . The Peloponnesian War, which set Greek against Greek in *polemos*, war, which was also

stasis, civil war, precipitated the crisis of language, of categories of difference" (Du Bois, pp. 118, 119, 120, emphasis in original).

27. Euripides, *Iphigenia in Aulis:* ". . . I a conspirator / Against my best
beloved and weaving plots / Against her" (lines 743–745).

28.

> CLYTEMNESTRA: Will he, if she resists, drag her away?
> ACHILLES: There is no doubt—and by her golden hair!
> (lines 1365–1366)

The suggestion of a rape in the woman dragged by her hair and screaming is
unmistakable.

29. See lines 1379–1400. Iphigenia offers herself as willing, sacred victim, as "savior of Greece," to uphold the critical difference as her father
offers it to her. After Agamemnon later presents her with an image of Greek
women raped by barbarians, Iphigenia says, "It is / A right thing that Greeks
rule barbarians, / Not barbarians Greeks." Agamemnon knows, however,
that the real conflict is "between brothers" (line 507).

30. In this, as in many other details, Lucrece is described in terms that
recall Philomela. Once raped, Lucrece also feels that she is polluted. Her
body is her soul's "sacred temple spotted, spoiled, corrupted" (line 1172). But
it is a temple built to male honor. Though Lucrece decides that only the
spilling of her own blood can purge her of pollution, for one moment it is
suggested that tears and the telling of her own tale might have served equally
well:

> My tongue shall utter all; mine eyes, like sluices,
> As from a mountain spring that feeds a dale,
> Shall gush pure streams to purge my impure tale.
> (lines 1076–1278)

But it is the poet, of course, who tells the tale, and not Lucrece. She feels
like a sacked city, like Troy; and like Iphigenia, she moves toward death by
learning to speak the language of the victim: she blames Helen for Tarquin's
violence.

31. "It is the knowledge of violence, along with the violence itself, that
the act of expulsion succeeds in shunting outside the realm of consciousness" (Girard, *Violence and the Sacred,* p. 135).

32. René Girard, *To Double Business Bound: Essays on Literature, Mimesis, and Anthropology* (Baltimore: Johns Hopkins University Press, 1978),
p. 188. Though Girard refers to the lynching of blacks in America in this
chapter, "Violence and Representation in the Mythical Text," he does not go
on to discuss that particular historical example of persecution. Had he done
so, he would have had to discuss the rape charge as the excuse commonly
used to lynch black men. A double process of scapegoating goes on in racist
violence, with tragic results for both categories of victim: the black person,
male or female, and the white female. As Ida Wells-Barnett, a militant and
peaceful civil rights leader, said in a speech to the 1909 National Negro

Conference, "Lynching is color-line murder," and, "Crimes against women is the excuse, not the cause." See Philip S. Foner, ed., *The Voice of Black America*, 2:71–75. Wells-Barnett's brief speech contains a superb example of a persecution myth generated by a white male racist who uses the image of the "mob" to his own ends. It has taken us a long time to see that actual rapes as well as the exchange of accusations of rape across the color line make use of the gender line within both groups, the line that precedes and also appears finally more intractable than the color line.

33. Frazer records, in a note to Apollodorus' text, that "Ovid . . . appears to have associated the murder of Itys with the frenzied rites of the Bacchanals, for he says that the crime was perpetrated at the time when the Thracian women were celebrating the biennial festival . . . of Dionysus, and that the two women disguised themselves as Bacchanals" (*The Library* 2:99). See Humphries' edition of the *Metamorphoses*, lines 585–607. To frame the rescue of Philomela and the murder of Itys with details of the Bacchanal is to suggest a likeness between Procne as unnatural mother and Agave, her counterpart in Euripides' *Bacchae*, who rends her son, the king Pentheus, under the spell of the Bacchic rites. Ovid presents the rites as degenerate: a festival that turns back into bloody and monstrous violence. He also trades on misogynist lore by making it clear that his Procne only pretends to be a Bacchante, suggesting that the rites are or were only a cover for the unleashing of female revenge against men. But Ovid cannot draw on the *Bacchae* or other Bacchic stories without drawing out the ambiguities within the whole tradition surrounding Dionysus. Greeks believed Dionysus' home was Thrace. The women in the myth are Greeks transported to Thrace. Among the reversals in the myth is this movement away from Athens, an actual center of Dionysian rites, back to the god's home, to represent the crisis in Greek culture when invaded by foreign religion.

Girard is shrewd in his analysis of the predominance of women in the Dionysiac cult. For his discussion of the displacement of responsibility for the sacrificial crisis and the ritual murder of the king onto women, see ch. 5, "Dionysus," in *Violence and the Sacred*, especially pp. 139–142.

34. See, for example, Achilles Tatius' novel *Leukippe and Kleitophon*: "Prokne, learning the rape from the robe, exacted an exorbitant revenge: the conspiracy of two women and two passions, jealousy and outrage, plan a feast far worse than his weddings. The meal was Tereus' son, whose mother *had* been Prokne before her fury was roused and she forgot that older anguish. For the pains of present jealousy are stronger than the womb's remembrance. Only passionate women making a man pay for a sexual affront, even if they must endure as much harm as they impose, count the pain of their affliction a small price for the pleasure of the infliction."

I would like to thank John Winkler for pointing out this passage to me and for providing me with his own translation in *The Ancient Greek Novels in Translation*, ed. Bryan P. Reardon (Berkeley: University of California Press), emphasis in original.

35. See Victor Turner, chs. 3, 4 in *The Ritual Process: Structure and*

Anti-Structure (Ithaca: Cornell University Press, 1969), and chs. 1, 6, 7 in
Dramas, Fields, and Metaphors: Symbolic Action in Human Society (Ithaca:
Cornell University Press, 1974). Turner says: "In human history, I see a
continuous tension between structure and communitas, at all levels of scale
and complexity. Structure, or all that which holds people apart, defines their
differences, and constrains their actions, is one pole in a charged field, for
which the opposite pole is communitas, or anti-structure . . . Communitas
does not merge identities; it liberates them from conformity to general
norms, though this is necessarily a transient condition if society is to continue to operate in an orderly fashion" ("Metaphors of Anti-Structure," in
Dramas, p. 274). Structure is coercive, but antistructure can be crisis *or*
peace. If Turner tends to spend more time looking at the peaceful dimensions
of *communitas* and Girard attends more to the violent, it is nevertheless
possible to find in the work of both the ground for symbolic or unbloody
sacrifice in art. Or, as Turner suggests, "metaphor is, in fact, metamorphic,
transformative" (*Dramas*, p. 25). The loom as instrument of transformation
and wool as the hair of the sacrificial beast which women, by a long and
careful process, transform into clothing suggest why weaving skirts the
sacred and the violent. It also suggests why women's power at the loom is
both derided and dreaded, transformed, like giving birth, into a sign of
weakness by patriarchal uses of language and symbol. I am arguing that
Philomela and with her feminist theorists and artists use an old instrument/
metaphor to new, positive ends. I am also arguing that this process need not
reproduce violence.

36. See Mary Douglas, *Purity and Danger*, ch. 6, "Powers and Dangers."
37. Euripides, *The Bacchae*, lines 118, 512–515.
38. See the exchange between Myrrhine and her husband, Kinesias.
39. Ovid, *Heroides*, line 15.
40. See Hazel E. Barnes, "The Myth of Medusa," *The Meddling Gods:
Four Essays on Classical Themes* (Lincoln: University of Nebraska Press,
1974), p. 6; and Jane Ellen Harrison, *Prolegomena to the Study of Greek
Religion* (Cambridge: Cambridge University Press, 1903), pp. 187–196. Douglas
notes that in some cultures strict taboo regulates when a woman can work
with fire. Girard notes that Hestia may be the locus of the early sacrificial
rites, but he does not ask why the common hearth should be given a female
identity and be identified with virginity. See ch. 9 of *Purity and Danger* and
pp. 166–167 (on masks) and pp. 305, 314–315 (on Hestia) of *Violence and
the Sacred*. If the common hearth was in fact the locus of ritual sacrifice, it
is all the more important that in myth Procne turns back to the hearth to
cook her own child as she undoes all of her female roles in culture.

41. Freud's formula can be found in "Medusa's Head," where it becomes
clear that his greatest dread is the woman as mother: Medusa's snaky head
is the sign of the mother's monstrous genitals. For a list of modern women's
poems about Medusa and their intense struggle to free themselves from the
mythic uses of her, see Ostriker, "The Thieves of Language."

42. Maxine Hong Kingston, *The Woman Warrior: Memoirs of a Girl-*

hood among Ghosts (New York: Vintage/ Random House, 1977), pp. 62–63.

43. Gabriela Mistral, *Selected Poems*, p. 204. This is not an exclusively feminist idea. See, for example, *"Revelation:* The Text as Acceptable Sacrifice," in Dennis J. Costa, *Irenic Apocalypse: Some Uses of Apocalyptic in Dante, Petrarch, and Rabelais, Stanford French and Italian Studies* (Saratoga, California: Anma Libri, 1981), 21:22–39. See also Costa's "Stuck Sow or Broken Heart: Pico's *Oratio* as Ritual Sacrifice," *JMRS* (Fall 1982), 12:221–235.

2
THE RHETORIC
OF ELISION

3

The Marquise's "O"
and the Mad Dash of Narrative

SUSAN WINNETT

Masters, they have exercised their rights as masters. They write,
of their authority to accord names, that it goes back so far that
the origin of language itself may be considered an act of authority emanating from those who . . . dominate. Thus they say that
they have said, this is such or such a thing, they have attached a
particular word to an object or a fact and thereby consider themselves to have appropriated it. The women say, so doing the men
have bawled shouted with all their might to reduce you to silence. The women say, the language you speak poisons your
glottis tongue palate lips. They say, the language you speak is
made up of words that are killing you. They say, the language
you speak is made up of signs that rightly speaking designate
what men have appropriated. Whatever they have not laid hands
on, whatever they have not pounced on like many-eyed birds of
prey, does not appear in the language you speak. This is apparent
precisely in the intervals that your masters have not been able
to fill with their words of proprietors and possessors, this can be
found in the gaps, in all that which is not a continuation of their
discourse, in the zero, the O, the perfect circle that you invent
to imprison them and to overthrow them.   Monique Witting

. . . hysterics are particularly constituted creatures . . . in whom
a shrinking from sexuality . . . is raised to a pathological pitch
and is permanently retained; that is, they are, as it were, people
who are psychically inadequate to meeting the demands of sexuality. But this view, of course, leaves hysteria in men out of
account.   Sigmund Freud

Toward the beginning of Heinrich von Kleist's *The Marquise of O,*
the heroine, in flight from the Russian troops laying siege to her
father's citadel, finds her escape blocked by a hoard of marauding
soldiers who undertake to sweeten their conquest by raping her:

"Here, just as she was trying to escape through the back door, she had the misfortune to encounter a troop of enemy riflemen, who as soon as they saw her suddenly fell silent, slung their guns over their shoulders and, with obscene gestures, seized her and carried her off. In vain she screamed for help to her terrified women. . . . Dragging her into the innermost courtyard, they began to assault her in the most shameful way, and she was about to sink to the ground."[1] At the crucial moment, a Russian officer arrives, repels "the lustful dogs," and kills one of them in a gesture that seems apt symbolic retribution for the attempted rape: "He smashed the hilt of his sword into the face of one of the murderous brutes, who still had his arms round her slender waist, and the man reeled back with blood pouring from his mouth . . ." (pp. 69–70). The novella's most famous nonscene follows; the screams, grunts, and savage gestures of war are momentarily forgotten, as the Count, who has seemed to the Marquise "an angel of heaven,"

> then, paying the lady his respects in French, offered her his arm and led her into the other wing of the palace which the flames had not yet reached and where, already speechless from all this turmoil, she lost consciousness and collapsed. Here—as the Marquise's frightened women arrived, he took measures to call a doctor; assured them, as he put on his hat, that she would recover soon, and returned to the war (p. 70, translation mine).

As most everyone knows, the nonscene to which I have referred is probably the most delicately accomplished rape in our literature.[2] After saving—and, we will find out later, raping—the Marquise and conquering her father's fortress, the Count departs with his troops. Later that day, it is reported, he falls on the battlefield. Some time later, after the Commandant and his family take up residence in a town house, the Count reappears and, quite out of the blue, makes the Marquise a marriage proposal. Despite the Marquise's stated resolution never to remarry, the Count is inexplicably insistent and is placated only by the family's promise to consider his proposal seriously after they have become better acquainted with him. After some negotiation, the Count leaves to accompany some dispatches to Naples. Soon after his departure, the Marquise is again plagued by the indispositions that had bothered her before the Count's reappearances and which remind her—bafflingly—of the morning sickness she experienced in her second pregnancy. As the signs of pregnancy become unmistakable, the Marquise, who, we are to believe, is truly unaware of how she could possibly have become pregnant, summons first a doctor and then a midwife, both of whom confirm the impossible. Spurned by her family, she retires with her children to the seclusion of her own estate, where she awaits the term of her pregnancy: "This splendid effort made her acquainted with herself, and, as if with her own hands, she raised herself up out of all the depths in which fate had thrown her. . . . Her reason was strong enough not to give way in her strange situation, and she submitted herself entirely to the great, holy, and inexplicable order of the world. . . . She decided to withdraw wholly into her innermost self . . ." (p. 93, translation mine). In her solitude, she resolves to discover the father of her child by advertising in the newspapers that ". . . unbeknownst to herself [she] had found herself in a certain situation, that the father of the child that she was expecting should disclose himself, and that, because of family considerations, she was determined to marry him" (p. 68, translation mine).

This advertisement provokes the Marquise's mother to test and prove her daughter's innocence and paves the way for the Marquise's reconciliation with her father. It also, of course, makes it the Count's duty to marry the woman he desires. On the appointed day, the Count presents himself in the Commandant's home; the Marquise is appalled by the identity of the baby's father (no one, of course, speaks of "her rapist") and at first refuses to go through with the wedding. Finally, however, the couple marries, on the condition that the Count relinquishes all the prerogatives of a husband. After the birth of a son, however, and after the Count bestows a fortune upon the child and declares its mother his sole heir, relations between the Marquise and her "husband" gradually improve. A year later, the Count proposes to the Marquise again and is accepted. Another wedding is celebrated, and in the course of the years, the text informs us, "a whole series of little Russians now followed, one after the other. . . ." In the final sentence of the novella, the Count asks why, on the day he had presented himself as the father of her child, she had fled from him as from the devil. She answers that "he would never have appeared to her then as a devil, had he not, at his first appearance, seemed like an angel" (p. 143, translation mine).

The trajectory of the narrative could be said to parallel the history of the Marquise's perception of the Count, were it not for the fact that he never appears to us as a devil. Indeed, the horror that I expect every reader feels about rape is as absent affectively as it is on the level of representation. Criticism of the novella has traditionally dwelt upon the courageous nobility of the Marquise, who defies her family in maintaining her innocence and is finally rewarded by the happy marriage, or it has stressed the courageous nobility of the Count, who recognizes the wrong he has done and risks ridicule and rejection to atone for it. More recent criticism has moved away from such exclusively thematic concerns and has proved itself more interested in abstract (and not necessarily feminist) reflections on how the text produces its construction of the feminine than in the rape.[3] And indeed, the text supports critical treatment of its main event as a trope rather than an action.[4] Reduced to a "dash" to which the reader will not pay any particular attention, the rape will achieve representation only through the narrative of its consequences, and this narrative will necessarily focus upon the mind and body of the (unconscious) victim rather than on the mind and body of the rapist. To the extent, then, that the reader ultimately "knows" about the rape without having had to encounter it in the text and thereby experience it affectively, s/he complies in what I hope to show to be broader cultural processes that relegate to the "heroine's plot" particular untold stories of male violence.

In the novella's opening scene, we too see the Count as the angel who delivers the innocent Marquise from the horde of soldiers seeking the usual reward for a successfully accomplished siege. To a hypothetical innocent reader, innocent, that is, of what s/he will later discover to have happened during the "dash," the sentence: "Here—he took . . . measures to call a doctor" ("Hier—traf er . . . Anstalten, einen Arzt zu rufen") makes perfect sense; the dash could be accurately accounted for by its German name, *Gedankenstrich* ("thought-dash"), representing mimetically the mental processes through which the "thoughtful" Count arrives at his decision to call a doctor. Such a reading is given greater credence by the different punctuation of the earlier sentence, also beginning with "Here," that chronicles the "thoughtless" soldiers' violent interruption of the Marquise's flight ("Here, unfortunately, she encountered . . . a troop of enemy riflemen" ["Hier, unglücklicherweise begegnete ihr . . . ein Trupp feindlicher Scharfschützen"]). In fact, it's unlikely that an unsuspecting reader's attention would be drawn to the dash, since the text is full of such typographical tics as asterisks, periods, and dashes, conventional eighteenth-century marks of discretion turning proper names into ciphers, lending authenticity to a story by masking the identities of those real people whose privacy the narrative would otherwise compromise. Much as the innocent Marquise's trauma-induced slumber continues through the Count's violation of her, the reader's preoccupation with the text's linguistic, typographic, and episodic density prevents her/him from seeing in the

Gedankenstrich anything crucial to the novella's denouement. It's not that a veil is being drawn over something the Marquise and/or reader knows is happening; rather, neither is conscious *that* anything of significance is happening at all—and this unconsciousness that the reader temporarily shares with the Marquise will be of the utmost significance in the novella's drive (one could say "dash") toward signification. The dash thus signifies not only the event upon which the existence of the narrative depends, but also the ideological complicities that permit the narrative to take its energies from this event without representing it. The intelligibility of *The Marquise of O* is in no way compromised by the suppression of the rape, although the Marquise's own credibility is most certainly compromised by its consequences. As the word "rape" remains unspoken, both the text's closural principles and family and community rituals accommodate its issue in a happy ending.

> . . . every story one chooses to tell is a kind of censorship, it prevents the telling of other tales . . .
>
> Salman Rushdie
> *Shame*

The closural processes that lead to the novella's happy end depend first upon our reading the rape as an accident, an unpremeditated, impulsive act about which the Count is subsequently truly remorseful, and second upon our regarding rape as something for which one can indeed adequately atone, something that, in the text's own words, can be assimilated into "the old order of things" (p. 73, translation mine).[5] If we decide that the Count was not in control of himself at the time of the rape, we can read the dash, the *Gedankenstrich*, as a sign of the temporary lapse of thought; the rest of the narrative would then chronicle the return of the Count's presence of mind, his attempt to fill in the blank, retroactively to make amends for a transport, a reckless act committed in the heat of battle that he will call "the only unworthy act he had committed in his life, unknown to the world" (p. 77, translation mine). This interpretation demands, moreover, that we condone a cultural reading of male sexuality as by nature—and *therefore* pardonably—beyond the control of even the otherwise most exquisite soul. Such an assumption has an enormous force in our constructions of sexuality and social organization: it subtends Rousseau's organization of sexuality in the *Emile* as well as such practices as the therapeutic (and ritual) castration of sexual offenders and stray male dogs. It is both the driving principle of our culture and the fact that culture is organized to obscure. When the Count claims that he is in the process of atoning for the "only unworthy act he has committed in his life, unknown to the world," he is articulating exactly an economy whose primary task is so to separate male sexuality from the man that the institutions of the latter (mankind, culture, marriage, even, as we will see, war) are policed by the threat of the former (our shorthand for which will be rape).

Nowhere does the delicacy of this transaction become more apparent than in war, and the juxtaposition of war and rape in Kleist's text gives us the opportunity to examine the way our culture negotiates the relations among sexuality, violence, and social institutions. In its thematics, *The Marquise of O* substitutes, in effect, rape for war. At the same time, by suppressing a rape that takes place in the midst of a battle whose gore is faithfully, if not hyperbolically, treated, it preserves the representational context of war, thus provoking reflection upon a representational economy that has to ignore the brutalization of women in war while allowing their bodies to tell the story of war's brutalization of men.

In a recent essay, Cora Stephan traces what she sees as the deterioration of war from a personalized, ritualized, profoundly regulated male game to an anonymous, technologized enterprise of unspecified gender.[6] She regards today's warfare as all the more murderous because its repertoire of martial arts—which differ from other forms of data processing only through their (usually) unseen and (fortunately) unimaginable consequences—no longer enable one plausibly to act out the drama of his (or her) honor. Stephan reflects on the apparently ludicrous martial pomp of earlier centuries and asks:

> . . . is it simply laughable, ridiculous, when a ritual of salutes, swords, and military discipline unfolds over the inferno; is it merely comical when a senseless massacre is decorated with plush, pomp, and banners? Why must men dress up when they attack each other? Why do they fall into regimental order; what good are the drills with weapons that are ultimately fired without any ceremony at all? What kind of peculiar dance of death inspires whole platoons to run directly at each other with drums and fifes and colorful uniforms and perform their curious pantomime: take up arms, fire, fall down dead; close ranks, take up arms, fire, fall down dead; resume positions, take up arms, fire, fall down . . .

In the midst of a bloodbath, an orderly [proper] proceeding.
(pp. 18–19)[7]

To this, what she calls "the heartbreakingly masculine endeavor to maintain forms, regardless of the obstacles" (p. 19), Stephan juxtaposes our contemporary notion of war: "We are no longer in the habit of regarding war as a business of culture. On the contrary: the wars of the 20th century . . . have lost all appearance of being based on any cultural achievement of channeling, enclosing, or limiting aggressive potential or 'basic instincts.' Instead, they appear to be the unchaining of unmitigated brutality, like the incarnation of force *sui generis*" (p. 30).

Stephan then proceeds to equate the brutality of technologized warfare with traditional male conceptions of female violence. In doing so, however, she betrays the extent to which her thought is governed by the cultural constructions of sexuality one would assume she wants to combat. I cite the following passage because of its clear demonstration of how serious reflection about male violence manages to exclude the violence against women which has always been the reward for the successful execution of the more elegantly choreographed variety practiced on (or with?) the enemy. Stephan begins by insisting upon a distinction between violence and war and continues:

> Modern war violates rules that are supposed to distinguish male violence [force][8] from everything that is held to be womanish. *It unchains the furor.* It is insidious and deceiving, it breaks with a gender-specific division of labor, it no longer differentiates between soldiers and civilians, and its modi operandi have robbed men of the privilege of bearing weapons.
>
> Modern war, as it has become conceivable, is everything that men have always claimed about female violence [force]: *It is formless, raw expression.* (p. 37, my emphasis)

The identification of the feminine as "formless, raw expression," while not endorsed by Stephan, does in fact receive the same sanction in her argument that it receives in the cultural constructions upon which she considers herself to be performing a critical operation: she *needs* it as much in her invective against war as do the advocates of war in their paens to military discipline. In her enumeration of traditionally "female" crimes (child murderers [especially "in other cultures and other epochs"], poisoners, killers of husbands, Salomé, Lady Macbeth, and the warrior Jeanne d'Arc are lumped together as representative of a typically female capacity for violence), she never pauses to wonder *why* a patriarchal culture designates these particular crimes as generically "female" (that a particular kind of cowardice inhabits even the woman with the courage to kill is demonstrated by the cases of Lady Macbeth and Salomé, who "let others do the killing"). What Stephan fails even to mention is that every crime here attributed to women by the cultural imagination is committed daily by very unimaginary men and that such crimes as child murders and poisonings have traditionally been "solved" by framing a woman who may or may not be culpable—or who may have been driven to it by such rituals as male bonding, wife beating, philandering, and rape.

If I began by claiming that the closural processes of *The Marquise of O* depend on our assuming the uncontrollable violence of male sexuality, my discussion of Stephan's argument would seem to suggest a cultural need for an equation of violence and the feminine. The institutions that express, regulate, and celebrate masculinity by calling violence strength (the military, sports, business, whatever) notoriously exclude women; discipline and strength are associated with a masculinity, which, given the absence of women in these spheres, appears to subsist naturally and blissfully outside the circuit of sexuality.[9] It is obvious that any ritual of order, especially such a ritual as war, where a real enemy has to be trusted to obey, as it were, a gentleman's agreement to abide by the rules, requires that its Other—uncontrolled violence—be clearly designated and gendered. As long as this Other is gendered female, war functions as a solemn ceremony of male bonding and a political institution at the same time as it remains a terrifying expression of violence and an aggressive, if unconscious, enactment of male fear of women.[10] In her nostalgia for a time when "war was an affair of culture," Stephan forgets to examine how the arrangements that encode violence into civilized gestures provide for the excesses that these gestures can neither accommodate nor negotiate.

As Klaus Theweleit makes clear in *Male Fantasies*, martial ideologies repress a male fear of women by celebrating ascetic male communion. Like football teams ("we don't think about women during practice"), armies do their serious work in a sphere from which (trivial) issues of sexuality are (conveniently) excluded. The celebratory copulation at the end of a tournament, like the successful occupier's conquest by force of all the enemy's women, has (the mythology has it) less to do with sexuality than with the economy of victory; it has less to do with women than with the spoils of war or "letting off steam."[11] This kind of sex is held, of course, to have nothing to do with love.

The Marquise of O maintains this distinction by juxtaposing the "lustful animals" who attempt to rape the Marquise in the heat of battle and the French-speaking gentleman who rescues her, only to rape her himself in a quieter (and less textually conspicuous) moment. The tact of the gentleman—and the tact due the gentleman—shroud his "unworthy deed" in silence. For not only does the Count conform to the rules of the game, he is himself the enforcer of them. Or rather, he obeys simultaneously the rules of *two* games: the rules of battle and the discrete manners of his class. We recall, for instance, the passage where the Commandant surrenders to the Count: ". . . the Commandant, who had only continued to resist because he had not been offered amnesty, was withdrawing to the main gate with dwindling strength when the Russian officer . . . called on him to surrender. The Commandant replied that this demand was all he had been waiting for, handed over his sword, and asked for permission to go into the castle and look for his family. The Russian officer . . . gave him leave to do so, accompanied by a guard" (p. 70, translation modified). Kleist's description of the battle constantly alternates between martial brutality and sociable politesses; when both the vanquished Commandant and the Russian commanding officer praise the Count for his "noble behavior," only the fact that he blushes betrays the conflict his rape of the Marquise has precipitated—a conflict that blurs and renders inoperative the distinctions between the battlefield and the drawing room that organize the life of the gentleman warrior.

It is this conflict, the fact that the Count cannot relegate the rape to the battlefield any more than he can visit the Marquise's drawing room without recalling it, that is responsible for his bizarre and abrupt proposal of marriage. The more passionately he presses his case, the odder his behavior appears. But with the insistence of a hysterical symptom, he restructures his hosts' intentions around his demand, announcing his resolution to abandon his mission in order that the Marquise get to know him as quickly as possible. Later, of course, we will realize that the Count's precipitousness has a real and compelling reason: he alone has grounds to suspect that the Marquise's slight indisposition is indeed a sign of pregnancy. But for the moment, the Count's behavior strikes everyone as thoroughly bizarre: "All agreed that his behaviour was very unusual, and that he seemed to be accustomed to conquering women's hearts by storm, as if they were fortresses" (p. 114, translation mine). This passage provides the first *textual* clues to the Count's motivations, likening his courtship of the Marquise to the kind of military scenario in which he first saved her from "being taken by storm" and then took her by storm himself. It also marks the limitations of the Count's military manners, suggesting the kind of traumatic conflict between the sociocultural and personal significance of a sexualized event that results in a hysterical attack. If "the hysteric suffers mainly from reminiscences,"[12] the Count suffers from the memory of a rape that means more to him than the rules of war admit. He alone harbors this memory, but he cannot atone for it alone. In order to make it clear why he needs to marry the Marquise, he would have to confess the rape. But the confession would so discredit him that a marriage would be out of the question. In his own way, then, the Count fits the description of the hysteric I cited in my epigraph and demonstrates how the psychic inability to deal with pathological sexual reticence describes the hysterical male as soon as we examine critically our constructions of male sexuality.

Not only the aetiology of the Count's "hysteria," but also its manifestations recall the kinds of disturbances reported in the psychoanalytic literature. Like a hysterical symptom, the Count's behavior disrupts the "order of things" restored after his siege of the fort. It causes the course of family life to reorganize itself around a set of largely incomprehensible demands: the Marquise, who had determined never again to marry, is pressured to abandon this resolution in order to reward her rescuer; the Count takes up residence immediately and unexpectedly in the Commandant's house. And these manifestations are, of course, but harbingers of a far more dramatic disruption around which the family will have to reorganize itself, namely, the Marquise's pregnancy. What is most striking about the Count's "hysterical" attack is its success; he more or less gets what he wants. His "hysteria" is far more effective, far less self-destructive, than that classically associated with women. Unlike hysteria in women that knows no representation that doesn't entirely disrupt familial, social, and narrative fabric, the Count's hysteria manages to be both manifested and contained by a syntax that, although bizarre, is never incorrect or incoherent.[13] Even though the Count's most conspicuous somatizing is linguistic, he does not fail to make himself effectively understood. Unlike the syntax of the hysteric, which, as Freud puts it in the "Dora" case history,[14] is by definition incapable of expressing a desire directly or articulating cause and effect, the Count's desire is presented in an indirect discourse (which is to say shared to some extent by the normative language of a narration upon whose authority we have no choice but to rely) that preserves hysterical affect at the same time as it exhibits an excessive, even precious grammatical and syntactical precision. Asked by the Marquise's mother how he came to survive the reportedly fatal injury, the Count explains

> ... that he had been carried to P . . . mortally wounded in the chest; that he had despaired of his life for several months; that during this time his every thought had been devoted to the Marquise; that he could not describe the pleasure and pain that embraced themselves in this idea; that after his recovery he had finally rejoined the army; that he had there been quite unable to set his mind at rest; that he had several times taken up his pen to release the agitation of his heart by writing to the Colonel and the Marquise; . . . that it had become impossible for him to continue living without having a clear conscience about a necessary demand of his soul; that as he was passing through M . . . he had been unable to resist the impulse to take a few steps towards the fulfillment of this purpose; in short, that he deeply desired the happiness of the Marquise's hand in marriage, and that he begged most fervently and urgently, that she answer him positively. (pp. 75–76, translation modified)

I have quoted at such length first to reproduce the melodramatic language of an affect for which the Count obviously has no experience and second in order to capture the texture of the syntax in which his communications are always narrated. The seemingly endless string of *"dass"* ("that") phrases ("he replied that . . . , that . . . , that . . . , that . . .") is not characteristic of the novella's prose in general; the sentences of indirect discourse relating comparable speeches by other characters are just as long, but are not punctuated by the *"dass"* that persists in the account of the Count's discourse like a nervous tic.[15] Each *"dass"* phrase strikes the reader as yet another inevitably inadequate attempt to explain the Count's motivations without revealing their true source and conveys nicely the anxiety accompanying his appeal. This anxiety is not without its contagion, and the Marquise's family, at a loss for how to deal with the Count's proposal and the self-destructive measures he takes in his insistence, negotiates a deferral by promising that the Marquise will marry no one else while the Count is delivering his dispatches in Naples. Frustrated by the impasse he has reached, the Count departs, leaving the family in a state of considerable confusion.

> And lucky you are, that your purpose is so simple and limited! Through you nature wants only to reach its goals; through us men, the state wants to reach its own. And out of this situation the most unholy contradictions develop.
>
> [Und wohl euch, dass eure Bestimmung so einfach und beschränkt ist! Durch euch will die Natur nur ihre Zwecke erreichen, durch uns Männer auch der Staat noch die seinigen, und daraus entwickeln sich oft die unseligsten Widersprüche.]
>
> Kleist
"On the Enlightenment of Woman"
(Über die Aufklärung des Wiebes")

In the Count's absence, the Marquise's pregnancy becomes unmistakable and her body takes over the telling of the story he cannot confess. In what amounts to a gesture of etymological downward displacement, the womb *(hyster)* of the Marquise becomes the locus of the representation and working through of the Count's hysterical conflict. We should note that the text has announced this downward displacement at its outset, in a parenthetical phrase following the title: *"The Marquise of O* (After a true occurrence, whose scene has been transfered from north to south)" ["Nach einer wahren Begebenheit, deren Schauplatz vom Norden nach dem Süden verlegt worden"]. The fictionalization of this "true story" lies in a *Verlegung* (transfer, relocation) of the scene from north to south, from the head to the body. Now the word *verlegt* not only means "transfer," but also "published," and recalls as well the adjective *verlegen*, which means "self-conscious" or "embarrassed." The novella's title thus announces the transformations through which the embarrassing event, the event that shatters the Count's self-consciousness, becomes socially representable (in the Marquise's pregnant body) and publishable (in *The Marquise of O*).

It is in this sense that we can speak of the "mad dash of narrative." The event suppressed by the dash and repressed in all the Count's appeals for the Marquise's hand is worked through in the ensuing narrative of pregnancy, disinheritance, reconciliation, marriage, birth, and remarriage. The generic laws of romance and the social laws governing marriage and inheritance conspire not only to make sufficient amends, but to domesticate the Count's madness and ensure that the rape itself remains enshrouded in tact, if not ultimately "unknown to the world." (When the Count marries the Marquise, anyone who's read the newspaper would be expected to draw the appropriate conclusions.)

The innocent Marquise, on the other hand, enjoys no such consideration. "A pure conscience and a midwife!" her mother exclaims when the Marquise summons a midwife to controvert the judgment of the doctor. Pregnancy and innocence are incompatible, and as long as she is held responsible for her pregnancy, the world insists on representing to her what it takes her to be denying. When the Marquise asks the doctor how she could possibly be pregnant, he replies "that he would not have to explain the facts of life to her" (p. 86, translation mine). The midwife who confirms the doctor's diagnosis is even more explicit in her insistence upon the Marquise's disingenuousness: "The midwife . . . spoke of hot-blooded youth and the wiles of the world; . . . she remarked that she had come across such cases before; young widows who found themselves in her ladyship's situation always believed themselves to have been living on desert islands; but that was no cause for alarm, and her ladyship could rest assured that the lusty corsair who had come ashore in the dark would come to light in due course" (p. 90, translation modified).

The midwife turns out to be right. The novella will of course ultimately restore to the Marquise both her "corsair" and the innocence she has lost in the eyes of the world. Yet there is an important respect in which the Marquise's pregnancy ravishes her of a different kind of innocence and in which she does indeed pass on the violence done to her. Like those notorious women Cora Stephan enumerates in her catalogue of female criminals, the Marquise (quite literally) *shows*. Her body makes visible what would otherwise have remained entirely hidden, revealing the universality of the practices of war associated with common soldiers and publicly execrated by the nobility; in her innocence, she divulges a cultural secret. In her very visibility she does violence to the social order in which she lives and which the novella always associates with a male figure, be it her father or brother or, finally, the Count. Moreover, it is not only her distended body that ruffles the complacency of a world that seems less disturbed by the enemy takeover than it is by her pregnancy. It is not, as we would assume, the scandal of the Marquise's pregnancy that occasions the novella's narratability, but rather, the advertisement in the newspapers of her willingness to marry the father of her child. Goethe described the novella as "a scandalous [unheard (of)] occurrence that has happened to take place" ("eine sich ereignete unerhörte Begebenheit").[16] In *The Marquise of O*, what provokes the telling (the making "told" ["erhört"]) of the scandalous ("unerhört") event is her advertisement in the newspapers.[17] The novella begins: "In M. . . , an important town in northern Italy, the widowed Marquise of O . . . , a lady of unblemished reputation and the mother of several well-brought-up children, had it be known through the newspapers that . . ." (p. 68). In the next sentence the Marquise is described as "the lady who took such a strange step with such assurance and provoked the derision of the world under the constraint of unalterable circumstances" (p. 68); in other words, here too her public deed, and not necessarily her pregnancy, is presented as exceptional enough to inspire a recitation of the events surrounding it: the battle, the Count's death and resurrection, his proposal, the pregnancy, her banishment, and the novella's concluding reconciliations.

When her appeal is answered, the Marquise is horrified and reviles the Count, calling him a devil. Although she marries him because of the "family considerations" mentioned in the advertisement, she does not seem to have gotten what she wanted. And indeed, according to my argument so far, the novella's euphoric resolution of the heroine's plot seems to accomplish itself mainly for the "hero's" benefit. To the extent that the happy end involves keeping secrets and upholding the status quo, its resolution bears the Count's signature. (We note that the multitudinous offspring alluded to in the penultimate sentence are "little Russians.") No protest about the rituals of arms and men disturbs the concluding mood of general contentment; never, of course, do we wonder seriously whether the Count's first son will become a pacifist or a feminist. The text has, indeed, restored the "old order of things" and so reconciled the family that they all move to the country together.

> Whatever they have not laid hands on, whatever they have not pounced on like many-eyed birds of prey, does not appear in the language you speak.
>
> Monique Wittig

At the end of *The Marquise of O*, nothing seems less appropriate than the talk of war, violence, or rape with which I began this discussion. Moreover, to say that *The Marquise of O* is the story of a rape is to decide that the novella is about something it takes conspicuously ingenious measures to exclude from representation. As I have tried to show, instead of suppressing stealthily the premises that would undermine its representational system, *The Marquise of O* overtly demonstrates its utter dependence upon both the rape and its suppression. Without the rape there would be no story —no story of the Count and no story of the virtuous widow. It remains to ask: Whose is the story of a rape? What is the relation between the tale told in the Marquise's name that is really the story of the Count and that other story, the Marquise's story, about which I've written far less? Is the Marquise nothing but a zero, an empty vessel through which the story of male hysteria achieves indirect representation? Or is there in the novella an analogue to Wittig's "O," the "zero, the O, the perfect circle that you invent to imprison them and to overthrow them"? I will go only so far as to suggest that the Marquise's matter-of-fact, practical attitude toward her pregnancy and the decision to publish her search for the child's father amount to a subtly violent assault on a world accustomed to a woman's hysterical sobs on the one hand and "confinement" on the other. The Marquise *does*, as the novella's final sentence tells us, get what she wants (she has "loved" the Count ever since the rescue), but she doesn't pretend to have gotten it her way. And her conduct throughout her ordeal has exposed the mechanics of an "order of things" that makes it possible for war to be regarded as an "orderly procedure," that assumes that a gentleman's sexuality is also gentle, and that arranges that his "follies" be atoned for by an other. In the course of the Count's fitful courtship of the Marquise, he tells her how she reminds him of a swan that he had seen on his uncle's estate: "that he had once thrown dirt at this swan, whereupon it had silently dived under the surface of the water and reemerged purified; that she had always seemed to be swimming around on fiery waves and that he had called her Tinka!, which was the name of this swan; that he was however never able to lure her towards him, since she took her pleasure in gliding around, arching her neck, and thrusting out her breast" (p. 82, translation modified).

The Marquise of O debunks the fantasy articulated in this anecdote. It suppresses the defilement of the Marquise (depriving the Count of the pathos of demonstrable guilt) while it demystifies the process of "purification" by exposing what takes place in secret, underwater, in the fantasy. The "unattainable swan" is a woman who becomes attainable because of the way pregnancy forces a woman to seek a husband. The Marquise's simultaneously passionate and sober pragmatics stand in sharp contrast to the hysterical pleas and rash theatrics of the Count. And although, as I have argued, the narrative bearing her name (necessarily) ends up telling the story of the Count's desire, it has circumscribed this desire (with an "O"?) and enabled us to question what our culture otherwise takes for granted. The next step would be for a man to tell the story of why men rape, critically to examine how a rapist comes to need to inflict himself so violently.[18] Until now the story of a rape has almost always been the woman's story: where she was attacked, how she did or did not defend herself, how she did or did not recover from the physical and emotional damage. We now need to know what struggles men are really waging when they take the easy way out and fight the next battle in their war against women.

NOTES

The first epigraph is from Monique Wittig, *Les Guerrillères*, trans. David Le Vay (New York: Avon, 1973), pp. 112–114.

The second epigraph: Sigmund Freud, "The Aetiology of Hysteria," trans. James Strachey, in Jeffrey Moussaieff Masson, *The Assault on Truth: Freud's Suppression of the Seduction Theory* (New York: Viking Penguin, 1985), p. 269.

1. Heinrich von Kleist, *The Marquise of O*, in *The Marquise of O and Other Stories*, trans. D. Luke and N. Reeves, (Harmondsworth: Penguin, 1978), p. 105. English translations, when not indicated as my own, are taken from this edition. In cases where I have used my own translation or modified the Penguin one, I have indicated the page number of the Penguin edition. For references to the German original I have used *Die Marquise von O* in *Sämtliche Werke und Briefe*, vol. 2 (Munich: Karl Hanser Verlag, 1984).

2. *Die Marquise von O* has often been compared to *Clarissa* and *La Nouvelle Héloise*, and indeed, Kleist read both works immediately prior to writing the novella and certainly had Rousseau's heroine in mind when he named the Marquise Julietta. Unlike Clarissa, who is also raped while she is unconscious, the Marquise has no idea that anything has happened. Unlike Lovelace, the Count has no erotic identity, no known designs on the Marquise. *Die Marquise von O* is the only one of the three works that is narrated from a third person perspective; whereas *Clarissa* and *La Nouvelle Héloise* have become synonymous with the expression and valorization of interiority, of the discourse of a Self whose authentic articulation is its only necessary justification, the *Marquise* steadfastly eschews any ambitions to represent the interior lives of its characters. Behind the Count's desire to marry the Marquise lies an act he wants to expiate, not a complex entity called the Self that has found itself inextricably involved with the vicissitudes of an-

other similar, equally complex entity. Similarly, the Marquise's perception of her pregnancy is entirely pragmatic: "If a woman told me that she had a feeling just like the one I just had, . . . I would think to myself that she was going to have a child. . . . The Marquise explained that she had just had a sensation similar to the one she had when she was pregnant with her second daughter" (p. 74, translation mine).

Like the rape of the Marquise, the rape of Clarissa is not represented directly, but we take this indirection to be a result of the discretion of the characters writing and not of the text itself. Interestingly, the discretion accorded the rape is indirectly proportional to that accorded the pregnancy. Or rather, Clarissa is raped and does not get pregnant; Julie is a willing accomplice to St. Preux's "seduction" of her; the Marquise is the only one of the three who is *both* raped and impregnated. Unlike Julie's, the Marquise's pregnancy reaches a happy term. Unlike Clarissa, the Marquise is reconciled with her father and welcomed back into the bosom of her family without having to set her sights on the metaphoric refuge of her "father's house." *Die Marquise von O* tells the story of a resurrection before death; *La Nouvelle Héloise* and *Clarissa* conform to the narrative tradition in which death is a prerequisite for transfiguration.

3. See, for example, Thomas Fries, "The Impossible Object: The Feminine, the Narrative (Laclos' *Les Liaisons dangereuses* and Kleist's *Die Marquise von O*)," *MLN* (1976), 91. 1296–1326, and John H. Smith, "Dialogic Midwifery in Kleist's *Die Marquise von O* and the Hermeneutics of Telling the Untold in Kant and Plato," *PMLA* (March 1985), 100:203–219.

4. Kleist also seems to have been tempted to diminish the gravity of the suppressed event. One of his epigrams reads: "Dieser Roman ist nicht für dich, meine Tochter. In Ohnmacht! / Schamlose Posse! Sie hielt, weiss ich, die Augen bloss zu" [This novel is not for you, my daughter. In a faint! / A shameless hoax! I know she simply kept her eyes closed]. In Heinrich von Kleist, *Sämtliche Werke und Briefe,* (Munich: Hanser, 1984), p. 1:22, translation mine.

5. It is interesting to note that one of the few changes Eric Rohmer made in the screenplay of his *Die Marquise von O* involved the rape scene (Eric Rohmer, "Notes on the Direction," and "Filmscript" in *The Marquise of O* [New York: Ungar, 1985]). Of course, the suppression of the rape in the text makes it impossible for him to be "true" to the text and show anything at all. Yet instead of filling in the blank by having the Count rape the Marquise during her fainting spell, Rohmer has him administer a sleeping potion and return some time later. "Here," we must assume, the rape takes place. The screenplay reads:

> The lamp still in his hand (and thus illuminating the area), the Count descends toward us and stops at the bottom of the steps (right medium shot). He looks down at the valet Leopardo, who, his back to the wall, is seated on the ground and sleeping next to a servant girl, equally exhausted. The Count also looks toward . . . Pan which moves to

frame the two children sleeping outstretched on a mat. Return to the Count; a dolly shot follows him up to the open door. He enters, back to us, and stops on the threshold.

. . .

Medium shot of the Marquise stretched out on an improvised bed, one arm dangling toward the ground; she is very beautiful and seems plunged in a deep sleep; nevertheless she sighs and spreads her legs slightly. A candle on a nightstand next to her feebly illuminates the room.

Medium countershot of the Count standing motionless at the threshold with the lamp in his hand. He looks toward the Marquise, who is out of the field; forward dolly toward him until a close shot. . . . Fade to black. ("Filmscript," p. 19, Rohmer's ellipses)

Like Kleist, Rohmer decides not to represent the rape, although he does have the Marquise spread her legs invitingly in her drug-induced sleep. And since the rape no longer takes place in the heat of battle, it seems far more considered and less impulsive than in Kleist's text.

I refer the reader to Rohmer's own discussion of this scene:

It may cause some surprise that in spite of our strongly affirmed intention to follow the text as closely as possible we take the liberty of modifying the circumstances of the heroine's rape: in the film it will no longer be a question of a fainting fit but of a drugged sleep. The fact is, we felt that a simple cinematic ellipsis could not without more ample care render the remarkable dash (—) that cuts the narration at this point in the German text. Unlike the reader of the book, whose imagination is more supple and whose thought is more abstract, the film spectator has a need to furnish this gap with images that do not jar with others that have come before or that will be proposed later. Let us hope that our solution will prevent him asking himself during the course of the film questions about the "how" of the matter— questions that will distract him from the real subject. It is so that we might better respect this subject and the liberty that Kleist allows to all psychological interpretations that we have effected this primary change. ("Notes," p. 10.)

6. "Mit Mässigung und Rücksichtslosigkeit nach hergebrachten Conven-ienzen: Kulturen der Gewalt, oder: Gegen die Feminisierung des Krieges," in Cora Stephan, *Weiterhin Unbeständig und Kühl: Nachrichten über die Deutschen*, pp. 17–74 (Reinbek bei Hamburg: Rowohlt, 1988). Further cita-tions appear in text, translation mine.

7. Emphasis mine. In the German, "Inmitten eines Blutbades ein ordent-liches Verfahren," the word "ordentlich" demonstrates the close relation between notions of "order" and "propriety."

8. It is worth noting that the German word for "violence" (and the word Stephan uses here), *Gewalt*, also means "power, force, authority, dominion."

9. Eve Kosofsky Sedgwick, *Between Men: English Literature and Male Homosocial Desire* (New York: Columbia University Press, 1985) and Klaus Theweleit, *Männerphantasien*, vol. 1 (Reinbek bei Hamburg: Rowohlt, 1985 and the translation, *Male Fantasies*, vol. 1 (Minneapolis: University of Minnesota Press, 1988) offer very different but compellingly complementary examinations of the homosocial continuum within our culture's most self-consciously heterosexual institutions. Theweleit's discussion of the autobiographies of members of the Freikorps addresses directly the male fantasy of a disciplined, desexualized, martial male paradise.

10. Book 5 of the *Aeneid* provides a dazzling example of the force of this economy. On the one hand, Aeneas sponsors war games in honor of the first anniversary of his father's death. In the course of the games there arise any number of conflicts, but there is no conflict so grave that Aeneas cannot find a fair, well-regulated solution that is accepted by all. Every man wins, even the loser. On the other hand, the Trojan women, excluded from the games, are incited by Juno, through her messenger Iris, to burn the Trojan ships so that the endless adventure may finally end. Iris, in the form of an old and venerable Trojan woman, tells the women of a dream in which Cassandra tells her that the new Troy should indeed be founded in Sicily. The women, in a kind of Bacchic frenzy, take torches to the ships, thus endangering everything for which Aeneas stands.

11. An epic example of this dynamic begins the *Iliad.* In order to placate the gods, Agamemnon must return a woman he considers his by right of the spoils of battle to her father. In order to compensate this loss, he commandeers Achilles' own prize, Briseis: "... I shall take the fair-cheeked Briseis, / your prize, I myself going to your shelter, that you may learn well / how much greater I am than you." *Iliad* 1:184–181, trans. Richmond Lattimore (Chicago and London: University of Chicago Press, 1951). When, at the end of the epic, Agamemmnon does return Briseis, he announces what the reader has always suspected: he hasn't touched her. If a squabble about a woman is enough to make Achilles withdraw from battle, it takes the death of his beloved Patroklus to make him reenter the fray.

12. Sigmund Freud and Josef Breuer, *Studien über Hysterie* (Frankfurt am Main: Fischer, 1970), p. 9, translation mine.

13. See Catherine Clément, "La Coupable," in C. Clément and H. Cixous, *La Jeune Née* (Paris: Union Générale d'Editions, 1975). Clément writes of the hysteric: "... the hysteric undoes familial ties, introduces disturbance in the regular course of everyday life." Yet Clément regards hysteria as essentially conservative: "... every hysteric ends up accustoming others to her symptoms, and the family closes itself around her whether she is curable or not" (pp. 13–14, translation mine).

14. Sigmund Freud, "Bruckstücke einer Hysterie-Analyse," *Studienausgabe,* (Frankfurt am Main: Fischer, 1982), 6:95–96.

15. Compare, for instance, the Commandant's reply to the Count's proposal: "... that he was certainly flattered by the proposal, if it was meant as seriously as it no doubt was. But on the death of her husband, the Marquise

of O, his daughter had decided not to embark on any second marriage. Since, however, the Count had recently put her under such a great obligation, it was not impossible that her decision might not be altered in accordance with his wishes" (p. 76, translation modified). Although the Commandant's (reported) speech is odd in its extreme formality, it has a flow that the Count's entirely lacks.

It is important to underline the fact that the utterances I am discussing are related in indirect discourse. This means, on the one hand, that we have no direct evidence of exactly what the Count said. On the other hand, we do have an entirely reliable record of the text's mode of presenting his speech and of contrasting it with the reported speech of others.

16. Conversation with Eckermann (January 29, 1827), cited in J. W. von Goethe, *Werke*, eds. Erich Trunz and Benno von Wiese (Munich: Beck, 1981), 6:744. Goethe's definition postdates *Die Marquise von O* and can therefore not have influenced Kleist (positively or negatively) in any way. Kleist's novella specifically presents itself as recounting "a true occurrence" ("eine wahre Begebenheit") and does, indeed, fit Goethe's description, at least as closely as Goethe's own novellas.

17. For the term *narratability* I am, as always, indebted to D. A. Miller, *Narrative and its Discontents: Problems of Closure in the Traditional Novel* (Princeton: Princeton University Press, 1982). Miller writes: "[The narratable] is meant to cover the various incitements to narrative, as well as the dynamic ensuing from such incitements, and is thus opposed to the 'nonnarratable' state of quiescence assumed by a novel before the beginning and supposedly recovered by it at the end" (p. ix).

18. Anyone who doubts that it is a story we need to hear, that we need to make men tell, should (re)read Eldridge Cleaver's *Soul on Ice* (New York: Delta, 1968). Cleaver's account of the genesis of a rapist demonstrates how women's bodies become the battlegrounds on which men fight the wars that most terrify them. Released from prison, "I become a rapist. To refine my technique and my *modus operandi* I started out by practicing on black girls in the ghetto . . . and when I considered myself smooth enough, I crossed the tracks and sought out white prey. . . . Rape was an insurrectionary act. It delighted me that I was defying and trampling upon the white man's law, upon his system of values, and that I was defiling his women—and this point, I believe, was the most satisfying to me because I was very resentful over the historical fact of how the white man has used the black woman. I felt I was getting revenge. From the site of the act of rape, consternation spreads outwardly in concentric circles. I wanted to send waves of consternation throughout the white race" (p. 14).

4

"A Little More than Persuading": Tess and the Subject of Sexual Violence

ELLEN ROONEY

The law distinguishes rape from intercourse by the woman's lack of consent coupled with the man's (usually) knowing disregard of it. A feminist distinction between rape and intercourse, to hazard a beginning approach, lies instead in the *meaning* of the act from women's point of view.

Catharine A. MacKinnon

My epigraph is drawn from an essay by Catharine MacKinnon that is relevant, I think, to the case of Tess. MacKinnon's primary concern is rape law, and so it is perhaps necessary to say at the outset that I recognize that law and literature are two very different practices.[1] The courtroom conventions of legal interpretation demand the production of a judgment, both in terms of a reading of the relevant statutes and in terms of an evaluation of the evidence— finding the Truth. Literary interpretation, on the other hand, has long been committed to the production of multiple and divergent readings; well before the advent of contemporary claims for the undecidability or indeterminacy of the literary as such, literature had been defined as a body of texts so rich in allusions and so subtle in their construction that they could sustain an infinite number of interpretations. As Stanley Fish suggests, "a text for which only one reading seemed available would be in danger of losing the designation literary."[2] This is literature defined as an inexhaustible source of truths.

The classic statement of this broad opposition between literature and the law appears in Plato's *Laws:* "When a poet takes his seat on the tripod of the Muse, he cannot control his thoughts. . . . When he represents men with contrasting characters, he is often obliged to contradict himself, and he doesn't know which of the opposing speeches contains the truth. But for the legislator, this is impossible; he must not let his laws say two different things on the same subject." In the case of *Tess of the d'Urbervilles,* many influential interpretations assume just such an opposition between the Truth of the Law and the truths of fictions. Hardy's representation of "contrasting" and "opposing" figures, his apparent self-contradictions and elisions have long been the topic of critical commentary. The multiple and often incompatible perspectives in the novel have been variously interpreted as signs of Hardy's rejection of all dogma and moral absolutism, as the scars of revisions and deletions demanded by his publishers, and as part of a general, epistemological effort to "undermine the authority of the whole notion of explanation."[3]

J. Hillis Miller's description of the critical debate engendered by *Tess* echoes the terms of the Platonic opposition between literature and law. He observes that "Hardy's insistent asking of the question 'Why does Tess suffer so?' has led critics to assume that their main task is to find the explanatory cause." By Miller's account, this task has been pursued in reductively "legalistic" terms: "Readers have . . . tended to assume that this cause will be single. It will be some one force, original and originating. The various causes proposed have been social, psychological, genetic, material, mythical, metaphysical, or coincidental"; "the problem is not that there are no explanations proposed in the text, but that there are too many. A large group of incompatible causes or explanations are present in the novel." Miller's disdain for these efforts to explain is literary precisely insofar as he rejects a legalistic notion of determination. In his reading, the multiplication of incompatible explanations is the point, the definitive expression of the "literariness" of the text: "It is wrong in principle to assume that there must be some single accounting cause." Literature is the operation of a structure of repetition that "produce[s] similarity out of difference and [is] controlled by no center, origin or end outside the chain of recurrent elements"; this operation can only generate "multiple valid but incompatible interpretations."[4] The radical force of *Tess of the d'Urbervilles*—as a *literary* work—is thus located in its multiplicity, in Hardy's ability to say "two different things on the same subject," that is, to abandon legalistic argumentation and a formal concept of proof. In the idiom of the *Laws,* Hardy is quintessentially the poet, "often obliged to contradict himself" and not bound to reveal which of his "opposing speeches contains the truth."

MacKinnon throws this very opposition between literature (truths) and law (Truth) into question. She criticizes—we might say from the perspective of literature—the legal presumption that a sexual encounter *can* be read objectively, from a "point-of-viewless" perspective, a perspective that is not caught up in the gender distinctions that produce sexuality and are reproduced by it. Although her example is the substantive law of rape, MacKinnon's larger analysis attacks objectivity as such: "the non-situated, universal standpoint, whether claimed or aspired to, [is] a denial of the existence or potency of sex inequality that tacitly participates in constructing reality from the dominant point of view."[5] In the context of male dominance, she argues, the ideal of objectivity and the epistemology that subtends it merely mask a masculine bias that is then (mis)taken for the human, beyond sexual difference. "The feminist theory of knowledge is inextricable from the feminist critique of power because the male point of view forces itself upon the world as its way of apprehending it"; "objectivity creates the reality it apprehends by defining as knowledge the reality it creates through its way of apprehending it" (p. 636). MacKinnon argues that this scenario, which unfolds from a metaphor of rape, is "metaphysically nearly perfect": "Its point of view is the standard for point-of-viewlessness, its particularity the meaning of universality" (pp. 638–639). Feminism—like literature in Miller's formulation—discredits this metaphysic by exposing its particularity, specifically by revealing the sexual differential that inhabits every perspective: "there is no ungendered reality or ungendered perspective" (p. 636). There is no disinterested (ungendered) party to pass legal judgment on the text of the real, no "single, accounting cause." Rather, that text itself is the subject of an essential dispute.[6]

MacKinnon's critique of objectivity in phallocentric culture grounds her perspective on the difficulty of adjudicating rape. The word that catches the literary critic's eye in her analysis is "meaning": "whether [or not] a contested interaction is rape comes down to whose *meaning* wins. . . . The problem is this: the injury of rape lies in the *meaning* of the act to its victims, but the standard for its criminality lies in the *meaning* of the same act to the assailants" (p. 652, my emphases). For MacKinnon, what is at stake in a rape case is a hermeneutic, a question of meaning, and a question of the power of certain readers—"under conditions of sexual inequality"—to make their point of view coextensive with the real, to universalize their particularity. Furthermore, she argues that "a feminist distinction between rape and intercourse . . . lies in the *meaning* of the act from women's point of view" (pp. 651–652). She thus insists that legal issues are always settled in interpretative arenas and demands that we rethink the legal process as one involving a choice between incommensurate meanings rather than one of uncovering a (temporarily hidden) fact,[7] the Truth.

In MacKinnon's view, "rape is a sex crime that is not a crime when it looks like sex"; "the law's problem, which becomes the victim's problem, is distinguishing rape from sex in particular cases." The question of who's looking is crucial, and MacKinnon argues not for interpretative relativism, but for the cultural constructedness of perception itself. She insists that "reality is split," much as the poet's thoughts when he composes, but gender is the principle of division. In terms of jurisprudence, Mackinnon's most radical conclusion is that "the deeper problem is the rape law's assumption that a single, objective state of affairs existed, one which merely needs to be determined by evidence, when many (maybe even most) rapes involve honest men and violated women. When reality is split—a woman is raped but not by a rapist?—the law tends to conclude that a rape *did not happen* . . . [The] subjectivity [that] becomes the objectivity of 'what happened' is a matter of social meaning, that is, . . . of sexual politics" (p. 654). When reality is split and its "terms are gendered to the ground," we face the possibility of an encounter, a "contested interaction," in which "a woman is raped but not by a rapist" (pp. 655, 654). The opposition rape/seduction breaks down, and the law is revealed as caught up in the very distinctions it claims to adjudicate.

This collapse of the opposition rape/seduction is, in a literal sense, MacKinnon's larger project. Her rejection of the opposition between violence and sexuality leads her to conclude that sexuality itself is "a social sphere of male power in which forced sex is paradigmatic" and to propose that the question "what is the violation of rape?" be replaced by the question "what is the nonviolation of intercourse?" (pp. 646–667). A similar use of the term *violation* characterizes readings of *Tess*. Critics acknowledge Tess' injury by blurring the distinction between seduction and rape. The novel's reviewers take this tack, referring to her "seduction" while asserting her innocence: thus "poor Tess falls a victim"; she is "soiled though guiltless," her "ruin . . . compassed in spite of herself." She is the victim of Alec's seduction.[8] The notion of violent seduction thus displaces the configuration of desire and power that characterizes rape onto seduction, in effect figuring rape as seduction. This trope persists in some twentieth-century interpretations, in readings that suggest Tess is "raped or seduced" or, even, "raped and seduced." For example, Ian Gregor argues:

In Alec, [Tess] senses both her creator and her destroyer. It is the attempt to do justice to the extent and range of these feelings that makes Hardy so calculatedly ambiguous about the nature of their encounter in the Chase; it is both a seduction *and* a rape. If it were merely a rape, than there would be no sense in Tess's profound feeling throughout the novel that her whole being has been invaded by Alec, so that in one sense she feels she "belongs" to him, belongs because he brought to consciousness her own sexuality. If it were simply a seduction, then there would be no sense in Tess's equally profound feeling that her past with Alec is a nullity. We could say that as a woman, Tess feels it to be a seduction in the way the strawberry scene hints at; as an individual person, she knows it was rape: 'There were they that heard a sobbing one night last year in The Chase.'[9]

Gregor's unselfconscious application of the double standard ironically evokes MacKinnon's model: he argues that reality is split *for women.* Tess lives as a woman, "in the way the strawberry scene hints at," and as an individual, a person for whom sexual assault is a "nullity." Doubtless, MacKinnon would not willingly align herself with this analysis. The representation of Alec as a demi-urge shaping the formless Tess, the misreading of the invasiveness of Alec's attack, the specious suggestion that his assault brings Tess to consciousness of her own sexuality, these are the signs of what MacKinnon sees as an essentially violating sexuality, that is, a (hetero)sexuality that is in its essence a violation. But there is an underlying continuity between Gregor's insistence that the encounter in The Chase is "both a seduction *and* a rape" and MacKinnon's claim that "contested interactions" may involve "honest men and violated women." In both readings, a fundamental link between rape and seduction is affirmed: Gregor and MacKinnon agree that seduction, like rape, is a matter of force and the appearance of consent. This unexpected coincidence of views suggests that we should interrogate the link between seduction and rape. How is this coupling connected to what we might call the problematic of consent, as well as to discourses, both phallocentric and feminist, which work to negate the desiring female subject? Phallocentric criticism of texts that pivot on scenes of sexual violence frequently engages the problem of sexuality in the form of the opposition between seduction and rape. It thus confirms MacKinnon's model, seeking to "distinguish rape from sex in particular cases." The many dilemmas this criticism faces only partially derive from the fact that representations of sexual violence are often characterized by silence, elisions, and ambiguities. The difficulty lies in the opposition itself, for the articulation that separates (opposes) rape from (to) seduction also serves to join them. The effort to distinguish rape from seduction, to fix rape and seduction in opposition, repeatedly falls short, its terms collapsing into one another, in part because to establish difference by opposing rape to seduction is often only to reinscribe—within rape and within seduction—the very patriarchal dichotomies we seek to escape. Thus Elizabeth Hardwick's conventional remark that a "seduction is the *very opposite* of the abrupt, which is, of course, rape," is blandly contradicted—in her next line—by her claim that "the most interesting seducers are actually rapists; for instance, Don Giovanni and Lovelace."[10] The difficulty lies in the founding opposition itself. The formulation of the problem of sexual violence (or sexuality) as the question of distinguishing rape from seduction works to reinscribe—within rape and within seduction—the very patriarchal dichotomies we seek to escape. The attempt to practice a sexuality without violation, a sexuality that cannot finally be reduced to the active/passive distinction, will be confounded if the rape/seduction opposition works to reassert the passivity of the feminine subject and thus forces her (and us) into a problematic of consent. A feminine subject who can act only to consent or refuse to consent is in fact denied subjectivity.

I want to suggest that what is ultimately at stake in any attempt to read the scene of sexual violence is the place and status of this subject. Such scenes may be privileged sites for investigating the construction of female subjectivity because they articulate questions of desire, power, and agency with a special urgency and explicitly foreground the opposition between subject and object. The intractable problems that dog our efforts to interpret these passages turn on our desire to fix this subject, to read from the privileged position of *the* subject of sexual violence, as if "a single, objective state of affairs existed."

Jane Gallop has suggested that "the possibility of valorizing seduction occurs either through some sort of equation between seduction and femininity, or at least through casting seduction as a threat to the uprightness of phallogocentrism." In *The Daughter's Seduction,* she proposes a subversive seduction that is "complicitous, nuanced, impossible to delineate into active and passive roles." But Gallop also invokes the rape/seduction opposition: "the dichotomy active/passive is always equivocal in seduction, that is what distinguishes it from rape."[11] This view implies that in rape the dichotomy active/passive is unequivocal. The difference between rape and seduction rests on this opposition of the unequivocal to the equivocal, which in turn generates a whole series of dichotomies: guilt/innocence, dominance/submission, Rake/Maiden, violator/violated, subject/object, presence/absence. The presence of equivocation, any acquiescent gesture, marks seduction. The absence of equivocation, unequivocal resistance, marks rape. Ultimately, the active/passive, male/female oppositions, which the valorization of seduction works to undermine, are reinscribed within rape, and the active resistance of the victim is obliterated.

In many readings of *Tess*, the problematics of seduction remain mired in an ambiguity where complicity is a crucial but elusive term: complicity is reduced to (feminine) acquiescence. These readings preserve feminine purity at the price of the totalization of feminine passivity: they treat rape as male sexual aggression met with unequivocal resistance and seduction as male sexual aggression met with equivocation. The passive object of seduction repeats the passive object of rape. A discourse that sees the seduced woman and the raped woman as two avatars of passivity easily adopts the locution "seduction and rape" because it thinks the woman in seduction as an object, paradoxically passive: she is always the *victim* of seduction. Thus, Gregor speaks of Tess' seduction and/or rape in The Chase, and MacKinnon asks, "what is the nonviolation of intercourse?" That the object of seduction—the female (or feminized) subject—might act is here unthinkable. The feminine part is to consent or refuse (to be taken) rather than to desire or will (to take). In this problematic, the "nuanced" and "complicitous" disruption Gallop desires is impossible. And the question arises: how does a discourse that thinks both the seduced woman and the raped woman as passive think the seductive woman?

The social text of phallocentrism decrees that women cannot rape. Yet the seductive woman remains an enormously threatening figure. In representations of this woman, we may again find the rhetoric of rape displaced into the rhetoric of seduction. The raped woman becomes the seductive woman; as such, she appears as an aggressor *provocateur*, paradoxically active. She is no longer an unambiguous/unequivocal victim, but an overpowering temptress/temptation, a species of rapist. Seduction is figured as rape, and the (Circean) woman is the paradigmatic aggressor. For MacKinnon, this seductive woman is merely another ruse of (hetero)sexuality; if sexuality is "a social sphere of male power in which forced sex is paradigmatic," the seductive woman as an agent of (her own) desire remains unthinkable. Donna Haraway has criticized this reduction of the social meaning of gender, suggesting that for MacKinnon woman "in a deep sense does not exist as a subject, or even potential subject, since she owes her existence as a woman to sexual appropriation." MacKinnon's insistence on the continuity between rape and seduction, violence and sexuality, leads her to negate the female (sexual) subject entirely. As Haraway puts it, this "radical theory of experience . . . is a totalization producing what Western patriarchy itself never succeeded in doing—feminists' consciousness of the non-existence of women, except as products of men's desire."[12] MacKinnon's emphasis on the split that constitutes the real promises an escape from the obsessive effort to read the scene of sexual violence from the position of *the* subject. But having argued that a contested interaction may involve two subjects, an honest man and a violated woman, she collapses her own distinction; honesty is violation as seduction is rape. The masculine subject is the only subject of sexuality.

MacKinnon retreats from the heterogeneity of reading in the direction of totalizing definitions, or what Frances Ferguson calls "stipulated states." Ferguson suggests that feminist critics such as Susan Brownmiller and Andrea Dworkin "share with ancient rape law the tendency to specify the male injury to the female in terms of formally identified and stipulated mental states. And thus they recapitulate, even though in a reversal of those early legal codes, the tendency of the law to negate particular psychological states and to substitute formal states for them. In other words, the process of reading an action as evidence of intention confines itself to stipulated states that are specifically detached from the notion of individual, actualizable psychological states."[13] MacKinnon has an uneasy place in this typology. She proposes the stipulation that heterosexual intercourse is formally rape, yet her insistence on the constitutive power of point of view holds open the possibility that a woman may contradict that stipulation by citing her own psychological state, that is, her desire.

Ultimately, MacKinnon preserves the purity of women by seeing them as objects; sexuality is entirely the work of men and sexual women wholly victims. The (desiring) feminine subject does not exist. I propose we read her text against its grain by considering *Tess* as a text that turns on a "contested interaction" of the sort MacKinnon describes. Penny Boumehla has observed that with the publication of *Tess*, Hardy came to be thought of as a writer with an ax to grind. One reviewer complained: "We are *required* to read the story of Tess (or Theresa) Durbeyfield as the story of 'A pure woman faithfully presented by Thomas Hardy.' Compliance with this request entails something of a strain upon the English language."[14] Hardy's later insistence that the book was "intended to be neither didactic nor aggressive" because "a novel is an impression, not an argument,"[15] only lends support to Boumehla's observation. The novel clearly contains a polemic for Tess as the "Pure Woman" of the subtitle, and some of the contradictions in the text result from revisions intended not to satisfy censorious editors but to strengthen Tess' case. Hardy's defense argument, as argument, is internally contradictory: it seeks both " to exonerate Tess and to secure forgiveness" for her (Boumehala 1982: 129). This is an obvious contradiction, but it just as obviously doesn't transform the defense into an indictment. Hardy asks his readers not to blame Tess too much and to believe in her innocence, but all of his arguments bend toward a single theme: Tess is a pure woman.[16]

The difficulty for readers persists. What, in this novel, is a pure woman? How ironic is Hardy's subtitle ("A Pure Women"), "appended," as he eventually claimed, "at the last moment, after reading the final proofs" (p. 8). Mary Jacobus and Boumehla agree that the effort to exonerate Tess is an obvious "attempt to rescue her for a conventionally realized purity" (Boumehla 1982: 129). Yet, in his 1892 preface, Hardy criticizes the "artificial and derivative meaning" of the word and chastizes those who "ignore the meaning of the word in Nature, together with all aesthetic claims upon it, not to mention the spiritual interpretation afforded by the finest side of their own Christianity" (p. 5). Finally, he characterizes the subtitle "as being the estimate left in a candid mind of the heroine's character—an estimate that nobody would be likely to dispute. It was more disputed than anything in the book. *Melius fuerat non scribere.* But there it stands" (p. 8). The disclaimer seems disingenuous. The use of Latin for the confession of error testifies to a certain reluctance to withdraw unambiguously from the dispute, and in the case of a book as heavily revised as *Tess* Hardy's hint that fidelity to the text requires him to allow the subtitle to "stand" strains credulity.

If we read *Tess* in light of MacKinnon's emphasis on *meaning* as the essential issue in a contested interaction, Hardy's "confusion of many standards" takes on a new significance. His apparently contradictory argument—Tess is pure because she "had been made to break an accepted social law" (p. 121), that is, raped against her will, *and* Tess is pure because she remains "unsmirched," despite her seduction—anticipates MacKinnon's claim that in many contested interactions reality is split and a single, objective state of affairs cannot be determined by the evidence. But Hardy's effort simultaneously to assert Tess' purity and to revise the meaning of purity itself traps him in the opposition between rape and seduction, between the unambiguous violence that would guarantee Tess' purity in even the most rigid patriarchal codes and the ambiguous and thus less pure space of complicity, desire, and reading. His text is contained by the problematics of consent once he accepts the opposition between rape and seduction as the mechanism for articulating Tess' purity. Ultimately, the meaning of purity hinges on the relation between seduction and rape; as Hardy attempts, without success, to clarify that relation, Tess' body is textualized, "converted into evidence" (Ferguson 1987: 91), and the relation between her body and her desire becomes the focus of intense representational anxiety. The impossibility of resolving that anxiety is the impossibility of representing Tess as a desiring or speaking subject.

The figure of the seductive woman is enormously important for any reading of *Tess*. *Seductive* is a word Hardy uses very sparingly in the final, 1912 edition of the text. He deletes it in a number of places: "And as Clare was oppressed by the outward heats, so he was burdened inwardly by a waxing fervour of passion for the *seductive* Tess" becomes "waxing fervor for the *soft and silent* Tess" (p. 210, my emphases). The "seductive Tess" is in fact the hinge of the novel, but *seductiveness* and *seduction* are two terms Hardy cannot articulate clearly. *Rape* is the third term that smooths over the aporia of the pure, seductive woman.

Given his commitment to her purity, Hardy's figuration of Tess as a seductive woman seems counterproductive. He fails to see what MacKinnon's argument makes most clear: he cannot articulate the *meaning* of the ambiguous encounter in The Chase as Tess—which is to say as one of the subjects of sexual violence—sees it. This is, in part, because the status of Tess' subjectivity is what is at stake, both in The Chase and in the whole of the novel. *Tess* critics generally discuss the heroine's "violated subjectivity" without considering how that subjectivity is first constituted or the degree to which Hardy's novel is about the production of female subjectivity.[17] (I stress female because Tess' efforts to escape the [strictly] feminine are harshly rebuffed: the subject exists here only in sexual difference.) Hardy believed at one point that the most "suitable title" for his novel would be "The Body and Soul of Sue," and, for Tess, subjectivity begins at the level of the body. Her subjectivity is structured as her flesh is structured: female, over and against the male. This construction fundamentally disrupts Hardy's effort to represent the scene of sexual violence from Tess' point of view, to make her a subject in the encounter in The Chase, even as his inscription of her subjectivity as structured by her body is an effect of this failure of representation.

Hardy is unable to represent the meaning of the encounter in The Chase from Tess' point of view because to present Tess as a speaking subject is to risk the possibility that she may appear as a subject of desire. Yet a figure who has no potential to be a desiring subject can only formally be said to refuse desire, to testify to the absence of her desire. Hardy is blocked in both directions. To preserve Tess' purity, he must insist on her passivity; as a "subject" who doesn't speak, her silence guarantees her right to our sympathy. Thus at three crucial moments in the plot we find elisions in the text: the sexual encounter in The Chase, Tess' misplaced letter, and her confession to Angel. Hardy's inability to represent Tess' narrative on her wedding night repeats his inability to represent the events in The Chase from her point of view. His failure to present her as a speaking or desiring subject forces him to figure her as the "seductive woman," a victim of her own sexuality. Tess embodies rather than acts her desire, but in the problematic of the seductive woman, all feminine behavior is seductive—as we shall see, she cannot escape the "risk" her own appearance constitutes (p. 387). Her very seductiveness is inevitably troped as a form of sexual violence: she is an overpowering temptress who ravishes men. The impossibility and the necessity of representing the events in The Chase from Tess' point of view impose a fundamental equivocation on the novel. Finally, these contradictions produce Hardy's equivocations on the topic of Tess' body—his insistence that her flesh *can* be read, that her soul appears to the eye, *and* that her body and soul, exterior and interior, depart from one another, that her body is not transparent. Ultimately, the scene of sexual violence, Tess and the female subject all appear as radically unreadable figures.

Hardy thematizes the problem of judging Tess, both within the novel and for its readers, and is immediately ensnared in the opposition of rape and seduction. The title of my essay cites an emendation Hardy made to the one-volume edition of *Tess* that appeared in September of 1892. The passage appears in the novel's Second Phase.

Tess returns home from Trantridge and bears a child, eventually to be baptized Sorrow;[18] after a period of mourning in which she retreats from the community, Tess emerges to help with the wheat harvest. Two field-women observe the young mother as she nurses Sorrow and then covers him with kisses, which, the narrator remarks, "strangely combined passionateness with contempt" (p. 127). The women then begin to discuss Tess' feelings for the child. The entire passage reads as follows, with the revision in italics:

> "She's fond of that there child, though she mid pretend *to hate en*, and say she wishes the baby and her too were in the churchyard," observed the woman in the red petticoat. "She'll soon leave off saying that," replied the one in buff. "Lord, 'tis wonderful what a body can get used to *o' that sort* in time." "*A little more than persuading had to do wi' the coming o't, I reckon. There were they that heard sobbing one night last year in The Chase; and it mid ha gone hard wi'a certain party if folks had come along.*" "Well, a little more or a little less, 'twas a thousand pities that it should have happened to she, of all others. But 'tis always the comeliest! The plain ones be safe as churches—hey, Jenny?" The speaker turned to one of the group who was certainly not ill-defined as plain. (p. 127)

This passage is interesting for several reasons. Tess' passionate contempt for her child hints at Hardy's plans for dealing with the infant. Sorrow dies by the chapter's end; Hardy refuses to redeem Tess by means of a heroically self-sacrificing motherhood. The allusions to Tess' beauty and to Jenny's plainness as a source of protection are chilling, and they form a persistent pattern of observation in the novel: Tess' sexuality—figured by her beauty—is a temptation to men that places her in almost constant danger. As this scene opens, the narrator speculates: "Perhaps one reason why she seduces casual attention is that she never courts it, though the other women often gaze around them" (p. 125). The seductive woman is a paradoxical figure who seduces (casual) attention precisely because she never "courts" or actively seeks it. In this phrase, Hardy captures the absolute divergence of Tess' experience (or practice) of her body and its effect on others; her seductiveness—where *seductive* describes her embodiment of sexuality—is here determined by her lack of seductiveness—the absence of the seducer's active courting.

"A little more than persuading," the woman in the red petticoat suggests; ". . . A little more, a little less," is the reply. This exchange strengthens the impression that the contested interaction in The

Chase was a rape; sexual violence, not seduction. Some evidence is adduced ("the sobbing"), but vaguely, without attribution ("they that heard"). Nevertheless, the speakers are clearly in sympathy with Tess and place the guilt or blame for her sorrow elsewhere. Hardy offers his readers these local judges as models; their sympathy for Tess and contempt for Alec are plain, although any anger they might feel is tempered by their apparent fatalism: " 'Tis always the comeliest.' "

Yet the expressions "a little more than persuading" and "a little more, a little less" expose the contradictions in the opposition of rape and seduction. They also disclose the degree to which Hardy's efforts to clarify the nature of Tess' "violation" are hindered by the rhetoric that links rape to seduction. The observation that "a little more than persuading had to do wi' the coming o't" defines sexual violence as something added to persuading, persuading and then some; seduction tips over into rape when force appears, when ineffective words give way to "irresistible" actions. Thus rape is an extension of seduction, of courting, in the direction of violence; rather than a radical break distinguishing rape from seduction, we have a continuity and an implied narrative of the movement from seduction to rape.

This blurring of the boundary between seduction and rape contradicts some feminist positions developed in the wake of Susan Brownmiller's *Against Our Will*. For those who define rape as "pure" violence, violence is necessarily excluded from discussions of seduction, that is, of sexuality. This position can lead to judgments, like Terry Eagleton's, that rape is a "virulently anti-sexual act." This characterization is essential to any diagnosis of misogyny, both in literature and at law. But it elides the eroticization of dominance and submission in favor of articulating feminism's ethical project. The radical edge of recent feminist work on sexuality is produced by the broad range of feminist thinkers (ranging from Susan Griffin to Gallop to MacKinnon herself) who acknowledge the violence *within* sexuality in our culture.[19] The term *rape culture* expresses this view that in our patriarchy "eroticism is wedded to power" and romantic "love finds erotic expression through male dominance and female submission" (Griffin 1979: 7–8).

Hardy seems to share the more ambivalent view. But the words "a little more, a little less" complicate this reading. In one register, they sound skeptical about the nature of the events in The Chase, weighing the possibilities, implying that perhaps there was more than persuading, but then again, perhaps not. Yet, this same remark can be read to suggest that rape should be defined as *less* than persuading; rape falls short of persuasion, is perhaps independent of the question of persuasion. In this reading, the link between rape and seduction might be broken. Rape and seduction would then appear as independent phenomena, with seduction at work in the realm of the sexual and rape relegated to the sphere of violence.

The final turn of the interpretation reads these lines with (or as) a shrug. The question of whether a "certain party" bothered (or even attempted) to persuade Tess is not compelling: the difference between rape and seduction is really no difference. No matter, it is a pity in any case, and the sorrow is the same. In this reading, the "little more" that is added to seduction is too trivial to bear mention; it is no longer a question of the violence within sexuality. Rape and seduction collapse into each other—at best, the project of separating them out, distinguishing them clearly, is a fruitless one.

Hardy repeats this ambiguous interweaving of the couple rape/seduction in revising the critical passages at the end of Phase One. In the pages leading to the notorious elision, from which Tess emerges "Maiden No More," he presents Alec as the lover-seducer. The "master" is a wheedling servant, who pouts, pleads, bribes, and tries to persuade: "Will you, I ask once more, show your belief in me by letting me clasp you with my arm? Come between us two and nobody else; now. We know each other well; and you know that I love you, and think you are the prettiest girl in the world, which you are. Mayn't I treat you as a lover?" (p. 98). Alec complains in a mode that is nearly Petrarchan: "For near three mortal months you have trifled with my feelings, eluded me and snubbed me," and he insists that Tess is "devilish unkind" (p. 98). His bribes include gifts for her family, and Hardy reports that he "steals" a "cursory kiss." When Tess dismounts, he makes her a "sort of couch or nest" and covers her "tenderly" with his overcoat, asking, "Tessy, don't you love me ever so little now?" (p. 100). A little more or a little less?

These attentions produce tears and embarrassed denials, but also more equivocal tones: " 'How could you be so treacherous!' said Tess between archness and real dismay." The scene demonstrates Tess' paralysis as a speaking subject. In response to Alec's request to treat her as a lover, she stutters, "writhing uneasily on her seat," "I don't know—I wish—how can I say yes or no, when—" Hardy reports that Alec slipped his arm around her and "Tess expressed no further negative" (p. 98). Her failure to express a negative—a practical negation of her refusal—is also her last reported gesture in this phase of maidenhood. Although she has managed to "reluctantly admit" that as for loving Alec, even a little, "But I fear I do not—" (p. 100), when he nearly stumbles over her sleeping form and calls her name, Hardy reports: "There was no answer" (p. 102). Tess fails to answer "yes or no." The final passages of the Phase read:

> Darkness and silence ruled everywhere around. Above them rose the primeval yews and oaks of The Chase, in which were poised gentle roosting birds in their last nap; and about them stole the hopping rabbits and hares. But, some might say, where was Tess's guardian angel? where was the Providence of her simple faith? Perhaps, like that other god of whom the ironical Tishbite spoke, he was talking, or he was pursuing, or he was in a journey, or he was sleeping and not to be awakened.
>
> *Why was it that upon this beautiful feminine tissue, sensitive as gossamer, and practically blank as snow as yet, there should have been traced such a coarse pattern as it was doomed to receive; why so often the coarse appropriates the finer thus, the wrong man the woman, the wrong woman the man, many thousand years of analytical philosophy have failed to explain to our sense of order. One may, indeed, admit the possibility of a retribution lurking in the present catastrophe. Doubtless some of Tess d'Urberville's mailed ancestors rollicking home from a fray had dealt the same measure even more ruthlessly towards peasant girls of their time. But though to visit the sins of the fathers upon the children may be a morality good enough for divinities, it is scorned by average human nature; and it therefore does not mend the matter.*
>
> As Tess's own people down in those retreats are never tired of saying among each other in their fatalistic way: "It was to be." There lay the pity of it. *An immeasurable social chasm was to divide our heroine's personality thereafter from that previous self of hers who stepped from her mother's door to try her fortune at Trantridge poultry farm.*

From "why was it" on, the passage is heavily revised, with most of it added after the serialization in the *Graphic*. Again, the revision's overall effect is to strengthen the argument that what is *not* represented *is* a rape, even while introducing certain ambiguities into the relationship between rape and seduction. Tess' "ancestors," as they are presented here, were definitely rapists; the analogy paints Alec as an assailant, ruthless and sinning: rape is unambiguous, large-scale violence. But the passage and the chapter as a whole also present the same *continuity* between seduction and rape that we saw assumed by the gossip in the fields. Alec first appears as a too ardent lover, then as a latter day d'Urberville. And, of course, we don't see him act the second role or act at all after kneeling at Tess' side and putting his cheek to hers—a gesture singular in its lack of aggression and its implicit equality.

Hardy's invocation of the brutal and "more ruthless" rapes committed by bands of armed men also works to reopen the distance between the ancient d'Urbervilles and the imposter Alec, between rape and seduction. At one level, Alec is very far from these "mailed" and "rollicking" knights, even as he is cited as their contemporary incarnation, revenging their violence. His "violation" of Tess is both radically different from the spectacular violence of knights in armor, that is, a seduction, and no different from the more obvious forms of rape, "the same measure." The parallel construction in his description of the "appropriation" in The Chase further complicates matters. When Hardy asks "why so often the coarse appropriates the finer thus, the wrong man the woman, the wrong woman the man," he sets Tess and Alec in rough equivalence, each appropriating the other against the odds, each mistaken or "wrong." His elision opens a space for the double reading that MacKinnon insists is necessary to represent the split reality of sexuality. He thus elaborates the conditions that would enable Tess to tell her story, to construe this interaction from her point of view. Ironically, he will make it impossible for her to do so.

Rape and seduction reappear in similarly tangled relations throughout the novel: sometimes presented as continuous, sometimes as radically opposed, and sometimes as practical equivalents. They are invariably invoked in tandem, as if the opposition could not finally be broken. Their coupling ensures Tess' violation and thus her purity; but it also confines her in a problematic of consent, to a passivity that renders her purity as constraining and silent as it is sure.

Tess' concern that she have the opportunity to tell "her story" is evoked at several points in the novel; she insists that she needs to relate "my history. I want you to know it—you must let me tell" (p. 270). Her commitment to the importance of "a woman telling her story" and her desire to tell "my experience—all about myself—all" (pp. 260, 255) provoke Angel to a "loving satire" on her inexperience. "Looking into her face," he agrees: " 'Your experiences, dear; yes, certainly; any number. . . . My Tess has, no doubt, almost as many experiences as that wild convolvulus out there on the garden hedge, that opened itself this morning for the first time' " (p. 255). Angel laughs at Tess' interest in "this precious history" and dictates its predictable form: " 'Yes; I was born at so and so, Anno Domini . . .' " (p. 271). As the wedding approaches, Tess' anxiety grows: "She resolved with bursting heart, to tell all her history to Angel Clare, despite her mother's command" that "on no account do you say a word of your bygone Trouble to him" (pp. 285, 275).

Tess finds the courage to offer her narrative in an intuition of equality that flares on her wedding night when Angel confesses his sexual adventure and asks forgiveness for his faults—"How strange it was! He seemed to be her double" (p. 316). His excuses and fears about admitting his past before the ceremony mirror her own, and after his confession, she celebrates her story's similarity: "O Angel —I am almost glad. . . . [It] cannot be more serious certainly, . . . because 'tis just the *same*" (p. 318)! Tess' resolve to tell her story is predicated on her (mis)perception that a woman's story may be the same as a man's; she begins to narrate in *imitation* of Angel. The reader is not in a position to agree with her, quite. The scene of "a woman telling her story" is elided, like the scene of sexual violence itself, and for the same reason: its meaning cannot be represented from Tess' point of view. It is that point of view that is finally excluded.

> "Say it is not true! No, it is not true!"
> "It is true."
> "Every word?"
> "Every word." (pp. 335–336)

Hardy all but mocks his readers' exclusion from the text of Tess' confession. "Every word" is erased from the scene, "even [the] reassertions and secondary explanations." We learn only that "there had been no exculpatory phrase of any kind" in her speech and no tears (p. 323).[20]

When Tess finishes what she mistakenly thinks is the same story Angel has told, she asks him for equal treatment, the same forgiveness. "Forgive me as you are forgiven," she argues. "I have forgiven you for the same." "*I* forgive *you* Angel" (p. 324). But Angel enforces difference. Tess is "not the same. No: not the same" (p. 329). With breathtaking self-righteousness, he asserts both that the same experience has rendered them hopelessly different and that she is no longer the same, no longer herself: "You were one person: now you are another. My God—how can forgiveness meet such a grotesque prestidigitation as that!" (p. 325) "The woman I have been loving is not you." "But who?" she asks. "Another woman in your shape," he replies (p. 325). Here the potential discontinuity between the flesh and the self, which operates throughout the novel as the mechanism of Tess' seductiveness, is revealed to a masculine reader with devastating effect.

"Shape" is perhaps a poor choice of words, as it is precisely knowledge of an alteration in Tess' body that alienates Angel. Yet his charge is originally one Tess levels at herself: "O my love, my love, why do I love you so, . . . for she you love is *not my real self*, but one in my *image* [my emphasis]; the one I might have been" (p. 304). Tess voices a similar anxiety about the status of what she calls her "self" at other points. She asks the Vicar to speak not "as saint to sinner, but as you yourself to me myself—poor me" (p. 137). At the moment of crisis, she says, "I thought, Angel, that you loved me —me, my very self"; "if it is I you do love, O how can it be that you look and speak so?" (p. 325). Tess also believes her body and this self are not identical, that she possesses a "very self," who survives "all changes," "all disgraces," but she cannot assert the meaning of that self in a way that eludes the mark that Alec has left on her flesh or, indeed, the seductiveness that is presented as an integral aspect of her flesh. Angel insists that he loved "another woman" in Tess' seductive "shape," but actually it is "soft and silent" Tess in another shape, intact rather than "unintact" (p. 464), whole rather than broken (into), whom Angel loves.

Hardy is unable to challenge Angel's refusal to see Tess' story from her point of view, to see the *meaning* of the events in The Chase as she sees them, that is, to see them as forgivable. Angel, like Hardy, persists in reading her flesh, even after her confession, when he might have begun to suspect the limits if not the complete inadequacy of his method: "She looked absolutely pure. Nature, in her fantastic trickery, had set such a seal of maidenhood upon Tess' countenance that he gazed at her with a stupefied air" (p. 335). The narrator intervenes to lecture Angel only for lacking confidence in his reading of the text of Tess' body: "[Alec] argued erroneously when he said to himself that her heart was not indexed in the honest freshness of her face; but Tess had no advocate to set him right" (p. 333). Her efforts to *speak* as her own advocate are useless. Her words have wrought a change not in Angel's vision, but in the trust he has in his reading of the form before him. The narrator comments that the "essence of things had changed" (p. 323) rather than their substance. The story that Tess had hoped would bring her self, her subjectivity, out into Angel's view, has only convinced him of the trickery of nature. "Her personality did not plead her cause so forcibly as she had anticipated" (p. 344); following Angel's interpretation with "dumb and vacant fidelity," she concludes that "the figurative phrase was true: she was another woman than the one who had excited his desire" (pp. 328, 344).

Hardy all but parodies his elision of Tess' story in the episode of her letter, written in defiance of her mother's command, but accidentally slipped beneath the carpet and thus unread. The exclusions of Tess' story are spectacular, grandiose; the lack her silences engender is filled by Sorrow. His brief presence is the material guarantee of Tess' sexual experience, an essential condition of the plot given her silence. The problem Hardy represents is thus a problem of reading, of locating in external form, in the "substance" or letter of one's text, its true meaning. The ambiguity of the scene of sexual violence is refigured as an ambiguity *within* Tess and as a fatal discontinuity that separates appearance from reality, external from internal, and leaves the reader hopelessly dependent on his own desire to ground his reading. MacKinnon's account of reality as split applies to Angel and Tess as it does to Alec and Tess: the meaning of the contested interaction from Tess' point of view is radically unassimilable, and so we face the problem of reading the silent, seductive Tess as a text, with the same difficulties that attended reading the scene of sexual violence.

It has been remarked that Tess is the least human of Hardy's protagonists. She is repeatedly compared to animals: birds, cats, snakes, a leopard, a fly (pp. 140, 175, 327). "Creature" is also a term used to describe her. At Talbothays in the dawn light, when Angel sees Tess as the "visionary essence of woman" and is most "impressed," he describes her as "ghostly, as if she were merely a soul at large" (pp. 185–186). By the novel's end, her breathing is "quick and small, like that of a lesser creature than a woman" (p. 538). An animal, a ghost, a vision, not quite human.

Tess is also persistently engulfed by the vegetation of the natural world she inhabits. The "social chasm" that divides the heroine's personality—and differentiates her sexual experience from Angel's —is partially defined by this well-known passage: "A field-man is a *personality* afield; a field-woman is a portion of the field; she has somehow lost her own margin, imbibed the essence of her surrounding and assimilated herself with it" (p. 124–125). This potential for the loss of personality is specifically feminine, and Tess sees herself in these terms at times. As Hardy puts it, "her quiescent glide was of a piece with the element she moved in. Her flexuous and stealthy figure became an integral part of the scene. At times her whimsical fancy would intensify natural processes around her until they seemed a part of her own story. Rather they became a part of it; for the world is only a psychological phenomenon, and what they seemed they were" (p. 121). The metaphors assimilating Tess to the natural world suggest the physical problem—which is ultimately a sexual problem—she faces throughout the novel. The "problem" of Tess' body is another figure by which Hardy distances her from ordinary (masculine) humanity, thus marking her peculiar lack of subjectivity as feminine.

Tess' body is a particular burden to her. And the status of that body—after her sexual experience and the birth of her child—is constantly in question. She herself wonders if lost chastity is forever lost. Joan Durbeyfield regards the "bygone Trouble" as a "passing accident." Hardy is of two minds on the matter. As many critics have observed, he insists on Tess' purity, but he is obsessed with that "immeasurable social chasm" that divides her *personality*—and not only her flesh—on that night in The Chase. He shifts from one view to the other, depending on his antagonist. Thus the narrator suggests that "Tess Durbeyfield, otherwise d'Urberville, [is] somewhat changed—the same but not the same; at the present stage of her existence living as a stranger and an alien here, though it was no strange land that she was in" (p. 125). At another point, he compares her experience to the acquisition of a Bachelor of Arts: "Almost at a leap Tess thus changed from simple girl to complex woman. Symbols of reflectiveness passed into her face, and a note of tragedy at times into her voice. Her eyes grew larger and more *eloquent*. She became what would have been called a fine 'creature'; her aspect was fair and arresting; her soul that of a woman whom the turbulent experiences of the last year or two had quite failed to demoralize. But for the world's opinion those experiences would have been simply a liberal education" (p. 139). Clearly the change in Tess is not simply a matter of the world's opinion. This reading of her body is a paradigm for Angel's reading in the aftermath of her confession. Hardy's aestheticization of her is complete; he makes her intensely literary, a text—symbolic, tragic, eloquent—in her flesh, her eyes, her voice, her face. Furthermore, he makes it clear that sexual experience is to a woman what literature (and looking at Tess) is to a man. Her body expresses all of the "changes" her "liberal education" has produced in her. The truth of her inner life is vivid in her appearance.

"True correspondence" between inner and outer is essential to Hardy's effort to represent Tess without taking the risk of allowing her to tell her own story. But this essential correspondence breaks down when Hardy approaches Tess' sexuality in a context where he cannot code it as beauty. We have seen that she is seductive, provocative, without even trying—without courting our attention. Insofar as this provocative quality is equated with her sexuality, it is a wholly external condition, an imposition. Tess cannot function as a subject of the discourse of desire. This was clear to Mowbray Morris, who in rejecting the book for *Macmillan's Magazine* observed that "even Angel Clare . . . has not yet got beyond a purely sensuous admiration for her person. Tess herself does not appear to have any feelings of this sort about her; but her capacity for stirring and by implication for gratifying these feelings for others is pressed rather more frequently and elaborately than strikes me as altogether convenient, at any rate for my magazine."[21] Tess' sexuality is this tempting quality, this unconscious and unwanted seductiveness. Alec sees her as a temptress and a witch, but admits she has "done" nothing; she is the innocent means of his backsliding. Tess herself reminds Angel, "You once said that I was apt to win men against their better judgment: and if I am constantly before your eyes I may cause you to change your plans in opposition to your reason and wish" (p. 345). To return to MacKinnon's formula, the meaning of Tess' sexuality is consistently determined elsewhere. Hardy defends her from at least some of those other meanings, from those that would challenge her purity, for example, but as he is unable to represent the meaning of her sexuality from her point of view without risking a slide into active desire, his narrator is the most persistent of the readers of Tess' body.

Hardy naturally has some difficulty negotiating the question of Tess' consciousness of her seductive beauty. He can't portray her as manipulating it; on the other hand, her "tragedy" depends on it, and he can hardly leave her ignorant of the account men give of her effect on them, especially after her experience with Alec. I have just referred to this effect as unwanted and unconscious, but of course, it can only be unwanted to the degree that some consciousness of it is forced on Tess. The awkwardness of Hardy's position is obvious in his commentary on Tess and Angel's discussion of their future:

Tess's feminine hope—shall we confess it?—had been so obstinately recuperative as to revive in her surreptitious visions of a domiciliary intimacy continued long enough to break down his coldness even against his judgment. Though *unsophisti-cated* in the usual sense, she was not *incomplete* and it would have denoted *deficiency of womanhood* if she had not *instinctively* known what an argument lies in propinquity. Nothing else would serve her, she knew, if this failed. It was wrong to hope in what was of the nature of *strategy,* she said to herself: yet that sort of hope she could not extinguish (pp. 342–343, my emphases).

Here Hardy argues that Tess' completeness depends not on her physical or emotional purity, but on her awareness of her seductive power. To seduce may be "to break down . . . coldness even against [another's] judgment." Alec hoped to wear Tess down by a combination of his proximity and bullying; Tess hopes, in the nature of a strategy, to weaken Angel by the argument of her seductive presence. Hardy balances this confession of Tess' capacity for stratagems with the assurance that her knowledge is inherent in her femininity, her "womanhood." She knows the force of her sexual appeal "instinctively." Instinct here is opposed to "sophistication" as the natural is opposed to the social. The latter is culpable: man-made and articulate, like the verbal persuasions of seduction. The former is pure: animal and dumb, like "soft, silent Tess."

Hardy explicitly posits Tess' consciousness of her sexuality only in the context of sexual violence. As a victim of her sexuality, which is her seductiveness, she can remain pure. The encounter in The Chase is elided, but we do see Tess "assaulted" once. Hardy tells us "there was something of the habitude of the wild animal in the unreflecting instinct with which she rambled on" after Angel's departure, "obliterating her identity" (p. 382). He adds that "among the difficulties of her lonely position not the least was the attention she excited by her appearance." Tess is addressed with "rude words" more than once, but she feels no "bodily fear" until the farmer who eventually employs her accosts her, demanding she admit the truth about her past with Alec and suggesting that she "ought to [beg] his pardon for that blow of [Angel's] considering" (p. 384). Tess flees into the woods and sleeps, again in a nest of leaves. She then "resolve[s] to run no further risks from her appearance"; she undoes her physical beauty to protect herself from "aggressive admiration" (p. 387). She dresses in her oldest clothing, wraps her jaw in a bandage, and cuts away her eyebrows. This disfiguration secures her a certain peace and the comfort of insults from passersby. Hardy remarks that she "walks on; a figure which is part of the landscape; a fieldwoman pure and simple. . . . There is no sign of young passion in her now" (p. 388). Tess remakes her body into a surface "over which the eye might have roved as over a thing scarcely percipient, almost inorganic" (p. 388).

"Obliterating her identity" by mutilating her face, Tess is no longer a "sign" to attract the aggressive admiration of others. She is safe, though shrunken, and she doesn't really fear the farmer: *"He's not in love with me"* (p. 436). But she has recovered, that is to say, grown beautiful again, before she travels to visit Angel's father. After Mercy Chant and Angel's smug brothers take her boots, Tess throws back her veil—"takes sufficient interest in herself" is how Hardy describes the gesture—"as if to let the world see she could at least exhibit a face such as Mercy Chant could not show." Yet, without Angel's desire, Tess insists, "It is nothing—it is nothing! . . . Nobody loves it; nobody sees it. Who cares about the looks of a castaway like me!" (p. 413).

This return to "self-interest," to the only subjectivity Tess achieves, a subjectivity that is an immediate extension of her flesh, leads to the renewed acquaintance with Alec. Many circumstances conspire to drive Tess back to Alec, not least among them her final acquiescence to the view that a physical change, the loss of virginity, is the definitive experience, in effect the meaning, of her life. Tess is the first character in the novel to wonder if the meaning of her encounter with Alec isn't equal to the meaning of marriage. She harbors "a religious sense of a certain moral validity in the previous union" and wonders: "She was Mrs Angel Clare, indeed; but had she any moral right to the name? Was she not more truly Mrs Alexander d'Urberville?" (pp. 261–262, 304). When Angel asks, "How can we live together while that man lives?—he being your husband in Nature and not I," and Alec claims, "If you are any man's wife you are mine" (pp. 342, 453), they are echoing Tess. Even as she rebuffs Alec, "the consciousness that in a physical sense this man alone was her husband seemed to weigh on her more and more" (p. 352). She explains her return to him in the same terms when Angel finds her in Sandbourne: "The step back to him was not so great as it seems. He had been as a husband to me: you never had!" (p. 519).

When Tess accepts this "physical sense" as *the* meaning of her experience, it is at the price of no longer recognizing herself as a subject.[22] She muses at Flintcomb-Ash that to have married Alec's wealth and position would "have lifted her out of subjection, not only to her present oppressive employer, but to a whole world who seemed to despise her" (pp. 436–437). When Angel returns, he finds her "lifted out of subjection" in another sense: "His original Tess had spiritually ceased to recognize the body before him as hers—allowing it to drift, like a corpse upon the current, in a direction dissociated from its living will" (p. 515). There is an irony, of course, in the word "original." Given his view that the original Tess ceased to exist once she had told her story, Angel's remark is ambiguous in its referent: where might we locate the original Tess?

Angel's account of Tess in this passage has an unexpected resonance with an earlier description of her, a passage in which Hardy comes close to representing Tess as a desiring rather than a desired/desirable subject:

> Tess flung herself down upon the rustling undergrowth of spear-grass as upon a bed, and remained crouching in palpitating misery broken by momentary shoots of joy, which her fears about the ending could not altogether suppress. In reality, she was drifting into acquiescence. Every see-saw of her breath, every wave of her blood, every pulse singing in her ears, was a voice that joined with Nature in revolt against her scrupulousness. Reckless, inconsiderate acceptance of him; to close with him at the altar, revealing nothing, and chancing discovery; to snatch ripe pleasure before the iron teeth of pain could have time to shut upon her; that was what love counselled; and in almost a terror of ecstasy Tess divined that, despite her many months of lonely self-chastisement, wrestlings, communings, schemes to lead a future of austere isolation, love's counsel would prevail. . . . "I shall give way—I shall say yes—I shall let myself marry him—I cannot help it." (pp. 255–256)

"Drifting," just as she is in her relation to Alec, Tess is here at the mercy of currents and waves and of her rebellious blood, succumbing to "love's counsel," giving way despite her chastisements. The context, of course, is radically different, and Hardy emphasizes Tess' joy and her sense of snatching pleasure. But her terrified subjection to external force—here Hardy names it Nature—is intensely realized. Tess' "desire," like her sexuality, is an imposition she ultimately consents to, moving in its currents, adrift.

Angel's remark echoes Tess' claim "that our souls can be made to go outside our bodies when we are alive" (p. 171). She encourages her listeners at Talbothays to lie in a field and stare up at the stars: "You will soon find that you are hundreds and hundreds o' miles away from your body, which *you don't seem to want at all*" (p. 171). That Tess should finally not want her body is a consequence of her inability to make her reading of it more potent in her world. Part of the difficulty Hardy creates by his double view of Tess and her relation to her body is captured by the contradiction in Angel's suggestion that the corpse before him—Tess—is "dissociated from its living will."

This dissociation follows inexorably from Hardy's commitment to reading Tess as body and his failure to allow her to speak as a subject; ironically, we might say that Tess dies when she accepts the complete association or identification of her body and her will. Finally, she doesn't "want [her body] at all," as she puts it at Talbothays. She abandons her struggle to distinguish her body from her "very self," to construct a subjectivity that speaks or desires in an idiom other than that of her flesh. As a subject, she finally has no experience to speak of; only her body is experienced, and her silence allows us to project meaning upon it. Alec's murder simply enables Tess to give over that body to the judges, silenced, not by Hardy's failure to see that she might speak, but by his unflinching inscription of the inexorable forces that produced her as the seductive object of the discourses of man.

NOTES

I would like to thank the Center for the Humanities at Oregon State University for a sabbatical grant that enabled me to complete this essay.

The epigraph is from Catharine A. MacKinnon, "Feminism, Marxism, Method and the State: Towards Feminist Jurisprudence." *Signs: Journal of Women in Culture and Society* (Summer 1983), 8(4):651–652.

1. At the same time, literary and legal scholars are increasingly interested in the relationship between their disciplinary practices. See Ronald Dworkin, "Law as Interpretation," *Critical Inquiry* (September 1982), 9 (1): 179–200, and Stanley Fish, "Working on the Chain Gang: Interpretation in the Law and in Literary Criticism," *Critical Inquiry* (September 1982), 9 (1): 201–216).

2. Stanley Fish, *Is There a Text in This Class?* (Cambridge: Harvard University Press, 1980), p. 312.

3. Robert C. Schweik, "Moral Perspectives in *Tess of the d'Urbervilles*," *College English*, vol. 24 (1962). See Bernard Paris, "A Confusion of Many Standards: Conflicting Value Systems in *Tess of the d'Urbervilles*," *Nineteenth Century Fiction* (1969), 24: 57–79, who argues that the multiplication of "partial and obviously limited perspectives" leaves the novel with "no real thematic core," and John Bayley, *An Essay on Hardy* (Cambridge: Cambridge University Press, 1978). See also Penny Boumehla, *Thomas Hardy*

and Women: Sexual Ideology and Narrative Form (Totowa, N.J.: Barnes and Noble, 1982), who celebrates the seemingly "disturbing discontinuities of tone and point of view" in Hardy's text as evidence of his "interrogation [both] of his own modes of narrative" and of the ideological project of representing and explaining woman in the figure of Tess (pp. 126–127). Further citations appear in text.

4. J. Hillis Miller, *Fiction and Repetition* (Cambridge: Harvard University Press, 1981), pp. 140–144.

5. Catherine A. MacKinnon, "Feminism, Maryism, Method and the State: Towards Feminist Jurisprudence," *Signs: Journal of Women in Culture and Society* (Summer 1983), 8 (4): 636. Further citations appear in text.

6. MacKinnon's view echoes with an unlikely pair of theorists: Stanley Fish and Luce Irigaray. Fish insists that disagreements "cannot be resolved by reference to the facts, because the facts emerge only in the context of some point of view. . . . Disagreements must occur between those who hold (or are held by) different points of view, and what is at stake in a disagreement is the right to specify what the facts can hereafter be said to be. Disagreements are not settled by the facts, but are the means by which the facts are settled" (*Is There a Text in This Class?* p. 338). Irigaray argues that phallocentric discourse secures its hegemony through "its power to *eradicate the difference between the sexes* in systems that are self-representative of a 'masculine subject'"; this scene of representation presupposes "the sexual indifference that subtends it, assures its coherence and its closure." See *Speculum of the Other Woman* (Ithaca: Cornell University Press, 1985). For a more complete account of MacKinnon's views, see *Feminism Unmodified* (Cambridge: Harvard University Press, 1987).

7. The claim that facts are "subject to interpretation" is hardly one that rocks the institutional foundations of the legal system in the United States. But the stricture that requires acquittal in cases of reasonable doubt expresses no more than the view that reasonable men (a crucial category for MacKinnon) may differ as to the *certainty* of the so-called facts: jurors weigh whether the evidence presented *as* fact *is* fact. MacKinnon raises the ante considerably by suggesting that fact—understood as an objective or neutral state of affairs—cannot exist.

8. R. G. Cox, ed., *Thomas Hardy: The Critical Heritage* (New York: Barnes and Noble, 1970), pp. 247, 189, 200. This notion of violent seduction is related to what Susan Estrich describes as "simple rape." In her excellent study, *Real Rape* (Cambridge: Harvard University Press, 1987), she documents the legal application of the distinction between simple and aggravated rape and the difficulties women who are attacked by men they know, however slightly, face in convincing prosecutors that these are real rapes.

9. Ian Gregor, *The Great Web* (Totowa, N.J.: Rowman and Littlefield, 1974), p. 182. Miller is within this tradition when he argues for the word *violation*, echoing the reviewers' notion of violent seduction and pointing to the power relations that would enforce Tess' acquiescence, whatever her

reluctance: "to call [her violation] either a rape or a seduction would beg the fundamental questions which the book raises" (p. 116).

10. Elizabeth Hardwick, *Seduction and Betrayal* (New York: Vintage, 1975), p. 185.

11. See Jane Gallop, "French Theory and the Seduction of Feminism," in Alice Jardine and Paul Smith, eds., *Men in Feminism* (New York: Methuen, 1987), p. 111, and *The Daughter's Seduction* (Ithaca: Cornell University Press, 1982), pp. 75, 56.

12. "A Manifesto for Cyborgs: Science, Technology, and Socialist Feminism in the 1980s," *Socialist Review* (March–April 1985), 15 (2): 77–78.

13. Frances Ferguson, "Rape and the Rise of the Novel," *Representations* (Fall 1987), 20: 91. Further citations appear in text.

14. Mowbray Morris, *Quarterly Review*, April 1892, reprinted in Laurence Lerner and John Holmstrom, *Thomas Hardy and His Readers* (London: Bodley Head, 1968), p. 85, my emphasis.

15. This disclaimer first appeared in the preface to the fifth edition. All references are to the Oxford variorum edition of *Tess of the d'Urbervilles,* eds. Juliet Grindle and Simon Gatrell (Oxford: Oxford University Press, 1983), pp. 4, 5.

16. Mary Jacobus details Hardy's "sustained campaign of rehabilitation" in "Tess: A Pure Woman," in Susan Lipshitz, ed.: *Tearing the Veil: Essays on Femininity*, pp. 75–92 (London: Routledge and Kegan Paul, 1978). Tess' purity and Hardy's polemic are revisited in Laura Claridge, "Tess: A Less than Pure Woman Ambivalently Presented," *Texas Studies in Language and Literature* (1986), 28 (3): 324–338. Claridge's sympathies lie with Mowbray. Defenses like Hardy's are heard in (literal) courtrooms: in Michael Deaver's recent perjury trial, the defense insisted that he had not lied under oath and that he was a recovering alcoholic whose memory of his activities was unclear during the period of his testimony.

17. Boumehla's very interesting work is an exception; another is Kaja Silverman's "History, Figuration and Female Subjectivity in *Tess of the d'Urbervilles,*" *Novel* (Fall 1984), 18 (1): 5–28. Silverman's essay focuses on issues very similar to those I take up here and offers a powerful account of figuration and nonfiguration as the poles of Tess' representation.

18. This scene and the whole of chapter 14 were deleted from the original serialization of the text, which ran in the *Graphic* from July to December 1891; the chapter was published independently under the title "The Midnight Baptism: A Study in Christianity" in the *Fortnightly Review* (May 1891); it was reinserted into the novel in the three-volume edition of 1891.

19. See Terry Eagleton, *The Rape of Clarissa* (Minneapolis: University of Minnesota, 1982), p. 63; Susan Griffin, *Rape: The Power of Consciousness* (San Francisco: Harper and Row, 1979); Gallop, *The Daughter's Seduction;* and MacKinnon, "Feminism, Marxism and the State: An Agenda for Theory," *Signs: Journal of Women in Culture and Society* (1982), 7 (3): 515–544 and especially pp. 646–647.

20. Silverman points out that in this scene Tess is subjected to overwhelming representational pressure: "At perhaps no other point in the novel is figural meaning so explicitly circumscribed by sexual difference. Angel is partly in the scene, on the side of the spectacle, as well as partly outside the scene, on the side of vision, but the narrator's gaze slides quickly past him ... it turns a searchlight on Tess, who remains all the time unseeing" (p. 20).

21. Ms. held at Dorset County Museum, to Thomas Hardy, 25 November 1889, cited in J. T. Laird, *The Shaping of Tess of the d'Urbervilles* (Oxford: Oxford University Press, 1975) p. 11.

22. This defeat contrasts with Ferguson's account of Clarissa's resistance to "recogniz[ing] herself in a new form as the result of the rape." Clarissa insists on the "inability of a form to carry mental states in anything but excessively capacious (that is, ambiguous) or potentially self-contradictory stipulated forms ... When Clarissa begins dying and Lovelace begins longing for her consent, the novel is literally haunted by the specter of psychology, in which mental states do not so much appear as register the improbability of their appearing" (p. 106).

5

Periphrasis, Power, and Rape in
A Passage to India

BRENDA R. SILVER

Periphrasis, defined most simply as "the use of many words where one or a few would do," has, like all figures, a more devious side. Rooted in the Greek "to speak around," described variously as a figure that simultaneously "under- and over-specifies" or "the use of a negative, passive, or inverted construction in place of a positive, active or normal construction," the circumlocution associated with periphrasis begins to suggest a refusal to name its subject that emphasizes the fact of its elision.[1] If we go further and describe it in Gerard Genette's terms as a figure that both opens up and exists in a gap or space between sign and meaning, a figure that is moreover "motivated" in its usage,[2] then we arrive at the association between periphrasis, power, and rape that structures both linguistic and social relations in *A Passage to India* and provides the space for rereading E. M. Forster's most enigmatic novel.

To introduce this association, we must move immediately to the event at the heart of the novel, Adela Quested's experience in the Marabar caves that leads to the trial of the Indian doctor Aziz for attempted rape. Or so we assume: the charge, like the event, is either elided completely or referred to by the English as an "insult," a clearly motivated circumlocution. Later, in a moment of vision during the trial, Adela returns to the caves and retracts her accusation of Aziz, but the reader never learns what, if anything, actually happened there. Where we would have the naming of the crime and its perpetrator exists only a periphrasis, a gap. Continually talking around this unspecified center, the text ironically generates more words to produce less meaning.

That Forster deliberately created this gap is clear from the original version of the scene, where the reader enters the cave with Adela and feels the hands that push her against the wall and grab her breasts; we too smash the assailant with the field glasses before running out of the cave and down the hill.[3] In the published version, not just the violent physical attack but the entire scene in the cave is elided. Into the interpretive space opened by this elision critics have not feared to rush, supported by Forster's statement that "in the cave it is *either* a man, *or* the supernatural, *or* an illusion."[4] "Illusion," translated into psycho-sexual terms, has proved the most persistent choice. These critics base their reading on Fielding's description of Adela as a prig, as well as Adela's realizations just before entering the cave that she feels no love or sexual passion for her fiancé, Ronny, and that Aziz is "a handsome little Oriental."[5] Later, responding to Fielding's hallucination theory, she compares her experience to "the sort of thing . . . that makes some women think they've had an offer of marriage when none was made" (p. 240). Thus it is that sexual desire and repression simultaneously enter the gap at the center of the novel. In this reading Adela becomes a later version of Henry James' governess in *The Turn of the Screw*; a hysterical, repressed, overly intellectual New Woman who fantasizes and is haunted by sex ghosts. In this reading, we might add, Adela wants to be raped.[6]

That Forster used his fiction to explore and expose prevailing sexual attitudes is a commonplace. On one level, he recognized the way in which society, in Michel Foucault's terms, had appropriated bodies and pleasure and deployed a sexuality that served to control individuals; Forster certainly would have understood the strategies, including "a hysterization of women's bodies" that Foucault associated with this deployment.[7] At another level, however, Forster's resistance to the system and his imagination were shaped by the sexual discourse of the period, including the concept of repression. In his fiction he continually evokes a scenario in which a darker, more sensual, usually foreign and/or lower class character initiates the repressed, often intellectual English man or woman into an awareness of his or her sexuality. An explicit example occurs in the heavily ironic fantasy titled "The Torque," which hinges on the homosexual rape of a Christianized Roman by a Goth: an act that undercuts the power of institutionalized chastity (the Church) and precipitates a realm of sexual freedom and fulfillment. Rape in this story becomes the pleasurable consummation of illicit desires experienced without guilt or subsequent suffering, a transgression of racial and sexual boundaries that unites rather than separating the two races.[8]

But *A Passage to India* tells a different story. For here, as Patricia Joplin would argue, rape becomes an act of violence, a transgression of boundaries, that enacts the rivalries at work within the culture upon the body of a woman who is herself potentially silenced, elided.[9] With this in mind, we can return to Adela's "unspeakable" experience in the cave—and the word is Forster's (p. 208)—the experience that she speaks as violation or rape, and read it not in terms of sexual desire or repression, but in terms of a deployment of sexuality within a system of power that posits a complex network of sameness and difference. Within this system, what is at stake is both gender difference and racial difference, with manifold lines of power crisscrossing the social and textual field. To read the novel from this perspective is to see it as a study of what it means to be *rapable*, a social position that cuts across biological and racial lines to inscribe culturally constructed definitions of sexuality within a sex/gender/power system.

In undertaking this exploration of race and gender in Forster's novel, I am keenly aware that both Forster's and my perspectives are rooted within Western, first-world, frameworks and that we both run the risk of appropriating the Indians in the novel—and defining their sexuality—for our own ends. No amount of analysis can or should alter the fact that Adela's accusation carries the weight it does because she is a white woman, a member of the colonizing group, or that a more accurate representation of the colonial experience would depict the rape of an Indian woman: the repressed term in the novel.[10] To the extent that Indian women are the one group denied a voice in the novel, the text replicates the complex intersections of racism, colonialism, and sexual inequalities that have consistently worked in Western discourses to erase the other woman's experience.[11] In attempting to write the silence of "the other woman" into my critique I wish neither to speak for her nor to substitute gender for race

—or to equate them. Instead, I will explore the multiplicity of discourses and structures that doubly silence the other woman in our culture—structures that Adela begins to understand and articulate —and locate them within the process of "social sexing" that feminist theorists associate with rape.

Starting from the assumption that the social construction of gender and the social division of power are grounded in sexuality and difference, these theories define social sexing as "that social process which creates, organizes, expresses, and directs desire, creating the social beings we know as women and men, as their relations create society."[12] If sexuality is the product of a power over the body, then "the system of power . . . has the bodies of women as its object of privileged appropriation,"[13] a *sexual* differentiation that affects every aspect of their being, including their ability to name or represent their perceptions and have them count as "truth." Within this epistomological system, Catharine MacKinnon notes, power includes the power to name the other as object, that which is objectively knowable, and "objectification makes sexuality a material reality of women's lives, not just a psychological, attitudinal, or ideological one" (1982:539). At issue is both the construction of the female subject and the effect of this construction on women's experience of their own being: the ways in which "women internalize . . . a male image of their sexuality *as* their identity as women," making epistemology and ontology one (1982:531, 538). The process of being reduced to an object, moreover, constantly aware of being looked at, acted upon, can cause women (and those placed in the feminized position) to split themselves in two, to watch themselves as women from the male perspective, affecting both their realization and their presentation of self.[14] Women, then, materially as well as psychologically, are both object and separated from themselves as object, a thing and nothing.

Within this formulation of sexuality, gender, and power, rape plays a central role, for it illustrates clearly both the congruence of knowledge, representation, and power at work in rape law, as MacKinnon has argued, [15] and the dynamic of objectification and appropriation that informs social/sexual relations. To recognize the social meaning of the encounter, the sexual politics, is also to recognize the categories "men" and "women" as gender/power designations, grounded in social, not biological, distinctions: to identify rape as an enactment of power. "Rape is sexual essentially because it rests on the *very social* difference between the sexes. . . . Men rape women insofar as they belong to the class of men which has appropriated the bodies of women. They rape that which they have learned to consider as their property, that is to say, individuals of the other sex class than theirs, the class of women (which . . . can also contain biological men)" (Plaza 1981:29). In MacKinnon's words, "To be rap*able*, a position which is social, not biological, defines what a woman *is*" (1983:651).

When applied to social relations in *A Passage to India*, the construction of the class, or category, woman crisscrosses racial as well as sexual lines. Illustrating Foucault's conception of power as the "interplay of mobile and nonegalitarian relations," the intersections of race and gender have "a directly productive role" on the discourses that simultaneously shape and sustain them.[16] Within this mobile discursive field, subject and object may shift, but the category of "object" and the category of "woman" remain identical.

For the first part of the novel English and Indian are locked into a power relationship and a discourse of race in which each objectifies the other, although in any direct confrontation the English maintain the position of subject. At the same time, however, English and Indian *men* share a discourse of sexuality that inscribes their subjectivity by objectifying and silencing women. After the "insult," relations shift to place the Indians explicitly in the category of woman, where their bodies and their subjectivity are appropriated for social ends. Within this latter discourse, both Adela, the Englishwoman, and Aziz, the Indian man, are elided in the English construction of the event through a deliberate act of periphrasis said by the narrator to be the result of the rape. When Fielding, the liberal schoolteacher who sides with the Indians, produces a "bad effect" at the English club by asking about Miss Quested's health, his transgression consists of pronouncing her name, for since the "insult" "she, like Aziz, was always referred to by a periphrasis" (p. 182). By reversing the figure, however, we can perceive the periphrasis as embedded in the *cause* rather than the *effect* of the rape. For periphrasis, the elision or negation of the individual human being, functions as part of a rhetoric of difference and power that objectifies the other and creates the space for rape to occur.

To a great extent, the rhetoric of power manifests itself within the novel in the use of synecdoche to reduce the other, the signified, to a physicality that denies the irreducibility and multiplicity of the individual subject. Rather than suggesting "relationship" or "connectedness,"[17] synecdochal representation opens up unbridgeable gaps.

Ironically, the Indians introduce this reductive rhetoric in the opening dialogue of the novel when they refer to Ronny, the new City
Magistrate, as "red-nosed boy" (p. 10), a usage motivated by the
belief, stated repeatedly in this conversation and confirmed by the
text, that the English are essentially indistinguishable: " 'They all
become exactly the same, not worse, not better. I give any Englishman two years be he Turton or Burton. It is only the difference of a
letter. And I give any Englishwoman six months' " (p. 11). What
differences the Indians sardonically allow are physical, not moral, a
representation of the political reality that the presence of the English
in India was itself immoral: " 'Red-nose mumbles, Turton talks
distinctly. Mrs. Turton takes bribes, Mrs. Red-nose does not and
cannot, because so far there is no Mrs. Red-nose' " (p. 11). Paradoxically, the "difference of a letter" in the first figure suggests the
possibility of opening a space between signifier and signified, individual and group, where individuals might meet, but when excep-
tions are introduced, they are immediately elided. As the narrator
remarks, they "generalized from [their] disappointments—it was
difficult for members of a subject race to do otherwise" (p. 13).

But what of the masters, the English? Caught up in a rhetoric of
power they initiated and control, they too generalize, unwilling to
break free of the by then historically well-inscribed characteristics
of the category "Indian" constructed through the representations of
generations of Orientalists. To the English the Indians are "types,"
and they "know" them all, as well as how to handle them. Equally
important, within this conceptual and stylistic framework, the English themselves become a type, the White Man, with a fixed set of
judgments, gestures, and language; those who do not conform are
not pukka.[18] Thus the first mention of Aziz by the English, located
within the center of linguistic and social conformity, the English
club, reduces the man, so vividly alive while chattering with his
friends and in the intervening encounter with Mrs. Moore, to "some
native subordinate or other" who had, typically, failed to show up
when needed. In the same breath Ronny is referred to as "the type
we want, he's one of us" (p. 25).

The mode on both sides, then, is reduction, a reduction that
claims as well the privilege of totalizing the other group. In addition,
both groups represent their synecdochal reductions as capturing "the
truth," including the truth of the other's moral state. For the English, however, the rulers, the mania for reductive categorizing goes
hand in hand with a dramatization of difference and superiority
inherent in their position of power: power not only to define the

categories but to enforce the "truths" they supposedly convey; for the English, knowledge, representation, and power are one. Fielding, a linguistic renegade long before the scene in the club following the "insult," experiences the strength of this discursive system, and his alienation from it, when he comments that "the so-called white races are really pinko-gray. He only said this to be cheery, he did not realize that 'white' has no more to do with a colour than 'God Save the King' with a god, and that it is the height of impropriety to consider what it does connote" (p. 62). More than a "manner of being-in-the-world" or a style (Said 1978:227), the linguistic structures practiced by the English inscribe the oppression of the Indians, both individually and as a group. The Indians' subversive rhetoric, at least in the early stages of the novel, produces rhetoric alone.

Not surprisingly it is Ronny, the newcomer, who enacts most explicitly the linguistic and ideological power inherent in the racial discourse, thereby satisfying the English desire for conformity and proving the Indians' perception of their sameness correct. To Ronny, the "higher realms of knowledge" to which he aspired were "inhabited by Callendars and Turtons, who had been not one year in the country but twenty and whose instincts were superhuman" (p. 81). In his zeal to learn the lingo and show his orthodoxy, he continually uses "phrases and arguments that he had picked up from older officials" (p. 33) to describe the Indians, phrases that simultaneously reduce them to a material state and equate this with their defective mental and moral character. In this way he illustrates the process by which synecdochal representation crosses the line described by Kenneth Burke between figurative language as used by poets and the scientists' belief that their representations are "real" (p. 507). At its most extreme, as in Ronny's remark during the Bridge Party that "no one who's here matters; those who matter don't come" (p. 39), this rhetoric effectively reduces the Indians present from the status of objects to nonexistence. The result is "to wipe out any traces of individual[s] . . . with narratable life histories" (Said 1978:229). Ultimately, inevitably, it is Ronny who provides the most painfully ironic example of synechochal reduction masquerading as truth: the representation of Aziz and all Indians by his missing collar stud— missing because he gave it to Fielding. To Ronny, this detail signifies "the Indian all over: inattention to detail; the fundamental slackness that reveals the race" (p. 82).

Within the gap opened by synecdochal reduction of the other to object rape finds its material and linguistic space. And when race is involved, the space increases exponentially. From Ronny's statement of the "fundamental slackness of the race" it is just a short step to the policeman McBryde's theory of the depravity of Indian men, which includes their sexual promiscuity and their attraction to white women. In this construction, the Indian man, reduced to his sexuality, becomes simultaneously rapist and rapable.[19] No matter that Aziz's missing collar stud signifies the space in which he and Fielding break free of the reductive generalities of the racial discourse to initiate their friendship; the established mode swallows such resistances in its representation of the Indian male. Perceived as a synecdoche, a "penis," he falls prey to the dictum that "whoever says *rape* says *Negro*."[20]

When Adela speaks rape, however, she says more than Negro; she speaks from within a discourse of sexuality that crosses racial lines and objectifies all women. While resting on similar rhetorical strategies, this discourse shifts the axis of sameness and difference, subject and object, from race to gender. Look, for example, at the moment during the Bridge Party when Mr. Turton, the highest-ranking Englishman, indicates to his wife her duty (that is, to speak to the Indian women); " 'To work, Mary, to work,' cried the Collector, touching his wife on the shoulder with a switch" (p. 41). The synecdochal details here, the shoulder and the switch, serve to place her in the subservient position of his horse, reducing her to a material adjunct of both the man, her master, and the empire he represents. Next to this moment we can place Turton's thought after the "insult" when his wife, voicing her hatred for the Indians, calls for the use of violence: " 'After all, it's our women who make everything more difficult out here,' ... Beneath his chivalry to Miss Quested resentment lurked. ..." "Perhaps," the narrator comments, "there is a grain of resentment in all chivalry" (p. 214). Perhaps, we could add, what we have here is the most significant aside in the novel, a glimpse into the misogyny, the contempt, characteristic of those who use " 'women and children' " (p. 183) as the rallying cry for their defense of women whom they in fact subordinate and elide by touches, however light, with a switch.

What, then, do these men resent? The rare moments when women, rather than allowing themselves to be objects of protection or exchange among those who have power, resist this structure by acting or speaking for themselves? In the case of Mrs. Turton and the other seasoned Englishwomen, the confinement of their roles and their limited contact with Indians evoke a racism more extreme than their husbands', but their outbursts only serve to underline the men's "contemptuous affection for the [Indian] pawns [they] had moved about for so many years" (p. 214). The threat posed by Adela and Mrs. Moore, however, differs, for their resistance threatens to destroy the status quo through intimacy, not hatred. One such moment of resistance occurs during the Bridge Party. Unlike Mrs. Turton, whose knowledge of Urdu consists only of the imperative mood and whose comments in English about the Indian women are glaringly reductive (p. 42), the two newcomers attempt to initiate a conversation with the Indian women, who form a third group in the social fabric, distinct from their men and the English alike. But the attempt fails; the Indian women remain silent. For one thing, the Indian men insist on talking for them. More significant, however, is the narrator's comment that "they sought for a new formula which neither East nor West could provide" (p. 42). Perhaps, then, men resent women as a disruption within the male discourse that controls social exchange, whether this exchange occurs officially or unofficially. Here even Fielding, capable as he is of seeing Indians as individuals, shares Turton's resentment. Motivated by his desire for the picnic at the caves to be a success for Aziz's sake, Fielding thinks, " 'I knew these women would make trouble.' " Mrs. Moore accurately identifies this reaction for what it is, scapegoating women: " 'This man, having missed his train, tries to blame us' " (p. 158).

A similar pattern of attributing power to women who in relation to their men have little or none occurs within the Indian community as well. For the most part, Indian women in the novel are nameless and invisible, represented only through their relatives' conversation about them. When we do go behind the purdah, as in the opening scene, we find Hamidullah's wife indicating her inferiority by the endless talk she sustains in order to show that she is not impatient for the dinner she cannot eat until her husband has eaten his (p. 13). When her talk begins to worry Aziz, Hamidullah considerately "[wipes] out any impression that his wife might have made" (p. 14). The woman is left behind the purdah with nothing but empty words at her command. Yet later, when his wife refuses to see Fielding— or, more accurately, refuses to let Fielding see her—Hamidullah claims that she wields the real power in the relationship (p. 271), a power we can define as the power to choose to remain invisible and thus to disrupt, however slightly, the male bonding achieved in this novel, as in patriarchal societies in general, through the exchange or mediation of women. Perhaps the clearest representation of women's power as refusal or negativity, however, occurs in the discussion of the "queer" events surrounding Aziz's trial. Here we learn that "a number of Mohammedan ladies had sworn to take no food until the prisoner was acquitted; their death would make little difference, indeed, being invisible, they seemed dead already, nevertheless it was disquieting" (p. 214).

Women, then, can disrupt or cause disquietude by their refusals, but their resistance is severely limited by the dominant rhetoric of power that reinscribes them as object of exchange or catalyst for rivalry within male conversation and male power struggles. Thus the alleged "insult" of one Englishwoman becomes the occasion for cloistering all Englishwomen, simultaneously reducing them to objects of protection and using them as an excuse to reassert white male power over both their women and their potential attackers. The pattern enacted in the novel, similar to that practiced in the American South, works to intimidate and coerce both Indian/black men and women and white women into accepting their subordinate positions.[21] Within this context, Fielding's refusal to elide Adela's name amidst the hysteria at the club surrounding "women and children" takes on heroic proportions. By speaking of her by name, by trying to reach her directly, he resists the periphrasis that destroys subjectivity and identity and reduces both her and Aziz to metonymic figures in a morality play of violated innocence and evil, whose end is to reaffirm the power of the white male. Fielding refuses their reduction to ciphers in the lengthening chain of periphrases leading to one possible closure only; he returns Adela to a virtual level of existence and focuses on the particular event.

When his attempt fails, however, Fielding, knowing the code, enacts his resistance to the group fiction by refusing to stand up for Ronny, the "insulted" fiancé, the "martyr" (p. 185) in this as in every drama of rape, in which the true victim is perceived to be the man whose boundaries and property have been violated through the usurpation of his woman's body. His resistance, that is, occurs within and is contained by a social system and a discourse of sexuality predicated on male bonding and male rivalry, in which the woman's experience, even of rape, is elided. Forced to choose sides, Fielding chooses Aziz, and in doing so, he reaffirms the power of their shared gender to mediate—at least potentially—racial difference.

Within the sexual discourse, Aziz and Fielding speak equally as subjects, as men, from the position of power, including the power to objectify and appropriate women. Thus Aziz, in his attempt to seal the intimacy between the two men, comments unabashedly that Adela " 'was not beautiful. She has practically no breasts . . . ,' " a synecdochal representation that reduces women to their physical attributes alone. For Fielding, he will "arrange a lady with breasts like mangoes . . . " (p. 120). In this scene, as elsewhere in the novel, Aziz's sexual objectification of women, the "derived sensuality that classes a mistress among motor-cars if she is beautiful, and among eye-flies if she isn't" (p. 241), alienates Fielding, who sees Aziz's valuation of women as commodities as a sign of "the old, old trouble that eats the heart out of every civilization: snobbery, the desire for possessions, creditable appendages" (p. 241). But however admirable this statement appears—however blind Fielding may be to his own ethnocentric biases—in committing himself to Aziz, Fielding acknowledges as well his place within the discourse of sexuality. When Aziz initiates their intimacy by showing Fielding the photograph of his dead wife, Fielding regrets that he has no woman or story of a woman to offer in exchange. The "compact . . . subscribed by the photograph" (p. 122) is completed by Aziz's statement that had his wife been alive, he would have showed the woman herself to Fielding, justifying this transaction to her by representing Fielding as his brother. Fielding feels honored.

It is not surprising, then, that in his attempt to reclaim Aziz from the periphrasis that threatens to engulf him after his arrest, Fielding tries to restore his status as subject by restoring his place within the sexual discourse shared by men. When McBryde, described as one of the most reflective and best educated of the English officials, offers Fielding a letter planning a visit to a brothel as evidence of Aziz's—and all Indians'—innate sexual depravity, Fielding responds by claiming that he had done the same thing at Aziz's age. "So had the Superintendent of Police," the narrative continues, "but he considered that the conversation had taken a turn that was undesirable" (p. 169). Why? Because by minimizing racial difference Fielding is "[leaving] a gap in the line" that these "jackels," the Indians, would exploit (p. 171). Fielding, that is, fills or bridges the gap generated by and necessary to the rhetoric of power by creating a gap in the barrier that ensures English self-representation and dominance.

But as Fielding learns from this exchange, more than racial stereotyping is in play here; social sexing is as well. In denying his complicity with Fielding and Aziz, in denying the sexual discourse that men share, McBryde refuses to recognize Aziz as man, as subject. And whatever Aziz's power to reduce women to commodoties, when spoken of as Indian within the discourse of English and Indian, sahib and native, he himself is objectified; he enters the category "woman" and becomes rapable. From the moment of his arrest, from the moment the door of the carriage is thrown open and the power of the state intrudes, Aziz is absorbed into a discourse that defines him by his sexuality alone. In contrast to the white man's position, which is coterminous with the (phallic) power of "the law," the position of the Indian man is to be symbolically "raped" by the accusation of rape, a position crucial for maintaining the white man's power and one that carries as much centrality in the intertwined discourses of sex and race as rape itself.

Once accused of rape, Aziz disappears as speaking subject; both his body and his possessions, including his letters, are appropriated by the police and used against him. For one thing, McBryde reduces Aziz to his body, his skin color, by implication his sexuality, which is by definition depraved. In discussing Aziz with Fielding, McBryde asserts that while the schoolmaster sees the Indians at their best, when they are boys, he, the policeman, "[knows] them as they really are, after they have developed into men" (p. 169). Later, in Court, "enunciating a general truth," he will state the "fact that any scientific observer will confirm," that "the darker races are physically attracted by the fairer, but not *vice versa*" (pp. 218–219).

From the perspective of McBryde's objective, "scientific," epistemological system Aziz, the object known by the observer, loses his status as man and with it the power to protect women, even his dead wife. When McBryde appropriates the photograph along with Aziz's other possessions, it ceases to signify Aziz's ability to exchange women in a ritual of male bonding; instead it indicates his reduction to sexual object. In response to Fielding's identification of the photograph, McBryde "gave a faint, incredulous smile, and started rummaging in the drawer. His face became inquisitive and slightly bestial. 'Wife indeed, I know these wives!' he was thinking" (p. 172). If the Indian man is reduced to a penis, Indian women are whores.

The photograph of Aziz's wife, then, becomes emblematic of woman both as object of exchange and as object of violation—violated here by McBryde's reading of her. He "knows" her, a metaphor that suggests clearly the relationship between knowledge, sexuality, and power—including the power to define, or name, the truth. While McBryde's statement illustrates the specific construction that metaphorizes the Orient as female, penetrated by the knowledge of the Western male Orientalist, the use of metaphors associated with sexuality or the violation of boundaries in discussions of the acquisition of knowledge is common in all "objective" or "scientific"—by definition "male"—discourses.[22] Even the existence of the photograph as "evidence" participates in the process, illustrating Susan Sontag's contention "the knowledge gained through still photography will always be . . . a semblance of knowledge, a semblance of wisdom, as the act of taking pictures is a semblance of wisdom, a semblance of rape."[23]

Photographs, if silent themselves, can be named; and the woman in this photograph is twice named and twice silenced—first by Aziz as woman, as object of exchange, and later by McBryde as object of an object, the sexualized Indian male. As such, her circulation reveals the shifting network of signification that elides the reality of the violation of woman and Indian through the periphrases at the heart of the novel. For if as woman she signifies the way in which all women are subject to rape by virtue of their gender—their sexual objectification and powerlessness to define themselves—she also signifies the rape practiced upon the Indians by virtue of their objectification and powerlessness. Her violation in her own right, however, remains an untold tale.

When Aziz regains his freedom, he reclaims his violated wife and with her his manhood (p. 261), setting the stage for the separation that ensues between Fielding and him, a separation precipitated first by Fielding's friendship with Adela after the trial and later by his marriage not to Adela—which is what Aziz mistakenly believes—but to Stella, Ronny's sister. Once the misunderstanding is cleared up, Fielding tries to recapture their previous closeness by "[forcing] himself to speak intimately about his wife"—by evoking, that is, the sexual discourse that had united them before. By now, however, Aziz no longer wishes intimacy with any English person and Fielding has "thrown in his lot with Anglo-India by marrying" a countrywoman (p. 319). However great Fielding's initial disregard of the racial discourse, he perceives his marriage as committing him to the system that defines him as English and male, and he accepts its limitations; he can no longer, in his words, "travel light," nor can he risk flirting with the other. Aziz is reduced to a "memento," a "trophy" (p. 319). Just as Fielding's defiance after Aziz's arrest was contained by the relations of power that made Ronny and him antagonists who spoke the same language, the form of his resistance corroborates rather than undermining the system. In this way it illustrates Foucault's belief that "resistance is never in a position of exteriority in relation to power"; it exists within the power/knowledge apparatus that "depends" upon it and is subject to its discourses.[24] In his defense of Aziz, for example, Fielding relies on the power of evidence and knowledge, which he believes will triumph, unable to recognize, as Hamidullah and the Indians do from the position of the feminized and colonized object, that even evidence and knowledge would not work to free them (p. 73; p. 269: "If God himself descended . . . into their club and said [Aziz] were innocent, they would disbelieve him"). Unable to cross the boundaries that separate subject and object, to enter fully into the category "woman," Fielding, for all his good intentions and his exposure of the system, enacts the story of the failure to identify with otherness.

Ultimately, it is Adela Quested, the woman, not Fielding, the man, who resists the "scientific truths" put forward by McBryde, simultaneously revealing and disrupting the mastery and violation that function as part of the rhetoric of knowledge and power. It is Adela who comes to represent the form of resistance described as "less a resistance, a force that can be set against power, than a non-force, an absolute difference with respect to power."[25] Edward Said has argued that the ending of the novel, where the landscape of India prevents Fielding and Aziz from bridging the gap that divides them, reinforces "a sense of the pathetic distance still separating 'us' from an Orient destined to bear its foreignness as a mark of its permanent estrangement from the West" (p. 244). But when viewed through the prism of gender, of social sexing, what separates the two men are their positions within the power grid that lock them into the discourse of male bonding and male rivalry, including racial rivalry. Adela, however, speaking from the gaps or interstices of the shifting power networks, speaks as woman for the category "woman." In this reading, the "mark of . . . permanent estrangement" that separates the two cultures is inscribed in the woman who enters the caves and returns speaking rape.[26]

The Marabar caves, the site of the rape, enclose in their empty, circular chambers the myth and the memory of the origin of difference that informs the novel. "Older than anything in the world," "flesh of the sun's flesh," the caves and the hills that surround them were "torn from [the sun's] bosom" at the time of creation (p. 123) and figure simultaneously sameness and difference, union and rupture. In the polished walls of their interior, with their suggestion of "internal perfection," the flame of a match becomes two flames that "strive to unite but cannot"; "[a] mirror . . . divides the lovers." Should the two flames finally "touch one another" in the beholder's eye, they simultaneously "kiss" and "expire" (p. 125). Union here becomes a form of extinction, while rupture opens the way for strife.

For Adela, the experience of the caves, the experience that she speaks as physical violation, represents her realization of the primal separation that makes difference and hence power possible; she is forced to recognize the social sexing that appropriates her body and names her woman. She experiences, we could say, the material and psychological reality of what it means to be rapable. Before the caves, Adela had defined herself, as Fielding does, through her intelligence, her honesty, and her belief in talk. If this self-definition constitutes a will to know, it manifests itself not in the "scientific" pronouncements endemic to the racial discourse but in a continual questioning of the givens of a situation and the desire to remove individuals from their position as figures in a frieze or typology. To the extent that Adela succeeds in having this self recognized, she believes she exists. But the obstacles are many. Ronny corrects her perceptions and language and circumscribes her actions; only a (male) background like his, he insists, produces usable knowledge in India (p. 81). Mrs. Turton labels her not pukka, Fielding calls her a prig and questions her sincerity, and Aziz, although he treats her as if she were a man, defines her by her lack of beauty. Despite her will to know, she increasingly figures in the narrative as an absence, a gap, created in part by the intrusion into her consciousness of her socially constructed status as woman: a thing and nothing. Ironically, she is first alluded to in the text as Ronny's not-yet-existent wife, the "Mrs. Red-nose" who cannot accept bribes, suggesting that for women existence is inseparable from marriage. But at the end of the Bridge Party, imagining her married life under the gaze of the Marabar hills ("How lovely they suddenly were! But she couldn't touch them. In front, like a shutter, fell a vision of her married life" [p. 47]), Adela experiences a radical diminution of self, the impossibility of knowing as woman within the social confines rapidly closing in on her. After the caves, having been absorbed by the male discourse that surrounds rape, she herself disappears: "The issues [she] had raised were so much more important than she was herself that people inevitably forgot her" (p. 216).

From this perspective, Adela's entrance into the cave affirms a crisis of identity that is both ontological and political. Coinciding with her doubts about her marriage and her perception that she lacks physical charm, it plunges her into consciousness of her place as woman: the place of sexual objectification, the place where being sexual object defines woman's existence. Within this realm, her intelligence, her desire to know, count for nothing. Within this realm, the refusal to accept her place, the refusal, for example, to marry, constitutes a refusal to be within the norms culture imposes upon her. Like the flame in the Marabar caves, she would experience union (marriage) as a form of extinction, while the rupture generated by her subversive refusal opens the space for social and political strife. That Adela ultimately represents this consciousness in the terms of a physical assault signifies both the materiality and the sense of powerlessness that accompany woman's objectification. She is, we could say, violated by the discourse, whether of rape or marriage, that reduces her to her sexuality alone.

Significantly, the words that precipitate Adela's experience by leaving her alone—her question to Aziz about the number of his wives—are not her own; they belong to Mrs. Turton (p. 153) and signify the unconscious absorption into the racial discourse that makes her speech an act of ventriloquism. This absorption begins immediately after her engagement when she speaks of the Nawab Bahadur, " 'our old gentleman of the car, ' " in exactly the "negligent tone" desired by Ronny (p. 96), and it can be attributed to the loss of self and voice, the reduction, that accompanies her impending marriage: "She was labelled now" (p. 94). Another way to describe her question is as an echo—an echo of the reductionism, the "singleness of vision and voice," associated with the echo in the cave and identified by Michael Ragussis as "the source of prejudice and egotism" in the novel.[27] By naming her experience rape, moreover, Adela activates the machinery and the discourse that violate Aziz and reduce the other Indians, even Hamidullah, to the condition of split beings, physically aware of the gaze of the other and the significance of one's self-presentation before those in the position of power—a reaction that profoundly annoys Fielding. When Hamidullah thanks Fielding for greeting him in public after the arrest, Fielding attributes this unaccustomed self-abasement to fear, not realism (p. 173).

Nevertheless, both Adela's original utterance and her subsequent withdrawal of Aziz's name during the trial can be read as a form of resistance, a resistance that resides in speaking her objectification. If the caves are for Adela "a reflexive place in which self divides into self and other"[28]—a division that makes her aware of her status as woman—they also allow her to speak as woman, in as much as division and self-differentiation characterize woman's authentic voice.[29] After the caves, lying passively in bed with her body full of cactus spines, while they are drawn out one by one, Adela literally becomes a split being, forced by the pain both to see and to experience herself as physical object, a vulnerable body. During the trial, when McBryde's lecture on "Oriental Pathology," the attraction of the darker races to the fairer, is interrupted by the comment, "Even when the lady is so uglier than the gentleman?," Adela's "body resented being called ugly, and trembled" (p. 219). This leads to the

first of the power plays initiated by the English, their insistence that
Adela's and their chairs be placed on the platform at the front of the
room. Adela herself, thus elevated, has the opportunity to see the
Indians involved, including Aziz. This vision returns him to the
material reality and the subjectivity denied him by the English, who
by refusing to speak his name had made him "synonymous with the
power of evil" (p. 202). With the understanding attained through
knowledge of her body, her sexuality, and the powers that control it,
Adela perceives him now for what he is: devoid of evil but subject as
Indian to a discourse of objectification and appropriation structured
in a similar way to that she experiences as woman.

It is this insight, perhaps, that allows her to recognize that whatever existed in the caves, Aziz was not there. What was there, still
unspeakable, because outside of or elided by the discourse that constructs the social/sexual category "woman," is the ontological shock
that accompanies the entrance into the gaps or interstices in the
culture where she simultaneously discovers and loses her self. Enclosed by the cave, she is enclosed as well by relations of power,
including gender, that make possible the discourse that represents
woman as pretense for male rivalry, token of exchange for male
bonding, or catalyst for male protection, even as it elides her being.

To understand the strength of her utterance it is necessary at this
point to invoke Mrs. Moore, the other woman who enters the caves
and returns not to speak rape, but to indifference and silence. For
Mrs. Moore, the experience of the caves, represented by the reductive powers of the echo, reveals not so much difference as sameness
—the radical sameness of all discursive systems and their failure to
escape the rhetoric of power and exclusion. From the beginning of
the novel, Mrs. Moore had refused the linguistic reductions that
characterize the speech of both English and Indian, even that
of Ronny, her son. After her first meeting with Aziz, after listening
to Ronny's reading of the scene, including his horror that her tone of
voice and choice of words had not indicated that she was talking to
a "native," she rejects the synecdochal mode. "Yes," she thinks, "it
was all true, but how false as a summary of the man" (p. 34). Later,
listening to Ronny justify the behavior of the English, she divorces
the words from the "self-satisfied lilt," perceiving, as the Indians do,
"the mouth moving so complacently and competently beneath the
little red nose," but rejecting the message as the last word on India
(p. 51). Mrs. Moore has, moreover, an uncanny ability to hear and
speak what is unspoken because unspeakable, illustrated, for example, by her naming the unknown force that attacks Ronny and

Adela on the way to the caves a ghost, a naming that places her within the racial memory of the Moslems. Her mode, we might say, is more metaphoric than metonymic or synecdochal; she makes no distinction between mosques and churches because "God is here" (p. 20), she calls wasps "Pretty dear" (p. 35), and she wishes for the union of all living things under a God who is love. At her strongest, she resists the totalizing rhetoric of power that reduces individuals to types and embraces a dual vision of particularity and union.

Plunged into the cave, however, terrified by the touch of flesh on flesh and by the echo that reduces all words, all language, all systems to "boum" (pp. 147–148), Mrs. Moore's double vision folds in on itself. Perceiving the horror of the void where distinctions and values disappear, the void beyond discourse and differentiation, she perceives as well that discourse itself, no matter how multiple or mobile its forms, has the potential to obliterate rather than unify individuals, even the discourse of love and marriage that she can no longer distinguish from rape: "Why all this marriage, marriage? . . . The human race would have become a single person centuries ago if marriage was any use. And all this rubbish about love, love in a church, love in a cave, as if there is the least difference" (pp. 201–202).

Despite her refusal to explain her vision ("Say, say, say. . . . As if anything can be said?" [p. 200]) or to declare Aziz's innocence, Mrs. Moore's uncanny knowledge communicates itself to Adela during her outburst about marriage in the form of Aziz's name, which until then had been completely elided by the English (p. 202). Adela, that is, hears Mrs. Moore say, "Dr. Aziz never did it," even though, as Ronny insists, "his name was never mentioned by anyone" (p. 204). "Aziz . . . have I made a mistake?" (p. 202), the younger woman asks, but Mrs. Moore no longer cares. Beyond marrying herself, encumbered by a body she feels enslaved to and children who demand things from her, including Adela, Mrs. Moore turns her back on the attempt to unravel the discourse of sexuality, possessiveness, and power, choosing instead indifference and annihilation. Nothing had happened to Adela, she feels, except fright, and even if it had, "there are worse evils than love" (p. 208). Described as a "withered priestess" (p. 208), she becomes, through the evocation of the myth of Persephone after her departure, a disillusioned Demeter, cynical about her daughter's violation and unwilling to intervene. Instead, she withdraws into the silence of the abyss and disappears.

Adela, the daughter, chooses to speak, and what she speaks is rape, the word that remains at the center of the novel even after she has withdrawn the charge against Aziz. Her discourse, moreover, is double, reflecting her discovery of differentiation and division. On the one hand, in speaking Aziz's name during the scene with Mrs. Moore, in restoring his subjectivity, she fills the gap opened by the rhetoric of power that objectifies the other and creates the space for violation to occur. She succeeds where Fielding had failed. "Dr. Aziz," she reiterates during the trial, "never followed me into the cave" (p. 229). On the other hand, by withdrawing his name without withdrawing the accusation of rape—that is, in refusing either to specify or deny what happened in the cave, a stance she maintains to the end (p. 263)—she creates another gap, one that disrupts rather than enabling the discourse of power and knowledge. Her refusal to specify, like the Indian women's refusal to be seen, generates a counter discourse, one that opens up gaps that those in power cannot control or afford, in part by undermining their claim to knowledge and truth. She generates as well the space between the material and the representational, between referentiality and textuality, where ideology and power are located, and she associates it with rape. Being English, she has the power to speak the position of otherness denied to the Indians in general and doubly denied to the invisible and silent Indian women, whose resistance resides in absence and negativity, and she uses this power to unsettle the dominant discourse.[30] In this sense she speaks what Aziz's dead wife cannot, naming the relationship between knowledge, objectification, and violation enacted by McBryde, the relationship that is elided in the periphrasis that surrounds Adela's experience even while it constitutes the reality of women's lives. However creative the elision of the proper term performed by periphrasis may be in literary speech, [31] when used as part of a rhetoric of power in *A Passage to India*, the elision emphasizes the refusal to name the reduction of woman and Indian that makes them rapable, the refusal to name it rape.

For Adela, then, to speak rape becomes an act of resistance. Her double discourse brings into representation woman's experience, the unspoken or unspeakable, that is left out of namings and ideologies even as it refuses the rhetoric of power that denies individuality and speech. For Forster, who spoke uneasily from within and without the discourse that appropriated his own sexuality, the periphrasis at the heart of the novel suggests the difficulty of his position. Unlike Fielding, with whom he clearly identifies, Forster understands the position of otherness inscribed in the woman, although finally unwilling to assert it himself. At the end he tries to recuperate the message of the caves through the marriage of Fielding and Stella and the temporary reconcilation of Fielding and Aziz, but he is unable to contain the woman's voice speaking from the interstices of culture the truth beyond the discourse of "the true,"[32] the truth that echoes throughout the novel, crisscrossing boundaries and prophesying violence and apocalypse unless we find new ways to respond when the other—whether woman or Indian—speaks violation.

NOTES

A longer version of this essay appears in *Novel* (Fall 1988), pp. 86–105. I am grateful to Mary Childers, Louise Fradenburg, Lynn Higgins, Marianne Hirsch, Nancy K. Miller, Sandy Petrey, and Nancy Vickers for their valuable criticism and suggestions.

1. In, respectively, *Webster's New World Dictionary of the American Language*, 2d College ed. (New York: Collins, 1978); Geoffrey Hartman, "The Voice of the Shuttle: Language from the Point of View of Literature," *Beyond Formalism, Literary Essays 1958–1970* (New Haven: Yale University Press, 1970), p. 352; *Webster's Third New International Dictionary* (Springfield, Mass.: Merriam, 1971).

2. Gerard Genette, "Figures," *Figures of Literary Discourse*, trans. Alan Sheridan (New York: Columbia University Press, 1982), pp. 47–49, 57.

3. E. M. Forster, *The Manuscripts of A Passage to India*, ed. Oliver Stallybrass (London: Edward Arnold, 1978), pp. 242–243.

4. Letter to G. L. Dickinson, June 26, 1924, quoted in Oliver Stallybrass, ed., *A Passage to India*, by E. M. Forster, Abinger ed. (London: Edward Arnold, 1978), p. xxvi.

5. E. M. Forster, *A Passage to India* (1924; reprint, New York: Harcourt, 1984), p. 152. Further citations appear in text.

6. The phrase "sex ghosts" comes from Mark Spilka's analysis of the governess's "prurient sensibility": "Turning the Freudian Turn of the Screw: How Not to Do It," *Literature and Psychology* (1963), 13:105–111. V. A. Shahane, summarizing various interpretations of Adela's experience, cites as "a minority critical view" that "Adela is sexually charmed by Aziz and that in her subconscious self she desires to be raped by him" (*E. M. Forster. "A Passage to India": A Study* [Delhi: Oxford University Press, 1977], p. 31). But the reading of Adela's experience in terms of repression, sexual hysteria, frigidity, or fear of the body is more widespread than Shahane implies. In addition, many critics associate Adela's experience with the condition of modern rationalism and the failure to recognize the importance of the heart or the passions or the instincts (revealed in part by the "new psychology" of Freud and Jung), but even here sexual repression enters the argument. Comparing Adela to D. H. Lawrence's Hermione Roddice, Lawrence Stone writes: "Both are catastrophes of modern civilization—repressed, class-bound, over-intellectualized" (*The Cave and the Mountain: A Study of E. M. Forster*

[Stanford: Stanford University Press, 1966], p. 382). A different perspective on Adela's perception of the experience as a rape, one closer to my own, associates it with the loveless or forced union symbolized by her engagement to Ronny: e.g., Gertrude M. White, *"A Passage to India:* Analysis and Revaluation," *PMLA* (1953), 68:641–657, and Elaine Showalter, *"A Passage to India* as 'Marriage Fiction': Forster's Sexual Politics," *Women and Literature* (1977), 5(2): 3–16. White also suggests an analogy between the relationship of Ronny and Adela and that of English and Indian in the novel.

David Lean's film version of the novel glaringly reinforces the view of Adela as sexually repressed. In an interview about the film, Lean remarked, "And Miss Quested . . . well, she's a bit of a prig and a bore in the book, you know. I've changed her, made her more sympathetic. Forster wasn't always very good with women": *Guardian* (January 23, 1984), quoted in Salman Rushdie, "Outside the Whale," *American Film* (1985), 10(4):70.

7. Michel Foucault, *The History of Sexuality,* vol. 1: *An Introduction,* trans. Robert Hurley (1978); reprint, New York: Vintage, 1980), pp. 44, 47, 104–105.

8. E. M. Forster, *The Life to Come and Other Stories* (1972; reprint, New York: Avon, 1976), pp. 160–176.

9. See essay 2 in this volume.

10. In his critique of the Raj revival in Britain, Salman Rushdie comments: "It is useless, I'm sure, to suggest that if a rape must be used as the metaphor of the Indo-British connection, then surely, in the interests of accuracy, it should be the rape of an Indian woman by one or more Englishmen of whatever class—not even Forster dared to write about such a crime" ("Outside the Whale," p. 70).

11. Like the black woman in Barbara Johnson's discussion of the intersections of race and gender, the Indian woman is "both invisible and ubiquitous: never seen in her own right but forever appropriated by the others for their own ends": "Metaphor, Metonymy, and Voice in *Their Eyes Were Watching God,"* in Henry Louis Gates, Jr., ed., *Black Literature and Literary Theory,* (New York: Methuen, 1984), p. 216. For the dangers inherent in Western feminist readings of "the other women," see Gayatri Chakravorty Spivak, "French Feminism in an International Frame," *Yale French Studies* (1981), 62:157, 179, and Chandra Talpade Mohanty, "Under Western Eyes: Feminist Scholarship and Colonial Discourse," *Boundary 2* (1984), 12/13:333–358.

12. Catharine A. MacKinnon, "Feminism, Marxism, Method, and the State: An Agenda for Theory," *Signs: Journal of Women in Culture and Society* (1982), 7:516 (hereafter cited in text).

13. Monique Plaza, "Our Damages and Their Compensation. Rape: The Will Not to Know of Michel Foucault," *Feminist Issues* (1981), 1(3):15 (hereafter cited in text).

14. See John Berger, *Ways of Seeing* (London: BBC and Penguin, 1972), pp. 46–47.

15. MacKinnon, "Feminism, Theory, Marxism and the State: Toward Feminist Jurisprudence," *Signs: Journal of Women in Culture and Society*

(1983), 8:654. See Ellen Rooney's essay in this volume for a reading of MacKinnon's analysis of rape law and its implications.

16. Foucault, *The History of Sexuality*, p. 94. See also *The Discourse on Language*, trans. Rupert Swyer, 1971, in *The Archaeology of Knowledge*, pp. 215–237 (New York: Pantheon, 1972).

17. I am following here Kenneth Burke's designation of synecdoche in "Four Master Tropes," *A Grammar of Motives* (New York: Prentice-Hall, 1945), pp. 507, 509. In the sense that synecdoche in this novel works towards reduction, it tends towards Burke's definition of metonymy.

18. For an analysis of what it meant to be a "White Man," see Edward Said, *Orientalism* (1978; reprint, New York: Vintage, 1979), p. 227. Further citations appear in text.

19. This is also the position of Hari Kumar in Paul Scott's *Raj Quartet: The Day of the Scorpion* (1968; reprint, New York: Avon, 1979).

20. Franz Fanon, *Black Skin, White Masks*, trans. Charles Lam Markmann (New York: Grove, 1967), pp. 169–170, 166. For Fanon, the black man exists for whites as a synecdoche, a penis.

21. See Nellie McKay's essay in this volume for an analysis of this phenomenon in the United States. See also Jacqueline Dowd Hall, *Revolt Against Chivalry: Jessie Daniel Ames and the Women's Campaign Against Lynching* (New York: Columbia University Press, 1979). The patterns are similar, not the same; Mrs. Turton's belief in the novel that Indian men "ought to crawl from here to the caves on their hands and knees whenever an Englishwoman's in sight . . ." (p. 216) not only reflects another of the negative effects of this "chivalry" on white women, but alludes as well to the actual treatment of Indians during the Amritsar riots after a white woman was attacked.

22. See MacKinnon, "Jurisprudence," p. 636; and Evelyn Fox Keller, *Reflections on Gender and Science* (New Haven: Yale University Press, 1985).

23. Susan Sontag, *On Photography*, cited in MacKinnon, "Jurisprudence," p. 637.

24. Foucault, *The History of Sexuality*, p. 95. See also Teresa de Lauretis' use of Foucault's formulation in her discussion of male power and male resistance as playing by the same rules: *Alice Doesn't: Feminism, Semiotics, Cinema* (Bloomington: Indiana University Press, 1984), pp. 91–92. Her text is Nicolas Roeg's film *Bad Timing*, which has a rape as its central narrative impetus.

25. De Lauretis, *Alice Doesn't*, p. 93.

26. Forster's " 'No, not yet' . . . 'No, not there' " is echoed in Julia Kristeva's definition of "women's practice as negative, in opposition to that which exists, to say that 'this is not it' and 'it is not yet.' " De Lauretis evokes this definition in her reading of the violated woman in *Bad Timing* who asks, 'What about my time' and 'what about now . . ." (*Alice Doesn't*, pp. 95, 98–99).

27. Michael Ragussis, *The Subterfuge of Art: Language and the Romantic Tradition* (Baltimore: Johns Hopkins University Press, 1978), p. 156.

28. Gillian Beer, " 'But Nothing in India is Identifiable': Negation and Identification in *A Passage to India*," in V. A. Shahane, ed., *Approaches to E. M. Forster: A Centenary Volume* (Atlantic Highlands, N.J.: Humanities Press, 1981), p. 18.

29. Barbara Johnson offers this speculation in her reading of the heroine's discovery of the power of voice in Zora Neal Hurston's *Their Eyes Were Watching God:* "The reduction of discourse to oneness, identity—in Janie's case, the reduction of woman to mayor's wife—has as its necessary consequence aphasia, silence, the loss of the ability to speak" (p. 212). We might add ventriloquism to this list.

30. De Lauretis associates Kristeva's perception that "women's practice can only be negative" with the concept of "a radical and irreducible difference," and "absolute negativity," that is not commensurate with the system that inscribes male power and resistance (p. 95). For de Lauretis, this difference is "much more radical than the lack of something, be it phallus, being, language, or power . . . an irreducible difference, of that which is elided, left out, not presented or representable" (p. 101).

31. Hartman, "The Voice of the Shuttle," p. 352. For Ragussis, in contrast to "the word," which "reports history," the recurring ellipses in the text "[pantomime] all that is outside history," establishing a space that can take on multiple meanings (p. 168). I would argue that when ellipsis becomes periphrasis, the space becomes a vacuum that denies those excluded by the elision their voice and their history.

32. Foucault, *The Discourse on Language*, p. 224.

3
WRITING THE VICTIM

6

Lucrece: The Sexual Politics of Subjectivity

COPP ÉLIA KAHN

Representation of the world, like the world itself, is the work of men; they describe it from their own point of view, which they confuse with the absolute truth.

Simone de Beauvoir,
The Second Sex

. . . the feminine . . . is not *outside* the masculine, its reassuring canny *opposite,* it is *inside* the masculine, its uncanny difference from itself.

Shoshana Felman,
"Re-reading Femininity"

The story of Lucrece, celebrated by Livy, Ovid, Chaucer, and Shakespeare, is one of the founding myths of patriarchy. Like so many of those myths, it entails the heroine's death, in this case accomplished by her own hand. While suicide marks Lucrece's exit from the story, though, it does not constitute narrative closure; that is accomplished with the expulsion of the Tarquins (the royal dynasty, to which the heroine's assailant belongs) from Rome, the abolition of monarchy, and the inauguration of the Roman republic. Rape authorizes revenge; revenge comprises revolution; revolution establishes legitimate government. In Lucrece's story, the personal is surely the political. Shakespeare's version of it is by far the longest, most fully dramatized one, in which the motives of Tarquin and the responses of Lucrece are given ample representation and subjected to keen moral scrutiny through richly elaborated language.

In this essay, I want to consider the representation of male and female subjectivities within a feminist problematic of rape, by looking closely at the language of power and the power of language with regard to the poem's two main characters, Lucrece and Tarquin.

Lucrece is notorious for her loquacity; while in comparison to Tarquin she says little before the rape, Shakespeare virtually turns the poem over to her after it. In copious lament, in apostrophe, sententiae, and ekphrasis, she explores the meaning of what has happened to her and her feelings about it. Yet, as I have argued elsewhere, Lucrece sees herself as a "patterne," a paradigm for all ages of the meaning of female chastity in a patriarchy.[1] Given the stridently patriarchal ideology in which the character is coded, then it is supremely pertinent to ask the question Mary Jacobus asks: "Is there a woman in this text?"[2] Or, to paraphrase similar questions asked by Jonathan Goldberg about "the Shakespearean text," who or what speaks in the character we call Lucrece?[3]

Does Lucrece as a female subject nonetheless speak like a man, for men and the world they control? Or does she voice a contending point of view not strictly framed by the dominant discourse? In her searching analysis of the poem's language, Nancy J. Vickers treats Lucrece as the voiceless creation of a rhetorical tradition through which the male gaze verbalizes itself, a tradition shaped by and shaping the linguistic and political rivalry of men, as exemplified in the blazon. She deals with that part of the poem, however, in which Lucrece is simply an object of description, before Tarquin enters her chamber, and not at all with the language Shakespeare gives the character herself.[4]

Before feminist criticism developed, for the most part readers avoided confronting the rape directly. They were also made uneasy by the poem's rhetorical luxuriance, particularly by the rhetoric accorded to Lucrece. This comment by F. T. Prince, the Arden editor of Shakespeare's poems, is representative: "Not only is she a less *interesting* character than Tarquin; she is forced to express herself in a way which dissipates the real pathos of her situation . . . After her violation, Lucrece loses our sympathy exactly in proportion as she gives *tongue*" [sic].[5] Prince's phrase links Lucrece's speech with a physical organ and makes it sound unseemly (even faintly obscene) for her to use that organ to speak about her violation. That violation, of course, also brought into prominence physical organs about which it was unseemly to speak; to be raped and to speak about it are thus similarly indecorous, alluding to matters about which women in particular ought to be silent. In giving Lucrece "tongue," Shakespeare perforce works *against* the patriarchal codes that, at the same time, he puts into her mouth. The text of *Lucrece* is a site of struggle between Tarquin and Lucrece, between lust and chastity, between male force and female resistance. The paradigm of all of these struggles, however, is the struggle between speech and suppression of speech, a struggle in which Lucrece figures not so much as Tarquin's antagonist but rather as the telltale sign of *his* subjectivity rather than her own.

While I agree with Jonathan Goldberg that "it is not necessarily a sign of power to have a voice, not necessarily a sign of subjection to lose it," I do not consider the speech of Shakespeare's characters removed from social practice and cultural signification, as Goldberg seems to. Shakespeare's text, I believe, is not a "mystic writing pad" from which male and female voices, untouched by constructions of gender outside the text, emerge and into which they also disappear.[6] Rather, the text exists interactively, reciprocally, with the social world in which the poet lived. It is no feminist catchword but merely accurate to term that world patriarchal, because it was patrilinear and primogenitural in the means by which it deployed power and maintained degree as the basis of the social order.[7] There as in the Rome of the poem, it is men who rape women and patriarchal constructions of gender and power that enable rape. As one feminist historian remarks of rape in sixteenth-century England, "whether regarded as a crime against property or a crime against the person, rape was a crime by men against women, and the law as an intrinsic and powerful part of patriarchy operated for men against women."[8] Yet the poem fascinates and moves me precisely because Shakespeare, I believe, tries to fashion Lucrece as a subject not totally tuned to the key of Roman chastity and patriarchal marriage and to locate a position in which he as poet might stand apart from those values as well. He fails, but his attempt reveals how narrowly the rhetorical traditions within which he works are bounded by an ideology of gender in which women speak with the voices of men. Despite the "tongue" with which Shakespeare provides her and the understanding with which he represents her, ultimately he inscribes her within the same constructs of power and difference as Tarquin.

Heroic Discourse and the Scopic Economy

Falling into two parts, the poem follows a structural pattern common in Shakespeare; in the portion preceding the rape, Tarquin's voice predominates as he struggles between conscience and desire; after the rape, we hear only Lucrece, who in a series of laments moves from grief to grievance and a determination to kill herself. In formal terms, Lucrece's laments are the counterpart of Tarquin's debates, but the two linguistic occasions place them in radically different positions.[9] Whether figured as a thief stealing another man's treasure, a predator seizing his prey, or a warrior besieging a fortified city, Tarquin is an agonistic competitor and as such, whether his aims are noble or despicable, inscribed within a heroic discourse (which is perhaps one reason why critics like Prince find him more "interesting" than Lucrece). Lucrece, identified with the besieged city and not the besieger, takes her traditionally feminine position in the same discourse as victim of and also witness to the pathos and grandeur of its agons. And when she determines to take action herself, even as the victim of a deed that Shakespeare condemns as a crime in terms that clearly subvert its heroics, her action nonetheless remains inscribed within heroic discourse, creating a contradiction at the heart of the poem. By comparing the rhetorical strategies of Tarquin's debate with those of Lucrece's lament, we can realize the extent to which Shakespeare, despite efforts to challenge the patriarchal structures that authorize rape (however much they may also imply disapproval of it), is pulled back into them.

As Vickers so cogently argues, Shakespeare conceives the precipitating causes of the rape—Collatine's boast of his wife's chastity and Tarquin's reaction to her beauty—within the poetic tradition of the blazon, "shaped predominantly by the male imagination for the male imagination . . . in large part, the product of men talking to men about women."[10] The term "blazon" means both a poetic description of an object and a heraldic description of a shield; when a woman is blazoned, then, she is incorporated into a certain heroic discourse. And when Lucrece greets Tarquin at Collatium, Shakespeare greatly intensifies this incorporation. Not only does he divide her body into parts in order to praise it, as blazon requires; he also employs heraldic terms to describe the parts as locked in chivalric combat. Virtue and beauty, liveried in the white and red of her complexion, create a "heraldry in Lucrece' face," "a silent war of lilies and roses" that extends over four stanzas (lines 50–77). This contest echoes the contest of description that took place in Tarquin's tent and impelled him to possess Lucrece and foreshadows the contest that concludes the poem with the expulsion of the Tarquins from Rome by Collatine's party. All these rhetorical moves inscribe Lucrece several times over within the linguistic domain of heroism, as prize of rather than participant in its agons.

They also construct Tarquin as a knowing male viewer for whom seeing means desiring and Lucrece as the innocent object of his gaze. The insistently visual coding of Lucrece in the first 575 lines as one who is seen but does not see, who is seen but not heard, can hardly be overemphasized. In the Argument, Collatine praises his wife only for her chastity; it is after Tarquin actually sees her that he becomes "inflamed with Lucrece' beauty," and from that moment on, to see her is to want her. In contrast to the possessive, dominating gaze of Tarquin, Lucrece's innocence is figured as a passive, superficial looking:

> . . . she that never cop'd with stranger eyes,
> Could pick no meaning from their parling looks,
> Nor read the subtle shining secrecies
> Writ in the glassy margents of such books . . . (lines 99–102)[11]

The contrast is intensified when, having secretly entered her chamber, he draws back the bed curtain and peers at her (lines 365–378), while her eyes "keep themselves enclosed." At this point, Shakespeare proceeds with a conventional blazon. The narrator names, describes, and praises parts of Lucrece's body: her cheek as it rests on her hand, her head, eyes ("canopied in darkness"), hair, and breasts. Finally he summarizes the whole, from Tarquin's point of view:

> What could he see but mightily he noted?
> What did he note but strongly he desired?
> What he beheld, on that he firmly doted,
> And in his will his wilful eye he tired,
> With more than admiration he admired
> Her azure veins, her alabaster skin,
> Her coral lips, her snow-white dimpled chin. (lines 414–420)

The sleeping Lucrece is both figuratively and literally unconscious of Tarquin's gaze "mightily" taking possession of her. Laura Mulvey's analysis of the male gaze in Hollywood films illuminates a connection between his gaze and his power over her:

> According to the principles of the ruling ideology and the psychical structures that back it up, the male figure cannot bear the burden of sexual objectification. . . . Hence the split between spectacle and narrative supports the man's role as the active one of forwarding the story, making things happen. . . . The power of the male protagonist as he controls events coincides with the active power of the erotic look, both giving a satisfying sense of omnipotence.[12]

No female character in Shakespeare is more decisively inscribed than Lucrece in a scopic economy that makes her an object for the

purpose of control and domination. At this point, the rape seems
inevitable and the story is Tarquin's, not Lucrece's, because he controls not only the gaze but also the story.

Transgression

Of course, it is true that according to the Roman reverence for family
lineage and the sacred precincts of the *domus*, Tarquin is breaking a
profound taboo. Nowhere in the poem is this sense of transgression
voiced more poignantly than by Tarquin himself as he struggles with
his desire:

> Fair torch, burn out thy light, and lend it not
> To darken her whose light excelleth thine;
> And die, unhallow'd thoughts, before you blot
> With your uncleanness that which is divine;
> Offer pure incense to so pure a shrine. (lines 190–194)

The imagery of shrine and holy fire is indebted to the cult of Vesta,
which replicated ancient Roman family rituals on a national scale
and centered on the maintenance of the sacred altar fire by the vestal
virgins. It was believed that catastrophe would befall Rome if this
fire were ever extinguished; thus the very existence of the state was
made symbolically dependent on the confinement of women's bodies within the institutional boundaries of marriage, family, and *domus*.[13] Lucrece, described throughout the poem in the imagery of
Vesta, is established as the very embodiment of the goddess even in
the Argument. When Collatine, Tarquin, and their comrades post
back to Rome to verify the claims they have made for their wives,
only Lucrece is found at home, spinning with her maids, chastely
guarding the hearth.

Shakespeare would have known about Vesta from the same book
in which he read the story of Lucrece: Ovid's *Fasti*. The cult of
Vesta, as Ovid conveys it (and his account is paralleled by that of
Cicero in *De Natura Deorum*), is curious in two ways.[14] First, it is a
virgin who is identified with the hearth fire, prime symbol of family
life, rather than a mother; second, of all the Roman pantheon, Vesta
alone is unrepresented: no images of her are permitted. Jean-Joseph
Goux remarks on the connection between these two elements of the
cult:

> Vesta's virginity and her unrepresentability are both protected
> at once. A man *(vir)* should neither penetrate, nor see, nor

imagine. The inviolable virginity and the strict unrepresenta-
bility are identical, as if there were a complicity, on some
opposing plane, between "rape" by manly sensual desire (the
Priapic appetite) and visualization which would be a phantasm
and an impious fraud.[15]

Even before the rape, then, when Tarquin penetrates Lucrece's
chamber and merely gazes upon her chaste and alluring body with
"manly sensual desire," he is symbolically raping her—and also
breaking what we might call the quintessential Roman taboo against
Vesta as goddess not only of *domus* but of *civitas*, in whose cult the
permanence and the sacredness of both are represented.

That Vesta is a virgin, that she guards a hearth fire, located at the
physical center of the *domus*, signifying the sacredness and permanence of home and state, that she must be unseen: all these motifs
combine to suggest that "she is the guardian of the innermost things
(rerum intumarum)," as Cicero says.[16] Goux links this inwardness
with "the idea of a *self* which is not identical to the ego" and which
he distinguishes from "the heroic will, the executive power of the
heroic ego (which turns outward)."[17]

What does it mean, then, for Tarquin's heroic will, turning outward toward Lucrece as a Vesta figure, a figure of the self, to rape
her? I suggest that it is precisely this transgression that allows
Shakespeare to create a heroic male subject in whom the contradictions of the dominant ideology are internalized and set at war. Even
as Tarquin reverences the sacredness of the Roman community, the
Vesta principle, he is driven to desecrate it in obedience to a principle equally strong and just as central, though not symbolized so
coherently in a single deity—the principle of *virtus*, which depends
on rivalry, agon, and conquest. His dividedness as a subject makes
him heroic in the tragic terms that Shakespeare, of all English poets,
has decisively established for our culture.

In contrast to Tarquin, Lucrece, because she is modeled on the
Vesta principle, is superbly unified; all that she says and does co-
heres around her chastity, and she dies in order to purify and reassert
it. It is also this unity, however, that keeps Lucrece from attaining
(as it were) the subjectivity that is Tarquin's. On the other hand,
unlike Vesta, Lucrece can be *seen*—she is not sequestered from the
agonistic rivalry just as important to Roman culture as its inviolable
unity. She is a woman, not a goddess, and her body is the site—and
sight—at which Shakespeare sets against each other these two contending aspects of the Roman ethos. Thus she divides the masculine

Roman self, yet in dividing it confers on it a dimension of subjectivity and a tragic potential, which we have learned to honor. Insofar as we can identify Lucrece with "the idea of a *self*" associated, as Goux argues, with "the innermost things," that "self" isn't hers. Rather, it is Tarquin's—but her capacity to stand for and set into play the ideological contradictions of Roman culture allows Shakespeare to create Tarquin as an inwardly divided, heroically torn subject.

Besieging Ardea, capital of the Rutuli, is considered a legitimate exercise of Roman military power; besieging Lucrece is not, and in punishment Tarquin and his family are stripped of power. But the same metaphors that validate the conquest of a neighboring people frame the conquest of Lucrece by Tarquin:

> Affection is my captain, and he leadeth;
>> And when his gaudy banner is display'd,
>> The coward fights, and will not be dismay'd. (lines 271–273)

> His drumming heart cheers up his burning eye,
> His eye commends the leading to his hand;
> His hand, as proud of such a dignity,
> Smoking with pride, march'd on to make his stand
> On her bare breast, the heart of all her land. . . . (lines 435–439)

> His hand that yet remains upon her breast,—
> Rude ram, to batter such an ivory wall!—
> May feel her heart, poor citizen! distress'd,
> Wounding itself to death, rise up and fall,—
> Beating her bulk, that his hand shakes withal:
>> This moves in him more rage and lesser pity,
>> To make the breach and enter this sweet city.
>>> (lines 463–469)

Does the metaphor of city and siege in these passages eroticize violence or militarize eros? One might argue that the difference of context—bedchamber, not battlefield—renders this heroic language ironic and suggests a critique of the rape, but the same sexual politics underlies both contexts. In the Rome of this poem, whether in bed or in battle, men are in command of physical force, political power, and the language that authorizes them; to none of these do women have free access. The transfer of language from one domain to the other does not challenge the structures of power that enable men to keep women hidden and mute. Shakespeare's language, at bottom, identifies rather than distinguishes erotic and military domination. Thus it elides and conceals that division within the Roman ethos of which Lucrece, as both incarnation of Vesta and object of masculine rivalry, is the metaphor, the trace.

The narrative moment in which the rape occurs specifically associates linguistic domination with the sexual domination of women by men through force. Tarquin interrupts Lucrece's pleas in midsentence (line 666) and in five compact lines reiterates his threat. With the ellipsis conventional in representations of rape, these lines narrate the act:

> This said, he sets his foot upon the light,
> For light and lust are deadly enemies:
> Shame folded up in blind concealing night,
> When most unseen, then most doth tyrannize.
> The wolf hath seiz'd his prey, the poor lamb cries,
>   Till with her own white fleece her voice controll'd
>   Entombs her outcry in her lips' sweet fold.
>
>   (lines 673–679)

Like a warrior marking his victory over an enemy, Tarquin stamps out his torch. The "shame" of line 677 is Tarquin's in that, like him, it "doth tyrannize"—but it is also Lucrece's, given her belief that she as much as Tarquin has "stained" Collatine, and this shame drives her to kill herself. The metaphorical design of lines 675–679 naturalizes that shame and along with it, the muffling of her voice.

The word Shakespeare's contemporaries often used for woman's sexual parts, *pudenda,* derives from *pudere,* to be ashamed. According to the standard of chastity to which she adheres, Lucrece's sexuality is held to be her shame and must be modestly concealed. Even when the shame of the rape is concealed by darkness, this shame "most doth tyrannize," because for Lucrece it resides not in what can be seen of her but in what is being done to her. When Tarquin seizes her and "entombs her outcry in her lips' sweet fold," in a single gesture he strips her of that modest concealment and robs her of language by using her nightgown to stifle her voice. In the phrase "her lips' sweet fold," we can discern an upward displacement of that "sweet fold" below, which when unmolested reflects—naturally as it were—the concealment dictated by Roman chastity. As Peter Stallybrass has argued, the chastity, silence, and confinement to the domestic realm urged on women in the Renaissance are parallel boundaries of containment: "the closed body, the closed mouth, the closed house."[18] In the patriarchal metaphors of this stanza, woman's shamefast body is folded back on itself, concealing her desire and her speech in its folds. When Tarquin muffles Lucrece's cries with the folds of her nightgown as he rapes her, though his act is brutal and unlawful, though he penetrates what ought to remain closed, at the same time he but repeats and reinforces the dominant tendency of the culture in concealing, sealing off, muffling women's desire and women's speech.[19]

Resistance

When Tarquin "shakes aloft his Roman blade" (line 505) before raping Lucrece, he performs a gratuitous but potently symbolic gesture.[20] The rape violates Roman law, yet the physical force implied in the sword is fully congruent with the Roman martial ethos. That force is truly exemplified not in his sword, however, but in the cunning threat that he then proceeds to utter. He makes it clear (in lines 512–539) to begin with that he will take her, no matter what her resistance. And if she resists, he says, he will kill her after he takes her. He adds a final element of coercion to this, however. After doing away with Lucrece, he promises to kill "some worthless slave" in her household, place him with her, and claim he slew them both because he found them together. This threat takes its force from the entire Roman ideology of male honor and female chastity. Tarquin is spurred to possess Lucrece by his competitive, agonistic Roman mentality even more than by her beauty per se. He wants her because she is Collatine's, and therefore every indication of her chastity—that is, her husband's rights over her body, which she affirms—paradoxically increases his desire. Nonetheless, to judge from this threat (which Shakespeare takes from Livy and Ovid), he appears to understand her chastity from her point of view as well as from his. He sees that she has perfectly identified herself with her husband, as the seal of his honor, and therefore will not risk resisting Tarquin because it would dishonor Collatine. To save her husband, Tarquin correctly guesses, she is sure to yield herself.

Whatever she does, Lucrece can't avoid being raped. Moreover, it is only by not *resisting* Tarquin that she can avoid disgracing her husband and herself, and Tarquin doesn't specify what he means by resistance. ("If thou deny, then force must work my way," he says in line 513.) Actually, Lucrece *does* resist Tarquin, in twelve stanzas of passionate argument terminated by the rape, which also silences Tarquin; he then simply vanishes from the poem, vanquished by guilt. The inner consistency and dramatic intensity of Lucrece's verbal struggle against her assailant arises from its anatomy of marriage as the institution that effects male control of women's sexuality and thus determines the sexual politics of Roman (and English) society. It is only in terms of that politics that Lucrece can construct her protests, however, only by invoking the very principles and institutions which also underlie Tarquin's threat:

> She conjures him by high almighty Jove,
> By knighthood, gentry, and sweet friendship's oath,
> By her untimely tears, her husband's love,
> By holy human law and common troth. . . . (lines 568–571)

> My husband is thy friend; for his sake spare me.
> Thyself art mighty; for thine own sake leave me.
> Myself a weakling; do not then ensnare me. (lines 582–584)

Her appeals to religion, the social hierarchy, friendship between men, marriage, law, etc., simply reinscribe Collatine's claim to her body and reinvoke the conflict between it and the Vesta principle of Rome as a unified body politic, the conflict in which Tarquin as a subject has been defined. Whenever Lucrece does not figure herself as belonging to Collatine, she uses metaphors that picture her as a typically weak and suppliant woman, the subject if not the victim of power held by men: "a poor unseasonable doe" (line 581); "a weakling" (line 584) capable only of sighs, moans, tears, groans (lines 586–588).

Lucrece's resistance, then, in effect cancels itself out, because it is inscribed within the same structures of power as the rape is. Such resistance can be contrasted to Kate's outspokenness in *The Taming of the Shrew*. In her interpretation of the play Karen Newman reads Kate's speech as a version of Luce Irigaray's "mimeticism," a self-conscious strategy of subverting the dominant discourse "so that metaphors, puns, and other forms of wordplay manifest their veiled equivalences: the meaning of woman as treasure, of wooing as a civilized and acceptable disguise for sexual exploitation, of the objectification and exchange of women."[21] Unlike Kate swearing to Petruchio that the moon is the sun if he will have it so, Lucrece doesn't mime the terms of her place in the Roman sex-gender system; she reiterates them with passionate sincerity. And unlike *Taming*, Lucrece lacks a dramatic frame (the Induction), which, as Newman says, "[calls] attention to the constructed character of the representation rather than veiling it through mimesis." Furthermore, as narrative poem rather than stage play, it lacks the subversive effect of transvestite boy actors. Whether Tarquin uses power rightly or wrongly, it is his power to use, and Lucrece does not question that; she only invokes the same structures of male authority and force that Tarquin will call upon to justify—however reprehensibly—the rape.

The Voice of Lucrece

Being raped does grant Lucrece a voice—the voice of the victim. But the terms of her victimage do not constitute a vantage point distinct from the patriarchal ideology that generated Tarquin's act. They merely emanate from another area of that ideology. Like Andromache and the other Trojan women, she laments the consequences of men's power, yet remains helpless to challenge it—even, I shall argue, in inciting revenge against Tarquin. Significantly, in an image that clearly foreshadows her suicide, Lucrece identifies herself with Philomel:

> Come Philomel, that sing'st of ravishment,
> Make thy sad grove in my dishevel'd hair. . . .
> And whiles against a thorn thou bear'st thy part
> To keep thy sharp woes waking, wretched I
> To imitate thee well, against my heart
> Will fix a sharp knife to affright mine eye,
> Who if it wink shall thereon fall and die. . . .
> (lines 1128–1129, 1136–1139)

As Patricia Klindienst Joplin suggests, in Ovid's story Philomel is robbed of her speech because she threatens to expose her male oppressors by speaking out. But by weaving her story, through "the voice of the shuttle," she fashions revenge and resistance.[22] Lucrece identifies herself not with this weaving woman, but with the Philomel who is metamorphosed into the nightingale, the Philomel who vainly laments her shame, under cover of night—wounding not her oppressor, but herself.[23] Her laments begin with the prayer that night may cover what she describes as disgrace, sin, guilt, and finally "helpless shame" (lines 750–756). This extended plea for concealment may be seen as the opposite and counterpart of the visual troping of Lucrece that prevailed before the rape; now, as a raped woman, she suffers to the fullest the penalty of being seen and wishes only to be hidden. As the prayer settles into an apostrophe to night, Lucrece begins to articulate her understanding of the rape. In doing so, she reworks exactly the metaphors in which Tarquin him-self constructed the crime as he contemplated it. He envisioned the dishonor of rape as an "eye-sore" or "loathsome dash" placed on his escutcheon by the herald (lines 204–210) to shame his posterity; she now sees it in the same heraldic terms, precisely and profoundly symbolic of the patriarchal family, as an "attaint" and "crest-wound-ing . . . mot," motto or device (lines 825, 827–831), which will bla-zon her now private shame to the world. The "ever-during blame," the "shame and fault" over which Tarquin agonized before the rape as his, are now hers (cf. lines 223–224, 238–239 with 750–756).

But even before the apostrophe to night gives way to an apostrophe to opportunity (at line 876), Shakespeare seems to shy away from the implications of Lucrece's language. The verse slides into sententiae that imply that the rape isn't a crime committed within a certain structure of power, but the result of a universal tendency:

> But no perfection is so absolute
> That some impurity doth not pollute. (lines 853–854)

> The sweets we wish for turn to loathed sours
> Even in the moment that we call them ours. (lines 867–868)

Specific references to Tarquin and Collatine are sparse; implicit connections are fitful. For more than a hundred lines (between, roughly, lines 848 and 967), the poem sinks into a bog of platitudes, as though Shakespeare can't allow Lucrece to mourn her injury in terms that would link it to patriarchal power and turn mourning into subversion. She blames night ("blind muffled bawd"), opportu-nity ("thy guilt is great"), and time ("be guilty of my death since of my crime") before she curses Tarquin and abandons "this helpless smoke of words" to form a plan of action.

That plan as first presented, however, does not entail action against Tarquin but solely against herself. Resolving to "let forth [her] foul defiled blood" (line 1029), she implies a symbolic quid pro quo, an exchange of her life for her shame. But as she explicates this sym-bolic act, an additional meaning emerges. According to Lucrece's thinking, suicide will substitute for the resistance that betokens perfect chastity—resistance she blames herself for not showing before:

> Poor hand, why quiver'st thou at this decree?
> Honour thyself to rid me of this shame:

For if I die, my honour lives in thee,
But if I live, thou liv'st in my defame.
Since thou could'st not defend thy loyal dame,
And wast afeard to scratch her wicked foe,
Kill both thyself and her for *yielding* so.
(lines 1030–1036, my emphasis)

But Lucrece *did* resist; as we saw, she argued against Tarquin at some length and when he seized her cried like a "poor lamb" until he smothered "her piteous clamours" with her nightgown (lines 673–686). In Lucrece's eyes, though, what *counts* as resistance? Evidently, not verbal protests or "piteous clamors," only physical action such as scratching her attacker, however futile it might be. But what about Tarquin's additional, more powerful and deadly threat, to rape and kill her first and then, *if she resisted*, implicate her in adultery with a slave, thereby besmirching her and, more important, Collatine irrevocably? In the light of this threat, *not* to resist physically really means to defend Tarquin's honor; apparent passivity, in this peculiar case, must be read as covert resistance. Shakespeare, however, seems to have forgotten the alternatives Tarquin allowed Lucrece and makes her conceive her suicide as though she had had only the choice of physical resistance, however futile, or submission to Tarquin's superior force, which would have compromised her integrity.

In dissecting the critical procedures commonly employed in the reading of sexual violence, Ellen Rooney argues

the *absence of feminine desire* in rape is read as simple (unequivocal) *passivity*. This maintains the valorization of the dichotomy of the rapist, the subject of the discourse of desire in rape. Because the "object" of rape is finally helpless, her defeat is read as passivity, and her passivity is totalized. As a consequence, her *resistance* (her *activity) goes unread.* Ironically, it is this activity—the resistance of the victim—that makes rape rape.[24]

Shakespeare makes Lucrece valorize the rapist's dichotomy between active resistance and passive submission, read her resistance as passivity, and totalize that passivity into "yielding." Thus it cannot be maintained, as some recent critics do, that even when she leaves off lamentation and takes action, she does so in a way that ceases to affirm her inscription into patriarchy, that establishes a "self" for her or gives that self a voice of its own.[25]

But let us turn, then, to that action as she finally orchestrates and accomplishes it. Summoning her husband and father to Rome by a letter that does not reveal the rape, when they are present she narrates the event, but before naming the rapist requires them to take an oath of vengeance. Only then does she sheathe the knife in her breast. In the narration preceding her suicide, she mentions Tarquin's sword, her cries, and his threat entailing "th'adulterate death of Lucrece and her groom" (lines 1625–1645). But in the final stanza of this account, she explicitly states that she didn't even resist verbally:

> Mine enemy was strong, my poor self weak,
> And far the weaker with so strong a fear.
> My bloody judge forbod my tongue to speak;
> No rightful plea might plead for justice there. . . .
>   (lines 1646–1649)

Again the text "folds up" Lucrece's voice and "in her lips' sweet fold," too; she herself reads her resistance right out of the story. Furthermore, she affirms Tarquin's claim that her beauty, not his lust, caused him to rape her:

> His scarlet lust came evidence to swear
>   That my poor beauty had purloined his eyes;
>   And when the judge is robb'd, the prisoner dies.
>   (lines 1650–1652)

As the Arden editor notes, in this metaphor lust is no longer the criminal; rather, it wears the scarlet robe of a judge and is a witness to boot. Though Lucrece believes her plea is "rightful," she accepts the verdict of the rigged trial she portrays and seeks only to make her "excuse":

> Though my gross blood be stain'd with this abuse,
> Immaculate and spotless is my mind;
> That was not forc'd, that never was inclin'd
>   To accessory yieldings, but still pure
>   Doth in her poison'd closet yet endure. (lines 1655–1658)

Any such "accessory yieldings" would have been accessory only in the sense of protecting Collatine from the "blot" on his honor caused by the rape.

When I wrote about this poem a decade ago, I cited three stanzas of authorial comment in the narrator's voice, lines 1240–1260, as evidence of what I called "Shakespeare's sensitive understanding of the social constraints which force Lucrece into a tragic role."[26] It now seems to me that his understanding of such constraints is itself constrained by the basic assumption underlying the entire passage— the assumption that women are "naturally" the weaker of the species. With their impressionable "waxen minds," their innocent "smoothness," their flowerlike beauty, they are more sinned against than sinning, not culprits themselves but "tenants" to the "shame" of men. In the comparison between male and female that structures the passage, women are always the subordinate term, creatures to be pitied rather than praised. Yet Shakespeare seems to want it both ways. He pities Lucrece for the (feminine) weakness that allows her waxen mind to be stamped with Tarquin's crime, yet also, and in equal measure, praises her for a (quasi-masculine) strength that empowers her to die like a later Shakespearean hero, "a Roman by a Roman valiantly vanquished."

The poem ends with the rout of the Tarquins, carried out by Collatine and his kinsmen but authorized by Lucrece's account of the rape and her suicide. Thus she as a woman plays a peculiarly heroic role in the foundation of the Roman republic. As Michael Platt points out, *Lucrece* can be seen as "a brief epic" resembling the *Iliad* or the *Aeneid* in centering on "the destruction and foundation of cities." Lucrece's body stands in the place of Troy; on its ruins is the new republic Rome built. As she gazes at the tapestry depicting the fall of Troy (lines 1541–1547), she realizes that "she is a city and her rape a tyranny."[27] In such a reading, the rape of Lucrece is seen as an aspect of Tarquin's overweening pride, associated with the tyranny of his house. The poem offers this view of the rape many times. But in another sense, given the metonymy of woman for city, the rape is, culturally speaking, inevitable; a continuation rather than a violation of the power held by men. The famous ekphrasis in which Shakespeare describes a tapestry depicting the furthest extent and final act of the siege of Troy suggests this sense.

In book 2 of the *Aeneid*, long recognized as the source of this episode, when the Greeks swarm into the inmost chambers of Priam's palace, their penetration is clearly imaged as rape. They tear off the portals leading to "the inner house," which creates "a gaping mouth" and leaves the long halls and private rooms "open, naked," as vulnerable to violation as the women, now wandering terrified amid the bridal chambers "that had such hopes of sons," will shortly be.[28] Neatly linking the end of the war to its beginning, Lucrece comments:

Had doting Priam check'd his son's desire,
Troy had been bright with fame and not with fire.
(lines 1490–1491)

Given the continuity between Homer's, Vergil's, and Shakespeare's epic poems, it is difficult to regard Tarquin's violation of Lucrece as a departure from the heroic norm. In the transformation of Rome from monarchy to republic men retain their exclusive command over force and over women. The "Roman blade" that Tarquin flourishes over Lucrece is the same one that she turns against herself, and her death sanctions the continuation of the same force.

NOTES

I would like to thank Mary Ann Doane, Christina Crosby, Karen Newman, and Naomi Schor for their helpfully stringent readings of this essay.

1. Coppélia Kahn, "The Rape in Shakespeare's *Lucrece*," *Shakespeare Studies* (1976), 9: 45–72.

2. Mary Jacobus, "Is There A Woman in This Text?" *New Literary History* (1982), 14(1):117–141.

3. Jonathan Goldberg, "Shakespearean Inscriptions: The Voicing of Power," in Patricia Parker and Geoffrey Hartman, eds., *Shakespeare and the Question of Theory*, pp. 116–137 (London: Methuen, 1985).

4. Nancy Vickers, " 'The blazon of sweet beauty's best': Shakespeare's *Lucrece*," in Patricia Parker and Geoffrey Hartman, eds., *Shakespeare and the Question of Theory*, pp. 95–115 (New York and London: Methuen, 1985). This essay is a somewhat different version of that cited in note 10 below.

5. F. T. Prince, introduction to *The Poems*, Arden Shakespeare Paperbacks (London: Methuen, 1969), p. xxxvi.

6. Goldberg, "Shakespearean Inscriptions," p. 130.

7. See Lawrence Stone's summary of the social practices by which patriarchy maintained itself in *The Crisis of the Aristocracy 1558–1660*, abridged ed. (London: Oxford University Press, 1971), p. 271.

8. For a critical reading of the legal records of rape cases, see Nazife Bazar, "Rape in England between 1550 and 1700," in *The Sexual Dynamics of History: Men's Power, Women's Resistance*, pp. 28–42 (London: Feminist History Collective, 1983).

9. I completed an earlier draft of this essay before Joel Fineman's "Shakespeare's Will: The Temporality of Rape" appeared, in *Representations* (Fall 1987), 20: 25–76. In arguing that the rape, *Lucrece*, and "heterosexual desire *per se*" are modeled on the figure of chiasmus, Fineman also notes that "Tarquin and Lucrece both speak the *same* language" (p. 43) and claims further that they "are inverse versions of each other, and for this reason

together make the rape of Lucrece" (p. 44). While I hold that patriarchy puts them in crucially different *political* positions, he sees them in terms of chiasmus as characters who occupy opposing but equal rhetorical positions.

10. Nancy Vickers, "This Heraldry in Lucrece' Face," in Susan Rubin Suleiman, ed., *Female Body in Western Culture: Contemporary Perspectives*, pp. 209–222 (Cambridge: Harvard University Press, 1986).

11. This and all subsequent quotations are taken from the Arden Shakespeare Paperback edition of *Lucrece* cited in note 5, above.

12. See Laura Mulvey, "Visual Pleasure and Narrative Cinema," *Screen* (1975), 16: 6–18.

13. See Kahn, "The Rape in Shakespeare's *Lucrece*," pp. 50–51.

14. Ovid, *Fasti* 2: 721–852, and Livy, *The History of Rome*, 1: 57–60, are Shakespeare's two main sources for the story of Lucrece. I believe that he also drew upon Ovid's descriptions of the observances connected with Vesta: 3:141–144; 4:949–954; 6:249–348. Cicero discusses Vesta in *De Natura Deorum*, 2: xxvii.

15. Jean-Joseph Goux, "Vesta, or the Place of Being," *Representations* (February 1983), 1:91–107.

16. Cicero, *De Natura Deorum*, 2: xxvii.

17. Goux, "Vesta," p. 100.

18. In his essay "Patriarchal Territories: The Body Enclosed," in Margaret W. Ferguson, Maureen Quilligan, and Nancy Vickers, eds., *Rewriting the Renaissance: The Discourses of Sexual Difference in Early Modern Europe*, pp. 123–142 (Chicago and London: University of Chicago Press, 1986), Peter Stallybrass observes that in Renaissance England "the surveillance of women concentrated upon three specific areas: the mouth, chastity, the threshold of the house. . . . Silence, the closed mouth, is made a sign of chastity. And silence and chastity are, in turn, homologous to woman's enclosure within the house" (pp. 126–127).

19. Fineman also notes the allusion to pudenda in "shame" but sees it as part of the same purely rhetorical chiasmic pattern that, he argues, informs the poem: "It is fitting that the rape, when it finally occurs, is figured in and as a simultaneously emergent and recessive in-betweenness forming and informing the fold of Lucrece's lips, for the smirky collocation of Lucrece's mouth with her vagina supports the formal implication that Lucrece is asking for her rape because her 'no,' as 'no,' means 'yes' " (p. 43). Thus his scrupulously formal, often fascinating interpretation of the poem arrives at the same reading of the rape as that dictated by a common misogyny: it's the victim's fault—she was asking for it.

20. See A. Robin Bowers, "Iconography and Rhetoric in *Lucrece*," *Shakespeare Studies* (1981), 14: 1–21. He notes that in Titian's painting of the rape, completed ca. 1570, a visual parallel between Tarquin's "phallic knee" thrust between Lucrece's thighs and the blade held high in his right hand emphasizes the violence of the rape (p. 7); I would read this parallel as a statement of the sexual politics of the poem. (This pose is repeated in five other versions of the scene attributed to Titian or his school.) Shakespeare

achieves a somewhat similar effect in punning on Tarquin's "falchion" and "falcon" (lines 505–511).

21. Karen Newman, "Renaissance Family Politics and Shakespeare's *The Taming of the Shrew*," *ELR* (Winter 1986), 16(1): 86–100.

22. Patricia Klindienst Joplin, "The Voice of the Shuttle Is Ours," *Stanford Literature Review* (Spring 1984), 1(1):25–53, reprinted in this volume.

23. See Katharine Eisaman Maus, "Taking Tropes Seriously: Language and Violence in Shakespeare's *Rape of Lucrece*," *Shakespeare Quarterly* (1986), 37 (1): 66–82, for a perceptive reading of the Philomel figure.

24. Ellen Rooney, "Criticism and the Subject of Sexual Violence," *Modern Language Notes* (December 1983), 98 (5): 1269–1277. See also Rooney's essay in this volume.

25. For this view, see Laura G. Bromley, "Lucrece's Re-Creation," *Shakespeare Quarterly* (Summer 1983), 34 (2):200–211. Heather Dubrow (*Captive Victors: Shakespeare's Narrative Poems and Sonnets* [Ithaca and London: Cornell University Press, 1987]) also thinks Lucrece has a "self" and holds that her passivity, innocence, emotionality, and belief in absolutes make her complicit, at least, in the rape.

26. Kahn, "The Rape in Shakespeare's *Lucrece*," pp. 67–68.

27. Michael Platt, "*The Rape of Lucrece* and the Republic for Which It Stands," *Centennial Review* (Spring 1975), 19 (2): 59–79.

28. See the *Aeneid* 2:645–679; I am quoting from *The Aeneid of Virgil: A Verse Translation*, trans. Allen Mandelbaum (Berkeley, Los Angeles, London: University of California Press, 1971). An unpublished paper by Lorraine Helms, " 'Still Wars and Lechery': Shakespeare and the Last Trojan Woman," clarified and deepened the analogies between woman and city for me, as did "The Divided World of *Iliad* VI," by Marilyn B. Arthur, in Helene P. Foley, ed., *Reflections of Women in Antiquity*, pp. 19–44 (New York, London, Paris: Gordon and Breach Science Publishers, 1981).

7

Rape, Repression, and Narrative Form in *Le Devoir de violence* and *La Vie et demie*

EILEEN JULIEN

The depiction of sexual violence in recent African fiction contrasts markedly with fiction in English and French before the late sixties, where rape and sexual violence are uncommon—a noticeable absence, given the pillaging of African resources, human and otherwise, under the slave trade and colonialism. And yet an understandable one, perhaps, when we consider the keen sense of decorum in indigenous and Islamic cultures, the conservative values imparted in colonial and missionary schools, and the politics of publication and reception. *Le Devoir de violence,* by Malian writer Yambo Ouologuem (Paris: Seuil, 1968), and *La Vie et demie,* by Congolese writer Sony Labou Tansi (Paris: Seuil, 1979), are formally innovative novels of the postcolonial period that expose the brutality of autocratic and totalitarian regimes. They mark turning points in recent literary history, and they practice the representation of sexual violence.[1]

Such violence is, of course, not the central issue of either *Le Devoir de violence* or *La Vie et demie* but is rather a measure of the sickness of social and political relations. This particular use of image may seem to ignore the particularity of female sexuality: sexual violence and rape become near transparent signs of something else. Yet sexual violence in these texts is elucidated, if we read carefully, by the context of political violence. Rape, these texts suggest, is not an aberration, not a singularly sick act, nor an individual problem in an otherwise healthy society. Rape is represented, then, not as an isolated, gratuitous instance of violence that can be read *metaphorically*—that is, as an *abstracted* image of human disorder, ugliness, and disenfranchisement. It is portrayed rather, as the French term *viol* makes clear, *metonymically*, as a *quintessential* act of violence in a context of rampant abuse, both political and sexual.

In this regard, Mary Douglas' study of the concepts of pollution and taboo offers a pertinent insight. She notes that "rituals enact the form of social relations and in giving these relations visible expression they enable people to know their own society. The rituals work upon the body politic through the symbolic medium of the physical body."[2] While the rapes that Ouologuem and Tansi depict may not be said to constitute *ritual* in the strictest sense, they nonetheless perform the same role in these texts: they enable characters and readers to know—not through simple analogy (metaphor) but because rape is a related manifestation (metonymy)—the society in which rape takes place.

With regard to sexual violence, *Le Devoir de violence* and *La Vie et demie* are especially interesting, then, because they contextualize rape: power, taken to its logical end, becomes brutality and asserts itself simultaneously in the political-military arena and in the realm of sexuality. For these writers, public life and private life are not separate domains. Yet the exposition or intimation of this dynamic in a text does not constitute in and of itself a challenge to it, for the very premises and form of each narrative express attitudes toward power, which in the case of Ouologuem's novel reinscribe it and in that of Tansi dispute it.

Yambo Ouologuem was born in 1940 in the Mopti region of Mali. His father was a school inspector and member of a traditional Dogon ruling-class family. Ouologuem is multilingual and, as his writing attests, he is widely read in literature, philosophy, and sociology. *Le Devoir de violence* is the first of Ouologuem's three books, all of which are characterized by a certain unorthodoxy. In 1969, one year after the publication of *Le Devoir*, Ouologuem published under a pseudonym a pornographic novel: *Les Mille et une bibles du sexe* (Paris: Editions du Dauphin) and in 1971 his angry *Lettre à la France nègre* (Paris: Edmond Nalis).[3]

Le Devoir can be viewed as a fictional response to the romanticized vision of "original" Africa, most often associated with L. S. Senghor, other négritude writers, and the European ethnologists who inspired them.[4] Their creed is summed up in *Le Devoir* by Shrobénius (caricature of the German anthropologist Frobenius) as follows: "African life was pure art, awesomely religious symbolism, a formerly glorious civilization—alas victim of the vagaries of the white man" (p. 102).[5]

An alternative reading and reconstruction of African history, *Le Devoir* is a compelling chronicle of the savagery and brutality of the fictional dynasty of the Saïfs in precolonial and turn-of-the-century West Africa: "But the colonizing powers were too late, even on arrival, since the colonizer long in place—along with the honorable aristocracy—was none other than the Saïf, whose game the European conqueror unwittingly played! Technical assistance, even then! So be it. Lord, may your handiwork be blessed. And exalted" (p. 31).

Colonization, Ouologuem posits, is not simply the victimization of a "good," helpless society by one that is technologically superior and morally inferior. Two partners elaborated colonialism and its structures: the Europeans and the African aristocracy who responded in an effort to maintain the privileges of their class. Although the latter obviously could not be held equally responsible, each had a hand in shaping colonial policy and practices to suit, as much as possible, its own needs. Thus Ouologuem's novel challenges time-honored essentialist views of Africa and Africans; he constructs a precolonial Africa that is not a garden of Eden, that contains its share of pitiable slaves and serfs, on the one hand, vicious nobles and rulers, on the other. Class divisions and interests are as integral to Ouologuem's precolonial and colonial Africa as they are in fictions of postcolonial Africa.

In its challenge to the myth of original innocence, the primitivism that often has dominated thinking about precolonial Africa, *Le Devoir* is not only violent but also sordid: there are gruesome murders and torture, and virtually all sexual relations are tainted by evil. The text itself is sadistic to the extent that Ouologuem makes of his readers the voyeurs of the Saïfs' cruelty and murders. Does this violence, one wonders, derive purely from political violence or also in large measure from Ouologuem's pyrotechnical *textual* violence, his intent to shock and outrage? Parodying the stylized language of oral historians and praise-singers, typical of West Africa, the narrator continually punctuates his tale (as in the passage above) with interjections of sorrow or pity, with Islamic terms of praise and allusions to Allah—all of which become, given the nature of the Saïfs' reign, not merely irreverential of Islam but cynical and grotesque.

For many readers, Ouologuem's ugly portrayal of precolonial Africa seems gratuitous and just as exaggerated as the extreme claims for "grandiose" Africa. It was, at the very least, the wrong story to tell in the late sixties, when most African nations had just become independent and others were still waging a battle for independence. Eurocentric reaction to the novel was favorable: *Le Devoir* was an exciting experiment in narrative, a parody of oral epic—ironic, satiric, compelling. Given the still vigorous ideology of colonialism, the shifting of the burden of responsibility in African discourse from European colonialism to African abuses of power was surely a welcome development. The novel was awarded the Prix Renaudot in 1972. This period of grace came to an end when Ouologuem's innovative novel was discovered to contain a number of unacknowledged excerpts from European, American, and African writers. His work was repudiated, of course, but its originality and brilliance are indisputable—evident in the very reworking and assembly of other sources and texts.[6]

Women, the Ultimate Pawns of Political Strategy

Le Devoir postulates brutality as an inherent dimension of the human condition. The leaders of the indigenous ruling class, the Saïfs (now Muslim but purportedly of black Jewish origin), are barbarous —and this seems to be Ouologuem's point—long before the arrival of the French. In time of war, as conquerors, they exploit violence, especially rape and sexual violence to men and women, as part of their military strategy; the subjugated masses, brutalized themselves, derive pleasure in brutalizing their conquered enemies: it is a self-perpetuating process.

In the superficially less turbulent colonial period, sexuality is still governed by the political and, in particular, the geopolitical struggles that ensue between Saïf and the French colonial administrators. The plight of the lower-class slaves and serfs and especially of women is tied to the workings of this political universe. Thus when the French arrive and create a colonial policy that requires African children to attend French schools, Saïf considers his and the children of noble caste to be above such instruction and decides that slave children only will be subjected to colonial schools, Catholic masses, and baptism. Saïf, precursor of the future American slaveholder, thus promotes marriage and reproduction among his subjects to serve these political objectives:

> That month, one thousand six hundred twenty-three marriages took place from province to province, from canton to canton. The aristocracy's campaign was under way.
>
> The people stupidly rejoiced; in reality, however, the aristocracy were making way for the future. From all these new, legitimate couples, children would soon be born. The aristocracy would send them—in place of their own children—to the French missionary schools. (p.64)

Still more important, Saïf maintains the support of his male followers by institutionalizing male power over women. By sharpening the ideology of masculinity, he offers to his potential opponents sexual rather than political power. Masculinity (the control of female sexuality) is a distraction, a sop that depoliticizes:

> Saïf had rallied aristocrats, servants, even the soldiers and interpretors of the "Fwench," by decreeing a customary law that definitively made women a tool of men. So that women would not be unfaithful, the practice of infibulation (fastening the genitals)—extremely rare until then—became law; so that, once married, she would not seek vengence by betraying her husband, excision of the clitoris, the dreaded punishment for all acts of adultery, greatly cooled the hotheaded negresses who consequently behaved themselves. (p.62)

It is thus in the contest of political wills between the French and the indigenous chief that female powerlessness and male power are not only encoded but extended.[7] Women become legitimate, recognized possessions of men, objects to be manipulated and mutilated at will. The double standard that Saïf promotes with regard to adultery further confirms this configuration of power: the betrayal of a husband is a public offense, and betrayal of a wife is no offense whatsoever. Adultery thus has little to do with either infidelity or religious principle but—like other sexual activities of procreation and female circumcision—serves Saïf's political ends, assuring him a loyal male following. In this society, designed by male political ambition and power, women, marriage, and kinship rules do indeed provide, as Lévi-Strauss has argued, "the means of binding men together."[8]

Le Devoir thus challenges the view of Africa as defenseless and unresponsive victim in the colonial and precolonial world. Its portrait of the hardiness and resourcefulness of the aristocracy is very convincing, but the narrative nonetheless promotes the categories of *the powerful* and *the powerless* in its pathetic image of the African populace and in its still more disabling treatment of African women. If *Le Devoir* demonstrates very clearly that class and male interests are conflated in the control of marriage and reproduction and in the institutionalizing of female circumcision and infibulation, it fails utterly in close-ups of female characters to accord them any but the most meager stature. Is the author merely "recording"—albeit scathingly—the view of the culture he constructs, or is he himself exhibiting a cultural or personal view? Women are everywhere pure victims, tools of men's objectives, testimonials to male conquest and prowess, and silent objects of the narrator's prying eyes. The uniform stature of women is apparent both in the "private" sphere of the home, where "nigger" women *(la négraille)* are instruments (wombs) of Saïf's reproductive policy, and in the public sphere of political intrigue, where women such as Awa are pawns in Saïf's game of rivalry with the French. Indeed, Awa's "public" role is quite private: she is enlisted to spy on *(seduce)* the French administrator Chevalier. The sex act is everywhere subsumed in a political system and is therefore expressive of it. Thus rape under the repressive regime of Saïf is neither an exceptional nor an accidental occurrence, for it epitomizes the dynamic of dominance and submission, voice and silence, agent and object that governs all aspects of life. The most gripping and revealing expression of this dynamic is the long, torturous rape of Tambira, the wife of Kassoumi, a slave of Saïf.

The Art of Dominance and Submission: Silence, Metaphor, and Narrative Time

Tambira is raped one day, first by Dougouli the sorcerer and then by Kratongo and Wampoulo, two henchmen of Saïf, who have witnessed the dirty business and who blackmail her as she returns home from the sorcerer's.[9] *Le Devoir* suggests the dynamic of dominance and submission both by the very act of rape (and Tambira's failure to assert herself) and the textual representation of the act, which also disempowers the female victim.

Tambira goes to the sorcerer in her capacity as mother, seeking a blessing for the success of her sons' exams. She finds herself in these circumstances, then, not only for reasons of gender but also for those of class (Saïf's policy of sending "slave" youth to French schools). Having few means to pay the sorcerer, Tambira will be asked to pay with her body.[10]

The respective strength and vulnerability of Dougouli and Tambira are revealed, first of all, in the quantity and types of sentences accorded to each. Dougouli speaks to Tambira fifteen times in all. Regardless of his mode of speech, his is the voice of power. He leads the conversation from first to last. Catching her unawares, Dougouli begins with a disarming hello and then proceeds to flatter and flirt with Tambira. From this rather seductive mode of speech he shifts to the imperative during the divination ritual and finally ends with curses and threats to Tambira and her children when she hesitates to gratify him sexually.

To the sorcerer's fifteen statements, then, Tambira makes only four replies. Her feminine modesty, her tenuousness before Dougouli's voice and power are manifest in the conditional tenses she uses and in the interrogative mode of her answers: "How could I not be distressed? My sons are taking their exams, which will bring me great happiness, and it is beyond my power to help them. . . . Why wouldn't I be nice, once my sons pass their exams?" (p. 149.) She fails to interpret Dougouli's condition that she "be nice" and an earlier remark as the veiled sexual advances that the reader grasps almost immediately ("By God, Tambira, I know what brings you. Come to me, persuade Dougouli, do good by him"). Dougouli's terms are ambiguous in the early moments of this encounter, but the author would have Tambira be either complicitous or utterly naive.

Her single emphatic statement is ironically a declaration of helplessness. Asked to take an active part in the divination, she says simply, "I'm too afraid." Once the divination ritual has ended and the sorcerer is stating the terms of payment ("a cock and two sheep, and your sons will pass. Unless . . ."), she echoes (naively, one presumes again): "Unless?" It is that casual, hypothetical conjunction that allows Dougouli to crystallize and voice his intention to violate her. The language (or nonlanguage) of Ouologuem's Tambira reveals a victim who is femininely simple, docile, fearful, and naive.

Tambira's four responses to Dougouli throughout this ordeal reveal weakness, but weakness is evident as well in what she does not say. In response to Dougouli's first abrupt remark, for example, the narrator notes: "Tambira's mouth twisted into a numb, humble smile; as if this sign of weakness had given the sorcerer complete license, he began to rant, that is, to make undisguised sexual innuendoes (p. 149). Tambira's inarticulateness, indeed, her lack of voice, corresponds presumably to her "inherent" powerlessness as female victim. But her silence renders her still weaker *textually*, for it becomes the occasion and justification for the narrator's intervention, an example of which we shall see further on. Thus while the sorcerer speaks his own thoughts, Tambira's mind is inhabited and voiced by the narrator. Almost all her thoughts and feelings are interpreted and uttered by this other, obviously male, voice in "free indirect" speech. Dougouli controls Tambira with his eyes and his spoken words, while the author does so—is it effectiveness or collusion?—through his mode of narration.

If a pathetic victimhood is suggested through a certain voicelessness, it is symbolized still more powerfully in the divination that also foreshadows the violence to ensue. The sorcerer, making sexual advances toward Tambira, commands her to stoop down, nude, over a puddle of water, to facilitate the divination:

> "Hey! Hey! Look! Sit straight. Hold your pubis still. See! Red as a cock's comb, it's opening, gaping, dancing around, quivering, see! What can you make out?"
>
> Tambira was fascinated by the puddle which danced before her; furiously, it enticed, gripped her drunken eyes; shapes were whirling around, laced in violence and lust in which her own degradation was insignificant. Suddenly a white cock rose from the puddle, then two white sheep with black heads. The cock cackled and the sheep bleated, then a whirlpool seized the puddle, whipping it around, licking it, filling its waters with hundreds of feathers from the cock's bleeding throat, from the necks of the slaughtered sheep. And then, nothingness. Nothing more but the reflection of Tambira's genitals, gaping above the puddle. Then the puddle itself disappeared, soaked up by the floor of compacted earth. (pp. 148–149)

In a ritual which clearly "enact[s] the form of social relations" (Douglas 1980:128), it is through the bloody cavity of Tambira's vagina that the vision of the future comes. Riveted by this vision and helpless to control it, she watches the blurred image of her own immolation. The sacrificial animals, superimposed on Tambira's reflection, are far more symbolic of Tambira herself than they are extraneous surrogates. Thus, as we saw above, the sorcerer at first asks for the rooster and two sheep; in a second, alternative request he proposes Tambira herself as their equivalent; finally, reconsidering, he asks all three. In this whirlwind of violence and lust, Tambira's loss of dignity is merely one insignificant sacrifice, insignificant because, unbeknownst to her, the hope for an individual success is belied by the structural problem of Saïf's tyranny (her sons will pass their exams only to play their part as Saïf's pawns), insignificant also —and this she may realize—because rape (and humiliation) is just one of countless sacrifices, all of which shall be forgotten, consumed by the earth.

Tambira is allowed one moment of rebellion in the face of this humiliation. Her resistance does not take the shape of a life and death struggle:

> The sorcerer's eyes flashed and, despite herself, the servant woman felt hypnotized. The man desired her. She hated him, this sorcerer, with his snake-like expression, his heavy lips, his crooked legs, his head shaking like a mule, his odor of blood and amulets made of badly tanned leather. Resolutely, she closed her eyes. All fascination then disappeared. And so it was as long as she avoided the sorcerer's glare. (p. 149)

The very first sentence pinpoints the dynamics of Dougouli's and Tambira's relationship ("Les yeux du sorcier lancèrent des éclairs, et malgré elle, la servante se sentit hypnotisée"). Dougouli's force does not derive primarily from the threat of immediate physical harm; rather, his power is authorial, assimilated to that of God or Zeus in his heaven *(lancèrent des éclairs)*. Tambira is appropriately referred to, then, as *servante:* she is both Saïf's lower-class maid and the handmaiden of the Lord/Dougouli. Characteristically helpless and despite her repugnance for Dougouli and his "unnatural" body *(malgré elle)*, she experiences herself as object *(se sentit)* of his charm *(hypnotisée)*. Dougouli's two vehicles of power are thus his incantatory voice and his hypnotic eyes. It is surely not by chance that the architect of this rape is a spiritual medium, practiced in the manipulation of words and the use of gesture and staring to create an aura of power.

It is worth noting once again that Tambira is not allowed to say, "I hate him," an *affirmative* statement, in the strict sense of the term—suggesting a new or full realization that presumably might enable her to act. Rather, her hatred is expressed *for her* ("She hated him" [Elle le détestait]) in a sentence that suggests an ongoing, passive condition (the French *imparfait*) and prepares the reader for resignation on her part. Significantly, before the moment of ultimate acquiescence Ouologuem imagines for Tambira one moment's respite from this diabolic charm when she closes her eyes. The retreat within herself, the refusal to be the object of another's sight and to be the inarticulate, lesser partner in this dialogue briefly restore her integrity, and she musters the courage to slap the sorcerer before he has uttered his final threat and curse. Yet Tambira's resistance can be only momentary, for in this chronicle whose form and content assume the triumph of power, the will to resist exists only to demonstrate the ultimate superiority of force: "So, full of anger, but fearing murder, supernatural revenge as much as the sorcerer's black magic, the woman sobbed softly like a faithful dog and, lying down on the ground, undid her cloth" (p. 149). Tambira's stifled feelings and thoughts, her inarticulateness find their symbolic equivalent in the text's assimilation of the woman's behavior to that of helpless animals continually evoked in the rape sequence.

While the narrator has "fondled" the first rape of Tambira, by Dougouli, in more than three pages, the second rape, by Wampoulo and Kratonga, is told with all dispatch in three paragraphs:

When she came out, her head down, her shoulders square, Kratonga and Wampoulo, who had followed her, were there. Facing her. Threatening to tell the entire story to her husband, they, too, had their revenge; long ago, the murderer Sankolo, their friend, had been squealed on by Kassoumi.

They ordered Tambira to follow them, and the woman complied. She experienced a cowardly, shameful fear. Fear of her husband, especially—he who was so good, betrayed by her—fear for him, as well—they would have killed him—and for herself also perhaps.

Wampoulo and Kratonga led her away behind the Yamé river waterfalls to a dense grassy spot. They took her, both of them. They took her and took her again all they wanted that day, frightening her. (p. 150)

The diminution in narrative time participates in forging this world in which masculinity and power are at the center, for it suggests that the subsequent rapes have less importance, they are but a footnote. Rapists and victim have become inherently less interesting: the rapists are less powerful men than Dougouli, and Tambira has already been exploited sexually and textually. Because Tambira can lose nothing more (from this point of view), there is no more seduction and thus nothing more to tell. Accordingly, Ouologuem's Tambira puts up no struggle whatsoever this time. As if to confirm this state of disgrace and the relationship of rape to violence, *Le Devoir* reduces Tambira to silence and effaces her completely with an ignominious death:

> Two mornings later, Kassoumi shuddered when Wampoulo and Kratonga came to get him.
> Tambira's body had been found. In the yard beyond the communal grave of Saïf's servants, above the serfs' excrement, a wide rectangular hole had been set up. Teeming with caterpillars and worms of all shapes and colors, it had been covered over with boards. The servants satisfied their needs there. It was in this hole that the body was discovered.
> It lay there, in a corner, all dressed and orderly, with worms crawling into the nostrils; the head rose above the excrement, held by a slipknot attached to one of the boards. (p. 150)

Tambira's life ends in a hole of life's wastes, like that of her vision at the sorcerer's. Her remains are taken back into the earth. She has existed all along in this text as a victim of her sex and as a sexual victim, the most pathetic martyr of violence. It is the Saïf's nefarious authority that dictates this end for her victimization.

Subject as Object

Both rapes of Tambira are acts in which men assert their power vis-à-vis the less powerful woman. She is an essential partner in the elaboration of that achievement—there can be no dominance without submission. Tambira is thus "collaborator" and addressee of each rape, but she is not represented as subject. Indeed in the rare moments when Ouologuem's Tambira sees herself at all, it is especially as a possession of or an appendage to her husband. When we read her thoughts, as they occasionally are spoken for her, it becomes clear that Tambira's sense of self (subjectivity) is shaped by a consciousness—that of the society in which she lives or that of the author—that perceives and constructs the world through male eyes.

In the prelude to the rape by Dougouli, as we saw above, the sorcerer requires Tambira to remove her *pagne* as part of the ritual of divination. The narrator explains:

> A horrible mixture of repulsion and fear strangled Tambira. The mindless prey of maternal love, she remembered the love

and poverty of her husband, ignored the excitement of the sorcerer's kisses against her neck, the softness of his caresses, the fire of his lips, the saliva of his mouth, the warmth of his chest, his hips, his underarms, his stomach, the fullness[?] of his penis *[satiété du sexe]*, the desire, the quivering of his legs: she took off her cloth and crouched down over the puddle of water on the ground. (p. 148)

Tambira is initially the victim of visceral feelings (repulsion and fear) that "strangle" her. Next—given the apposition of "mindless prey" *(bête, bête éreintée)*—she is *in her essence* consumed stupidly and instinctually, like an animal, by her motherhood. She has no ability to make a self-interested judgment, much less a moral decision. Finally, Tambira is granted the role of subject-actor in this passage, and her response is, of course, neither self-affirming anger nor the will to walk out of Dougouli's hut: "She remembered the love and poverty of her husband." Because she is mother, because she is wife, she has little consciousness of herself apart from these roles and is pure self-sacrifice. She consequently will proceed to let the sorcerer have his way and will close off her senses to his excitement. Thus at the same time that the text deprives Tambira of a will of her own, it also seems to make her all too present to the sorcerer's sensuality. The fact that she must "ignore" the excitement of Dougouli's body, that the textual description, regardless of its hyperbole, is detailed and seductive, suggests a depth of physiological response on the part of the perceiver (presumably despite herself). Indeed, *where is* the excitement of Dougouli's kisses—in the kisses or in the reception? This foul play on the part of the narrator compromises Tambira's integrity once again; she is a tabula rasa for the narrator's script as she is for that of the sorcerer.[11]

During the second rape by Wampoulo and Kratonga, her indifference toward her own being and her sense of guilt vis-à-vis her husband (that is, her sense of her value in relationship to him) are made explicit. The narrator, of course, stands between her thoughts and the reader, and it is unclear why Tambira's fear should be characterized as cowardly and shameful: "She experienced a cowardly, shameful fear. Fear of her husband, especially—he who was so good, betrayed by her—fear for him, as well—they would have killed him—and for herself also perhaps."

Tambira's fear *of* her husband is motivated both by her misplaced sense of responsibility for the transgression and her sense of having become a soiled and unworthy token, in contrast to his enduring virtue. Thus she responds to the violation of *her* person as though it were first and foremost an affront *to her husband* and she blames herself for this act that violates him.

Of course, in this cultural universe, Tambira is not alone in perceiving herself as an extension of Kassoumi. Kratonga and Wampoulo rape Tambira not only to affirm their power over her but also to punish her husband: "They, too, had their revenge: long ago, the murderer Sankolo, their friend, had been squealed on by Kassoumi" (p. 150). Once again, as in Saïf's control of marriage and reproduction, women are "signs ... to be communicated between men" (Lévi-Strauss 1969:496). The second rape of Tambira, then, like Saïf's first night right to all brides, is a demonstration to Kassoumi of the pecking order, a masculine language whose words are women.

Tambira's fear *for* her husband during the second rape is a further index of her self-effacement. Having failed to be pure enough for Kassoumi, she then measures her self-worth by her capacity to protect him. Thus she fears for herself last of all and only "perhaps." Several meanings suggest themselves in the text's "perhaps": Is the narrator unsure of Tambira's fear for herself? Or is the doubt Tambira's: she too *might* be killed? Still another meaning that may be present in this narrative hesitation is that rape is itself a near-death, that Tambira has been exhausted, has become indifferent to her fate. She matters less and less, is effaced more and more, until she finally disappears.

Le Devoir thus presents facets of the experience of rape and femaleness perceived, as it were, in a specific ideology of masculinity: silence, immolation, and an absence of subjectivity. The novel replicates this victimhood unquestioningly and even with complacency. Just as sexuality and women are conditioned by the political struggle within the narrative, they are similarly governed by the rules of the narrative itself, which tells the triumph of power. *Le Devoir* is as bound to an admiration of force as is Saïf to violence. The novel would critique what it portrays, but it nonetheless respects the intelligence and cunning of Saïf, disdains the ignorance and naiveté of lower-class men, and is, finally, indifferent to women of those classes— seemingly beneath contempt. Thus Ouologuem succeeds in dismantling the myth of African powerlessness, but only to replace that myth, with another, equally insidious, powerlessness and depravity of the African populace. Nowhere is this more obvious than in his construction of women.[12]

Object as Subject

La Vie et demie is, like *Le Devoir,* the chronicle of a fictional African country, neocolonial Katamalanasia, its savage dictators, and, this time, its insurgents, in particular Chaïdana, the beautiful daughter of the rebel leader Martial. *La Vie et demie* and *L'Etat honteux* (Paris: Seuil, 1981), a kindred work, are the first of several novels by Sony Labou Tansi, who also directs and writes for the Rocado Zulu Theatre troupe of Congo-Brazzaville. Born in 1947 in Zaïre, Tansi is, perhaps, the most visible of the "new generation" of African writers of French expression, who abandon both the naturalistic mode of first-generation writers and the nearly ubiquitous theme of earlier fiction, the crises of colonial domination. Tansi writes of contemporary neocolonial life, and his active involvement in live and popular cultural productions clearly affects his style and vision as a novelist.[13]

In the foreword to the novel, Tansi refers to his story as a fable, and indeed it has an allegorical character. The opening sequences consist of Chaïdana's memories; her story is interwoven with that of the general civil revolt outside the palace walls. The story begins as the head of state, the "Providential Guide," murders Martial before the latter's children and wife and forces them to eat Martial's remains. To the consternation of the Guide, Martial—stabbed, shot, and poisoned—stubbornly refuses to die and, on the contrary, returns frequently to haunt the Guide as he sleeps. The Guide's fortune-teller recommends marriage to Chaïdana, with whom the Guide must abstain from sexual relations, however. Chaïdana later flees the "excellential" palace with the help of the presidential physician; before going off in seclusion to the countryside, she takes advantage of her nearly perpetual youth to assume 243 identities, seduce and poison dozens of cabinet ministers, and take a great many husbands, including the Guide himself. On one occasion she is nursed back to health by her father and subsequently raped by him—presumably because she is preparing to seduce (and poison) the Guide. As she makes her way to the countryside, she is again raped by 333 soldiers on the side of the road.

The liberation struggle will be taken up by her daughter, Chaïdana, who, as beautiful as her mother, will find herself also the wife of a future dictator, Jean Coeur de Père. Exiled to Darmellia first by her husband and later by her son, Jean Coeur de Pierre, Chaïdana the younger will be joined by her grandsons, Jean Canon, Jean Coriace

(Tough), Jean Calcium, Jean Camera, Jean Caoutchouc (Rubber), and so on (all conceived in the first annual week of Virgins and thus members of the C series of Jeans). Bright, savvy, inventive, the Jeans will secede from Katamalanasia and wage war against their father and his successors (their half-brothers) and later against the superpowers.

Tansi's fable evokes any number of traditions, all of which care little for the supposed boundaries of reality. The motif of the dead who will not die, for example, is basic to many traditional African stories. *La Vie et demie* is reminiscent also of Rabelais, in its textual love of plenty (Chaïdana is pregnant for eighteen months and six days) and its wordplay: in addition to the fifty Jeans of series C, for example, there are those of series V—Jean Vérole (Syphilis), Jean Vautour (Vulture), Jean Vocabulaire, Jean Vide-Cave (Wine Guzzler) —as of all the alphabet. The mixture of fantasy and "reality" recalls Gabriel García Márquez, and the greedy, pouting, and tantrum-prone dictators resemble Jarry's voracious, childish Père Ubu. There is also a certain similarity to *Candide* in the peripatetic and perilous journey of innocence in a callous world of evil and in the narrator's understated response to it. Finally, Tansi's story evokes the cartoon and comic strip, in which extremes and exaggeration are the rule and finality and disaster are most often taken with a grain of salt. Through hyperbole and absurdity, then, Tansi pushes his tale beyond the limits of the rational, provoking laughter and ridiculing power. Related to the suppleness of plot is his incessant play on words, evident, for example, in the last names of the countless grandsons, cited above. *La Vie et demie* is as much about language in a time of tyranny as about tyranny itself. Tansi both reveals the ploy of dictatorship to impose and censor language and subverts that language through the discourse of the novel, which highlights the jingles and jargon of government-approved speech.[14]

In *La Vie et demie*, sexual abuse is in metonymical rapport with politics as it is in *Le Devoir*. Not only does it symbolically enact the political order of domination and submission, but it clearly derives from that order and plays a role in maintaining it. The most obvious instances are Chaïdana's rape by the militiamen and her first marriage to the Providential Guide. In the first instance, Tansi records the rape journalistically, even statistically:

That evening, as she hadn't budged [from the side of the road], a group of fifteen militiamen came and soothed themselves with her. As a result, she passed out. At the first crow of the cock, another group of militiamen arrived. They left her for dead, and in the wee hours there came a final group who were more impetuous because time was short. She lay there inanimate for three nights and during three nights she lasted through thirteen rounds of militiamen, for a total of three hundred thirty-three men. (p. 72)

The boxing jargon ("she lasted through thirteen rounds" *[encaissa]*) and the improbably numerical count banalize rape and thus convey that arrogant view of the world in which this rape is one of many routine military acts. As in *Le Devoir*, rape is the assertion, the prerogative, of power.

A still more important index of the ties between the sexual and political is Chaïdana's marriage to the Guide, which presumably ratifies the political power of one man (the Guide) by another (Martial). In an absurd adaptation of literary and mythological traditions, the warring factions (dictators and insurgents) are united in marriage but—given the fortune-teller's prohibition—are unable to consummate their union. Thus marriage rites are represented once again and mocked as a form of man-to-man communication. Inasmuch as this is a marriage "forced" by the other side, Martial has not given up his stake in his daughter, and so the marriage is form without substance. It becomes a hollow institution like so many others in this autocratic state.

Martial's subsequent rape of Chaïdana makes sense in light of the struggle for power between himself and the dictator. Political struggle is displaced in the battle for sexual union with Chaïdana. Chaïdana is punished by Martial, first of all, for her postmarriage attempt to seduce and murder the Guide. Martial has the habit of slapping Chaïdana whenever she engages in such sexual vigilantism, and on this occasion "Martial had such a fit of anger that he beat his daughter like an animal and had sex with her, undoubtedly so as to slap her internally" (p. 69). Even were Martial's rape read as a mere "corrective," it does not, for that reason, cease being the enactment of male domination and female submission, a lesson Chaïdana understands all too well. Simultaneously, the rape of Chaïdana is read by the reader (if not by the Guide himself) as Martial's symbolic attempt to wrest power from the dictatorship, as his declaration that he has not surrendered.

Sony Labou Tansi suggests yet another relationship between political order and sexuality. When Chaïdana devises her vigilante strategy of poison-laced "champagne receptions" for government officials, she begins her secret campaign with a visit to the Minister of Internal Security. The minister has offered a commission to his secretary for every beautiful young woman ushered in and is already beside himself with anticipation as Chaïdana enters:

> —I saw you on television, said Chaïdana, and your physique gave me ideas.
> . . . His Excellency had never thought that his poses on television, the masculine fervor with which he extolled the Providential Guide, his everyday words, his national gestures, his artificial conviction, and his battering of words had any effect whatsoever on that mysterious landscape, the opposite sex. He vaguely recalled his last appearance on Télé-Yourma; it was after the last arrests. He'd spoken as though they were at war. Maybe it wasn't that time. He thought of the other times, and the thought almost made him unhappy because now that he dared take a look at himself for the first time, he saw only the sad profile of a man of hate, a man whose heart was fueled by schemes, he saw something resembling human refuse, a figure whose core was ultimately low and inhuman. He thought of all the times, not one of them . . . Unless women, with their particular eyes that don't see what everyone else's eyes see, with their particular ears that don't hear what everyone else's ears hear . . . (p. 47)

Chaïdana thus makes her first conquest easily, appealing to and flattering an already finely developed sense of masculinity, reinforced by power and the purse. This masculinity, as the minister begins to grasp, however, is nationalistic and bellicose in character; it is ultimately hateful and inhuman. Thus the feminine becomes a necessary complement to the masculine: it is the mirror in which the masculine looks at itself, both for affirmation of visible, superficial prowess and for hidden, deeper humanity. As with Estelle and Garcin in Jean-Paul Sartre's *Huis-Clos,* the minister hopes that Chaïdana will see beyond a certain exterior—in this instance, a masculinity forged of aggression and hatred—to a core of goodness and lovability. Feminine submission thus can affirm and sustain the ideology of masculinity, reassuring men that they may be both beauty and the beast. *La Vie et demie* thus intimates that sexuality and love —in certain forms, at least—may fuel a political order of domination and brutality.

It is not surprising that *La Vie et demie* does not represent the rapes and attempted rapes of Chaïdana but rather recounts them in brief sentences. Given its departure from realism, the lurid details, the horror and fear are not of primary importance. Rape is not an occasion for voyeuristic pleasure, anger, or anguish. But more especially, rape is not paralysis, the end of life. To the extent that rape itself is absent, Tansi makes space for and privileges Chaïdana's response to rape as to abuses of political and male power.

Curiously, there are two methods of subversion possible for Chaïdana: writing and sexual intercourse. Chaïdana's revolt in its first phase consists of arming bands of young boys with spray guns and black paint:

> She bought black paint for three million [African francs[15]]. . . . She recruited three thousand boys who, on Christmas night, were to write on all the doors in Yourma her father's famous saying: "I don't want to die this death." The handsome batallion of pistolwriters worked marvelously: they'd managed to write the saying even on the third set of gates in the wall of the excellential palace. A few of them, the boldest undoubtedly, had succeeded in writing the sentence on the body of several military officers such as General Yang, Colonel Obaltana, Lieutenant-Colonel Fursia and quite a few others. Amedandio said he'd written the saying on one thousand-ninety uniforms.
>
> On Christmas while the city drank and danced, the pistolwriters did their all to put Martial's saying everywhere. And Amedandio vaguely proclaimed "there'd be fire the next time," promising he'd write the saying on the Providential Guide's ass. (pp. 44–45)

In this comic episode, the form of Chaïdana's revolt is male, phallic, aggressive—a kind of reverse rape. In order to "speak" in the public forum, Chaïdana assumes male form by hiring young *boys*, whom she arms with *pistols*, to *spray* the entrances to the sanctuary that is the male palace. Chaïdana herself will write memoirs, poems, and fiction later on in life when she has retired from her career in the city. Few of her works, of course, will survive censorship; they will be burned. Thus language and writing in this context are the site of a constant struggle for power. When Chaïdana writes, writing becomes especially subversive because writing is male. Chaïdana's experience echoes that of other heroines in African literature, Buchi Emecheta's heroine in *Second Class Citizen*, for example.

Of course, writing is not sufficient. And Chaïdana turns to more active participation in the power struggle, as we saw above. Her actions clearly are directed toward dismantling the political struc-

ture of Katamalanasia, but they must also be read, given the antago-
nism with her father, as an attempt to undo simultaneously the
subjugation that she knows as the experience of femaleness. If Chaïdana's rage is in part the rage of a female object of exchange between
two rival men, Martial and the Guide, then her acts of vengeance are
not only a bid to wrest power from the villanous dictators, but also
an attempt to inveigh against the system of domination that also
reduces women to signs between men. Her anger is directed, then,
against the state whose domination and hierarchy brutalize all, against
the system that makes of her a token of communication and against
her father, of whom she says, "You've won the first round. . . . Let's
see if you'll win the second" (p. 69). Chaïdana challenges power in
its dual manifestations, political dictatorship and masculine domination of women.

The Lens of Narrative Form

If *Le Devoir* exposes the workings and abuses of power, the novel
nonetheless pays homage to them, for Ouologuem's premise—the
implacable destiny of violence—requires it. The novel thus takes
tyranny, barbarity, and, more important, hierarchy as given, as simple facts to which we all must submit. Women are the most abject
expression of that stuck, "natural" state of affairs. In this system,
which Ouologuem shows to be brutal, the only issue is *which tyrant
will prevail*—not *whether any tyrant should*. The game of chess
with which the novel ends is therefore an appropriate metaphor for
this chronicle of undefeatable rank and power. The dominion of the
king over the pawns is never in doubt. The only question is which
king will dominate. The "reality" of hierarchy and domination is
the very assumption on which the narrative is built.

Tansi is, from this point of view, more subversive. For he not only
shows the abuses of tyranny but challenges the very concept of
dominance. He questions the very notions of dictatorship and hierarchy by refusing to replicate them in his text, by submitting them
to the playfulness and irreverence of fable and cartoon. Thus *La Vie
et demie* is able to explode the myth of power as "natural." As
Chaïdana says, "a naked ruler is the height of ugliness." The novel,
then, like the child in the fairy tale, points its finger at an emperor
without clothes and reveals the frailty of authority, once we are no
longer blinded by the accoutrements of power. Hierarchy, *La Vie et
demie* shows, is a sham, an intolerable absurdity. So it is that Chaï-

dana the elder and Chaïdana the younger are *agents*, not merely victims. Tansi does not posit utopia as the solution, but he nonetheless wrestles with power in his text, as do the heroines in his story.

Some quarrel with the role of women as saviors of one's race, kin, or clan, seeing therein a tired cliché; it is a virtuous role but not innocently assigned. Yet the originality of *La Vie et demie*'s vision lies precisely in opposing an *essential* femininity. It is not a privileged femaleness per se that invests women with virtue and strength. It is rather that from their position of marginality they perceive the nakedness of power. And it is that perception that enables them to envision, to challenge. If the women of *La Vie et demie* are once again the voice of imagination, it is surely not as muses to let men sing. Women are the voice of subversion because they see that what passes for the natural order of things is merely, but ever so persuasively, contrived.

NOTES

Early versions of this paper were presented at the Harvard African Studies Seminar (April 1987) and at meetings of the African Literature Association (April 1988) and Modern Language Association (December 1988). I am grateful to Ava Baron, Margaret Burnham, Sally Moore, Nellie McKay, Emmanuel Sédi Zadi, Sandra Zagarell, and the editors for suggestions and comments made at various stages of its writing.

1. Other recent African novels that depict or allude to rape are Jean-Marie Adiaffi's *La Carte d'identité* (Abidjan: CEDA, 1980); Buchi Emecheta's *Rape of Shavi* (1983; reprint, New York: Braziller, 1985), Nuruddin Farah's *From a Crooked Rib* (London: Heinemann, 1970), and Ahmadou Kourouma's *Les Soleils des indépendances* (Paris: Seuil, 1970).

2. Mary Douglas, *Purity and Danger: An Analysis of the Concepts of Pollution and Taboo* (1966; reprint, London: Routledge and Kegan Paul, 1980), p. 128. Further citations appear in text.

3. For further information on Ouologuem, see Hans M. Zell et al., eds., *A New Reader's Guide to African Literature*, pp. 455–457 (New York: Africana, 1983).

4. Stanislas Adotevi dubbed them "négrologues" in his famous invective, *Négritude et négrologues* (Paris: 10/18, 1972).

5. This and all subsequent translations of *Le Devoir de violence* and *La Vie et demie* are mine. *Le Devoir* is available in translation by Ralph Manheim as *Bound to Violence* (New York: Harcourt, Brace, Jovanovich, 1971). To my knowledge *La Vie et demie* has not been translated.

6. See, for example, Eric Sellin, "The Unknown Voice of Yambo Ouologuem," *Yale French Studies* (1976), 53:137–162; Wole Soyinka, *Myth, Liter-*

ature and the African World (Cambridge: Cambridge University Press, 1976), pp. 98–106; Bernard Mouralis, "Un Carrefour d'écritures: *Le Devoir de violence* de Yambo Ouologuem," *Recherches et Travaux* (1984), 27:75–92; Christopher L. Miller, *Blank Darkness* (Chicago: University of Chicago Press, 1985), pp. 216–245.

7. A similar argument is made in Tobe Levin, "Women as Scapegoats of Culture and Cult: An Activist's View of Female Circumcision in Ngugi's *The River Between,*" in Carol Boyce Davies and Anne Adams Graves, eds., pp. 210–211. *Ngambika*, (Trenton: Africa World Press, 1986).

8. Claude Lévi-Strauss, *The Elementary Structures of Kinship*, trans. James Harle Bell, John Richard von Sturmer and Rodney Needham (Boston: Beacon Press, 1969), 480. Further citations appear in text.

9. Prior to this, Tambira has already been raped, of course, by Saïf, who grants himself the right to his subjects' brides. This rape is not seen as such, however. Because it is institutionalized, because sovereigns will be sovereign, the perception of rape is impossible, as is a revolt against sovereign violence. In Dougouli's rape of Tambira, violation is displaced from the political to the medico-religious arena—the two are not without parallels.

10. It should be noted, however, that in the political crossfire between Saïf and the French, women are subject to rape, regardless of their class, race, or nationality. At the dinner the French administrator organizes in order to poison Saïf, the latter "adroitly placed his foot near Mme Vandame's, caressing it; then, quietly—being a little anxious about the quivering he noticed on her part—he stared at her, tenderly, attentively, carefully, because, at that very moment he knew he was raping her slowly, irresistibly and calmly" (p. 75).

11. There are other occasions in the novel in which women welcome sexual violence done to themselves and "love" the perpetrators of that violence. Thus with regard to infibulation "quite a few men, living with women by common law, were happy on their wedding night to have the right to a new, sadistic pleasure, voluptuous and painful, when they deflowered— genitals pricked with thorns, thighs splattered with blood—their mistress, *herself in ecstasy and exhausted for the most part from pleasure and fear*" (p. 62, emphasis added). Notice once again the ambiguity of the description *(sexe picoté d'épines, flancs éclaboussés de sang)*, which may refer to the male or female body.

Similarly, the narrator says of Awa, as she is strangled by her boyfriend, whom she has caught masturbating, "Awa's hands were useless; they/she didn't try *[elles ne tentait pas (sic)]* to return the blows; tortured by the horror and degradation of this physical struggle, *she liked it/loved him [elle l'aimait]*" (p. 108, emphasis added).

12. For an opposing point of view, see *Emitaï* (1971), Ousmane Sembène's film on Senegalese village women during the colonial era.

13. For further information on Tansi, see Zell et al., *A New Reader's Guide to African Literature*, pp. 495–497.

14. See Eileen Julien, "Dominance and Discourse in *La Vie et demie* or How to Do Things with Words," *Research in African Literatures* (1989) 20:371–384, and Georges Ngal, "Les Tropicalités de Sony Labou Tansi," *Silex* (1982), 23:134–143.

15. An equivalent of sixty thousand French francs.

8

Rape and Textual Violence in Clarice Lispector

MARTA PEIXOTO

Clarice Lispector is known to feminist literary audiences in France and the United States mainly through Hélène Cixous' mediation. As Cixous tells us in *Vivre l'Orange*, she first read Lispector in October 1978, almost a year after the Brazilian writer's death.[1] Cixous' critical and fictional texts about Lispector (the boundary between them is tenuous) reveal a deep, though somewhat suspect, sympathy. With the words of another woman from a foreign place Cixous establishes a tender dialogue, and in these words she discerns multiple mirrorings of the dynamics of her own texts. I take as an example one of many passages where Cixous both describes and enacts the generative receptivity toward objects and beings she finds in Lispector:

> A patience pays attention. A tense, active, discreet and warm attention, almost imperceptible, weightless like the slight warming of glances, regular, twenty one days and twenty one nights, at the kitchen window, and at last an egg is. Patiences pay attention: do nothing, do not agitate, fill in, replace or occupy space. But let space be. Think delicately about. Direct

a mixture of wise glances and loving light towards. A face.
Surround it with a discreet questioning, confident, attentive.
Allow, watch over it, for a long time, until penetration of the
essence.[2]

A superlative reader of the nuances of gentleness in Lispector, Cixous nevertheless presents a tamed version of her texts, stripped of
their disturbing pull toward violence. Although she sets up Lispector
as an exemplary practitioner of *écriture féminine,* possessor of a
feminine libidinal economy "more adventurous, more on the side of
spending, riskier, on the side of the body,"[3] Cixous privileges in
Lispector traditional and ideologically conservative feminine stereotypes (woman as mediator, as benevolent nature, as Good Mother).[4]
Yet the context for gentleness in Lispector is often a field of textual
interactions charged with violence. I would like to examine this
textual violence by focusing on a persistent issue in Lispector's
fiction: writing the victim.

Starting with her earliest fiction, Lispector turns an acute gaze to
the exercise of personal power, to the push and pull of the strong and
the weak, and particularly to the dynamics of victimization. Sometimes the line between victim and victimizer blurs or, in a sudden
reversal, the two exchange places. Lispector places these interper-
sonal struggles in the broader context of the individual subject's
contact with impersonal cosmic forces, termed *reality* or *God* (though
not in any conventional religious sense), a contact that seems not
entirely voluntary, fraught with violence, and also cast as an interaction between self and other. In one of Lispector's best-known
novels, *The Passion According to G. H.* (1964), this "reality" inheres
in a cockroach: a female narrator watches it closely, kills it, then, in
a sort of mystical communion, tastes its substance. In this tense
encounter, observation yields repulsion, identification, and dizzying
reversals of relative power as the woman feels engulfed by the cockroach, which is in turn victimizer and victim. I think it fair to say
that in Lispector narrative demands a victim or, conversely, the
victim demands narrative.[5]

But how, from what perspective and with what investments, does
one write the victim's experience? Of the many answers Lispector
gives to this question in the practice of her writing I would like to
examine two. First, I will look at three short narratives about rape,
to define and interpret the curious moves whereby Lispector distances and naturalizes violence against women. Second, I will turn
to the last narrative Lispector published before her death, *The Hour*

of the Star (1977), where the strategy for writing the victim no longer entails a containment within ideological and narrative structures that minimize the violence, but involves, on the contrary, an unleashing of aggressive forces. While the rape stories show the workings of representation as a construct that further oppresses the victims by diminishing and justifying the assaults they suffer, *The Hour of the Star* calls into question the suspect alliances of narrative with forces of mastery and domination.

The three stories about sexual assault, "Mystery in São Cristóvão," "Preciousness," and "Pig Latin," the only representations of rape among the many instances of transgressive sexuality and physical violence in her fiction, depict a symbolic, a partial, and a deflected rape. She wrote these stories at different stages in her career and collected them in volumes published in 1952, 1960, and 1974 respectively.[6]

In the earliest story, "Mystery in São Cristóvão," a third-person narrator tells of the encounter in a lyrical and tranquillizing tone. The violence, mostly psychological (its slight symbolic manifestation deflected onto an object), occurs in the setting of a family's home in a middle-class neighborhood of Rio. Late at night, three young men on their way to a party, dressed up as a rooster, a bull, and a knight with a devil's mask, trespass into "the forbidden territory of the garden" (FT: 135) to steal some hyacinths. They have barely broken the stalk of one flower when the "defloration" begins. "Behind the dark glass of the window, a white face was watching them" (FT: 137). The men feel as frightened as the nineteen-year-old woman who watches them. "None of the four knew who was punishing whom. The hyacinths seemed to become whiter in the darkness. Paralyzed, they stood staring at each other" (FT: 137). The encounter provokes deep but unspecified resonances in each participant. The young woman, whose white face becomes *her* mask, appears no more a victim than the trespassers. "The simple encounter of four masks in that autumn evening seemed to have touched deep recesses, then others, then still others . . ." (FT: 136). This ritual-like confrontation, while not naming the specific motive for the powerful feelings, hints that they spring from the fascination with and fear of sexual contact.

Although fear strikes all four, the confrontation touches the young woman most deeply. She leaves the window and screams, but can explain nothing further to her alarmed family. "Her face grew small and bright—the whole laborious structure of her years had dissolved and she was a child once more. But in her rejuvenated image, to the horror of her family, a white strand had appeared among the hairs of her forehead" (FT: 137). The white hyacinth, her white face, and finally the white strand of hair represent the vulnerable female body that bears the marks of the assault. It is the grandmother, "her white hair in braids," who finds the only "visible sign" of the incident: "the hyacinth—still alive but with its stalk broken" (FT: 137–138). The young men, also shaken, cling together at the party, "their speechless faces beneath three masks which faltered independently" (FT: 137). Their costumes seem a flimsy façade of masculinity. The hyacinths—"tall, hard and fragile" (FT: 135)—also have a phallic import: the initiation involves a fearful rupture and is curiously disempowering for both sexes. The four characters act in the grip of an impersonal force that surges from their "hollow recesses" yet seems somehow alien, like their masks. In a convergence of culture and nature, masks and inner forces work together to determine the actions of the uncomprehending and frightened subjects. The characters come to no rational understanding of the encounter; the violation remains unacknowledged, unspoken. The young woman soon forgets or represses whatever the confrontation led her to intuit (the better to proceed with the "real" violations it foreshadows?): "She gradually recovered her true years" (FT: 138).

In this encounter, a mysterious violence aligns itself with inner and outer nature, appearing as natural as the evening, the moon, and the flowers. The masks of masculine aggressiveness represent cultural roles, but their animal guises (rooster, bull) link them back to nature, and the mythic figure (devil) stands for equally unquestioned psychic impulses. Distance and impersonality characterize the narrative mode of this story. The narrator stands back from the nameless characters to tell of their actions. In the postsymbolist climate of this theatrical, stylized, and aesthetically pleasing world, masks, sounds, looks, and the play of light and darkness bear suggestive meanings. The encroachment upon a woman's body and its repercussion back on the aggressors seem justified as an inevitable part of growing up and as a component of the postsymbolist repertoire that the narrative deploys.

"Preciousness," a longer and more complex story, takes up again an initiatory encounter between strangers. Two frightened but predatory young men briefly attack an adolescent on her way to school in the darkness of early morning by reaching out to touch her body. A third-person narrative, unwaveringly centered on the young woman, conveys her feelings and fantasies and only "reads" those of the young men in the sound of their footsteps and their gestures. The sexual assault is embedded in a subtle and many-layered account of the girl's adolescent conflicts. Timidity and arrogance, pride and shame in her body, sexual curiosity and revulsion, gender role rebellion and compliance alternately determine her thoughts and actions. The narrative follows a double movement. First, it presents the girl's daily routine of going to school and back, when the fear of a sexual attack weaves in and out of her thoughts. Second, the narrative retraces that routine on one specific day, when an attack in fact does take place. As in the first story, the violation, rather slight in its outer manifestation, occurs in a dreamy atmosphere, close to that of sleep. It is as if inner fantasies and outer events converged: the girl on her way to school spends an hour of "daydreams as acute as a crime" (FT: 103).

Questions of power, gender, and sexuality are at the center of this story. The "preciousness" of the title refers to the girl's feelings about herself, which echo and prolong society's positive valuing of nubile virgins. Yet she is precious to herself mainly for other reasons: "She was fifteen years old and she was not pretty. But inside her thin body existed an almost majestic vastness in which she stirred, as in a meditation. And within the mist there was something precious. Which did not extend itself, did not compromise itself nor contaminate itself. Which was intense like a jewel. Herself" (FT: 102). If she is precious or interesting to men as a brand new sexual object, untouched and touchable, she is precious to herself for an as yet imprecise but "vast" potential, which she protects by her aloof, self-enclosed manner. The girl's newly developed body bestows upon her an as yet untapped "vast" power over men yet also results in a new sort of vulnerability to sexual advances.

Although the girl mainly fears the milder and more common assaults by looks or words (even men's thoughts she considers invasive and wishes to control), in the incident she suffers an attack by touch. As the two men come toward her, she feels compelled not to turn back and flee an encounter where pride and power are at issue. The narrator describes the girl with a kind of respectful exaltation: she walks on "heroic legs," "with a firm gait, her mouth set, moving in her Spanish rhythm" (FT: 108). Her courage is more than courage: "It was the gift. And the great vocation for a destiny. She advanced, suffering as she obeyed" (FT: 108). It is as if this assault followed a predetermined plan, to which the individuals involved must submit. Yet the attackers overstep the boundaries of that plan:

What followed were four awkward hands, four hands that did not know what they wanted, four mistaken hands of people with no vocation, four hands that touched her so unexpectedly that she did the best thing that she could have done in the world of movement: she became paralyzed. They, whose pre-meditated part was merely that of passing alongside the dark-ness of her fear, and then the first of the seven mysteries would collapse; they . . . had failed to understand their function and, with the individuality of those who experience fear, they had attacked. It had lasted less than a fraction of a second in that quiet street. Within a fraction of a second, they touched her as if all seven mysteries belonged to them. Which she preserved in their entirety and became the more a larva and fell seven more years behind. (FT: 110)

In this ritual gone wrong, the error seems to lie in the rush to appropriate too many mysteries too soon. Only youth, awkwardness, and lack of understanding and vocation characterize these anony-mous attackers, presented with remarkable sympathy and some dis-dain. "From the haste with which they wounded her, she realized that they were more frightened than she was" (FT: 110). Where and how they "wound" her remains unspecified, but the impact seems severe. The attack at first impedes the girl's inner growth; she "falls behind" and experiences a paralysis on which the narrative dwells at length.

The assault seems to have proved to her that she is not, after all, precious to anyone else. Alone in the school lavatory, she cries out loud, "I am alone in the world! No one will ever help me, no one will ever love me! I am all alone in the world! (FT: 112.) She has exchanged the solitude of the special being, the elect, for the solitude of someone whose power has been cut back. She moves out of the world of missions and sacrifices; the narrative abandons those ag-grandizing metaphors. As she looks in the mirror to comb her hair, she sees herself as an enclosed animal: "The expression of her nose was that of a snout, peeping through a fence" (FT: 113). The cer-tainty of the disparity between her external and internal value moves her to practical gestures of self-protection, which includes demand-ing new shoes of her family: "Mine make a lot of noise, a woman can't walk on wooden heels, it attracts too much attention! (FT: 113.) This request reconnects her obliquely to the assault. As the men approached her, she focused her fear on the sound of their footsteps and of her own. By demanding new shoes, she counters the insight that followed the violation: She extracts tangible proof of her family's love and care. The "quiet" shoes would put her in a relationship of dissimilarity both to her own previous self and to her assailants. By associating "quiet" with womanliness she internalizes a traditional feature of femininity and seems to give up her fantasies of specialness and power.[7] Yet the language of ritual returns in the paragraph that concludes the story with an almost celebratory tone:

> Until, just as a person grows fat, she ceased, without knowing by what process, to be precious. There is an obscure law which decrees that the egg be protected until the chick is born, a bird of fire. And she got her new shoes. (FT: 113)

The attack seems to begin a process that ultimately results in the loss of her preciousness, now appearing as a self-protective fantasy, and in the girl's recognition of her true vulnerability as a woman and human being. Sexual assault, here as in the first story, is mitigated by appeals to "obscure laws" that govern human nature and social conduct. The attack nudges forward the protagonist's growth: the suffering of violence brings with it inner progress and social adaptation, turning ugly chick into "bird of fire."

The story "Pig Latin," published in *The Stations of the Body* (*A Via Crucis do Corpo*, 1974), is an example of Lispector's later short narratives, where the plot enacts literally the violence previously contained in her characters' feelings and fantasies and in the figurative language that describes them. The stories are brief, brisk, their simple syntax and occasional vulgarisms a stark contrast to the involutions and periphrases of Lispector's earlier style. They also dismiss the psychological scrutiny at the center of her earlier work. Yet this story about rape repeats in a different register certain configurations of the two earlier ones. It is also a violent initiation, since the protagonist, Cidinha, is on the brink of entering a larger world. An English teacher from the provinces, she is traveling to the metropolis: first Rio, then New York. "She wanted to perfect her English in the United States" (PL: 68). Two men sitting opposite her in the train look her over and begin talking to each other in a strange language. Suddenly she understands they are speaking pig latin, planning to rape her in the tunnel and kill her if she tries to resist. She does not consider using her advance warning—pig latin was the language "they had used as children to protect themselves from the grownups" (PL: 60)—to defend herself; getting up and changing seats might have been enough. Her response is more devious:

... if I pretend that I am a prostitute they'll give up, they wouldn't want a whore.

So she pulled up her skirt, made sensual movements she didn't even know she knew how to make, so unknown was she to herself—and opened the top buttons on her blouse, leaving her breasts half exposed. The men suddenly in shock.

"Eshay's razycay."

In other words, "she's crazy." (PL: 61)

This act of self-defense masked as seduction reveals the hidden motives of the men. Cidinha correctly sees that they desire not sexual pleasure but inflicting cruelty and humiliation. When she offers to give freely (or perhaps for a fee) what they were about to take, the men are amused and put off. The ticket collector also takes her for a prostitute, and she is turned over to the police. Because, like other of Lispector's protagonists, she cannot explain—"How could she explain pig latin?" (PL: 62)—she spends three days in jail. "Finally they let her go. She took the next train to Rio. She had washed her face. She wasn't a prostitute any more. What bothered her was this: when the two had spoken of raping her, she had wanted to be raped. She was shameless. Danay Iay maay aay orewhay. That was what she had discovered. Humiliation" (PL: 62). When she left the train under arrest, still in her prostitute mode, a young woman about to board looked at her with scorn. Several days later, Cidinha comes upon a newspaper headline: "Girl Raped and Killed in Train." The presumably virtuous and unyielding young woman dies at the same assailants' hands. Cidinha saves herself by pretending to be what in her own severe self-judgment she really is.

Her successful strategy hinges on the recognition of her double oppression in society. She is "rapable" to the extent that she is "pure," for in order to be a particularly desirable object of sexual violence, she must have done prior violence to herself, by suppressing her own sexuality. Yet Cidinha agrees with her attackers, complicitly acquiescing in the brutal equations that oppress women: having sexual desires equals being a whore; wanting sexual contact equals wanting to be raped. The men still manage to humiliate her by making her aware of her sexual desires.

The protagonist's escape is a small battle won in a losing war. After she reads the headlines, "she trembled all over":

It had happened, then. And to the girl who had despised her.

She began to cry there in the street. She threw away the damned newspaper. She didn't want to know the details.

"Atefay siay placableimay."
Fate is implacable. (PL: 62)

The protagonist's complicity with a gender ideology that oppresses her becomes clear in her adoption of the rapists' pig latin. In it, she accuses herself of being a whore and sees the rape and murder of her substitute not as the result of certain human arrangements but as an instance of implacable fate. The naturalization of violence persists in this story. No longer seen as a ritual that helps girls and boys grow up, the confrontation with sexual violence is presented as an initiation into the brutality a woman faces in the "real world" by virtue of her gender. The men's own fear, their youth, or their compliance with mysterious "obscure laws" no longer mitigate the display of violence on the part of the assailants, briefly and stereotypically described: "One was tall, thin, with a little mustache and a cold eye, the other was short, paunchy, and bald" (PL: 68). Although these two are certainly the most ridiculous, made fools of by the girl (though she does not thereby permanently disarm them), all the men come off badly in these stories, even the earlier assailants that had been sympathetically described. The configuration of two or three men against one woman at first seems an obvious symbol of the unequal balance of power between the sexes. In the unfolding of the stories, however, the numerical imbalance also points to the weakness of men, who gather together for strength in order to impose their dominance. The protagonist of "Pig Latin" manages only to deflect the violence. The farcical elements here—the comic improbability of a plot where criminals speak pig latin, where rape and murder occur in broad daylight in a normally occupied train—serve as a distancing device in a story that proceeds as a morality tale, laying bare the cruel workings of a rigidly unjust world.

These three narratives figure sexual assault in a progression that goes from a mildly toned and "aesthetic" symbolic representation to literal and farcical plot events. Yet all the stories share narrative devices that minimize violence. Effaced third-person narrators interpret the victim's experience, only in the case of "Preciousness" occasionally merging with the protagonist, but never implicating themselves in the violent acts. There are no encoded readers; these texts suggest for their reception the position of discreet, impersonal observation. These stories focus on specific incidents of aggression that are explained and assimilated by ideologies about personal growth, adolescent sexual fantasies, initiation into the harshness of male-female relations, and woman's place in a world governed by "implacable fate." *The Hour of the Star*, the ninety-page novella Lispector published just months before her death, offers a new and challenging perspective on writing the victim, where violence is no longer naturalized and contained.[8] In this work, Lispector represents overlapping systems of oppression and a victim absolutely crushed by them. At the same time, she accuses writer, narrator, and reader of participating in and profiting from that oppression.

In an elaborate fiction within a fiction, the narrator of *The Hour of the Star*, a male writer, discusses his creation of a female protagonist. This young woman, a bona fide social victim, is a native of the Northeast, a region that in its tortured landscape and harsh reality of droughts and severe economic ills, has attracted the imagination of many Brazilian writers. The protagonist, recently arrived in Rio, hungry, marginalized, displaced, represents others in her situation, a fragment of a vast social reality. In this text, Lispector opens up the scope of her depiction of the experience of oppression beyond the scrutiny of gender-role conflicts and spiritual crises of middle-class women (and the occasional man). Simultaneously she calls into question the process whereby literature represents oppression.

The protagonist, Macabéa, a barely literate typist, has joined the urban poor of Rio. Like the four shopgirls with whom she shares a room, she belongs to an underworld of those who, severed from their families, live in cramped quarters and subservience in exchange for enough to eat. Her improbable job as a typist—this text also has many farcical elements—provides her with a modicum of dignity but exposes her to ridicule, since she types word for word and can't spell. An orphan, her growth stunted by poverty, Macabéa was raised by an aunt who enjoyed beating her. Chaste, proud of her virginity, Macabéa murmurs each morning, "I'm a typist and a virgin, and I like Coca-Cola" (HS: 35). She confides to her boyfriend an incongruous dream: "Do you know what I really want to be? A movie star. . . . Did you know that Marilyn Monroe was the color of peaches?"—"And you're the color of mud," her boyfriend retorts. "You haven't got the face or the body to be a movie star" (HS: 53). Macabéa, moreover, is infertile: "Her ovaries are as shrivelled as overcooked mushrooms" (HS: 58). Yet she is sensuous without knowing it. "How could so much sensuality," the narrator asks, "fit in a body as withered as hers without her even suspecting its presence?" (HS: 73.) With the rude bluntness of caricature, Lispector makes clear that Macabéa is victimized by everything and everyone:

her socioeconomic origins have weakened her body (which the multinational purveyors of Coca-Cola further malnourish), her brutal aunt broke her spirit, her boyfriend insults her, while patriarchy neutralizes her sensuality and foreign stereotypes of beauty encourage her and others to despise her body and its color. The movies also provide an outlet for her self-hate: "Macabéa had a passion for musicals and horror films. She especially like films where women were hanged or shot through the heart with a bullet" (HS: 58). Macabéa is "raped" not by one individual man but by a multitude of social and cultural forces that conspire to use her cruelly for the benefit of others.

The plot takes Macabéa through a series of large and small misfortunes, which relentlessly beat her down. First, her boss puts her on notice to be fired. Next begins a desultory courtship, where Macabéa is the object of Olímpico's insults and audience for his fantasies of grandeur. He soon abandons her to take up with her officemate Glória. Finally, a fortune-teller predicts for Macabéa a happy ending, complete with marriage to a rich gringo. But this Cinderella outcome is no sooner suggested than brutally cut short. Stepping out of the fortune-teller's house, Macabéa meets her death in a hit and run accident: the gringo, driving a Mercedes, turns out to be her killer, not her groom.[9] On one level, then, these "feeble adventures of a young woman in a city all set up against her" (HS: 15) compose a plot that parodies the sentimental stories of ill-used innocence and shattered dreams of many literary and nonliterary texts. On another level, this novella, "a fiction of fiction making" in Peter Brooks' term,[10] concerns itself with narration, especially with the possibility of mimesis and with the charged authorial investments in the creation of characters. We are given not only the story of the victim, but a meditation on writing the victim, a process that itself duplicates and inscribes the act of victimization.

Macabéa is both a grotesque *other* and a repository for subtle processes of identification by which the narrator claims to gain access to her interiority and her reality. "I use myself as a form of knowledge," the narrator remarks, addressing Macabéa. "I know you to the bone by means of an incantation that goes from me to you" (HS: 82). Macabéa herself does not engage in quests. She lacks practical ambitions and insight into what the narrator claims is her "true" condition. Her inwardness is empty: "She was only vaguely aware of a kind of absence of herself in herself. If she were someone who could communicate her feelings she would say: the world is beyond me, I am beyond myself" (HS: 24). The narrator is the questing character, who pursues a verbal construct: writing the victim's story and through it his own. "Even though I have nothing to do with this young woman, I will have to write myself through her, amazed at every turn" (HS: 24).

In the dramatization of the storytelling act, three textual interactions emerge as central. All are unstable and often aggressive, hinging on identification and rejection, sympathy and repulsion: first, the implicit connection between Lispector and her male narrator, Rodrigo S. M. (given the context of cruelty, it is difficult not to think of the sadomasochism these initials sometimes signify); second, the narrator's relationship to Macabéa, whom he invents, but whose "truth" he also claims to "capture"; third, the interaction between Rodrigo S. M. and the encoded reader, whom he frequently—and contentiously—addresses. References to narration fragment the plot, interrupting it on almost every page. There is nothing seamless about the text and much that is abrupt, excessive, and grotesque. The grid through which Macabéa is written, itself fictional, of course, remains firmly in the foreground.

From the midsixties on, autobiographical references frequently intrude in Lispector's fictional narratives, disrupting systematically the fictional pretense with what we might call the autobiographical pretense. In the preface to *The Hour of the Star*, "Dedication by the Author (actually, Clarice Lispector)," she assumes a masculine voice and makes the preface stylistically indistinguishable from Rodrigo S. M.'s narrative. If her narrator is a mask, Lispector seems to imply, then so is her autobiographical "self." The preface begins: "Thus, I dedicate this thing here to Schumann of long ago and his sweet Clara, who are now bones, woe to us. I dedicate myself to a shade of red, very scarlet like my blood of a man in his prime and therefore I dedicate myself to my blood" (HS: 7). In these dizzying reversals of subject/object relations, the disdain implicit in "I dedicate this thing here" quickly subsides and the verb becomes reflexive: "I dedicate myself." The giving of something external to someone else collapses, in a vertigo of self-involvement, into the giving of oneself to oneself (but also to a male other residing in one's very blood). These alternations of rejection and identification between the first person, the text, and those whom it addresses continue to be dramatized as points of friction in the novella. But why, we might ask, the equivocal cross-gender connections between Lispector and her male narrator? She gives *him* a masculine identity; he gives *her* male blood: "my blood of a man in his prime." The author is a woman who assumes a male mask and the narrator the mask of a female author.

The blurring of gender demarcations continues in the novella when the narrator in turn creates a fictional female as his mask and his double. The insistent recourse to a male subject of discourse—both in the autobiographical preface and in the fictional narrative—functions as a distancing device that opens up textual space for various kinds of irony. Rodrigo S. M. again and again refuses the rhetoric of pity. To this end his individuality may be irrelevant, but his gender matters: "Come to think of it, I discover now that I am not at all necessary either and what I write another could write. Another writer, yes, but it would have to be a man because a woman writer might get all tearful and cloying" (HS: 14). With irony, Lispector at once curiously rejects and endorses the cultural myth of the sentimental woman writer. While the "real" author is of course a female writer, she insists that the fictive author must be male. The male mask, by increasing the distance between narrator and character, also points up the outrageous presumption that writing the other, especially the oppressed other, implies. "It is my passion to be the other. In this instance, the female other. I tremble, emaciated, filthy, just like her" (HS: 29).

The interaction between Rodrigo S. M. and Macabéa, the most pressing concern of the metatextual commentary, entails two main issues. First is a sustained though in part implicit questioning of the status of a novelist's invention of fictional characters. How much of it originates in valid apprehension of personal and social truth, as the narrator in his more optimistic moments believes? "Can it be that it's my painful task to imagine in my own flesh the truth that no one wants to face?" (HS: 56.) Writing, in this view a generous gift, gives voice to those who would otherwise be silent. In much of the metatextual commentary, mimesis appears urgent and attainable.

A second set of metatextual commentaries contradicts the possibility of mimesis or at least sees representation as more complicated and charged. One obstacle to mimesis stems from class differences between narrator and characters. These disparities in economic status and cultural presuppositions are not smoothed over but played up as points of friction. Prejudice, repugnance, fear, and guilt animate the cruelty so pervasive in this text, lodging, for instance, in the narrator's remarks about the street where Macabéa lives: "Acre Street. What a place. The big fat rats of Acre Street. I wouldn't go there for the world because I'm shamelessly terrified of that drab piece of filthy life" (HS: 30). The narrator constructs Macabéa and the other characters by calling upon openly displayed class prejudices. The characterization of Olímpico and Glória, especially, relies with strident glee on the clichés through which the upper classes typically view the poor: Olímpico's gold tooth, proudly acquired, and greasy hair ointment; Glória's cheap perfume disguising infrequent baths, her bleached egg-yellow hair.

Other pressures also undercut social mimesis and intrude into the narrator's resolve to see Macabéa. How much of the novelist's invention originates in the murkier waters of self-concern? In self-seeking, self-abasing, expiatory, or malevolent investments? The narrator loses focus on his protagonist and deviously, compulsively takes her place: "I see [Macabéa] looking in the mirror and—the ruffle of a drum—in the mirror my face appears, weary and unshaven. So thoroughly do we take each other's place" (HS: 22).

Images of victim and victimizer alternately define the relationship between narrator and Macabéa. His masculine gender allows for double entendres that sometimes propose for this "liaison" the model of a typically exploitative sexual affair between a man and a woman of disparate social circumstances: "Before this typist entered my life, I was a reasonably cheerful man" (HS: 17). Although the social context of his discourse may implicate him as the exploiter, he often sees himself as victim. "Well, the typist doesn't want to get off my back. Why me, of all people? I find out that as I had suspected poverty is ugly and promiscuous" (HS: 21). Although Macabéa in the text's fiction knows nothing of her narrator—like Borges' dreamer in "The Circular Ruins" she believes she is real—she possesses a peculiar power as a site for the narrator's investments. Provoking his guilt, forcing him to live in her skin, she drags him through the misfortunes he invents for her. The attraction of the narrator to Macabéa is compulsive, involuntary. Lispector offers this equivocal commerce between narrator and character as a parable on a basic motivation of narrative and on the obstacles to social mimesis.

Two contradictory but interwoven languages govern Macabéa's characterization. The language of the grotesque fixes Macabéa's life and appearance in cruelly degrading poses but is periodically displaced by another language that rewrites her in lyrical terms. Narrator and characters seem equally drawn to defining Macabéa in disparaging metaphoric and descriptive epithets that favor essentializing predicates following the verb *to be*. The following quotations are representative of the narrator's deflating definitions:

She was all rather dingy, for she rarely washed. (HS:26)
Nobody looked at her in the street; she was like a cup of cold coffee. (HS:27)

> She was born with a bad record and looked like a child of who knows what, with an air of apologizing for taking up space. (HS:26)

> She was a chance event. A fetus thrown in the garbage, wrapped in newspaper. (HS:36)

> She had no fat and her whole organism was dry like a half empty sack of crumbled toast. (HS:38)

Other characters contribute to this insistent chorus. "You, Macabéa, are like a hair in a bowl of soup," her former boyfriend tells her. "No one feels like eating it" (HS:60). This generalized textual impulse to demean the protagonist continues down to the scene of her death: "Did she suffer? I believe so. Like a chicken with a clumsily severed neck, running around in a panic, dripping blood. Except that the chicken flees, as one flees from pain, with horrified cluckings. And Macabéa struggled in silence" (HS:80).

Bakhtin, in a chapter of his book on Rabelais, points out that "of all the features of the human face, the nose and mouth play the most important part in the grotesque image of the body. . . ."[11] Although images of absence, insubstantiality, and lack usually define Macabéa, Lispector, in two mirror scenes, contrives to provide her with a grotesque nose and mouth. In the bathroom of her office building it seems to Macabéa at first that the dull and darkened mirror reflects nothing at all. "Could it be that her physical existence had disappeared? This illusion soon passed and she saw her whole face distorted by the cheap mirror, her enormous nose like the cardboard nose of a clown." (HS:24–25). A later mirror scene, which likewise stresses this text's attachment to a deforming mimesis, focuses on her mouth. She puts on bright red lipstick, on purpose going beyond the contours of her thin lips, in a futile attempt to resemble Marilyn Monroe. Afterward, "she stood staring in the mirror at the face staring back in astonishment. It seemed that instead of lipstick thick blood oozed from her lips, as if someone had punched her in the mouth, broken her teeth and torn her flesh" (HS:61–62). Blood and vomit, obsessively frequent in this text, signal the opening up of the body and the rupture of its self-enclosed system. Like other "acts performed on the confines of the body and the outer world,"[12] bleeding and vomiting contribute to the grotesque image of the body as Bakhtin describes it. Macabéa suffers from permanent hunger and equally permanent nausea, indexes of her position in a world she cannot incorporate and which refuses to accept her. Blood and vomit mark the hour of her death, which the narrator had mistakenly predicted would bring her a moment of glory: "She would surely die one day as if beforehand she had learned by heart how to play the star. For at the hour of death a person becomes a brilliant movie star, it's every one's moment of glory" (HS:28). The promise of stardom —of height, of exaltation—is reversed, debased, materializing in a star-shaped pool of blood on the pavement. Eating (and the contrasting states of hunger and nausea), several forms of elimination, and bleeding, dispersed throughout the text, point up Macabéa's pathetic lack of glory and adaptation in contrast to the other characters' vigorous if repugnant incorporation into and of the world.

In counterpoint to this grotesque inscription of Macabéa, an equally insistent though less dominant language of lyricism emerges. The narrator exalts her, proclaims his affection: "Yes, I'm in love with Macabéa, my darling Maca, in love with her homeliness and total anonymity, for she belongs to no one at all. In love with her fragile lungs, the scrawny little thing" (HS:68). Her physical thinness at times becomes airy, delicate. He reveals her spiritual bent: she has faith, believes in the goodness of others, and falls into ecstatic states upon contemplating a rainbow, a particular play of light, hearing Caruso sing on the radio, or looking at a tree. Her subjectivity is not entirely empty, after all. Yet it is through her inner emptiness that she approaches saintliness: "Most of the time she possessed without knowing it the emptiness that fills the soul of saints. Was she a saint? It would seem so" (HS:37). Irony lurks at the edges of this lyrical language but does not totally undercut its effect. In sketching Macabéa, the text proceeds by disconcerting juxtapositions of the "high" and the "low," in the plot, in descriptions, and in clusters of metaphors. These contradictory forces of exaltation and abasement, which at times include a gratuitous violence, appear again and again.

Berta Waldman, one of Lispector's insightful readers, remarks about Macabéa: "In her simple nature, she represents a being without fissures, continuous with herself, who exists at the center of the savage heart [an allusion to Lispector's first novel, *Close to the Savage Heart*] in the paradisiacal space where beings participate in the inner nucleus of things, a space which proved impenetrable to Lispector's other characters."[13] Waldman accounts here for only one side of Macabéa's portrayal, an unstable one at that, for Macabéa's paradisiacal self-identity is not constant. The critic neglects to acknowledge how irony and the grotesque constantly undercut her presentation as a being without fissures. But in one sense, and this is an aspect of the text some readers may find offensive, Macabéa is a privileged soul when set against the gallery of Lispector's seekers of truth and inner harmony. Her simplemindedness attenuates anguish and self-division; she believes she is happy. As the quintessentially vulnerable being, ideally open to existence, she possesses, like a holy fool, an unsought, unconscious wisdom. Macabéa's musings echo those of Lispector's serious thinkers, with a parodic edge, in terms significantly askew. Curious about the cultural artifacts that surround her and yet escape her, Macabéa collects odd bits of information and words whose meanings she doesn't know ("algebra," "electronic," "culture," "ephemeris"). She asks questions, both weighty and idiotic, without necessarily expecting answers:

> How do I manage to make myself possible? (HS:48)
> Is the sky above or below? (HS:31)

In his own tortured way, the narrator also questions and despairs of finding answers:

> As long as I have questions to which there are no answers, I'll go on writing. (HS:11)
> This book is a silence. This book is a question. (HS:17)

And Lispector, in turn, also refracts this same questioning mode when she writes in the preface: "This is an unfinished book because an answer is missing. An answer I hope someone in the world will provide. You?" (HS:8.) Macabéa, both a subject without fissures and a truncated, grotesquely charged version of Lispector's questing characters, carries their typical moves to a reductio ad absurdum.

The dramatization of the text's reception provides no relief from the tense interactions of the other participants in the narrative act. The encoded reader, source and recipient of violence, offers a particularly uncomfortable position for any real reader to occupy. Frequently addressing the reader as *vós* (the formal pronoun, now archaic), the narrator assumes various tones: ceremonious, religious, lyrical, or mocking. The narratee shares the narrator's niche of economic security and comes to the text with motives not entirely clean: "(If the reader possesses some wealth and a comfortable life, he must step out of himself to see how the other at times can be. If he is poor, he won't be reading me because reading is superfluous for those who feel slight and permanent pangs of hunger. I function as an escape valve for the crushing life of the average bourgeoisie. . . .)" (HS:30.) This "coming out of oneself," not a pleasant escapism, involves a degrading identification that the narrator wishes to force upon the narratee: "If there is any reader for this story, I want him to soak up the young woman like a mop on a wet floor. This girl is the truth I wished to avoid" (HS:39). In another passage, the aggression against the encoded reader reaches a shriller pitch: "Let those who read me, then, feel a punch in the stomach to see if they like it. Life is a punch in the stomach" (HS:82–83). As a perpetrator of violence, the "you" collaborates with the forces that crush Macabéa and the narrator: "I have to ask, though I don't know who to ask, if I must really love whoever slaughters me and ask who among you is slaughtering me" (HS:81). The narratee, then, provides a fictional space for participation in the main activities figured in the text: repulsion and identification, violence and the reception of violence. Reading the victim, like writing the victim, entails a symbolic engagement with the pressures of her life. That engagement is doubly uncomfortable, doubly suspect, in the role this text proposes for the reader: sympathy slides into suffering and disengagement into the wielding of a malevolent power.

In her dramatization of the production, transmission, and reception of a fictional text that attempts to write the victim Lispector allows none of the dramatis personae of author, narrator, character, and reader to occupy a comfortable position. With hyperbole and uncompromising detail, Lispector stresses the particular agencies of that victimization. Macabéa, as we have seen, is not simply or perhaps even mainly a social victim. The novella presses this point in the implicit contrast between Macabéa and her two false friends. Olímpico, also a displaced migrant from the Northeast, displays will and an evil forcefulness. Glória, a sensuous female, combines vigor with a smug self-satisfaction. Macabéa's position as a victim transcends motivations of gender, class, and what might be loosely called race, factors that nevertheless contribute to her oppression. This hyperbolically naive, unprotected, bewildered young woman—"adrift in the unconquerable city" (HS:80)—signifies the shared human helplessness of beings engulfed in the brutality of life, "life which devours life" (HS:84).

Macabéa's hunger is both a product of material deprivation and a metaphor of that totally vulnerable and denuded existence that Lispector sets up as an ideal in many texts. In this polyvalent encoding of poverty Lispector questions the dubious moral and psychic forces at work in the representation of oppression. She points up the absurd hubris of the well-off writer who imagines the position of someone who goes hungry, stressing—and giving in to—the urge to engage in just such an act of the imagination. For a writer in a city crowded with the poor, perhaps especially for a woman writer who enters into daily intimate contact with attenuated poverty in the person of the domestic servant (I think here of the many maids, shadowy or acerbic presences, in Lispector texts), the compulsion to write the victim is in no way innocent or simple:

> In a street of Rio de Janeiro I caught a glimpse of utter disaster in the face of a young woman from the Northeast. (HS:12)

> Care for her, ladies and gentlemen, because my power is only to show her so that you will recognize her in the street, stepping lightly because of her fluttering thinness. (HS:19)

These initially simple, lyrical acts of seeing, showing, and recognizing quickly absorb violent energies, as Lispector implicates, melodramatically, even histrionically, both in the misfortunes of the victim and in the powers that crush her, all the subjects who engage in the narrative transaction.

One may question whether the construction of Macabéa as both social and existential victim may not overload the circuits and disrupt any effective social criticism. A character whose "wisdom" consists of meek acceptance—"things are the way they are because that's the way they are" (HS:26)—is written by a narrator who agrees with her: "Could there possibly be another answer? If someone knows a better one let him speak up for I have been waiting for years" (HS:26). And in the preface the "real author" echoes this statement, placing the burden of an answer on someone else. Yet if we read this novella in the context of the three stories about rape that soften the implications of sexual assault and women's oppression, we see that the very refusal to provide answers underlies the disturbing effectiveness of *The Hour of the Star*. Macabéa dies in utter abjection, learning nothing from her trials. The narrator finds no moral in his tale and with reluctance and relief detaches himself from Macabéa in the end. Lispector refuses to naturalize the oppression of one class or gender or race by another or, for that matter, to see human life in heroic terms.

We might also read this novella as a parable on the motivations of narrative and on Lispector's own creative process. Peter Brooks, in *Reading for the Plot*, affirms his belief that "narrative has something to do with time boundedness, and that plot is the internal logic of the discourse of mortality."

> Walter Benjamin has made this point in the simplest and most extreme way, claiming that what we seek in narrative fictions is that knowledge of death which is denied to us in our own

lives: the death that writes *finis* to the life and therefore confers on it its meaning. "Death," says Benjamin, "is the sanction of everything that the story teller can tell."[14]

A similar view about the generative connection between death and narrative drives the plot and perhaps also other instances of textual violence in *The Hour of the Star*. The narrator seems to engage through Macabéa in a kind of sacrificial rite that culminates in the killing off of the protagonist. "Death is my favorite character in this story" (HS:83), he says. In the ritual performed by the narrative, symbolic self-immolation plays a part. The narrator remarks in one of his more histrionic moments: "I want to be a pig and a chicken, then kill them and drink their blood" (HS:70). Macabéa dies in a slow motion scene that takes up seven pages. The narrator watches her suffer, gloating strangely over his power to save or kill her. He decides she must die, yet acknowledges her death as his betrayal of her. "Even you, Brutus?!" (HS:84), he says to himself. He claims to accompany her at the moment of dying: "Don't be afraid, death happens in an instant and is quickly over. I know because I just died with the young woman" (HS:85). Although in Lispector's fiction the ritual sacrifices, the charged commerce between victimizer and victim, narrator and double, do not bring about enduring illumination, much less result in dramatic change, they are essential acts that set her narratives in motion.

The Hour of the Star offers, then, a lucid representation of the aggressive investments narrative entails. Violence is no longer limited, as it was in Lispector's earlier fiction, to intrapsychic conflicts, clashes between characters, or the mimesis of social forces. Violence is no longer justified, contained, and subdued by ideological and narrative strategies. Instead, in this text and elsewhere in her later fiction the act of narration itself appears problematic, aggressive, guilt-provoking. A textual violence permeates the vertiginous doublings and mirrorings in which author, narrators, characters, and readers engage. I propose this interpretation in contrast to Hélène Cixous', which privileges in Lispector a matrix of mild and generative identifications and a narrative subject who assumes a position of innocence: "just looking with beneficent eyes," seeking "to overrule the ego and the pretense of mastering things and knowing things," as Cixous defines it in a recent article.[15] But Lispector questions, I believe, the very possibility of innocence: she enacts a knowing, guilt-ridden struggle with the mastering and violent powers of narrative.

NOTES

1. Hélène Cixous, *Vivre l'orange / To Live the Orange* (Paris: Des femmes, 1979).

2. This is from another of Cixous' early texts on Lispector, published in the same year as *Vivre l'orange:* " 'L'approche de Clarice Lispector, Se laisser lire (par) Clarice Lispector, A Paixão segundo C. L.," *Poétique* (November 1979), 40:412, my translation.

3. "voice i. . . ," an interview with Hélène Cixous by Verena Andermatt Conley, *Boundary 2* (Winter 1984), 12(2): 54.

4. Cixous attempts to give to these stereotypes a liberating slant. See, for instance, Toril Moi in *Sexual / Textual Politics: Feminist Literary Theory* (London: Methuen, 1985), p. 115: "Cixous' mother-figure is clearly what Melanie Klein would call the Good Mother: the omnipotent and generous dispenser of love, nourishment and plenitude. The writing woman is thus immensely powerful: hers is a *puissance féminine* derived directly from the mother, whose giving is always suffused with strength . . ."

5. I modify here Laura Mulvey's sharp formulation, "sadism demands a story," quoted and discussed in its possible reversibility by Teresa de Lauretis ("Is a story, are all stories to be claimed by sadism?") in "Desire in Narrative," *Alice Doesn't: Feminism, Semiotics, Cinema,* (Bloomington: Indiana University Press, 1982), p. 102.

6. "Mystery in São Cristóvão" was later republished in *Family Ties.* The page numbers after all quotations of Clarice Lispector are from the published English translations, which I modify occasionally for reasons of accuracy. I use the following abbreviations:

FT:—*Family Ties,* trans. Giovanni Pontiero (Austin: University of Texas Press, 1972).

PL:—"Pig Latin," trans. Alexis Levitin, in *Soulstorm: Stories by Clarice Lispector* (New York: New Directions, 1989), pp. 59–62.

HS:—*The Hour of the Star,* trans. Giovanni Pontiero (Manchester: Carcanet, 1986).

7. Naomi Lindstrom, "A Discourse Analysis of 'Preciosidade' by Clarice Lispector," *Luso-Brazilian Review* (1982), 12 (2): 193.

8. The following commentary on *The Hour of the Star* is a revised and modified version of my discussion of it in the article "Writing the Victim in the Fiction of Clarice Lispector," K. David Jackson, ed., in *Transformations of Literary Language in Latin American Literature: From Machado de Assis to the Vanguards,* pp. 84–97 (Austin: Department of Spanish and Portuguese, University of Texas at Austin / Abaporu Press, 1987), reprinted by permission.

9. The Brazilian film *The Hour of the Star* (1986), directed by Suzana Amaral and available in the United States, is a very interesting adaptation of Lispector's novella. Considerably less corrosive than its literary counterpart, the film stresses the failed Cinderella plot and (wisely) omits the mediated narration and metafictional mediations.

10. Peter Brooks, *Reading for the Plot: Design and Intention in Narrative* (New York: Knopf, 1986), p. 315.

11. Mikhail Bakhtin, *Rabelais and His World*, trans. Helen Iswolski (Cambridge: M.I.T. Press, 1968), p. 316.

12. Ibid., p. 317.

13. Berta Waldman, *A Paixão Segundo C. L.* (São Paulo: Brasiliense, 1983), p. 69, my translation.

14. Brooks, *Reading for the Plot*, p. 22.

15. Hélène Cixous, "Reaching the Point of Wheat, or the Portrait of the Artist as a Maturing Woman," *New Literary History* (Autumn 1987), 19: 20.

4
FRAMING
INSTITUTIONS

9

The Poetics of Rape Law
in Medieval France

KATHRYN GRAVDAL

In studying the status of women in medieval society, scholars traditionally consulted the texts of "courtly love," a practice that perpetuated the commonplace that women achieved a higher status during the period of the courtly love discourse. Thus courtly love came to fulfill the same function for modern critics that it did for medieval society: it became a self-authenticating discourse.

In the nineteenth century, medievalists' judgments of the historical status of women derived primarily from studies of the new type of literature that appears in twelfth-century France. It was commonly held that in these poems and romances the feminine constituted a new cultural ideal. Traditional commonplaces held that the sympathetic depiction of women in courtly literature and the literary focus on emotional and psychological relationships between men and women marked a shift in historical attitudes toward and treatment of women.

Since the 1960s revisionist studies have raised doubts both about the actual effect of courtly love discourse on medieval society and about the ideological value of this literary glorification of women.[1]

Historians have begun to show that the ideals of courtly love had little positive effect on the historical experience of women in the Middle Ages.[2] Many literary critics even question whether female characters in medieval texts are placed on pedestals at all or rather insidiously disempowered.[3] In point of fact, the new sentimental and moral stature for women accompanies a marked restriction of women's role in society. In *Mâle Moyen Age,* Georges Duby attempts again to dispel the belief that courtly literature was a female phenomenon.[4] He does so by broadening the field of investigation to the study of societal relations in medieval France, particularly the institutions of marriage and of chivalry. Duby reveals courtly love to be a game: a masculine game of power, property, and violence.

To explore the status of women in medieval France, we will turn away from the texts of courtly love to study "noncourtly" texts, as well as other types of documents and discourses, describing the condition of women. Our own work contributes to the revisionist positions by drawing on different types of discourse surrounding rape and in particular the treatment of sexual violence in medieval law, both canon and civil, and courtroom records of rape trials in northern France.

The discursive representations or constructions of rape, whether as romantic "ravishment" or slapstick comedy, reflect, refract, and even reify the power structures of female and male in society. Further, attitudes toward sexual violence may be shaped and justified in a layering of discourses: fourteenth-century legal practices may have been authorized or legitimized by thirteenth-century literary practices, which may themselves have been justified by twelfth-century lawbooks. Despite the ways in which male-authored texts attempt to mystify rape as romance or as a game, the female reader may decipher textual representations of rape quite differently from the way they were meant to be read.

The text to which we will first turn is a "noncourtly" French literary genre, the thirteenth-century pastourelle.[5] The pastourelle is a lyrico-narrative genre, based on three poetic moments: a bucolic meeting between a knight and a shepherdess; a debate about love; the lament of the abandoned shepherdess.[6] While most of the extant pastourelles are anonymous, those that are signed were, interestingly enough, composed by many of the same troubadours who wrote courtly lyric: Marcabru, Gui d'Ussel, Jean Bodel, Gautier de Coinci. Among the signed pastourelles we also find the names of aristocrats and royalty: Thibaut IV, Count of Champagne and King of Navarre; Jean de Braine, Count of Mâcon and Vienne; Henri III,

Duke of Brabant; Hugh, Count of La Marche.[7] The label *noncourtly* is therefore misleading in its implicit reference to social class of authorship and audience. Since the pastourelles were composed by the same authors as other types of courtly love lyric, it is possible to surmise that they were written (and performed) for the same audience.

Nothing in the critical studies written on French medieval literature prepares the female reader for the sexual violence in the pastourelle. Discontinuous with the classical tradition of pastoral poetry, these medieval song-and-dance pieces are poetic celebrations of the social practice of rape: a knight is riding down a road, sees a shepherdess all alone with her flock, and attempts to seduce her. The knight promises love, jewels, cloaks, belts, purses, in exchange for the shepherdess's sexual compliance. But always unspoken in his bargaining is the threat of rape: they are alone in the fields. Indeed, the narrative setting of the pastourelle (a pretty peasant girl alone in the field) almost calls for rape. While not staging rape themselves, the majority of the pastourelle texts set the scene for those that do: the shepherdess yields to the knight's seduction and accepts the promises of clothing or jewels. The pastourelles in which the shepherdess "is seduced" set up a kind of sexual overcoding: the portrayal of her compliance helps to blur the boundary line between seduction and rape. In one-fifth of the Old French pastourelles the knight tires of cajoling the unwilling girl, throws her to the ground, and rapes her. The pastourelle then closes, frequently with the same gaily nonsensical refrain with which it began: tu-re-lu-re-li, tu-re-lu-re-lay.

In the pastourelle, rape is presented as acceptable, indeed institutionalized, and quite funny. What is noteworthy about the representation of rape in the pastourelles, however, is not the matter-of-fact acceptability of the sexual violence, but the fact that the word "rape" has scarcely if ever appeared during two centuries of pastourelle scholarship. Critics point out that these are literary texts, fictional knights and shepherdesses, that this is poetic language and no reflection of or on the reality of medieval society.[8] Others argue that these texts constitute the projection of the female desire to be "ravished." The recurring scene of sexual assault in the pastourelle can be explained away in more or less convincing fashions: a textual return of the repressed, now that male sexual violence has been stamped out by courtly ideology, a collective wish fulfillment on the part of poor, unmarried knights, an allegory of political structures in feudal society, a satire of social class relations in medieval France, or even sexual projections of the romantically inclined ladies who fuel this poetic production and are said to be responsible for the popularity of the genre.[9]

Let us, *arguendo*, assign to the rapes in the pastourelle the status of fictional metaphors, whether allegorical, satirical, or psychological. Where then are we to discover the history of sexual violence in the French Middle Ages, and how can we contrast that poeticization to the place of rape in medieval society? If we turn to Old French literature we find conflicting images of sexuality, from the fabliaux to troubadour lyric. Other texts, such as those that define and describe criminal sexuality, can offer a largely unexamined perspective on the history of sexuality.[10] Our study will examine two nonliterary examples of the discursive practice of rape: the texts of medieval law, both canon and civil, and the records of medieval courts, both church and state. Ultimately we discover that the history of rape is a symptomatic part and a continuing chapter of the history of women and of the relations between gender and society. Recent work on sex crimes in thirteenth- and fourteenth-century Italy serves as a point of comparison to highlight the specificity of attitudes toward sexual violence against women in medieval northern France. Guido Ruggiero finds that rape is treated as an extension of the customary victimization of women, a fact of life that is accepted and not particularly troubling in fourteenth-century Venice. Penalties are minimal. Cases involving minors, the elderly, or incest are taken seriously; cases involving girls of marriageable age, wives, widows, or lower-class women are punished by a mere slap on the wrist.[11]

Rape law in medieval France is complex and can sometimes appear to be contradictory, because two legal systems coexisted in the twelfth and thirteenth centuries: the law of the church, on the one hand, and the law of France's King on the other.[12] Canon law was maintained by ecclesiastical courts and lawyers; civil law was the province of the king and of the feudal lords. Canon law draws initially upon Roman law, in which the punishment for *raptus* (abduction of a woman, usually but not necessarily followed by sexual violation) was death and confiscation of property.[13] Death and/or castration was the form this punishment took in feudal law throughout the early Middle Ages.[14] But the church, preaching Christian love, abhorred death and mutilation in principle. In the midtwelfth century, during the start of "courtly love" discourse, Gratian and other canonists established a variety of penalties for rape: excommunication, pillory, imprisonment, whipping, monetary fines, or marriage to the victims as penance.[15] The new leniency was to the advantage of the accused rapist and scarcely protected the rights of women.

In perusing the texts of law we must ask whether they have a privileged status as facts or are simply texts that may or may not represent the true practices and attitudes of society. That question can find a partial answer in medieval court records, both ecclesiastic and state. Records of actual trials reveal valuable information about the application of law during this period. Furthermore, the language used to represent rape in the courtroom reveals much about cultural attitudes toward women and violence.

In northern France, where, we should note, the pastourelles achieved greatest popularity, we find the *Registre de l'Officialité de Cerisy*, the court records of the Abbey of Cerisy, in Normandy.[16] The records do not begin until the fourteenth century (1314–1457), but they are the earliest remaining texts of rape trials and as such remain precious as an index for approximating the medieval understanding of and response to rape. Since they are the records of regular inquiries, almost inquisitions, into the behavior of the community, they also constitute a dramatic representation of life in four fourteenth-century towns: Cerisy (200 households), Littry (150 households), Deux-Jumeaux (40 households), and Saint Laurent-sur-mer (29 households) in a difficult period: from the time of the plague to the English occupation of the Hundred Years' War. We find a picture of poverty, broken family structures, quotidian sexual violence, incest, demoralization, and social instability. The court is notably lax in sentencing, practically flaunting canon law. The names of the jurors in any given sitting frequently include those of men convicted of criminal behavior in the preceding sessions.

The local churches of the area, symbolic centers of these communities, are themselves in shambles, as the records reveal time and again. On May 16, 1332, during the visitation to Deux-Jumeaux the Cerisy court makes note of a chronic situation: "Primo defectus est in ecclesia quia in eadem pluit et tantus ventus descendit quod luminaria ardere non possunt" (Dupont 1880: entry 385). The roof is so damaged that it rains during services, and the wind extinguishes the candles, making it impossible for the priest to conduct services. As for the roof of Littry church, it suffers indignities of another sort. In 1410, Fr. Jean Bequet, local priest, is fined for playing tennis on the roof of Saint-Germain de Littry. He is typical of many in the register in that he is a recidivist: in 1413 he is arrested again for playing tennis, this time on top of Littry monastery.[17] It is the spiritual state of the clergy itself that is most startling in these records. The local priests and rectors are frequently and repeatedly cited for infractions more troubling than illicit tennis: keeping concubines despite repeated fines, having children, seducing the wives and especially the widows of the parish, chronic drunkenness, and brawling.

From 1314 to 1399, an eighty-five-year period, we find twelve rape and attempted rape cases.[18] The figure is low, doubtless because in the Middle Ages, as in our own day, many rapes go unreported. In ten of the twelve trials, the accused rapists are churchmen. They belong to one of two classes. The first consists of young clerics, who undertake collective rape almost as if it were a sexual rite of passage.[19] We know that the medieval church is more lenient than the state in its dealings with rapists; it is not therefore surprising to discover the leniency with which the church courts try their own representatives in rape cases.

On August 12, 1314, four clerics: Colin de Neuilly, Raoul Roger, Jean Onfrey, and Henri Goie, alias le Panetier, are convicted of the collective rape of a widow, la Gogueree de Littry (Dupont 1880: entries 6 and 7). Sentence: Colin is fined twenty-five sous. Because Colin is poor, his father, Pierre, pays the fine. Raoul is fined twenty-five pounds. The fine is paid by Raoul's father, Richard Roger, who states that he does not want his son to be in debt. Richard Roger also pays the twenty-five pound fine of Jean Onfrey.[20] Sexual assault appears to be less shameful than financial debt in fourteenth-century Normandy: these fathers step forward to pay for their sons' collective attack.

While the Cerisy register is too incomplete to establish any systematic table of fines, it does allow us to compare fines levied in the same year for nonsexual crimes. Jean de Altovillari, rector of Littry church, is fined ten pounds for frequenting taverns (entry 9h). Guillaume de Tomeris, rector and master of Littry school, is fined one hundred sous for flogging a student, Philippe Malherbe (entry 18b). The student is fined ten pounds for retaliating in kind. A comparison of all fines levied in 1314 indicates that the church is less concerned about rape than other forms of misconduct.

In 1399, Geoffroi and Pierre, known as "Les Guillours," clerics and first cousins, are held for the collective rape of Katherine, wife of Guillaume Goubert (entry 3731). Fine: fifteen pounds. As in the 1314 trial, the fathers of the young men step forward to pay their fine. In this case, the two fathers are themselves brothers, a fact that raises questions about the role of sexual violence in the family structure. The fine is relatively heavy for a rape charge, perhaps because the Guillors are notorious recidivists known for terrorizing these hamlets. By way of comparison to fines for nonsexual crimes, we can point out that in the same year, Jeanne, wife of Yvon Anglici, cleric, and Philippote, wife of Geoffroy de Cantely, cleric, will be fined ten pounds for insulting one another (entry 374). (The fining of these two women is all the more ironic as, according to canon law, Yvon and Geoffroy are the ones who should be punished, for being married clerics.)

These collective rapes give the impression of being youthful crimes. But patterns in the record indicate that when young clerics eventually become priests and rectors, they continue to practice sexual violence and constitute the second largest group of rapists in the Cerisy jurisdiction. Given the power of their office, they practice sexual abuses with even greater impunity.[21] One example will suffice to illustrate the complicity of the church in the misconduct of its priests. On September 20, 1339, Richard Quesnel, rector of the church of Saint Marcoule, broke into the house of Mathilde la Chanteresse and, with the aid of an accomplice, raped her daughter (entry 205). The court's pronouncement is breathtaking: "super quibus omnibus debemus conscientiam nostram informare." Sentence: none.[22] Meanwhile, as the church examines its conscience, Quesnel appears to retaliate as best he can: on the same day Mathilde la Chanteresse is charged with keeping a house of prostitution. The accusation is dismissed as false.[23]

Church sanctions against rape are more grudging than forceful. Conversely, women are punished harshly for sexual infractions and often receive heavier fines than their male partners. A striking but not atypical example is the 1391 sentencing of Bertin Quenet, for breaking into the home of Alicia, the widow of Jean Hoquet, with an accomplice and raping her (entry 363k). Quenet is fined five sous, one of the lightest fines meted out in 1391. Then, despite the fact established by the court that the men used violence to break into her home, Alicia is fined fifteen sous, three times more, for allowing the two men to have carnal knowledge of her (entry 363l).

Canon law was well known to be more lenient than civil law in the matter of rape; if rapists managed to flee to the sanctuary of churches, they could be tried in ecclesiastical courts, where the punishments were less harsh.[24] In the Middle Ages, the French state continued to maintain the Roman tradition: rape was punishable by death. Philippe de Beaumanoir, an important thirteenth-century expert on custom law in northern France, states in the *Coutumes de Beauvaisis* that the punishment for rape is the same as that reserved for the most serious crimes, such as murder and treason: to be dragged through the streets and hanged.[25]

In the case of civil law, we are able to study legal practice in a document from the 14th century (1332–1357), a summary of actual trials held in a wealthy seignorial court in Paris, the *Registre Criminel de la Justice de Saint-Martin-des-Champs à Paris*.[26] Just as the Cerisy register belies commonplace assumptions about the enlightened attitudes of the medieval church, so the Saint-Martin-des-Champs record reveals a striking contradiction between the text of the law, in these days of chivalry, and that of the courtroom.

The Saint-Martin record is far more complete and systematic than the Cerisy register. Written in the vernacular, rather than the impoverished Latin of the church scribes, it presents a more articulate representation of daily existence in fourteenth-century France. It also reveals that life in Paris was marked by preoccupations different from those of rural Normandy. The Cerisy church court is obsessed with questions of marriage and sexuality and with controlling the behavior of the clergy. The Cerisy register includes endless lists naming those husbands sleeping with someone else's wife and those priests who have children by various concubines. The focus of the Saint-Martin court is on urban crime and violence.

In a period of twenty-five years, the register lists six cases of rape.[27] In the six trials, one rapist receives the death penalty, two disappeared, and three were absolved for a variety of reasons.

The first recorded rape case is as sensational as it is moving. On July 13, 1333, Jacqueline la Cyriere is accused of luring a ten-year-old girl, Jeannette Bille-heuse, into her home to do housework. There Jacqueline helps a Lombard soldier to rape the child. The court orders not one but two sworn matrons to examine Jeannette. Their testimony is chilling: the child has been deflowered, wounded, tortured, and cruelly mutilated. Sentence: Jacqueline la Cyriere is burned at the stake. Every element indicates that the seignorial court took Jacqueline's complicity with the utmost seriousness. However, there is no mention of the Lombard soldier.

The second rape case in the Saint-Martin records suggests again that the seignorial court does take the rape of minors seriously. On January 21, 1337, Jean Agnes, tailor, is accused of deflowering two twelve-year-old girls, Perrete de Lusarche and Perrete la Souplice, both apprentices in a relative's care. The tailor is dragged through the streets and hanged, in strict accordance with the law. Jean Agnes is the only man, in this record, to receive the death penalty for rape. It is likely in this, as in the sentencing of Jacqueline la Cyriere, that the court prosecuted to the full extent of the law because of the tender age of the little girls.

A 1342 case is remarkable by all accounts. On September 29, Jean Pinart is taken into custody, accused of the rape of Jeannette, daughter of Pierre Legage. The court orders a sworn matron to examine the girl. The sworn matron, Emmeline La Duchesse (who figures repeatedly in the twenty-five-year register), reports that Jeannette had been deflowered and raped in the past week to ten days. Pinart is absolved. The court offers no comment. Even the laconic Louis Tanon, who edited and published these records in 1877, cannot resist stating: "Cette affaire est remarquable en ce que l'accusé est absous malgré la précision des faits dénoncés contre lui et le rapport de la matrone jurée quis semblait confirmer la dénonciation" (Tanon 1883:188, note 2).

In the last Saint-Martin case, the accused had been arrested by the King's men in Paris. On March 10, 1340, Angelot Burde, Lombard, is brought from Châtelet prison and tried for the deflowering of Ennesot La Brissete. Emmeline la Duchesse testifies that Ennesot is healthy and intact. Based on la Duchesse's testimony, the accusation is judged slanderous and Ennesot la Brissete can now be fined for damages.

The French seignorial court, known for its stringent rape law, much harsher than the fines and jail sentences of the church court at Cerisy, seems reluctant to prosecute. Because of the severity of the penalty, punishment is rarely meted out. It could be argued that the state courts in France deem human life precious and feel capital punishment to be unchristian. But in comparing the convictions and sentencing of rape trials with those of other crimes, we discover a surprising corollary to minimal rape sentencing. In the years 1332–1338, 18 of the 203 men brought (on any charge) before the court receive the death penalty (1.97 percent); 10 of the 39 women brought before the court receive the death penalty (7.7 percent). The figures available from the Saint-Martin register, limited though they are, clearly suggest that women, who commit far fewer crimes, receive the death penalty three times more frequently than men.

Punishments for nonsexual crimes by women are literally barbaric: the death penalty for women is not hanging, which would be an offense to their female modesty, but burial alive (for lesser offenses) or burning at the stake (for grave offenses).[28] In March 1340, Angelot Burde was absolved for raping Ennesot La Brissete. In August of that same year Perrete Cotelle was buried alive for stealing 57 "mailles blanches de 8 deniers"; in December of the same year Phelipote La Monine was buried alive for stealing nine ounces of silk, and in that same month of December Perrete d'Avenant was buried alive for stealing a dress and a purse. In September 1342 Jehan Pinart is inexplicably absolved of rape, perhaps out of Christian charity or perhaps through plea bargaining. In that same month Ameline La Soufletiere is buried alive for the theft of a man's purple cloak.[29]

The Saint-Martin register indicates that medieval French law was interpreted to support a long-standing tradition of indifference to the violation of a woman's sexuality and personality.[30] Conversely, the Saint-Martin court punishes women consistently and to the full extent of the law. Slow to protect and quick to punish, this society gives every sign that it values female life less than male.

Turning from the question of the application of the law, we must examine the language and composition of the records. The notion that the texts of criminal records demand analysis and interpretation is borne out by the presence of "fictive elements" in historical documents. Recently historians have begun to study the fictional or literary qualities of archival documents and discover the extent to which authors give narrative shape to the events of a crime.[31] The medieval courtroom records examined here are fictional to the extent that they are the compositions of clerks who could choose which words would be recorded verbatim, what statements would be summarized, what language would be used to summarize them, and what phrases would represent the things actually said and done in court. The court records bear witness to the discursive practices of law clerks in fourteenth-century France. As such, they call for interpretation.

Scrupulous attention to rape rhetoric in Venetian court records demonstrates that, in the early fourteenth century especially, the language used to report rape in Venetian records is "curiously distant and antiseptic." Ruggiero argues that such laconic reportage made minimal penalties easier to impose: "A close physical description of what individual rapes entailed might well have added considerable weight to the . . . penalties."[32]

The ecclesiastic court of Cerisy also reveals a curiously technical and cursory tone in its description of rape trials. Is it because the court notaries struggle with the constraints of a Latin they master very poorly? The vividness of entries describing violent fights and tavern brawls suggests that the court recorder could shine in flashes of poetry and drama when the case managed to catch his attention (394k, r).

The first quality the reader notices in the Cerisy rape entries is that of clinical distance. In the collective rape by the Guillour brothers, the clerk antiseptically notes: "Unus in presencia alterius carnaliter cognovisse, et hoc perpetrando unus alterum scienter adjuvit" [they knew her carnally, each in the presence of the other, and in this way each helped the other perform better.] (3731). In 1391 the recorder eschews any terms referring to the violence of an assault by two men *(raptus,* for example, or *violenter)* and sparely notes that Bertin Quenet: "infra domum relicte J de nocte intrasse contra voluntatem ejus et jacuisse cum ipsa, et Johannes Guellin secum" [went into the house of Jean Hoquet's widow at night and lay with her against her will, and the same for Jean Guellin] (363k). Again, the notary avoids any term connoting force and chooses the more neutral "iacere" (to lie with).

The second quality we notice in the rape entries is a vagueness so consistent that it eventually raises the suspicion that the resulting ambiguity is deliberate. One example is the frequent use of the verb "volere" (to want to), not only in attempted rapes but in almost all the attacks: "volebat dictus Ricardus filiam dicte Matilidis suponere vi et violencia et quod debuit frangere domum dicte Matilidis . . ." (205). Fr. Richard Quesnel went to the trouble of finding an accomplice to break into the girl's home, but the presence of "volebat" casts doubt on the seriousness of the attack.

The tendency to minimalize descriptions of sexual violence will be equally pronounced in the fifteenth century. In 1405 a case that includes all the elements of an attempted rape is reported as a simple break-and-enter incident: Guillaume Vitart, cleric, is arrested for breaking a side window and entering the home of the widow of Richard de Fourmegni at night (383c). What is left unsaid is that widows are the most frequent victims of rape in these communities, unprotected as they are by father or husband. The court notary remains complicitously silent as to the intention of Richard. In 1413, the attack by Pierre le Prevost, cleric, is described in vague terms: He violently entered the home of Guillaume le Guillor, where he attacked Guillaume's sister, Agnes, with his knife, wounding her several times "quod predicta Agnes voluntati sue consentire nolebat" (because the aforesaid Agnes would not agree to do his will). The scribe coyly refuses to say what it was that Agnes refused to consent to do with this man who broke into her home and stabbed her repeatedly. The cleric is fined five sous, a derisory sum in this year in which Yvon Anglici is fined five sous for throwing a loaf of bread at Pierre Siart's head (3941).

The major features of rape entries in the Cerisy records are laconism and ambiguous vagueness. The stylistic habits of the court secretary could be attributed to any number of complex factors: judicial, linguistic, material, geographic, or psychosocial. But this survey would not be complete without noting that in 1373 Etienne Bernart, rector of Littry church, listed as *notarius curie nostre,* our court notary, is arrested and fined for the rape of Guillemete de Costentino (235a, 292).

In the same year that the court notary is arrested for rape, we discover one exception to the rule of stylistic vagueness in the Cerisy register. It deserves mention because it is strikingly similar to the linguistic habits we will encounter in the Saint-Martin register. In 1369 an extremely curious entry states that two men are fined for the seduction and possible rape (the entry is ambiguous) of a minor (245a and b). Etienne de Molendino and Guillaume le Deen, priest of Littry, are accused in unusual terms, perhaps because their case involves a young girl. The scribe troubles himself to record the words of the witnesses. The mother of the girl testifies that Etienne de Molendino, sitting by the fire, took her daughter in his arms and seduced her with the following words: "Mea pulcra netis, ego dabo tibi unam tunicam burelli mei" [my lovely little child, I will give you one of my burlap gowns]. This "text" is striking in that the blandishments echo distinctly those of the knight in the thirteenth-century pastourelles.

> *Douce bergerete,*
> *soiies m'amiete,*
> *je vos donrai de brunete*
> *cote trainant. . . .*
> *Tot maintenant l'acolai.*[33] (Bartsch 1967, vol. 3, text 23,
>   lines 17–20 and 45)

[Sweet little shepherdess, be my little love, I will give you a long cloak of brunete,[34] that sweeps the ground. . . . And without further ado I kissed her].

In the same 1369 entry, Jean Alain testifies that he heard Guillaume, the priest, sitting by the fire, using similarly lyrical words of seduction: "Pulcra neptis, oscula me, et ego dabo tibi unam tunicam burelli mei quando factum fuerit." [Lovely child, kiss me, and I will give you one of my burlap gowns when it is done]. It is as if the priest were humming scraps of a popular song or the court scribe were remembering a pastourelle:

> *bele, vostre amor demant. . . .*
> *por ce vos proi et apel*
> *que vos faciez mon voloir,*
> *et je vos donrai mantel*
> *de brunete taint en noir . . .* (Bartsch 1967, vol. 2, text 64,
> lines 18, 40–43)

[Beauty, I am asking for your love . . . That is why I ask and beg that you do as I say, and I will give you a cloak of brunete].

Could popular songs offer the linguistic paradigm for the tolerance of sexual violence? Sentence for Molendino and Le Deen: none noted.

It would seem that we have come upon discursive structures existing prior to the event in the minds of the fourteenth-century participants: "possible story lines determined by the constraints of the law and approaches to narrative learned in past listening to and telling of stories or derived from other cultural constructions."[35]

That court clerks consider themselves to be writers, just as surely as the authors of the pastourelles, is clear when we turn again to the *Registre de Saint-Martin*. In reading through these trials we find a tendency quite opposite to the practices of the Cerisy churchmen. Unlike the records of Cerisy, the rape trials of Saint-Martin seem to inspire the professional scribes to their greatest literary efforts. Many of the rape accounts in civil records show unusual attention to narrative development, to the reproduction of direct discourse, and to chilling detail. The scribes cast their texts in the stylistic and narrative codes available to them in their culture.

In the *Registre de Saint-Martin*, Ymbelot Roussel, the court recorder, enters most trials in an economical fashion: three to six sentences can describe the prisoner's arrest, the charges, the testimony, and the sentencing. But in entries recording a rape trial, the character of the writing is transformed. The record goes on for one, two, or three pages; the scribe plays with direct discourse and describes details of the rape scene with a literary effort that appears in no other type of case.

In the 1333 trial of Jacqueline La Cyriere, the court clerk records in fascinated detail the gestures, conversations, and movements involved (Tanon 1883: 40–43). With a theatrical flourish, the scribe shows how Jacqueline sets her perfidious trap for the child, sitting on the stoop of her father's house: "La vint ladicte Jacqueline, qui la prinst par la main et lui dist: Vien si, me soufle mon feu, et laveras mes escuelles" [there came the said Jacqueline, who took (the girl) by the hand and said to her, "Come along with me, you can tend my fire and wash my dishes].

The scribe vividly relates how Jacqueline and the soldier forced the child to drink a "vile green potion" intended to render her mute and threatened her life if ever she told what had happened. It is as if the scribe suddenly felt inspired to compose a text with suspense, drama, and detail.

In the case of Jehan Pinart, tried for deflowering a thirteen-year-old girl, the scribe creates a flourish of drama and a suspenseful pause in the narration of what must have been an agony for Jehan-nete Le Gage. The secretary describes how Pinart drags her into his room and throws her on his bed. She screams so loudly that he stuffs his cape in her mouth. She struggles so effectively that he cannot completely violate her on the bed. He drags her to another room and pulls her onto a table in the hope of gaining better traction. Here the poet-scribe pauses: "Et la, sys ycelle table, la corrompy et despucela tout oultre" (Tanon 187) [and there, on that very table, he corrupts her and deflowers her completely]."

Even more striking than the rhetorical flourishes of the Saint-Martin records is the way in which they, like Fr. Guillaume le Deen and his friend, seem to rework the language of popular medieval song. The Saint-Martin trials focus on the same elements found in the pastourelle rapes: the rapist's effort to pull the woman to the ground, the victim's cries for help, the names of the garments that are pulled away, the rapist's attempts to silence the victim, the necessity of force to violate the victim. In the trial of Jacqueline la Cyriere the scribe focusses on the physical force required of the impatient Italian soldier:

> . . . et la geta sur un lit, et s'efforça de gesir aveques lui, et entra entre ses jambes. Et pour ce que il seul ne pot faire son vouloir, et que elle croiot trop fort, ladicte Jaccqueline vint . . . et adonques ledit Lombart la geta jus, et entre entre ses jambe, et hurta contre sa nature, et s'efforça de entrer en lui. (Tanon 1883:41–42)

[. . . he threw her on a bed, and forced her to lie with him, and entered between her legs. And because he could not do his will alone, and because she cried out very loudly, the said Jacqueline came . . . thereupon the said Lombard threw her down, and entered between her legs, and hurled himself against her private parts, and forced himself into her.

The construction of that text is not unlike the thirteenth-century pastourelle "Chevachai mon chief enclin" [I went riding, my head bowed], which offers the same configuration of narrative details:

Ne vo plux a li tencier,
ains l'ai sor l'erbe getee;
maix as jambes desploier
lai fut grande la criee.
Haute crie goule beee. (Bartsch 1967, vol 2, text 4, lines 49–53)

[I did not want to quarrel with her anymore, so I threw her on the grass; but when I tried to pull her legs apart, oh, what a cry she let out. At the top of her lungs she cried aloud.]

In the trial of Jehannin Agnes, the record portrays the gestures of the rapist as he brutalizes the twelve-year-old girl:

Là, en un selier, fist entrer, oultre son gré et par force, ladicte
Perrete La souplice, et al jeta à terre, et avala see braies, et se mist
sus lui, et s'efforça contre sa nature tant comme il pot, et pour ce
que elle crioit, il la bati et feri, et la laissa. (Tanon 1883:88)

[There in a cellar he forced her to go, against her will and by force, the said Perrete La Souplice. He threw her to the ground, and pulled down her underwear, and got on top of her, and forced himself against her private parts as hard as he could. And because she cried out, he beat her, struck her, and left her there].

Thirteenth-century songs could have presented a ready paradigm for an archetypal rape scene, like "En mai la rosee que nest la flor" [In May, at dawn, when the flower springs forth]:

Quant vi que proiere ne m'i vaut noient,
couchai la a terre   tout maintenant,
levai li le chainse,
si vi la char si blanche
tant fui je plus ardant;
fis li la folie . . . (Bartsch 1967, vol. 2, text 62, lines 25–30)

[When I saw that my prayers were worthless, I laid her down on the ground right away, lifted her shirt, and saw her flesh so white that I burned all the more. I did the trick to her.]

Could it be that the pastourelles offer preexisting linguistic materials of which the court scribe builds his own text?

We already noted the poetic efforts of the scribe in the case of Jehannete, the thirteen-year-old who fought Jehan Pinart so fiercely. The text goes on:

La prist par la main et la mena en sa chambre, et la geta sus son lit, et se efforça de la despuceller; et que ce que elle crioit harou, lui avoit mis son chapperon sus sa bouche, afin que l'en ne l'oïst crier. (Tanon 187)

[He took her by the hand and led her into his room, and threw her on his bed, and tried to take her virginity. And because she called for help, he put his hood in her mouth, so that no one would hear her scream.]

The thirteenth-century pastourelle entitled "Quant voi la flor nouvele" [When I See a Fresh Flower] sketched out the poetic rape of a thirteen-year-old who resists her attacker angrily:

*Pris la par la main nue,
mis la seur l'erbe drue;
ele s'escrie et jure
que de mon geu n'a cure.
"Ostez vostre lecheure,
dex la puist honir;
car tant m'est asprete et dure
ne la puis soufrir."* (Bartsch 1967, vol. 2, text 67, lines 33–40)

[I took her by her bare hand, put her on the green grass; She cried out and swore that she did not care for my game. "Leave your lechery, may God put it to shame; so harsh and rough is it that I cannot bear it.]

After the rape in "When I See a Fresh Flower," the girl gets on her feet and cries out that she is thirteen years old (line 53).

The Saint-Martin records reveal a poetic troping of rape reminiscent of that of the pastourelles. The daily spectacle of violence against women is made tolerable and even compelling as it is made literary. Like the popular songs that inscribe rape as poetic, the legal representation of rape detracts from its brutality through its literariness and engages the imagination of a society that seeks to justify violence against women in a number of ways. Ymbelot Roussel, the court scribe in Saint-Martin, seeks to be identified with the inscription of violence against women, for he twice signs his name to the records with a flourish: autograph and paraph. When Philippote la Monine is sentenced to execution for theft in 1340, he takes the unusual step of writing: "Procès fait par Robert Neveu, notre maire, et je. Y. Roussel." When Perrete Cotelle is also sentenced to death for theft in 1340, we read: "Procès en a esté fait par moy, Y. Roussel."

In the Cerisy records, the scribe minimalizes the representation of rape almost to the point of dismissing its violent character, through clinical and distant summary. Such a discourse makes it easier, as Ruggiero argues for Venice, to lighten sentencing. In the Saint-Martin register, the text works to make images of violence against women tolerable by troping them poetically. Medieval law, like medieval literature, creates a generous space for the cultivation of discursive strategies that rationalize male violence against women.

Is literary rape pure imaginative sign, or is it related in some way, whether psychological, symbolic, or ideological, to the sexual behaviors and practices of a society? This study of legal writing shows that figures of literary discourse travel, move, and can be reemployed and reinvested. Linguistic paradigms first identified in lyric texts reappear in legal documents, reconverted but bearing an equal affective weight. Poetry, song, story, all can offer men and women, judges, lawyers, plaintiffs, the words to circumscribe and perhaps institutionalize experiences that are complex and difficult to comprehend. To this extent it is necessary to acknowledge the direct relation between literary discourse and the world of deeds. When translated into a discursive domain such as the legal document or the courtroom hearing, poetic topoi and narrative paradigms can affect the way acts are perceived, authorized, or penalized. Such linguistic fragments, such "pure poetry," can be come the tools of judgment and power.

NOTES

An initial version of this article was presented at the Congress of Medieval Studies at Kalamazoo, Michigan, in May 1986, and I am grateful to Roberta Krueger for her invitation. I wish to thank James Brundage for his careful reading, bibliographical suggestions, and his invaluable seminar on women, family, and law in the Middle Ages, conducted at the Newberry Library,

Chicago, during the winter of 1986. I also thank Guy Mermier and the Medieval and Renaissance Collegium of the University of Michigan for enabling me to participate in that seminar. Early drafts could not have been written without the help of Katharine Jensen. E. B. Vitz was generous with her ideas and a valuable interlocutor, even when our interpretations of these texts differed.

1. In 1964 Georges Duby published an important article in *Annales* 19: "Les 'Jeunes' dans la société aristocratique dans la France du Nord-ouest au douzième siècle," later reprinted in *Hommes et structures du Moyen Age* (The Hague: Mouton, 1973). In 1968 a seminal revisionist article appeared by John Benton, "Clio and Venus: An Historical View of Courtly Love," in F. X. Newma, ed, *The Meaning of Courtly Love* (Albany: S.U.N.Y., 1968).

2. Joan Kelly's theory, that medieval women did have power, greater power and status than women during the Renaissance, has been challenged by the recent work of the historian Penny Schine Gold. See *The Lady and the Virgin: Image, Attitude, and Experience in Twelfth-Century France* (Chicago: University of Chicago Press, 1985).

3. One of the finest examples of this new literary criticism is a volume edited by E. Jane Burns and Roberta L. Krueger, *Courtly Ideology and Woman's Place in Medieval French Literature, Romance Notes* (1985), 25(3).

4. Georges Duby, *Mâle Moyen âge* (Paris: Flammarion, 1988).

5. Kathryn Gravdal, "Camouflaging Rape: The Rhetoric of Sexual Violence in the Medieval Pastourelle," *Romanic Review* (1984), 76 (4): 361–373. That article was inspired by Joan Ferrante's important article: "Male Fantasy and Female Reality in Courtly Literature," *Women's Studies* (1984), 11: 67–97. See also Kathryn Gravdal, *Ravishing Maidens: Rape in Medieval French Law and Literature* (Philadelphia: University of Pennsylvania Press, forthcoming in 1991).

6. Pierre Bec, *La Lyrique française du moyen âge (XIIe–XIIIe siècles): Contribution à une typologie des genres poétiques médiévaux* (Paris: Picard, 1977–78), p. 120.

7. The edition used here will be that of Karl Bartsch, *Romances et Pastourelles Françaises des XIIe et XIIIe Siècles* (1870; reprint, Darmstadt: Wissenschaftliche Buchgesellschaft, 1967), p. 187. All translations mine. See also William D. Paden, ed., *The Medieval Pastourelle*, vols. 1 and 2 (New York and London: Garland Publishing, 1987), which includes avatars of the French pastourelle in Latin, English, German, and Italian and antecedents in other languages.

8. William Paden, Jr., "Rape in the Pastourelle," *Romanic Review*, forthcoming.

9. See, for example, W. T. H. Jackson, "The Medieval Pastourelle as a Satirical Genre," *Philological Quarterly* (1952), vol. 11; W. Powell Jones, *The Pastourelle: A Study of the Origins and Tradition of a Lyric Type* (Cambridge: Harvard University Press, 1931); and Michel Zink, *La Pastourelle* (Paris: Bordas, 1972).

10. Guido Ruggiero, *The Boundaries of Eros: Sex Crime and Sexuality in Renaissance Venice* (Oxford: Oxford University Press, 1985), chs. 1 and 5. See also Ruggiero's earlier book: *Violence in Early Renaissance Venice* (New Brunswick: Rutgers University Press, 1980), especially ch. 10.

11. Ruggiero, *The Boundaries of Eros*, pp. 89–108.

12. James A. Brundage, "Rape and Marriage in the Medieval Canon Law," *Revue de droit canonique* (June–December 1978), 28: 62–75, and also "Rape and Seduction in the Medieval Canon Law," in Vern L. Bullough and James Brundage, eds., *Sexual Practices and the Medieval Church*, pp. 141–148 (Buffalo: Prometheus Books, 1982).

13. *Corpus Iuris Canonici*, ed. E. Friedberg, 2 vols. (Leipzig, 1879), (Causa 36, quaestio 1, dictum post capitulum 25.

14. "Fame esforcier si est quand aucuns prent a force charnel compaignie a fame contre la volenté de la fame et seur ce qu'ele fet son pouoir du defendre," no. 829, p. 130; "Quiconques est pris en cas de crime et atains du cas, si comme de murtre, ou de traïson, ou d'homicide, ou de fame esforcier, il doit estre trainés et pendus et si mesfet quanqu'il a vaillant, et vient la forfeture au seigneur dessous qui li siens est trouvés et en a chascuns sires ce qui en est trouvé en sa seignourie," no. 824, p. 129, both in Philippe de Beaumanoir, *Coutumes de Beauvaisis*, ed. A. Salmon (1899–1900; reprint, Paris: A. & J. Picard, 1970).

15. *Corpus Iuris Canonici*, Causa 36, quaestio 2, capitulum 1 and 4. On the newly revived custom of marriage to the victim as penance, see Simon Kalifa, "Singularités matrimoniales chez les anciens germains: le rapt et le droit de la femme à disposer d'elle-même," *Revue Historique de droit français et étranger*, 4th ser. (1970), 48: 199–225, and also Pierre Lemercier, "Une curiosité judiciaire au moyen âge: la grâce par mariage subséquent," *Revue Historique de droit français et étranger*, 4th ser. (1955), 33: 464–474.

16. M. G. Dupont, *Le Registre de l'Officialité de Cerisy 1314–1457*, in *Mémoires de la Société des antiquaires de Normandie* 3rd ser. (1880), 10: 271–662. English translations mine. Further citations appear in text. For a useful study (although filled with incorrect references) of sexual behavior in the Cerisy records, see Jean-Luc Dufresne, "Les Comportements amoureux d'après le *Registre de l'Officialité de Cerisy*," *Bulletin Philologique et Historique*, (1973): 131–156.

17. "... luserant ad palman supra ecclesiam de Listreyo" (3901). "... luderant ad palmam supra monasterium de Listreyo" (394d).

18. Entries 3; 6–7; 150; 188b; 205; 235b and d; 245a and b; 292 and 293; 363k and l; 3731; 383c; 394c.

19. On collective assault as a rite of initiation in the French Middle Ages, see Jacques Rossiaud, "Prostitution, Youth, and Society in the Towns of Southeastern France in the Fifteenth Century," in Robert Forster and Orest Ranum, eds., *Deviants and the Abandoned in French Society*, pp. 1–46 (Baltimore: Johns Hopkins University Press, 1978).

20. The livre or pound was originally a measure of silver weighing one pound. It is impossible to fix the value of these sums in the High Middle

Ages, but one pound (livre tournois) was worth approximately twenty sous (although a livre parisis was worth twenty-five sous). One sou was worth twelve deniers, and one denier was worth two mailles, a small brass coin.

21. Dufresne, "Les Comportements amoureux," pp. 149–53.

22. In his preface, Dupont himself expresses surprise over this case for, "d'après les aveux même des coupables": the attackers' sole goal was the rape of the daughter.

23. Dufresne, "Les Comportements amoureux," p. 143.

24. See Brundage, "Rape and Marriage," p. 63. Dufresne shows that the fines levied by the Cerisy court are rare and light: "de 5 à 10 sous en général, pas plus que pour un soufflet ou une injure" (p. 151).

25. Beaumanoir, Coutumes de Beauvaisis, entry 824, p. 129.

26. Louis Tanon, Registre criminel de Saint-Martin-des-Champs, in Histoire des Justices des Anciennes Eglises et Communautés Monastiques de Paris (Paris: Larose et Forcel, 1883), pp. 455–556.

27. 13 July 1333; 21 January 1337; 23 February 1338; 20 April 1338; 10 March 1340; 29 September 1342.

28. "Enfouissement," or burial alive, is the official penalty for repeated larceny, but it is applied to women only. See Tanon's introduction, Registre Criminel de Saint-Martin-des-Champs, pp. xciii–xcvi.

29. 11 August 1340; 7 December 1340; 11 December 1340; 12 September 1342.

30. Ruggiero reaches similar conclusions in studying Renaissance Venice (The Boundaries of Eros, p. 108).

31. Nathalie Zemon Davis, Fiction in the Archives: Pardon Tales and Their Tellers in Sixteenth-Century France (Stanford: Stanford University Press, 1987), p. 105. Davis looks at the rhetorical crafting of pardon letters and also compares them to literary texts of the sixteenth century.

32. Ruggiero, The Boundaries of Eros, p. 90.

33. It is not until Guillemete de Costentino married one Colin Osmont that she comes forward to tell her story, a factor that may have weakened her case.

34. The garment mentioned here and frequently in the pastourelles, "mantel de brunete," is a luxury item, made of an expensive fabric, tinted not quite black. Godefroy points out that it was worn by "gens de qualité" and that councils frequently prohibited the wearing of a "mantel de brunete" by monks (Frédéric Godefroy, Dictionnaire de l'ancienne langue française (Paris, 1880; New York: Kraus Reprint, 1961], 1: 747). Indeed, the men of Cerisy promise the girl a coat of burelli, or burlap.

35. Davis, Fiction in the Archives, p. 4.

10

Rape's Disfiguring Figures: Marguerite de Navarre's *Heptameron*, Day 1: 10

CARLA FRECCERO

... which is exactly like South Africa penetrating, so to speak, into Namibia penetrating into Angola.
June Jordan, "Poem About My Rights," p. 87

A revolutionary act!? Shiiiiiiit. Don't be gettin' back at the hunky by rapin' Sisters, and kinda Sisters.
Carlene Hatcher Polite,
Sister X and the Victims of Foul Play, pp. 55–56

These epigraphs by Black feminist women in the United States underscore the complex political and economic meanings with which "rape" is invested. June Jordan depicts Pretoria's imperialist invasion of the frontline states as a rape. She implicitly connects the political and aesthetic meanings of representation suggested in Craig Owens' discussion of representation as aesthetic practice:

> Among those prohibited from Western representation, whose representations are denied all legitimacy, are women. Excluded from representation by its very structure, they return within it as a figure for—a representation of—the unrepresentable (Nature, Truth, the Sublime, etc.). This prohibition bears primarily on woman as the subject, and rarely as the object of representation, for there is certainly no shortage of images of women. Yet in being represented by, women have been rendered an absence within the dominant culture.[1]

For women, suggests Jordan, as for Black southern Africans, "rape" is the experience of the inability to represent themselves. "Rape" is not rape if its victim can be portrayed as territory to be colonized, as "consenting," as somehow "wrong" ("then I consented and there was / no rape because finally you understand finally / they fucked me over because I was wrong I was / wrong again to be me being me where I was / wrong / to be who I am"), nor is there rape without "proof" ("I mean how do you know if / Pretoria ejaculates what will the evidence look like"), and proof, she demonstrates, depends, for its visibility (its representability) on the colonizer-subject's representation.[2] Her poem brings the "dark continent" of female sexuality and Black southern Africa into lucid alignment to point out that gender and class/race oppressions are political oppression and that political oppression is, like rape, a matter of representation.

Carlene Hatcher Polite directs her critique toward the specifically sexual politics of rape. She points out the absurdity of a masculinist revolutionary politics that forgets its solidarity with the oppressed ("Sisters, and kinda Sisters") and accepts the terms of phallocracy in its definition of women as symbolic objects in a masculine economy. These women, whose legal power of representation depends on the eradication of both phallocratic and racial oppression, represent violation as rape in order to reappropriate its definition and thus to demystify its political force as symbolic action performed upon the bodies of women.[3]

Roy Porter, in a collection of articles titled *Rape*, asks the question: "Does Rape Have a Historical Meaning?" and concludes that, differently from its contemporary all-pervasive presence, ". . . rape has flourished mainly on the margins; at the frontiers, in colonies, in states of war and in states of nature . . . Rape has also erupted on the psycho-margins, amongst loners, outsiders, who fail to be encultured into normal patriarchal sex."[4]

Porter's argument suggests that, historically and legally, "rape" does not become politicized until patriarchal control is itself destabilized to the extent that direct violence becomes a necessary means of maintaining dominion. As an isolated occurrence socially regarded as violation (theft), rape defines its perpetrator as an unassimilable element to be purged from patriarchal society. Porter thus qualifies some feminists' view of rape as systematic patriarchal terrorization by noting patriarchal society's historical collusion in the criminalization of rape.

The historical account of rape based on a legislative definition of the term articulates the position of the patriarchal subject from within patriarchal society. But just as Jordan and Polite tell a very different story with respect to the patriarchalism of the colonizer and the revolutionary, so too may we expect to find, in history, representations of "rape" marked by nonhegemonic subject-positions. For as Jordan notes, the experienced violation may not figure as "rape" in the privileged subject's (legal) representation of what constitutes such violation. Porter says that in "listening for rape fears in the past, we are surprisingly often met by silence" (p. 222) in reference to nineteenth-century feminist writings. In the spirit of skeptical inquiry, I would like to analyze an early modern representation of (attempted) rape that articulates within a hegemonic ideology similar to that of Porter (Western patriarchalism), but also inscribes feminine difference. What happens when the subject of representation, although not deliberately counterhegemonic, as in the case of Jordan and Polite, is, nevertheless, a woman?

Marguerite de Navarre, a sixteenth-century aristocratic author, foregrounds the issue of representation in the matter of rape, where rape constitutes an extreme moment in the politics of courtly love.[5] She stages a feminine narration of a story of failed seduction; the narrative itself alternates viewpoints between the knight's and the lady's perspectives. The story is told to a mixed audience; they respond to it in predictably and significantly gender-marked fashions. This dialogic approach disarticulates the ideology of courtly love by opening up a space within it for feminine perspectives to be heard.[6] Ultimately, however, those perspectives remain divided, leaving unresolved the ideological contradictions exposed by the dialogism of the discourse.

Courtly love has always figured power relations in sociopolitical terms, from Capellanus' scenarios classified according to the class positions of lover and beloved to Jean de Meun's image of the lady as fortress to be assailed. There is social inequality between knight and lady and oedipal rivalry between landless youth and noble lord. Marc Bloch, though inattentive to the fact that, in the courtly relation, gender difference complicates class inequalities, suggests this in commenting that "when the Provençal poets invented courtly love, the devotion of the vassal to his lord was the model on which they based their conception of the fealty of the perfect lover. This fitted the fact that the lover was often of lower social rank than the lady of his dreams."[7]

Renaissance discourses of courtliness, while frequently evoking "woman," begin to expose courtly ideology as a political program for class relations among men and often use the idiom of sexual politics to figure masculine political struggles. It is no accident that, in the sixteenth century the *querelle des femmes* coincides with a period of nation-state consolidation in France and redistribution of political power in the Italian city-states.[8] Castiglione's *Courtier* focuses on the codified relation between courtier/knight and lady as a figure for the relation between the courtier and his prince.[9] In the third book, examples of feminine resistance to rape function allegorically to designate a course of action for courtiers struggling against tyrants.[10] One example of such an allegorization uses the topos of woman as fortress to make a political point about "retainers of princes," or courtiers:

> ... there is no fortress so unassailable that, were it attacked with a thousandth part of the weapons and wiles as are used to overcome the constancy of a woman, it would not surrender at the first assault. How many retainers of princes, made rich by them and held in the greatest esteem, who were in command of fortresses and strongholds on which that prince's state and life and every good depended, without shame or any fear of being called traitors, have perfidiously and for gain surrendered those to persons who were not to have them? ... And again how many do the vilest things from fear of death! And yet a tender and delicate girl often resists all these fierce and strong assaults, for many have been known who chose to die rather than to lose their chastity.[11]

The comparison elides fundamental asymmetries between the retainer's situation and that of the girl; the former may yield for gain, whereas the latter, in doing so, loses whatever status she may originally have had. The appeal to courtiers to exhibit the courage of a virgin exposes the third book's *querelle des femmes* as a discourse about political power, with rape glorified as the proving ground for the resistance of the feminized powerless.

In the longest novella of the *Heptameron* and one that, writes Marcel Tetel, constitutes "un microcosme de l'oeuvre entière" Marguerite de Navarre reanimates the politics of courtly love, not by figuring the relation as an allegory for other power relations, but by focusing on sexual politics in juxtaposition with the warrior ethos of political struggle among men.[12] By articulating the perspectives of both the subject and object of representation in courtly discourse, she exploits contradictions in the discourse that lead to a narrative and discursive impasse.

The tenth novella is the story of a "gentil homme," Amadour, who has all the qualities of a perfect knight: he is beautiful, graceful, eloquent, and a brave warrior. He falls in love with a noblewoman, Floride, who is only twelve at the time. He decides to love her, though he knows he could never marry her, for she is far above him in social station. He insinuates himself into her household by marrying her lady-in-waiting, Avanturade, declares his love, and becomes her "loyal serviteur." She in turn accepts him as her "amy," who, of course, will respect her honor. Their relationship continues over time, he performing valiant deeds in battle, she doing virtuous work at home. Her mother, the countess, marries her to someone she does not love, but Avanturade goes with her, so she and Amadour continue to see each other. Frontier wars between France and Spain are interspersed with visits to the duchy of Cardonne, Floride's abode. Amadour's wife dies of grief upon hearing of one of his departures, and despairing of ever seeing Floride again, Amadour feigns illness so that she will minister to him, at which point he "[begins] to pursue the path that leads to the forbidden goal of a lady's honor."[13] Floride is shocked. Amadour tries to justify his action, saying that since she is married she no longer needs to preserve her honor, then claims he was only testing her, but to no avail. She rejects him, and he leaves for battle in despair. Amadour later confesses his love to her mother, the countess, who is sympathetic.

While Amadour is away, he decides to rape Floride, because, by her rejection, she has become his enemy. He gets the countess to arrange for Floride to receive him alone in her room. Floride, meanwhile, fearing that her beauty had led him astray, disfigures her face by smashing it with a stone, hoping thereby to quell his desire for her. Amadour is intent on raping her nevertheless; the narrator, Parlamente, makes clear that his motive is hatred. Floride tells him he will not succeed and, at the crucial moment, calls out to her mother. Amadour tells the countess that he had merely attempted to kiss her hand and in the face of Floride's silence her mother believes him, so much so that she does not speak to her daughter for seven years. Floride wins her mother back with a ruse that causes Amadour to court another woman and thus appear unfaithful.

Finally, unable to persuade Floride to love him, Amadour goes off to war, this time seeming more reckless than brave. The Spanish army is defeated; Amadour rescues the Count of Arande (Floride's father) and sends the corpse of the Duke of Cardonne (Floride's husband) back to his home. Rather than be captured, he preserves his honor by falling on his sword. The newly widowed Floride, in turn, retreats to a convent, where she remains till her death.

Amadour, whose courtly posture is at first perfect (too perfect, according to Marcel Tetel, who reads Marguerite's hyperbolic praise as irony 1971: 199) experiences an abrupt turnaround when Floride frustrates his first attempt to consummate their love. While at war, he "devised his grand scheme—not a scheme to win back Floride's heart, for he deemed her lost forever, but a scheme to score a victory over her as his mortal enemy, for that was how she now appeared" (p. 145). The scene of the attempted rape depicts him in terms of the physiognomy of anger: "His whole expression, his face, his eyes, had changed as he spoke. The fair complexion was flushed with fiery red. The kind, gentle face was contorted with a terrifying violence, as if there was some raging inferno belching fire in his heart and behind his eyes. One powerful fist roughly seized hold of her two weak and delicate hands." (p. 147) It is all the more surprising then when, during the frame discussion, Hircan comments, "And as for Amador, if he'd been more of a lover and less of a coward, he wouldn't have been quite so easily put off . . . I still maintain that no man who loved perfectly, or who was loved by a lady, could fail in his designs, provided he went about things in a proper manner" (p. 153).

Hircan is often described as the demystificatory materialist who opposes a sensualist notion of the erotic experience to the neoplatonic transcendentalism of his wife, Parlamente, narrator of the tenth story. Yet love of a woman is clearly not the issue in the attempted rape. Hircan, in fact, interprets the story from Amadour's perspective. Jules Gelernt, in his *World of Many Loves*, inadvertently offers a clue to the puzzle when he remarks of Hircan's statement: "Such a position is that of the aggressive male who insists on the primacy of his erotic drive. The masculine code of honor Hircan espouses requires the lover to banish all fear, to use force if necessary to achieve his end; it applies to love the principles of war."[14]

In the mystified and mystifying rhetoric of the kind that Gelernt refers to as "the position of the aggressive male," war is to politics what rape is to seduction. But rather than an application of the same set of principles to two different phenomena, "love" and "war," Hircan's comment demonstrates, from the perspective of the tale itself, the inseparability of these categories as they are subsumed into the "multiplicity of force relations" that constitutes the ethos of the courtly warrior.[15] Furthermore, these force relations operate within a political economy that, in the social sphere, depends on a notion of woman-as-property, where class positions mask gender oppression.[16] "Love," the narrative suggests, is not at all that different from war in the case of knighthood. In the tenth novella the two are juxtaposed, revealing the contradictions in a chivalric ethic that would embody love and war as separate principles, producing an appearance of difference while operating according to the same logic.

Saffredent, another male member of the company, "explains" the rhetorical dissimulation of courtly practice:

> ... all the credit goes to the ladies, because they put on such haughty expressions and adopt such refined ways of speaking, that people who see nothing but their external appearance go in awe of them, and feel obliged to admire and love them. However, in private it is quite another matter. Then Love is the only judge of the way we behave, and we soon find out that they are just women, and we are just men. The title "lady" [maistresse] is soon exchanged for "mistress" [amye], and her "devoted servant" [serviteur] soon becomes her "lover" [amy]. Hence the well-known proverb: "loyal service makes the servant master." (p. 153)[17]

The displacement of class conflict onto courtly seduction and the passage from courtship (politics) to rape (war) have a long genealogy in political philosophy. The discourses of erotic pursuit and political power intersect in that most famous of Renaissance political treatises, Machiavelli's *Prince*. I cite it here, not as imputed subtext, but as a formidable branch in the textual genealogy of the figure of rape for the sixteenth century. In the penultimate chapter of *The Prince*, Machiavelli polemicizes man's relation to fortune with a striking allegory:

> Since Fortune is fickle and men are fixed in their ways, I therefore conclude that men are successful while they act harmoniously with Fortune and unsuccessful while they act inharmoniously with her. I am absolutely convinced that it is better to be impetuous than circumspect, because Fortune is a woman and you must, if you want to subjugate her, beat her and strike her. It is obvious that she is more willing to be subjugated that way than by men with cold tactics. Therefore, like a woman, she always befriends the young, since they are less circumspect and more brutal: they master her more boldly.[18]

Machiavelli's portrait of man's relation to fortune demystifies Dante's deification of Lady Fortune in canto 7 of the *Inferno*: "ma ella s'è beata e ciò non ode: / con l'altre prime creature lieta / volve sua spera e beata si gode."[19] This passage, in turn, echoes the poet's description of Beatrice in the *Vita nuova*, thus setting up a parallel between the unapproachability of Fortuna and that of the courtly beloved: "Ella si va, sentendosi laudare, / benignamente d'umiltà vestuta; / e par che sia una cosa venuta / da cielo in terra a miracol mostrare."[20] Machiavelli opposes this aristocratic notion of court-ship by proposing rape. In later versions of courtly love, persuasion replaces Dante's acceptance of the lady's unapproachability. But what Machiavelli does, through the figure of rape, is to preempt the strat-egy of persuasion with an assertion of force.[21] From politics to war-fare. In more contemporary rhetoric, "rape [is] an insurrectionary act," defined, from the rapist's perspective, in the context of class revenge.[22] Whether figuratively or literally employed, "woman's body [is] imagined as the passive terrain on which the inequalities of masculine power [are] fought out."[23]

Amadour, the perfect knight, is, from the outset, described as a potentially self-made "prince": "Although he was only 18 or 19 years of age, he had such confidence, and such sound judgement, that you could not have failed to regard him as one of those rare men fit to govern any state" (p. 122). He is also a disinherited youngest son; Parlamente underlines his status as class aspirant with eco-nomic metaphors: "avecq les dames de Barcelonne et Parpignan, . . . il avoit tel credit que peu ou riens luy estoit refusé" (p. 56).[24] One passage in particular brings the description of Amadour into the realm of a Machiavellian political economy: "But Love and Fortune, seeing him ill-provided for by his parents, and resolving to make him their paragon, bestowed upon him through the gift of virtue and valour that which the laws of the land denied him. He was experi-enced in matters of war, and much sought after by noble lords and princes. He did not have to go out of his way to ask for rewards. More often than not, he had to refuse them" (p. 124).

Love and Fortune adopt Amadour and "vertu"—that Roman no-tion of masculine prowess adopted by Machiavelli, rather than that virtue which, for Floride, consists in honor and chastity—provides him with means he would otherwise be denied.

But Amadour is a failed prince, as are all of the great Machiavel-lian exempla in *The Prince*. Up until a certain point, his strategy for advancement is politically persuasive; he consciously aims for the top and proceeds systematically toward the achievement of his am-bition:

For a long while he gazed at her. His mind was made up. He would love her. The promptings of reason were in vain. He would love her, even though she was of far higher birth than he. He would love her, even though she was not yet of an age to hear and understand the words of love. But his misgivings were as nothing against the firm hope that grew within him, as he promised himself that time and patient waiting would in the end bring his toils to a happy conclusion. (p. 123)

His marriage to Avanturade and his insinuation into the countess' good graces are all part of this strategy, as is his rhetorical eloquence, repeatedly emphasized and displayed in the narrative ("there was not a man in Spain who could express his mind more eloquently than Amador" [p. 125]). As Parlamente puts it, "he won the day" (p. 134).

Amadour's change of tactics, his attempt to seize fortune, precipitates his failure: "He made up his mind to make one last desperate gamble—to risk losing all, or to gain everything and treat himself to one short hour of the bliss that he considered he had earned" (p. 140). His is a calculated risk: "now you are a married woman. You have a cover and your honour is safe" (p. 141). In this first attempted rape of Floride, the rhetoric of courtliness begins to break down, for Floride does not participate in the masculine political economy whereby "victory" through an assertion of force preserves honor and produces glory. Against the masculine assertion that to preserve appearances is to safeguard honor, Longarine, a female member of the company, protests: "But you are not talking about true honour . . . which alone gives true contentment to this world" (p. 154). Honor is here exposed as a gendered concept that produces an impasse in the courtly relation.

Amadour's move from politics to warfare begins to undermine his rhetoric of persuasion, preventing him from successfully maintaining the distinction, so essential to his strategy, between apparent and effective motive. He betrays himself as rivalrous with the other men who possess this "female" territory, using the argument of justified reward more appropriate to the relation between vassal and lord where Floride, like property, is a gift exchanged for service:

It is I who have really won you, through the power of my love. The man who first won your heart so irresolutely pursued your body that he well deserved to lose both. As for the man who now possesses your body—he's not worthy of the smallest corner in your heart. So you do not really belong to him, even in body. But consider, my Lady, what trials and tribulations I have gone through in the last five or six years for your sake. Surely you cannot fail to realize that it is to me alone that you belong, body and heart . . ." (p. 141)

The narrative exposes the "erotic drive" in the "lover" as a commonplace in the rhetoric of seduction that masks Amadour's ambition.

As Stallybrass notes, "within literary discourse, class aspiration can be displaced onto the enchanted ground of romance, where considerations of status are transformed into considerations of sexual success."[25] For Floride the attempted rape and Amadour's ensuing speech partially reveal the rhetorical nature of the courtly posture. Although Amadour attempts to recuperate his losses "avecq le plus fainct visaige qu'il peut prendre" (p. 75) ("putting on the most convincing expression he could manage" [p. 143]), Floride "was beginning to understand the evil ways of men. If she had found it had to believe that Amadour's intentions were bad, she now found it even harder to believe him when he said that in reality they were good" (pp. 143–144). The second scene of attempted rape no longer borrows this rhetoric, either in its narration or in its dialogue; Floride is an enemy, and Amadour is attempting to win the war.

The struggle for advancement whereby the woman's body mediates as battleground between male rivals fails in this woman-authored text. War alone accomplishes the leveling of status Amadour seeks between himself and other men.[26] What has been called by critics a perfunctory ending becomes, in fact, the apotheosis of the knight in a bloodbath that confirms his relative power and effects the phallic union that the narrative reveals as the goal of male political struggle:

> When the wounds were examined, however, it was found that the Count of Aranda was still alive, so he was carried back in a litter to the family home, where he lay ill for a very long time. The Duke's corpse was sent back to Cardona. Amador, having rescued the two bodies, was so heedless of his own safety that he found himself surrounded by vast numbers of Moors . . . Commending his body and soul to God, he kissed the cross of his sword, and plunged it with such force into his body that he killed himself in one fell blow. (p. 152)[27]

Although the narrator indicates that Amadour's motives are less than heroic ("his exploits during that campaign were so extraordinary that they had more the appearance of acts of desperation than acts of bravery" [p. 151]), his excess wins him glory within the warrior economy. Geburon comments, at the end of the story, "In my opinion Amador was the most noble and valiant knight that ever lived . . . he's a man who never experienced fear in his life, a man whose heart was never devoid of love or the desire for courageous action" (p. 154).

Floride receives a lesson in strategy from the dissimulation practiced by her suitor, but hers is also a story of rhetorical failure. Just before Amadour comes to exact revenge, she disfigures her face with a stone. The defacement masks her beauty; it is the shield she holds up to deflect his blows: "If you will look at the way my face is now adorned, you will lose all memory of the delights that once you found there, you will lose all your desire to approach it nearer!" (p. 148.) A once beautiful face that dazzled its beholder into speechlessness ("he, the most eloquent man in Spain, was speechless as he stood before her" [p. 124]), now held up as a hideous shield against the enemy, evokes the figure of Medusa, another woman whose beauty, according to Ovid, incited rape.[28] Medusa's severed head is a figure for eloquence, from Plato's *Symposium* through Coluccio Salutati's *De Laboribus Herculis*. Nancy Vickers notes that: "As the woman's face that one carries into battle, that reduces eloquent rivals to silent stone, the apotropaic power of the 'Gorgon's head of Gorgias' eloquence' resides in its ability to stupefy a male opponent."[29]

In the merging of shield and enemy, Floride hopes to deflect Amadour's attack on what she believes is the source and object of his desire ("she could not bear the thought that this beauty of hers should kindle so base a fire in the heart of a man who was so worthy and so good" [p. 146]). Her (self-)defacement is rhetorically motivated; by putting on a "fainct visaige" (the false face used by Amadour to persuade her) she dissimulates her own desire (for she is "unable to love him less than before" [p. 144]) in order to represent herself as undesirable. In *Sexuality and the Psychology of Love,* Freud notes that the Medusa is also a representation of the female genitals and that "displaying the genitals is familiar in other connections as an apotropaic act. What arouses horror in oneself will produce the same effect upon the enemy against whom one is seeking to defend oneself."[30] Floride becomes, in this economy, a victim of masculine representation by locating in herself the source of Amadour's madness, the "horror" of desire. In holding up the metonymic sign of her own defilement (and once again, according to Ovid, Medusa's deformed face is her punishment for having been raped), Floride simultaneously disfigures a figure (her dazzling face) and figures the disfigured (her raped body); face and figure converge in this emblem of the (feminine) self.[31]

Floride's gesture is a literal (dis)figuring. Her attempt at rhetorical (self-)presentation merely reiterates what is, behind her beauty, the obvious "truth" for Amadour: that she is symbolic property, a married woman possessed by another man. Medusa cannot function as the signifying "proper" of the woman's "self"—the rhetorical power

of the figure is lost on him for whom it only signifies catachresti-
cally. He responds to Floride's act of self-representation by negating
the power of her subjective agency. She is indeed, for Amadour, a
"dead" metaphor: "Nor am I going to be deterred because you've
disfigured your face! I'm quite sure you did it yourself, of your own
volition. No! If all I could get were your bare bones, still I should
want to hold them close! (148).

The Medusan shield of eloquence fails in the hands of she who is
herself the Gorgon, and Floride must cry out to her mother to be
saved. She demonstrates her rhetorical inadequacy once again when,
in a Cordelian moment, she cannot master "that glib and oylie art"
to answer her mother's question, thus bringing about a seven-year
estrangement between them.

The failure of Floride's "éducation sentimentale," as Tetel calls
it, does delineate, however, a different path for the woman's "éducation politique." I noted that she eventually learns the art of dissimulation, a point emphasized in the narrative through facial imagery, "visaige estrange" and "dissimulé visaige" (p. 81). In order to
prove to her mother that she is not perverse (for her mother "was
convinced that Floride . . . had taken it into her head to dislike
anyone that her mother was fond of" [p. 50]), Floride tricks Amadour
into courting another woman, Lorette. Although this event serves to
show Floride's ultimate incapacity to dissimulate her feelings, for
when she hears that Lorette's husband has sworn to kill Amadour,
she warns him ("incapable of wishing arm on Amadour, however
harsh a mask she might wear" [p. 151]), it also effects the reconciliation of mother and daughter. Floride adopts the rhetorical strategies
she has been taught by Amadour, but to a different end, reconciliation rather than conquest.

Mothers, as Freud noted, are never very far away from Medusas.
In the tenth novella, the mother is a powerful and ambivalent figure
who mediates the transactions and transitions of the tale. Like Fortune, who is Amadour's adoptive mother, the countess provides the
knight with opportunities denied him by birth. Her travels provide
the occasion for Amadour and Floride to meet; her influence facili-
tates Amadour's marriage to Avanturade. The countess' affection for
Amadour wins him a place in her household and in Floride's heart;
indeed, when he confesses his love for Floride the Countess she
encourages, then forces her daughter to write to him. She also forces
her daughter to marry the duke of Cardonne. The Countess provides
the occasion for Amadour's attempted rape, and she also rescues

Floride from its consummation. And finally, it is to the Countess that Floride must prove herself by learning to dissimulate.

Fortune is indeed a lady in this text authored by a queen and mother, and a resolutely aristocratic one at that (the question of marriage between Amadour and Floride is never entertained). She can be courted but not coerced. Against a Machiavellian politics of class aspirant self-determination, the maternal figure in this novella guarantees the preservation of a social order. She is a collaborator, obeying patriarchalist class dictates at the expense of her daughter's happiness: "Pressed by the King to agree to the marriage, the Countess, as a loyal subject, could not refuse his request ... once the agreement was concluded, she took [Florida] on one side to explain how she had chosen for her the match which was most fitting" (p. 137). She colludes in the system that makes of daughters objects of masculine desires and exchange without counseling, nevertheless, the politics of rape. Amadour's failure and his eventual death testify to this. Even the territorial wars that populate this novella are massive failures, playgrounds for men's narcissistic death wish, ending in defeat. These contradictions describe the maternal text in patriarchy, informed by the powerful ambivalence of the mother-daughter relation.[32]

The Countess's refusal to hear her daughter's silence teaches Floride to wield a Medusan shield of eloquence to her own advantage, to use rhetorical strategies to expose the dissimulation of their practitioners.[33] She counsels the politics of pragmatic "negotiation," practiced up to a point by Amadour, for her daughter as well. Parlamente, at the end of the tale, displays such maternal pragmatism when she comments, "I would beg you to be less harsh, and not to have so much faith in men that you end up being disappointed when you learn the truth" (p. 152).

The tenth novella of the *Heptameron* is deeply troubled by a figure, the French "figure" par excellence: the face. Metaphors of face and masking throughout the tale accompany references to that suspect art of eloquence: rhetoric. Floride's "staged scene" of disfigurement is, both thematically and tropologically, a gesture of feminine self-representation in the text, an inscription. In an essay on women's writing, "Arachnologies: the Woman, the Text, and the Critic," Nancy Miller proposes that in female-authored texts can be found "the embodiment in writing of a gendered subjectivity" and that "within representation [are] the emblems of its construction."[34] She goes on to invoke a practice of "overreading" that "involves a focus on the moments in the narrative which by their representation of writing itself might be said to figure the production of the female artist" (pp. 274–275). In an invocation of violence that seems particularly apt to this text, she notes that through this practice "we may discover in the representations of writing itself the marks of the grossly material, the sometimes brutal traces of the culture of gender; the inscriptions of its political structures" (p. 275). She designates these gender-coded representations of writing as the "feminine signature" in women's writing.

In Marguerite's tenth story, the feminine signature takes the form of a disfigured face, the disfigured face of the feminine. As Paul de Man has shown, the trope whereby name (signature) becomes face, prosopopoeia, designates the "autobiographical moment" of the text: "Voice assumes mouth, eye, and finally face, a chain that is manifest in the etymology of the trope's name, *prosopon poien*, to confer a mask or face *(prosopon)*. Prosopopeia is the trope of autobiography, by which one's name . . . is made as intelligible and memorable as a face."[35]

The already prosopopoeic "face" of the Medusan shield in this text is defaced to figure the voice of a feminine subject. This autobiographical moment in Marguerite de Navarre's writing also figures the impossibility of feminine autobiography, if the latter is taken to mean the product of a "subject" with an "identity." Prosopopoeia, as de Man points out, confers neither voice nor face, for it is represented in language and "language, as trope, is always privative," in other words, mute. De Man concludes his powerful essay by describing the cognitive negativity of the autobiographical project:

> As soon as we understand the rhetorical function of prosopopeia as positing voice or face by means of language, we also understand that what we are deprived of is not life but the shape and the sense of a world accessible only in the privative way of understanding. Death is a displaced name for a linguistic predicament, and the restoration of mortality by autobiography (the prosopopeia of the voice and the name) deprives and disfigures to the precise extent that it restores. (p. 81)

It is perhaps not surprising that, in the context of this Renaissance novella, the subject "we" of de Man's passage seems particularly gender-limited. For what can be said of the double prosopopoeia doubly disfigured that is Floride's face? It is a feminine signature of the feminine, a trope of femininity based on femininity as trope. A literal disfigurement takes place to produce a rhetorical figure, a literal disfigurement of what is already, so to speak, a figure. That "privative way of understanding" that is written can be, for "woman," herself prosopopoeically constructed by masculine representation, restorative *only* to the extent that she becomes the agency of her defacement. Marguerite's text stages the failure of feminine self-representation and the perpetuation of a phallocracy with a "brutal trace" of the "culture of gender." Yet mutilation, the feminine signature *par excellence,* is a sign of textual and political resistance. It remains for the rest of us to translate that resistance into action.

The epigraphs to this paper are meant to complicate my own subject position as a white female academic who has been raped and for whom the experience was a lesson both in gender subjection and in class privilege. Writing on rape in Marguerite de Navarre is deeply connected to these lessons. The rapist was a white man of a lower socioeconomic class than myself, and the police, counselors, and doctors all stated at a certain point that my claims to having been raped were justified because I was a graduate student at Yale University and because I was white in the city of New Haven, Connecticut. I must assume from what they said that Black and poor women are not so readily believed when they report this crime and that the rapist would not have been so readily prosecutable had he not been poor. In analyzing Marguerite de Navarre's narrative about an attempted rape of an aristocrat by a class aspirant, I sought, in critiquing phallocracy, other alliances to help me understand the class complications of my position and of the noblewoman Marguerite de Navarre's narrative.

As a U.S. citizen, I can best understand class difference through the oppression of African Americans, because "race" and class share a history in this country. Many Black women writers have taught me, through their focus on differences, that to be blind to my class/ "race" privilege is to betray a feminism that seeks revolutionary praxis. Furthermore, African Americans have a historical relation to rape that implicates me. I wish to seek a theoretical way out of the political impasses of that implication (not historically, of course— that cannot be done) by a political analysis of rape as a specifically phallocratic practice that benefits no oppressed person, that reinscribes, rather, the hierarchies of domination constitutive of the *status quo.*

Marguerite's text, which underscores the gender-specific contradictions of the phallocratic ethos of courtly love, operates within the contradictoriness and confusion of conflicting class and gender positions. Jordan and Polite suggest, in very different ways, that complicity with one form of domination entails complicity with others and that rape is always the mobilization of patriarchalist property claims that victimize. Marguerite de Navarre dramatizes that problem in the staging of a mother-daughter conflict and a conflict of interpretive commentary. Her text contains an emblem of that complicity, the self-mutilation that results from "blaming the victim." But although the text makes clear that the discourse of love is, in a context of gender oppression, a political matter, it does not successfully subvert the complicity that has continued to reproduce that discourse as ideology and that continues to reproduce phallocracy. Would this text ever have been canonized had it done so?

The *Heptameron* is part of my inheritance as a feminist literary critic of what is called the Renaissance in Western European literary history. In seeking a way to understand my experience as a survivor of rape I brought its theme into my work of the moment, which included teaching the *Heptameron* in a class. Androcentric critics of the text seemed to have focused exclusively on love as affect in Marguerite's stories.They failed to see how courtly love is politicized, at least in this story, by a focus on the feminine response to its ideological extreme: rape.[36] Roy Porter's view of rape may help to explain why. By privileging gender difference as a category of reading and of writing, I hope to have shown how Marguerite's text resists phallocratic appropriation and dismissal to a "purely" private domain of affective (read feminine) experience. This is, necessarily, a gesture of empowerment, although, prefaced as it is by the words of Jordan and Polite, such a gesture must remain self-critically provisional.

NOTES

1. Craig Owens, "The Discourse of Others: Feminists and Postmodernism," in H. Foster, ed., *The Anti-Aesthetic: Essays on Postmodern Culture*, pp. 57–82 (Port Townsend, Wash.: Bay Press, 1983), p. 59.

2. June Jordan, "A Poem About My Rights," *Passion, New Poems 1977–1980* (Boston: Beacon Press, 1980), p. 56.

3. Carlene Hatcher Polite, *Sister X and the Victims of Foul Play* (New York: Farrar, Strauss & Giroux, 1975).

4. Roy Porter and Sylvana Tomaselli, eds., *Rape* (London: Blackwell, 1986), p. 235.

5. Marguerite de Navarre, *L'Heptaméron*, ed. M. François (Paris: Garnier Frères, 1967).

6. Toril Moi, in her analysis of Andreas Capellanus' *De Amore*, notes the extent to which courtly discourse depends on the lover's linguistic domination of the lady. See "Desire in Language: Andreas Capellanus and the Controversy of Courtly Love," in David Aers, ed., *Medieval Literature: Criticism, Ideology and History* (New York: St. Martin's Press, 1986), pp. 11–33.

7. Marc Bloch, *Feudal Society*, trans. L. A. Manyon (1966; reprint, Chicago: University of Chicago Press, 1974), 1:233. Kate Millett's "reply" to a statement such as Bloch's introduces the gender analysis that provides an ideological critique: "One must acknowledge that the chivalrous stance is a game the master group plays in elevating its subject to a pedestal . . . both the courtly and the romantic versions of love are grants which the male concedes out of his total power. Both have had the effect of obscuring the patriarchal character of Western Culture . . ." *Sexual Politics* (London: Virago, 1977), p. 3. Kathryn Gravdal has recently contributed to the ideological critique of courtly love from a feminist medievalist perspective. See her "Camouflaging Rape: The Rhetoric of Sexual Violence in the Medieval Pastourelle," *Romanic Review* (1985), 76:360–373. I would like to thank Kevin Brownlee for bringing this article to my attention.

8. Peter Stallybrass explores the Renaissance discursive deployment, economic and political, of "woman" and the bodies of women in "Patriarchal Territories: The Body Enclosed," in Margaret W. Ferguson, Maureen Quilligan, and Nancy J. Vickers, eds., *Rewriting the Renaissance: The Discourses of Sexual Difference in Early Modern Europe*, (Chicago: University of Chicago Press, 1986), pp. 123–142. For an emergent bourgeois discussion of woman in relation to property, see Leon Battista Alberti's *The Albertis of Florence: Leon Battista Alberti's Della Famiglia*, trans. Guido Guarino (Lewisburg, Pa.: Bucknell University Press, 1971), book 3: "Oeconomicus."

9. Pierre Jourda explicitly compares Castiglione's work to the *Heptameron*; "Il [Castiglione] avait conté de même qu'une femme, mal mariée, n'avait pas cédé aux instances de celui qu'elle aimait. N'est-ce point là l'histoire de Floride?" *Marguerite d'Angoulême, Duchesse d'Alençon, Reine de Navarre (1492–1549), Etude biographique et littéraire* (2 vols. 1930; reprint, Paris: Champion, 1966), 2:749.

10. In this context see Dain Trafton's essay, "Politics and the Praise of Women: Political Doctrine in the *Courtier*'s Third Book," in R. Hanning and D. Rosand, eds., *Castiglione: The Ideal and the Real in Renaissance Culture* (New Haven: Yale University Press, 1983), pp. 29–44. Stephanie Jed has also written on the deployment of the rape of Lucretia story in Italian Renaissance discussions of tyranny. See "Salutati's *Declamatio Lucretiae*: The Rape of Lucretia and the Birth of Humanism," *Genre* (1987):209–226; also

Chaste Thinking: The Rape of Lucretia and the Birth of Humanism (Bloomington: Indiana University Press, 1989).

11. Baldesar Castiglione, *The Book of the Courtier*, trans. C. Singleton (Garden City, N.Y.: Anchor, 1959), p. 250. Further citations appear in text.

12. Marcel Tetel, "Une réevaluation de la dixième nouvelle de l'Heptameron, *Neuphilologische Mitteilungen* (1971), 72:564.

13. Marguerite de Navarre, *The Heptameron*, trans. P. A. Chilton (Middlesex, England, and New York: Penguin, 1984), p. 140. Further citations appear in text. The French text will be cited where the translation inadequately reflects the choice of vocabulary in French.

14. Jules Gelernt, *World of Many Loves: The Heptameron of Marguerite de Navarre* (Chapel Hill: University of North Carolina Press, 1966).

15. Michel Foucault notes that politics and war are separable only insofar as they represent differing strategies within a "multiplicity of force relations": "If we still wish to maintain a separation between war and politics, perhaps we should postulate rather that this multiplicity of force relations can be coded—in part but never totally—either in the form of 'war,' or in the form of 'politics'; this would imply two different strategies (but the one always liable to switch into the other) for integrating these unbalanced, heterogeneous, unstable, and tense force relations." *The History of Sexuality*, vol. 1: *An Introduction*, trans. R. Hurley (New York: Vintage Books, 1980), p. 93.

16. Elsewhere in the *Heptameron* Hircan remarks, "You mean to say then . . . that if there were no ladies, we would all be merchants?" (p. 533), thus revealing how the lady is used in the ideology of courtliness to maintain an aristocratic class position.

17. Ann Jones and Peter Stallybrass have examined the political structuring of the courtly love relation and its inversion in the poetry of Sidney. They write: "By a peculiar double reflexiveness, love, modeled upon an idealization of court hierarchies, could refashion in mystified form those very relations of power and submission that had structured it in the first place" (p. 54). Such a stragey depends, for its effectiveness, upon the opposition between public and private, an opposition that, Marguerite demonstrates, produces an untenable concept of honor for the lady. See "The Politics of *Astrophil and Stella*," *Studies in English Literature* (1984), 24:53–68.

18. Niccolò Machiavelli, *The Prince*, trans. J. Atkinson (1976; reprint, Indianapolis: Bobbs-Merrill, 1977), pp. 369–371.

19. Dante Alighieri, *Inferno*, trans. John Sinclair (New York: Oxford University Press, 1939), canto 7, lines 94–96.

20. Dante Alighieri, *Vito nuova—Rime*, Ed. Fredi Chiappelli (Milan: U. Mursia, 1965–1973), p. xxvi, lines 5–8.

21. John Freccero in a recent talk, "Machiavelli and the Myth of the Body Politic" (MLA, 1987), examined Machiavelli's use of sexual imagery to construct a myth of political empowerment. Machiavelli's use of the Medusa

myth is especially relevant as a contrast to the appearance of the literalized figure of Medusa in Marguerite's text.

22. Eldridge Cleaver in *Soul on Ice* (New York: Dell, 1968), analyzes the relation between rape and class revenge: "Rape was an insurrectionary act. It delighted me that I was defying and trampling upon the white man's law, upon his system of values, and that I was defiling his women—and this point, I believe, was the most satisfying to me because I was very resentful over the historical fact of how the white man had used the black woman. I felt I was getting revenge" (p. 26). He also notes: "I started out by practicing on black girls in the ghetto" (p. 26).

23. Stallybrass, "Patriarchal Territories," p. 141. In the third book of *The Discourses* Machiavelli devotes a chapter to "How States Are Ruined on Account of Women," in which he locates "woman" as a site of class conflict (ch. 26).

24. The English translation does not preserve the economic metaphor of "credit." See p. 123: "His reputation stood so high [he had so much credit] there [with the ladies of Barcelona] that there was little or nothing anyone would refuse him."

25. Stallybrass, "Patriarchal Territories," p. 134.

26. As Nancy Vickers points out, elaborating upon Eve Sedgwick's theory of homosexual desire in literary representation in *Between Men: English Literature and Male Homosexual Desire* (New York: Columbia University Press, 1985):

"In *Lucrece*, occasion, rhetoric, and result are all informed by, and thus inscribe, a battle between men that is first figuratively and then literally fought on the fields of woman's 'celebrated' body. Here, metaphors commonly read as signs of a battle between the sexes emerge rather from a homosocial struggle, in this case a male rivalry, which positions a third (female) term in a median space from which it is initially used and finally eliminated." " 'The Blazon of Sweet Beauty's Best' Shakespeare's *Lucrece*," in Patricia Parker and Geoffrey Hartman, eds., *Shakespeare and the Question of Theory*, pp. 95–115 (New York: Methuen, 1985), p. 96. The language describing Amadour's behavior and motives and the alternating narratives of courtship and war in Marguerite's story suggest such a homosocial struggle, but here the woman can be said to remove herself, as ground, from the battlefield.

27. Julia Kristeva, in *Le Texte du roman: Approche sémio-logique d'une structure discursive transformationelle* (The Hague: Mouton, 1970), claims that sixteenth-century (phallocentric) discourse constructs woman as "pseudo-Other." Marguerite allegorizes this construction in her story, figuring the erotics of war as a homoerotics. Writes Kristeva: "Lieu d'occultation ou de valorisation, la femme sera un pseudo-centre, un centre latent ou explicite, celui qu'on expose . . . ou bien qu'on camoufle . . . le centre présent ou absent du discours romanesque (psychologique) moderne, dans lequel l'homme cherche l'homme et s'y divinise . . ." (p. 160).

28. In the *Metamorphoses*, book 4, the tale goes as follows: "she was very lovely once, the hope of many/An envious suitor, and of all her beauties / Her hair most beautiful . . . / One day Nepture/ Found her and raped her, in Minerva's temple . . ." (Ovid, *Metamorphoses*, trans. R. Humphries [Bloomington: Indiana University Press, 1972], p. 106).

29. Vickers, " 'The Blazon of Sweet Beauty's Best,' " p. 110.

30. Sigmund Freud, *Sexuality and the Psychology of Love*, ed. Philip Rieff (New York: Collier, 1963), p. 213. For a further exploration of masculine representations of Medusa, see Neil Hertz, "Medusa's Head: Male Hysteria under Political Pressure," *Representations* (Fall 1983), 4:27–54. Catherine Gallagher's response, in the same issue, offers both a historical corrective and a feminist analysis, suggesting that Medusan emblems may not only signify absence but also chaotic plenitude ("More about 'Medusa's Head,' " pp. 55–57). As Helene Cixous playfully notes of the Freudian text: "Wouldn't the worst be, isn't the worst, in truth, that women aren't castrated, that they have only to stop listening to the Sirens (for the Sirens were men) for history to change its meaning? You only have to look at the Medusa straight on to see her. And she's not deadly. She's beautiful and she's laughing." "The Laugh of the Medusa," in E. Marks and I. de Courtivron, eds., *New French Feminisms, an Anthology*, pp. 245–264 (New York: Schoken, 1981), p. 255.

31. It is interesting in this connection to read Cixous' description of a woman in an oratorical situation: "Listen to a woman speak at a public gathering (if she hasn't painfully lost her wind) . . . Her flesh speaks true. She lays herself bare. In fact, she physically materializes what she's thinking; she signifies it with her body. In a certain way she *inscribes* what she's saying . . . Her speech, even when 'theoretical' or political, is never simple or linear or 'objectified,' generalized: she draws her story into history" (ibid., p. 251).

32. My notion of the maternal is derived from the philosopher Sara Ruddick's essay "Maternal Thinking," in J. Trebilcot, ed., *Mothering: Essays in Feminist Theory* (Totowa, N.J.: Rowman & Allanheld, 1983), and her later "Preservative Love and Military Destruction: Some Reflections on Mothering and Peace," in Trebilcot, *Mothering*, pp. 231–262, as well as her recent book, *Maternal Thinking: Toward a Politics of Peace* (Boston: Beacon Press, 1989). Ruddick defines maternal practice as the engagement in a discipline, mothering, that is a form of social thought. She identifies three principal interests governing maternal practices: the preservation, growth, and acceptability of the child both to herself, her values, and to those of the society in which she lives. Under the economic, political, and social conditions of phallocracy, the third of these interests, acceptability, produces the internal contradictions constitutive of the collaborator. See also the work of Marianne Hirsch, *The Mother/ Daughter Plot: Narrative Psychoanalysis, Feminism* (Bloomington: Indiana University Press, 1989).

33. In the earlier of two articles on Shakespeare's *Lucrece*, Nancy Vickers proposes the solution to representation counseled by the maternal voice in Marguerite's text, "that the secret of survival is clearly neither to be a shield,

nor to see a shield, but to know how to use one" (" 'This Heraldry in Lucrece's Face,' " in S. Suleiman, ed., *The Female Body in Western Culture: Contemporary Perspectives* (reprint, Cambridge: Harvard University Press, 1986), pp. 209–222.

34. Nancy K. Miller, "Arachnologies: The Woman, the Text, and the Critic," in Nancy K. Miller, ed., *The Poetics of Gender*, (New York: Columbia University Press,1986), p. 272. Further citations will appear in text.

35. Paul de Man, "Autobiography as De-Facement," *The Rhetoric of Romanticism* (New York: Columbia University Press, 1984), p. 76. Further citations appear in text.

36. Marcel Tetel, in his often astute study of Marguerite de Navarre's *Heptameron*, remarks at a certain point that "the subject matter of the *Heptameron* is first and foremost love." *Marguerite de Navarre's* <u>Heptameron</u>: *Themes, Language, and Structure* (Durham, N.C.: Duke University Press, 1973), p. 15]. In calling "love" the subject mater of the work he, like most (male) critics of the text, falls prey to a peculiarly modern mystification with regard to the discourse of love, a mystification that has often led to a dismissal of women writers. "Love," in these critical discourses, becomes the means by which the text is trivialized and relegated to the realm of pastime romance. See also the conclusion to Lucien Febvre, *Amour sacré amour profane: Autour de l'Heptaméron* (Paris: Gallimard, 1944), also Tetel in his conclusion and Jules Gelernt *(World of Many Loves)* in his. This is an error that no one seems to commit in the case of Boccaccio's *Decameron*, although he writes, in the preface: "I intend to provide succour and diversion for the ladies, but only for those who are in love . . ." (Penguin translated by G. H. McWilliam), p. 47, thus explicitly designating "love" as the subject of his work.

11

Alice Walker's "Advancing Luna—and Ida B. Wells": A Struggle Toward Sisterhood

NELLIE Y. MCKAY

"The cultural meaning of rape is rooted in a symbiosis of racism and sexism that has tolerated the acting out of male aggression against women and, in particular, black women. An important part of the task of deconstructing the consciousness of rape is revealing the linkages between the social [and cultural] mechanisms that empower violence against both racial groups and women and insure the fragmentation of marginalized and oppressed groups to consolidate the power of the patriarchy."[1]

In this essay, on rape, power, and relationships between black and white women, I assume rape as a crime of violence and intimidation with intrinsic connections to sexual aggressiveness and political and economic power. The implications of these connections are even more politically charged when the act occurs across racial boundaries. In spite of this, for generations, the most direct and common threat that black and white women continually face is the victimization of intra- and interracial rape. How then do we account for the fact that the most irreconcilable angers, jealousies, and hostilities plaguing relationships between women of color and white women have their genesis in the politics of sexuality and, to a large extent, in those of rape? A large part of the answer to that question resides in the male perception of women as property, which transforms the rape of any woman into an attack on the property of a man. In an essay on " 'Social Equality,' Miscegenation, Labor, and Power [in the South]," Nell Irvin Painter cogently sums up the social development of woman-as-property in the United States this way:

> Sex was the whip that white supremacists used to reinforce white solidarity . . . [since] nearly all white men could claim to hold a certain sort of property, in wives, sisters, and daughters. . . . [The threat of] "social equality" [the bugbear that white supremacists used as their "come-on"] invited all white men to protect their property in women and share in the maintenance of all sorts of power."[2]

For a long time this psychology supported white male fascination with the nature of power and control associated with interracial rape, readily observable in that group's perpetuation of white-on-black rape and its too often exaggerated violent reactions to allegations of black-on-white rape. In a demonstration of this power, for centuries men in this group have raped black women with impunity, while they responded not only to actual incidents of such violations, but even to suspicions or imagined threats of the interracial rape of white women with swift mob violence that made criminal punishment secondary to the destabilization of the entire black community.

Alice Walker's "Advancing Luna—and Ida B. Wells" gets to the heart of these issues.[3] This story, of the death of a friendship between a black and white woman, critiques the politics of female silence and the struggle for the "word" over black-on-white rape. In her analysis, Walker examines how, in the manner in which black women perceive the power of language as a weapon for racial and sexual oppression, conflicts between race or sex unity develop. Her text largely addresses the emotional and intellectual tensions growing out of this moral dilemma for black women. The story provides a crucial space in which we see how women's cross-racial relationships are held hostage by the self-interests of systems of white male power. In exploring the inner conflicts and ambivalences of black women confronting actual or alleged black-on-white rape, "Advancing Luna" does much to illuminate such phenomena as black women's lack of group support for the contemporary (white) feminist antirape movement, in spite of their own historical oppression by rape.

The narrator's ambivalences toward race *or* sex loyalties create the psychological complexities of "Advancing Luna." These are partly represented in the story's blend of autobiography, fiction, history, and essay, partly by the nature of the narrator's dialogue with herself and partly in the fragmentation of the narrative's inclusion of writer's notes: "Afterwords, Afterwards Second Thoughts" and "Luna: Ida B. Wells—Discarded Notes," and two alternate endings appended to the story: "Imaginary Knowledge" and "Postscript: Havana, Cuba, November 1976." These many disjunctions symbolize the author's tortured search for resolution to a moral and spiritual dilemma and invite us to reckon with the difficulties that black women perceive in black-on-white rape at the intersection of white women's (conscious and unconscious) racism and white male legal and extralegal racism and sexism toward black America.

Put another way, transformed into a question, the title of Walker's text probes the moral dimensions of black women's ambivalences toward sisterhood with white women especially on the issue of black-on-white rape. Is it possible, she is asking, for black women to "advance Luna" (raise their voices in unconditional outrage for the white-woman victim) without violating the meaning and memory of the lives of Ida B. Wells and the myriad other named and unnamed black men and women who devoted lifetimes and careers to the campaign against lynching or the innocent black victims of that bloody crime? [4] The politics of raising voice or remaining silent, of fully comprehending the significance of the "word," and the power of language are major elements in women's cross-racial experiences.

For in the black mind, white male rape of black women and white male lynching of black men are inextricably linked to the power and violence of race domination. In calling the lynchings of black men "symbolic rapes," Painter dramatically highlights the interconnectedness of rape, race, and power for black people as a group:

> Like actual rape against women, [these symbolic rapes] were rituals of power and degradation, as white men burned, whipped, and murdered in an attempt to close the circle of their power over black men. Aping the forms of legal executions, these symbolic rapes constituted the bodily aspect of the maintenance of white men's physical power over black men, and by extension, all black people. [5]

With this concept deeply engraved on their psyches and the realization that white women's words remain empowered to unleash such violence, it is extremely difficult for black women to separate themselves from the history of race and to link their oppression by rape to that of white women. For in the psychology of the entire black community, the terror of lynching underlines the relationship between white power and black powerlessness.

In "Advancing Luna—and Ida B. Wells," two narratives develop simultaneously: a frame story with three choices of an ending, the third taking shape a decade after the first and second, and a story within the story: the narrator's internal debate over the psychological and moral conflicts that the frame story raises for her. This gives the piece its "essay" quality. The frame story moves through the meeting, development of, and disintegration of a close friendship between two young women, one black and the other white, in the wake of the white woman's allegation of rape by a black man. The story within the frame focuses on the dilemma of the oppositions (mentioned above) in the title of the piece. In this, the narrator confronts three issues: 1) her private individual response to a difficult personal situation, 2) the responsibility of the black woman writer to speak honestly and truthfully, even on black-on-white rape, and 3) her commitment to search for the meaning of rape in the lives of all women.

The friends in "Advancing Luna" are opposites to each other in many ways. The nameless black narrator is a native Georgian from a sharecropping family who, on scholarship aid, attends a prestigious northern white women's college. She is physically attractive, alert, and outgoing in her relationships with others. The rape victim, Luna, a northern white woman, described as sexually unattractive and passive toward others, is the offspring of divorced upper-class parents with (she tells the narrator) superficial moral and aesthetic values. Luna's involvement with the Civil Rights Movement and her relationship with the narrator are her attempt to find an identity for herself separate from that of her family. The women meet in Georgia, in the summer of 1965, when they work together in a black voter registration drive in the South. In spite of their differences, a warm friendship develops between them that successfully spans differences of race and class and appears firmly grounded in mutual respect. A year later, the narrator, by then a college graduate intent on a writer's career, moves to New York City. Having only limited financial resources, she accepts Luna's offer that they share the latter's apartment, a run-down junkie-and-wino–infested tenement building on East 9th Street. Appalled that rich-girl Luna would choose to live in such a place, she nevertheless moves in with her.

While they live together in New York, Luna confidentially informs the narrator that in the South, during the previous summer, she was raped by a less-than-notable black Civil Rights worker, Freddie Pye, someone whom the narrator previously held in low esteem. The narrator does not doubt Luna's story. On the basis of their shared past and present relationship, she accepts it as truth.[6] Yet soon after the revelation the relationship between the women deteriorates: "a cooling off of our affection for each other" takes place, the narrator reports. Nor do they discuss the rape again or Luna's "remaining feelings" on it. While silence shrouds the deed, the "rape" becomes a powerful force, a "thing" that tears them apart from each other.

At first, the narrator, unwilling to face the major issue in their failed relationship, attempts to justify its end with other circumstances. "Luna was becoming mildly interested in drugs, because everyone we knew was," she tells us (suggesting she was not), and "I was envious of the openendedness of her life. The financial backing of it . . . [when] she was tired of working, her errant father immediately materialized" (Walker 1981:96). But these are not honest reasons. Although race and class privilege permit Luna no need for immediate goals or purpose for her life, the narrator feels superior to her in this respect. Without race, class, and sex privilege, she is proud of her self-directed focus and her ability to support herself on meager resources. She anticipates that her financial and social difficulties are temporary and characterizes this era in her life as "dissolute . . . [but] pleasurable existence." After all, she assures us, she was a "Sarah Lawrence girl 'with talent,' " who would not permit herself to "rot" in a building that had no front door. Facing the truth, she admits that "the knowledge of the rape, out in the open, admitted, pondered over [yet paradoxically silenced], was [the thing] between [them]" (p. 95). But why and how had this come to be? These are questions the narrator attempts to answer in her dialogues with herself as she journeys to the painful center of black women's fears of and angers toward the race and class privilege that give white women's words authority over all black people's lives.

On this, the narrative's psychological level, Walker explores her deep-seated emotional responses to the meaning of black-on-white rape to her life and her friendship with white women. In the beginning, in order, she registers three reactions to the account: surprise, embarrassment, and intense (silent) anger toward the white woman. For Freddie Pye she has only contempt. She is surprised because she expected that even a passive Luna would have screamed at the violation of her person. "I felt I would have screamed my head off," she notes in an aside to the reader (p. 92). Her embarrassment signifies empathy and sympathy for her friend—for the sexual vulnerability and social impotence of all women to alter their situation. Surprise and embarrassment indicate a level of shared friendship between the women; anger creates the raison d'être for "Advancing Luna—and Ida B. Wells."

Anger precipitates the narrator's confrontation with the conflicts of race, sex, and power; compels her to reevaluate the grounds on which friendships between black and white women occur; and tears apart what both previously thought existed between them. The political dimensions of Luna's silence and, in converse, her voice are undeniable. "You know why [I did not scream]," she responds to the narrator's initial surprised query of her silence. The simple answer speaks volumes and removes the actors in this scene from the personal terrain—two friends, equal in their relationship to each other —to the arena of the historical context, where the currency is the power of race and class vested in Luna's word. "I began to think," the narrator angrily notes, "that perhaps—whether Luna had been raped or not—it had always been so; that her power over my life was exactly the power *her word on rape* had over the lives of black men, whether they were guilty or not, and therefore over my whole people" (p. 95). Furthermore, if in confiding the rape to her friend Luna intended to strengthen their mutual female bonds, she failed. From the narrator's historical perspective, this revelation reinforces the power imbalance between black and white women and casts Luna in the role of seeking an alliance with the black woman. Such sex loyalty on the part of black women would separate them from black men and further erode the morale of the already powerless community.[7]

For what the narrator takes seriously is that the survival of the black community depends heavily on its women. How can the black woman be an ally of the white woman as long as the white woman's "word" remains a sword of Damocles over all black people? How can the narrator, in a world in which the unsubstantiated words of white women remain a powerful force against all black people, "advance" Luna without denying (rejecting) her history embodied in the struggles of the life of Ida B. Wells? She notes black women's traditional responses to these situations: "Whenever interracial rape is mentioned a black woman's first thought is to protect the lives of her brothers, her father, her sons, her lover" (p. 93). Although no black woman denies that some black men rape white women, unquestionably race and sex together constitute a "Great Divide" between black and white women's relationships. How can the black woman writer, who wrestles with the integrity of her calling, and black women, who face intra- and interracial rape daily, remain silent on this outrage against anyone?

In dialogue with herself in search of answers to such vexing questions, the narrator seeks counsel and advice from the wisdom of the spirit of Ida B. Wells, the black woman who devoted most of her career to the antilynching campaign in the late nineteenth and early twentieth centuries: *"Write [say] nothing,"* remain silent, Ida B. Wells seems to counsel, write, say *"nothing at all. It will be used against all black men and therefore against all of us"* (p. 94, author's emphasis). The response confuses the narrator even though she knows that in her (the narrator's) thoughts Ida B. Wells recalls the violence and atrocities of the lynching of black men, the rape of black women, and the power of race and sex on the lives of all black people. For black women and men it is a history of shame to be always remembered.[8]

For black women in the United States specifically, all black women know that rape and sexuality became synonymous as soon as the first African woman set foot on a slave ship bound for the New World. Thus the American experience for Afro-American women began with the subordination of race and sex in the rape of their ancestral mothers during the horrendous Middle Passage. That nightmare gave way to another, as slavery proved to be the continuous horror of what many African women must have hoped at the outset was only a bad dream from which they would awaken. The large number of mixed-blood Afro-Americans by the end of the Civil War attests to the degree to which slave masters' rape of slave women was an integral part of the institution of black servitude and confirmed that the dynamics of racial and sexual oppression enhanced white male authority and emphasized black male and female powerlessness. On the one hand, black slave men were the property of their masters for purposes of their labor and for economic and political control; on the other, the sexuality of black slave women was also property over which the master exercised full authority. Furthermore, cultural presumptions continue to reinforce majority public perceptions of rape as the violation of white women, to the exclusion of black and other women of color.[9] And so, struggling with the conflicts created by the clash between the call to silence (race loyalty) and speaking truth, her moral obligation, the narrator grapples for an understanding not only of the meaning of loyalty to the history of the black struggle against the oppression of race and sex, but for the roots of the oppression that precipitates her angry outcry: "Who knows what the black woman thinks of rape? Who has asked her? Who cares? Who has even properly acknowledged that *she* not the white woman in this story is the most *likely* [author's emphasis] victim of rape?" (p. 93). For hundreds of years the answer to these questions was no one.

While the storm of conflicting emotions still rages in her, one morning the narrator is startled to see Freddie Pye emerge from Luna's bedroom and unceremoniously leave the apartment. In spite of her surprise and curiosity (similar to what she experienced when she first learned about the rape), the incident spawns another silent space between the women. They never "discuss [Freddie's presence in Luna's bedroom]. . . . It was as if he was never there" (p. 97). A month later each woman goes her own way, losing forever the chance to reconstruct their intimacy. Although they correspond periodically with each other, they meet only once again, years later, when Luna visits the narrator, who by then is living in the South again. She brings with her a "lovely piece of pottery." In time, the gift breaks in an accident, but the narrator glues it "back together in such a way that the flaw improves the beauty and fragility of the design" (p. 98). By then, rejecting the advice of Ida B. Wells, she writes the story, with the broken and mended pottery as its first ending.

For the narrator, however, such an ending does not resolve her dilemma. Why had she not felt the freedom to openly express outrage against Freddie Pye and to confirm strong female bonds with Luna? From her notebook (the postscripts to the text) we learn that although she had written an alternate ending, had pondered the issues for years, even discussing them with a loved and trusted friend, neither ending satisfied her. Instead, she spent years unable or unwilling to finish or publish the story. The broken-and-glued-together-pottery ending, her notes reveal, was the best she thought she could "afford to offer a society in which lynching is still reserved, at least subconsciously, as a means of racial control" (p. 98).

The second ending, "Imaginary Knowledge," reserved for a country "committed to justice" for all, was different from the first in its treatment of Freddie Pye's New York visit. Here the narrator, taking control of the story, makes Luna and Freddie into "characters" in a script. In their world, honest relationships between black men and white women are possible. When Freddie visits New York, Luna confronts him and speaks, explaining her confusion over *"whether, in a black community surrounded by whites with a history of lynching blacks, she had the right to scream"* about the rape. For her, *"this was the crux of the matter"* (p. 101, author's emphasis). They talk through the night, of history and sexual politics, until they remove the "stumbling block" of rape/race/power between them. At this stage they renounce conscious and unconscious participation in the tripartite victimization of race, sex, and power. Together they demand a world in which "Luna's word alone on rape [could] never [again] be used to intimidate an entire people, and where, an innocent black man's protestations of innocence of rape [would be] unprejudicially heard" (p. 102). Still, without immediate hopes for honest cross-racial relationships, the narrator concedes this ending is unrealistic. For in the world we inhabit, she thinks, "relationships of affection" between black men and white women and black and white women will continue as they have been, and solidarity among black and white women is only rarely likely to exist" (p. 102).

The third ending to the story, "Postscript: Havana, Cuba, November 1976," directly addresses patriarchal manipulation of rape to subordinate all women and men of color. More than a decade after the narrator and Luna lived in New York, on a trip to Havana with a group of black American artists the narrator discusses her story and its unresolved endings with an Afro-American muralist, a former radical activist of the 1960s. His response to the meaning of the rape and Freddie Pye focuses on "evil, power, [and] corrupted human beings in the modern world" (p. 104). Freddie Pye, he tells her, might have been "raping white women on the instructions of his government" (p. 103). He explains that he too had once been offered such "work" when he was indigent. The muralist's Freddie Pye is a "man without conscience," someone who is "simply evil, a disease on the lives of other people," a black man "beyond lust and rage [and] . . . aggression and purely racial hatred," who for money will do anything, including murdering other black people (p. 103).

The muralist's conclusions confirm the idea that rape has direct links to social and political mechanisms that empower violence against racial groups and women. The limits of this power are clear in the naming of the government, the authority of law, as its source. In the muralist's analysis, Luna's rape was not an isolated incident based on Freddie Pye's sexual desires for her (the narrator's early detailed description of the unattractiveness of Luna's body implies this). The narrator's recall of the boasts that Eldridge Cleaver and Imamu Baraka made of raping black and white women for political revenge further substantiates the theory. The rape of Luna might well have been part of a pattern of violent aggression against all women and radical black men for the consolidation of white male power. The lynching of black men on accusations of their sexual desires for white women historically served two purposes. (1) It promoted white female dependence on white men, the only group who could protect them against such bestial assaults, and (2), it directly intimidated the black community into submission to race power. Following this line of reasoning, white men were willing to surrender the bodies of white women to black men as sacrifices on the altar of white male race and gender supremacy. Thus the rape of white women associated with the Civil Rights Movement was "the perfect disruptive act" to destroy a black political movement and to continue to control the lives of white women.

Where does "Advancing Luna—and Ida B. Wells" leave us in our need to resolve the sisterhood between black and white women? A history of differences in experiences, class privilege, and racism, even in the contemporary women's movement, exacerbates many continuing difficulties between these groups. Still, black feminists in our time excoriated the failings of and join their voices to those of white women in many areas of the struggle for women's equality. Yet sexuality, and rape in particular, remain almost impervious to meaningful discourse in women's cross-racial understanding. As Walker perceives it, this situation is the outgrowth of a social system in which the "affiliations" between black men and white women and between black and white women are poisoned from within and without by historical fear and the threat of violence (p. 102). Her solution promotes the idea that those affected develop an understanding of and actively engage the power that generates, controls, and prescribes negative interactions between white women and people of color. For the successful resolution to this story, which we must write, depends on achieving honest relationships between black and white women and between white women and black men. We can then empower our own words and language, rejecting absolutely the silence of oppression (even of history) that "empower[s] violence against racial groups and women" by exploiting *all* female sexuality.

Walker gives us a model in the structure of "Advancing Luna—and Ida B. Wells." Much like the "No Name Woman" story in

Maxine Hong Kingston's *The Woman Warrior*,[10] "Advancing Luna" evolves from a confidence held between women: Luna's language, silenced for fear of its violent potential; to the writer's script with characters: the fictitious "Imaginary Knowledge," in which the narrator assumes control of language but remains dissatisfied with the ending; to the artifact, her final text, with its multiple endings and which many people now read and discuss. Like Kingston, who must tell the story to give meaning to her aunt's life, in spite of her initial resistance—"more than a little of Ida B. Wells's fear of probing the rape issue was running in [me]"—Walker cannot avoid telling her story: The implication of this fear would not let me rest" (p. 98). In its final version, the narrator approaches her text objectively, speaking out to claim the power of the female voice in her language as well as Luna's—language that reverses the fear and need for silence that destroyed their friendship.[11]

NOTES

I especially wish to thank Susan Stanford Friedman, Linda Gordon, Lynn Higgins, Gerda Lerner, Florencia Mallon, Deborah McDowell, Nell Irvin Painter, Benita Ramsey, Mary Helen Washington, and Craig Werner, whose encouragement, criticism, and wise words helped to make this essay possible.

1. Kristin Bumiller, "Rape as a Legal Symbol: An Essay on Sexual Violence and Racism," *University of Miami Law Review* (September 1987), 42 (no.1): 88.

2. Nell Irvin Painter, " 'Social Equality,' Miscegenation, Labor, and Power," in Numan V. Bartley, ed., *The Evolution of Southern Culture*, (Athens: University of Georgia Press, 1988), p. 49. Although not the first to note the link between rape and woman-as-property, Painter significantly points out sex as the most effective "whip" southern white supremacists used to reinforce racist ideology. She writes: "Political slogans that spoke straightforwardly of property or wealth . . . failed to rally . . . [poor white men]," but all (more or less) "owned" women, whom they could perceive as being protected from "social equality."

3. Alice Walker, *You Can't Keep a Good Woman Down* (New York: Harcourt Brace Jovanovich, 1981), pp. 85–104. (Further citations will appear in text.) Walker also addresses black-on-white rape in her novel *Meridian,* 1976. The difference between the two accounts is in the details in the novel versus lack of details in the story. In *Meridian*, the rapist commits the act against the white wife of a black friend in anger at losing an arm due to a murder attempt on Civil Rights workers by white racists. The rape is known

in the black community and becomes a point of stress within the Movement community.

4. Ida B. Wells, a nineteenth- and early twentieth-century feminist and the nation's first black female journalist, spent the major part of her public career in the antilynching campaign against the terror that intimidated the black community for almost fifty years. I thank my friend and colleague Craig Werner, who helped me to clarify the tension in the title of Walker's story—one that indicts the racist, patriarchal society for effectively separating black and white women by marginalizing them in each other's eyes.

5. Painter, " 'Social Equality,' Miscegenation, Labor and Power," p. 63. Also see Trudier Harris, *Exorcising Blackness, Historical and Literary Lynching and Burning Rituals* (Bloomington: Indiana University Press, 1984), for literary representations of lynchings.

6. In Georgia the women had "assumed a lifelong friendship ... that [they assured each other] would be truer than everything, [and would] endure even ... marriages, children, [and] husbands" (Walker 1981:95).

7. Other contemporary black women writers, like Toni Morrison, address black and white women's alliances in this way. Pauline Breedlove in *The Bluest Eye* does not understand why her white female employer withholds wages and continued employment from her because she (Pauline) does not leave her husband, Cholly. The employer advises Pauline to compel Cholly to pay the household bills and give her alimony as well. Pauline thinks: *"It didn't seem none too bright for a black woman to leave a black man for a white woman ... I seen she didn't understand that all I needed from her was my eleven dollars to pay the gas man so I could cook," The Bluest Eye* (New York: Pocket Books, 1970), p. 95–96, author's emphasis).

8. Walker's subsequent rejection of Wells' advice as "useless" recalls an incident in Jean Toomer's *Cane*. The protagonist of his play *Kabnis* seeks advice from old man Father John, the spirit of the past. Kabnis is angry and berates the old man when he receives no useful information from him. On the contrary, Walker knows that Wells can give us no answers for today's world. We must find our own way to make our world better.

9. Many feminists of color note the development of negative literary and cultural images of nonwhite women in the United States. The sexuality of these women inferred promiscuity and immorality, suggesting these women were eager to offer sexual favors to all men. Thus were not raped. Even today, women of color rape victims are often treated in this way.

10. Maxine Hong Kingston, *Woman Warrior: Memoir of a Girlhood Among Ghosts* (New York: Vintage Books, 1975), p. 3. Kingston begins her story with a story that her mother told her. In China, many years earlier, her father's sister, whose name she had never heard before, disgraced their family and upset the villagers by taking a lover and bearing a child. Subsequently, she committed suicide but had her revenge by drowning herself in the well that was the community's only source of water. Even as she tells the story, Kingston's mother cautions, "You must never tell anyone. ... We say that

your father had all brothers . . . it is as though she [the sister] had never been born." But Kingston writes of her nonconformist aunt, and her words shatter the silence surrounding the life and death of her aunt.

11. My reading of the story justifies this optimistic ending. Although a situation of rape, as Linda Gordon pointed out to me, it is a women's story, reclaiming women's bodies and women's voices. In this way, Walker's "speaking out" empowers all female language in opposition to patriarchy.

5

Unthinking the Metaphor

12

The Rape of the Rural Muse: Wordsworth's "The Solitary Reaper" as a Version of Pastourelle

NANCY A. JONES

Literary historians who discuss the origins of courtly love poetry or comment on the historical dearth of woman poets tend to discuss women and folk songs in one breath. They see the masculine art lyric as emerging from an anonymous, collective folk art. In this perspective folk songs appears as a primitive backdrop to the self-conscious artistry that impels male poets to write down their songs. To an earlier generation of scholars, equating masculinity with culture and femininity with nature, it seemed obvious that "masculine Art-Poetry" gradually emerged from "feminine Folk-Song" during the Middle Ages. This view is itself part of a deep-seated tendency to subsume a female voice of the folk, the earth, or nature into a masculine voice of artfully shaped, controlling song. It is behind the pastourelle's own hidden ideology and its continuation, albeit much transformed, in Wordsworth's celebrated lyric.

In the medieval lyric genre known as the pastourelle, male and female lyricism meet in a strophic, quasi-dramatic dialogue. This poetic form is not merely a burlesque of courtly love, transposing the exchange between knight and lady to that between knight and shepherdess. Rather, it is a highly self-reflexive genre, wherein the medieval lettered poet can express—and repress—his anxieties over his relationship with folk songs and folk art. This tension between art and the folk, the literary and the popular, extends far into the cultural heritage from which the interpretive studies of medieval poetry emerge.[1]

Literary Romanticism, as is well known, is deeply indebted to folk genres such as the ballad and the fairy tale. Thomas Percy's *Reliques of Ancient Poetry*, published in 1765, may well have inspired the revival of lyric poetry at the end of the eighteenth century. The English Romantic poets regarded the folk ballad as "pure poetry," for it appeared untouched by sophisticated rhetoric and artifice and the "artificial" themes of literature. The ballad became a model for poets striving to recover "something more simple, sensuous, and passionate than the standards of neoclassicism had allowed."[2] Romantic pastoral poetry, therefore, inspired by the vogue for folk songs and folksingers, might be seen as an attempt to bridge the gap between what William Empson calls "proletarian literature" and literary pastoral.

A study of the past, however, suggests that this union of the two forms is not so simple. One particular form of literary pastoral represents the boundary between art lyric and folk songs as the site of a mythic conquest of song, gendered as female, by poetry, gendered as male. Taking inspiration from Empson's analysis of pastoral, I suggest that we broaden the definition of pastourelle. It represents not only a medieval lyric genre, but also a changing, yet persistent, impulse on the part of the male poet to bring the female folksinger into an imaginary relationship with himself, sometimes forcibly.

The comparison of this medieval genre with a poem drawn from a radically different tradition may appear eccentric, if not wrongheaded. I will justify my unreverential (but not irreverent) reading by demonstrating striking analogies between Wordsworth's poem and the medieval pastourelle. First, there is a rural encounter between a wandering male character and a woman working in the fields. Second, this encounter is told from the man's point of view. Third, the female figure in the medieval pastourelle is initially overheard singing a lament, much like Wordsworth's solitary reaper. Fourth, a social and ethnic difference separates the man and woman. Finally, the speaker transfers his own sense of difference onto the reader. I offer this list as an analysis of the basic elements underlying the narrative situation of the pastourelle, not as a full account of the literary genre.

Kathryn Gravdal has recently shown us how not to deny the reality of the rape narrative in the medieval pastourelle.[3] Her analysis, however, can be carried a stage further. The knight forcibly takes the woman's body; the male poet, more subtly but no less forcibly, takes the woman's voice. The poems to be discussed dramatize an encounter between male *poet* and female *singer*. In each the woman's inferior social status is equated with sexual vulnerability and sexual vulnerability, I shall argue, becomes a figure for song's inferiority to poetry.

The typical pastourelle presents itself as a knight's reminiscence of a fortuitous springtime encounter. As he rides along through the countryside, the knight comes upon a lovely shepherdess and wastes no time in approaching her and asking for sex, in the form of a euphemistic *demande d'amour*.[4] In some versions the shepherdess instantly accepts his overtures; in others she resists. When faced with resistance, the knight tries to gain her favors through bribes, persuasion, or force. In the end he has his way, often brutally. Occasionally, however, he withdraws his suit, and in the more farcical versions he is beaten off by angry shepherds. More rarely the dialogue between the knight and the shepherdess becomes a lively debate in which the shepherdess displays superior wit and verbally outduels her physically intimidating aggressor.

Critics often overlook the crucial difference between the two speakers in pastourelle. Although both the knight and the shepherdess are stock characters, the knight appears as a kind of narrator-protagonist. His experience establishes the poem's perspective, however ironical that perspective may be. Posed by a tree or spring, the shepherdess appears as part of the landscape and remains unaltered throughout the action. (The knight persona has even more power when the poet is himself a knight.) Furthermore, the knight, as narrator, is in full control of the poem's matter. The poem begins with his entrance onto the scene and closes with his departure. One might say that the genre is animated by male desire and closed by the woman's humiliation.

The shepherdess' voice does not emanate from a female poet, nor does her voice have the same double dimension as the knight's.[5] In the pastourelle, the poet often speaks in his own name, while the shepherdess is a fictional voice, a conventional lyric puppet that the poet animates according to his comic purposes. Only in the exceptional versions composed by the troubadours Marcabru and Giraut

Riquier does the shepherdess appear as a partner in a genuine debate that undercuts the genre's built-in narrative closure.

With its often brutal misogynist humor and type characters, the medieval pastourelle may, in the eyes of the modern reader, seem to be a poetic relic reflecting the tastes of a remote society inured to sexual violence and a rigid social hierarchy. And yet remote as such poetry seems, something of its spirit has survived in modern lyric. Long after knights ceased their pursuit of shepherdesses, male writers (and critics) continued to find enticing nymphs by the roadside and, later, in the city.[6] The shepherdess' charm is explicitly erotic, but her attraction also derives from her song and the male lyric poet's desire to master it. This desire to possess the rustic muse and her song is the subject of this study. In the second portion of this essay I will examine one of the emblematic poems of English Romanticism, Wordsworth's "The Solitary Reaper," as a transmutation of the lyric pastourelle.

By signaling his superiority to the reaper and her song in the very act of proclaiming his awe and solicitude for her, Wordsworth offers us a poem that enacts a similar pattern. The male poet experiences spiritual transcendence through the mediation of a female figure who as earth mother personifies nature and as rural muse represents the power of pretextual song. At the same time, however, the encounter reveals the poet's need to master this mythicized female voice (which threatens to overwhelm his own) and to incorporate it into his text. Once her song's power has been tapped, the songstress-muse is left behind. In Wordsworth's version of pastourelle, the discovery of folk song by the literary poet in terms of a conquest/abandonment myth is subtly displaced by a new set of hierarchical oppositions.

In the medieval pastourelle, the poet treats the rural encounter in the comic mode and travesties the peasant woman from the point of view of the male aristocrat confident of his physical, social, and aesthetic superiority. In the medieval poetic system, the pastourelle functions as the genre that "corrects" the excessive refinements of courtly poetry, allowing the courtly lover to indulge himself in an entertaining erotic adventure among the simple folk who live more completely under nature's rule. The Romantic poet Wordsworth mythicizes the encounter as a moment when the poet's vision fuses the principles of nature and imagination.

As versions of pastourelle, both the medieval and the modern poems reveal the strategies adopted by lettered poets of different eras to embrace and simultaneously silence peasant women's sexual and cultural difference. The strategy consists in a distorting of a peasant woman's singing into a sirenlike song that in turn conceals the male poet's fantasy of self-generation through rape. Once this strategy is recognized, however, the poems can be made to reveal the male poet's discomfort with his true, less flattering relationship to the peasant woman's art and labor.

By casting "The Solitary Reaper" against the rough comic back-drop of the pastourelle, I have already cast suspicion on the self-styled "Bard of hill and dale." The poem's speaker is obviously not literally a rapist, nor is Wordsworth consciously celebrating men's power to rape. The modern male poet's subjective, idealizing re-sponse to a peasant woman's singing, however, displaces physical to metaphoric conquest, namely the male, leisure-class appropriation of a peasant woman's power to create poetry. He takes not her body but her body's relationship to nature through work that creates spontan-eous song. Wordsworth exercises his gender and class prerogatives by recreating the peasant woman as nature's songstress. The desire beneath this vision has both sexual and political dimensions.

The narrative of "The Solitary Reaper" can be reconstructed thus: A peasant woman's singing halts the lyric speaker on his way through the countryside (here an English tourist traveling through Scotland). He stops to admire her and to muse about her song before moving on. For convenience, I will quote the poem in its entirety:

> Behold her, single in the field,
> Yon solitary Highland Lass!
> Reaping and singing by herself;
> Stop here, or gently pass!
> Alone she cuts and binds the grain,
> And sings a melancholy strain;
> O listen! for the Vale profound
> Is overflowing with the sound.
>
> No Nightingale did ever chaunt
> More welcome notes to weary bands
> Of travellers in some shady haunt,
> Among Arabian sands:
> A voice so thrilling ne'er was heard
> In spring-time from the Cuckoo-bird,
> Breaking the silence of the seas
> Among the farthest Hebrides.

Will no one tell me what she sings? —
Perhaps the plaintive numbers flow
For old, unhappy, far-off things,
And battles long ago:
Or is it some more humble lay,
Familiar matter of to-day?
Some natural sorrow, loss, or pain,
That has been, and may be again?

Whate'er the theme, the Maiden sang
As if her song could have no ending:
I saw her singing at her work,
And o'er the sickle bending, —
I listened, motionless and still;
And, as I mounted up the hill,
The music in my heart I bore,
Long after it was heard no more.[7]

As is well known, Wordsworth's poem was not composed spontaneously upon his encounter with a solitary reaper. The story of its
genesis appears in Dorothy Wordsworth's *Recollections of a Tour in
Scotland*, the account she wrote of the trip she, Wordsworth, and
Coleridge made in the early autumn of 1803. Two years after their
return, Wordsworth composed the poem and Dorothy inserted it into
her recently finished *Recollections*. The poem appears as an entry
for September 13, following Dorothy's description of a scene she and
Wordsworth came upon as they walked through a Highland valley:
"It was harvest-time, and the fields were quietly (might I be allowed
to say pensively?) enlivened by small companies of reapers. It is not
uncommon in the more lonely parts of the Highlands to see a single
person so employed. The following poem was suggested to Wm. by a
beautiful sentence in Thomas Wilkinson's Tour in Scotland."[8] She
refers to a passage in the then unpublished travel diary written by
her brother's friend, the gentleman farmer Thomas Wilkinson. To
his touristic account of the harvest season in the Highlands Wilkinson had added the following note: "Passed by a Female who was
reaping alone, she sung in Erse as she bended over the sickle, the
sweetest human voice I ever heard. Her strains were tenderly, and
felt delicious long after they were heard no more."[9]

Wordsworth's editors note that Wilkinson himself later copied
the sentence into a commonplace book kept by Wordsworth.[10] Critics cite this information as evidence of Wordsworth's famous process
of "remembered recreation," which they treat as a cerebral process.

Yet one could also argue that Wordsworth's debt to Wilkinson represents his identification with the masculine tenor of Wilkinson's text. While Dorothy Wordsworth's account of the scenes above Loch Voil does not specify that the reapers were women or that they were singing, Wilkinson's text clearly conveys a masculine response to a woman and her voice described in culturally loaded terms as "sweet," "tender," and "delicious." Did Wordsworth receive more than this "beautiful sentence" about Highland women from Wilkinson? Was this borrowing part of a larger, less ethereal masculine exchange of impressions? We will never know for certain.[11]

At first glance, sexual politics and even sexual desire seem to be conspicuously missing from Wordsworth's poem. "The Solitary Reaper" appears to turn male adventure into pure reverie over the resonant, yet indistinct, singing of the lone woman reaping grain in a field. Whereas the knight appears as an experienced seducer, Wordsworth's speaker seems simply admiring. Strictly speaking, no encounter takes place. The action consists of the poet's observation and description of a woman reaping and singing in the field. Between the observer and the observed nothing happens. The reaper is (apparently) unaware of her observer's presence. "Stop here, or gently pass!" the speaker bids himself and his reader. Something, evidently, creates a mysterious barrier between them that both silences and privileges the speaker so that he may speak of, but not to, the reaper.

What makes the reaper so solitary? Her solitude—reiterated three times in the opening stanza—would seem to identify her with the numerous female solitaries of other Wordsworth poems, those sad, sometimes deranged figures who roam the countryside begging for food and lamenting lost children or lovers.[12] Likewise, the sorrowful character of her song (described as "a melancholy strain" and a flow of "plaintive numbers") might recall their complaints. The poem's speaker, however, characterizes her song's sorrow only in generic terms as either that of ballads or a "humble lay" (stanza 3). The reaper, furthermore, belongs to a georgic world of work and song, and so her solitude must be explained as a function of the curious distance maintained between her and the speaker. Furthermore, once we recognize "The Solitary Reaper" as a version of pastourelle, the voyeuristic nature of this pleasure should become clear.

Knight and tourist both enjoy their class prerogative to wander idly over hill and dale among the "backward" countryfolk. (English disdain for the "primitive" Scottish Highlanders during the eighteenth century is a relevant factor here.) Furthermore, they seek to possess something that resists possession. Thus while the seduction-rape narrative is *literally* absent from Wordsworth's poem, the pastourelle scenario is implicit: an errant male comes across a lone woman in the fields and pauses to "satisfy" himself before moving on.

That Wordsworth's pastourelle-alias-pastoral presents a particularly gender- and class-determined view of the rural world is revealed, I would argue, by the very effort to de-eroticize what is traditionally an erotic and predatory encounter. Wordsworth follows tradition in personifying the bucolic world as an anonymous, vulnerable, and beautiful woman.[13] Perhaps the sexual plot is the only avenue back into the pastoral world for the modern poet (and novelist). For Wordsworth, it was important to disclaim any erotic relationship with nature and the women he identified with it. By avoiding plots and themes associated with sexual desire, Wordsworth appears to desexualize his own pastoral persona. And yet, in such poems as "To a Highland Girl" and "The Poet and the Caged Turtledove," Wordsworth half-confesses, by denying, the erotic elements in his nature poetry. Not surprisingly, given his discomfort with sexual themes, he never repeated the direct exploration of his own aggressive impulses toward a feminized nature found in the early poem "Nutting."[14]

The encounter between the passerby and the reaper is predicated on desire, but this is not a man's desire for a woman's body. It is a more general desire for mastery, whereby the man denies or conceals the true nature of the differences he half-consciously perceives between himself and the woman singer. Wordsworth's attempt to aestheticize the reaper (to "reap and bind her song," as a recent critic notes approvingly[15]) can be seen as a desire to treat both her and her song as vessels into which he will pour his own poetic power.

The poet-traveler's seemingly spontaneous outburst over the beauty of the reaper's song is in fact highly contrived. The device of the dumb character, addressed through repeated imperatives ("Behold"/ "Stop here, or gently pass!"/ "O listen!"), turns the reader into a complicit spectator. The first stanza contrasts two realms of discourse, one perpetual and impersonal, the other momentary and subjective. The reaper's song is endless and inexhaustible, whereas the speaker's rejoinders, inspired by her singing, are broken. Temporal and spatial hyperbole further widen the gap between them. She is rooted in a single time and space; he commands a wide vista of both geography and history. For the male traveler, the linguistic barrier intensifies the sense of the woman's relationship to nature. The (for him) incomprehensible Erse lyrics serve to conflate her song with wordless birdsong, as we see in stanza 2. Here the highly conventional comparisons of her voice to those of the nightingale and the cuckoo transport us to the antipodes of Europe, where man, we infer, feels his own solitude most keenly. Both birds "console" a lonely mankind amidst nature's deserts. The speaker's rhetorical plea, "Will no one tell me what she sings?," justifies his inability to comprehend her song by universalizing the weary (male) traveler's need for feminine "solace."

The forms "singing" and "bending" denote a timeless present, in contrast to the preterite form ("bore") that signals the birth of Wordsworth's poem. This contrast in verb tense and aspect implies that her labor is to be seen as an ongoing activity, whereas Wordsworth's metaphorical harvest—the movement of consciousness—presents itself as an act. Similarly, while her singing and her labor appear as simultaneous activities, fused by the coordinate positioning of the forms "singing and bending," Wordsworth's poem emerges at a later moment, in an act of "consciousness." This verbal contrast opposes the poet's conscious art of composition to the artless singing of the reaper. (He does not differentiate between her song and her labor.) Furthermore, one notes an implied contrast between the restricted range of her song and the permanence of his poem, which fixes forever the encounter as he has experienced it. Her literal voice fades from hearing as he strolls on, but he claims to carry off within himself its "music," i.e., its essence.

For all her obliviousness to the speaker, the singing reaper resembles the Homeric siren, a female figure whose alluring song lures the male wayfarer to abandon his journey and draws him to his death. The mythical siren is also a winged creature who conducts souls to the Other World. Of the siren one historian of Greek religion writes: "The Sirens stand, it would seem, to the ancient as well as to the modern, for the impulses in life as yet unmoralized, imperious longings, fantasies, whether of love or art or philosophy, magical voices calling to a man from his 'Land of Heart's Desire' and to which if he hearken, still sing on."[16] It is the song in particular that pulls a man toward his doom.

We can perhaps take the implication of the siren figure a stage further when we recognize that its appeal to modern culture rests in part on the oedipal master myth. In this view, the song represents "the love of the mother in all its allurement, holding forth the promise of the Land of Heart's Desire which symbolizes the possession of the beloved mother; but the end of that song is death (castration)."[17] On this reading, Wordsworth would emerge from his encounter with the reaper/castrating mother as a triumphant Odysseus:

> I listened, motionless and still,
> And, as I mounted up the hill,
> The music in my heart I bore,
> Long after it was heard no more.

Such an analysis, however, offers only a limited perspective on the reaper—the poet's. Her symbolic value is a key to the poetic myth of the man-child artist that informs the poem. In his process of maturation, he must pass through the castration anxiety brought on by his accidental glimpse of nature exposed as female (i.e., minus a phallus). His success is confirmed in the past tense of the lines just cited. Momentarily caught by the inexplicable charm of her voice, he breaks free and "mounts" up the hill, carrying off the woman's song. This final ascent implies the speaker's heroic repossession of the phallus as he incorporates the latter ("in my heart I bore") into his poetic identity. He becomes again potent in his implicit sexual mastery of the woman and in his male overcoming of sexual difference.

The poem he writes about the reaper, nevertheless, is engendered by *his* reaping of something that he himself does not possess. The final stanza, moreover, indicates that a fundamental shift in relations has taken place. After listening to her song, the hitherto motionless onlooker triumphantly sets off up the hill, having gathered an intangible harvest. Here at the poem's close he returns to the outer world bearing inside himself the power, if not the meaning, of her song.

Instead of the reaper's song, we have Wordsworth's poem about listening to it. He has made off with her music to ascend to literary fame, much as the knight makes off with the shepherdess' virginity. While the pastourelle maintains the façade of courtship or, more accurately, seduction, here there is no dialogue that would bring the reaper out of the background and onto the same plane as the poet. His apparent concern to leave her undisturbed is actually a refusal to acknowledge her relationship to her song. For her, after all, song serves to accompany, lighten, and even beautify hard labor. Wordsworth ignores this dimension of her song. By keeping her one step removed from us, clothed in anonymity, he is able to carry out a poetic violation. (Rape is, after all, an act that denies a woman's sexual autonomy). She becomes the basis of his own Romantic poetic myth, the personification of folk song, the song of the earth, which he has to encounter, experience, internalize, and ultimately leave behind.

Wordsworth's "gentle" solicitude toward the singer (line 4) enables him to romanticize and appropriate her solitude (that is, her personal and cultural autonomy) as a mirror of his own poetic process. In the second stanza, he declares her more beautiful than the traditional emblems of song, the nightingale and the cuckoo. He can only speculate about the subject of her song. His question, "Will no one tell me what she sings?," is a question about the subject of woman herself. She is presented here as a mythical being on the boundary of nature and culture, just outside man's approach. The voice of imagination (the nightingale) and the voice of love (the cuckoo) refresh and humanize man's existence. As the speaker pauses before this scene of pure movement and song, continuous and unselfconscious, he seems to have brought us to the primal scene of poetry.

The accentuated distance between the speaker and the reaper has yet another significance. Behind the reverent awe expressed by the lyric speaker lies an effort to turn historically specific economic and social distance into a quasi-religious barrier and the reaper into an object of veneration. And yet the sexual and cultural differences that the reaper and her song represent are not in themselves absolute. Instead of attempting to bridge them, Wordsworth mythicizes the gap of class and gender as a timeless divide, crossed only by the poetic imagination conceived as a transcendent principle. Thus he can endow the peasant woman's song with its sirenlike mystery through his privileged denial of her labor. The combination "bending and singing" denotes a musical fusion of work and song, but the poem effaces both the effort and the material value of this labor that he, as a member of the middle class, reaps.[18]

The medieval pastourelle, as we have noted, creates semidramatic characters or dramatized voices. Wordsworth's poem addresses the reader through a textual voice. The textual voice is literally a borrowed voice, in the sense that it emerges only intermittently and is dependent upon the reader's voice for full realization as an utterance. But the lyric's textual voice has a certain autonomy or freedom. Wordsworth's poem, in implying the fortuitous and illicit nature of its own engendering, as the child of rape, casts itself against what is to be seen as the limited, conventional signifying power of the reaper's traditional song. His poem nominally celebrates her song, but in fact celebrates its own textuality, its own signifying potency.

Like the knight, the poet-wanderer claims to be under the spell of female beauty in its harmony with nature. As a poet, however (and the poet always stands behind the knight), he is experiencing his textual privilege to recuperate an ideal unity of labor and song. His rapturous response to folk song as pure music and his lack of interest in its content and cultural function leads to the more far-reaching discovery of his own capacity as a writer to assert the superiority of his own poem by virtue of its power to move from the mythic to the historical order. Provoked by the literary innocence (i.e., the metaphorical virginity) of the reaper's song, which has no textual existence, Wordsworth, like Apollo with Daphne, forcefully embraces it to create a text of great cultural prestige, which is in turn monumentalized by a virgin sister-amanuensis.

The act of simplifying and idealizing an experience or object is central to poesis; Wordsworth's poem reveals a hidden but not infrequent strategy of Western poetics, namely the use of woman as a vehicle of transcendence. In pastourelle, however, a trace of the woman's song remains. If recognized, it can disrupt the metaphoric economy of the pastourelle whereby women's bodies and voices become the currency of male artistic self-assertion and prestige.

By keeping the poem a monologue, Wordsworth defuses and displaces some of the sexuality of the pastourelle, whose dialogue form gives a greater individuality to the woman. Wordsworth's reaper, aestheticized and mystified as a voice of the countryside, is also (in part) desexualized. Yet the historical moment of the meeting of art song and folk song cannot entirely suppress the play of genres in the meeting of the two isolated figures in this rural landscape.

"The Solitary Reaper" presents a particular turn on the basic paradox of pastoral poetry. In seeking to evoke the unsophisticated beauties of the rustic world that he so admires, the pastoral poet necessarily transmutes them by casting them into the sophisticated idiom of poetry. Wordsworth, as a pastourelle poet, cannot fully disguise the fact that his poetic tribute to a solitary peasant songstress originates in a displaced but nonetheless intense desire to assert his power over her, and this remains a form of violation. The reaper's enticing solitude, like that of her medieval predecessor, therefore, is not simply the imaginary romantic one projected onto her by the poet. Rather, it hints at the historical marginalizations of women, peasants, and their arts within the violent adventures of male poetic desire.

NOTES

1. The classic scholarly speculation about the "female" origin of poetry can be found in W. J. Entwistle, *The European Ballad* (Oxford: Clarendon

Press, 1939), pp. 37–38. On the gradual emergence of "masculine Art-Poetry" from "feminine Folk-Song" see E. K. Chambers' review essay, "Some Aspects of Medieval Poetry," in *Sir Thomas Wyatt and Some Collected Studies* (London: Sidgwick and Jackson, 1933), pp. 46–63. On the subject of medieval women's songs, see Theodor Frings, *Die Anfänge der europäische Liebesdichtung im 11. und 12. Jahrhundert.* (Munich: Bayerischen Akademie der Wissenschaften, 1960).

2. See Kenneth MacLean, *Agrarian Age: A Background for Wordsworth* (New Haven: Yale University Press, 1956), p. 51.

3. Gravdal has convincingly demonstrated how critics have isolated the shepherdess as a figure for interpretation and in doing so have completely overlooked "the celebration of rape in the corpus." See her "Camouflaging Rape: The Rhetoric of Sexual Violence in the Medieval Pastourelle," *Romanic Review* (1985), 76(4):369. As the first feminist analysis of the medieval pastourelle, Gravdal's article presents a powerful corrective to the often sexist interpretations of pastourelles. In her essay for this volume she gives documentation on the incidence of sexual violence in medieval France showing that the supposedly fictive rapes in pastourelle were all too real. The basic elements of the knight-shepherdess encounter can be found in the Greco-Roman myths where a god rapes a woodland nymph or mortal woman who has unwittingly exposed herself to his view. As Gravdal's work suggests, such stories may be displaced versions of a social reality.

4. See, for example, Jean-Claude Rivière, *Pastourelles II* (Geneva: Droz, 1975), no. 58.

5. One should not conflate the pastourelle with the debate genre known as the *tenso,* where a debate takes place between two poets who name one another. A small number of male/female tensos exist, for example the debate poem between the troubadour Gui d'Ussel and the *trobairitz* Marie de Ventadour.

6. Michael Zink, *La Pastourelle: Poésie et folklore au moyen âge* (Paris: Bordas, 1972), pp. 104–116; 119–120. Also see Mark Johnston, "The Shepherdess in the City," *Comparative Literature* (1974), 26(2):124–141.

7. Text from William Wordsworth, *The Poetical Works,* ed. E. de Selincourt and Helen Darbishire (1952; reprint, Oxford: Clarendon Press, 1968), 3:77.

8. E. de Selincourt, ed., *Journals of Dorothy Wordsworth* (New York: Macmillan, 1941), 1:380–381.

9. Thomas Wilkinson, *Tours to the British Mountains* (London: Taylor and Hessey, 1824), p. 12.

10. William Wordsworth, *The Poetical Works,* eds. E. de Selincourt and Helen Darbishire, 3:444–445.

11. In this context, a comparison of Wilkinson's text with Dorothy Wordsworth's travel diary, *Recollections of a Tour in Scotland,* is suggestive. Whereas Dorothy writes frequently and at some length about her attempts at communication with Highland women across the linguistic barrier, Wilkinson is constantly riveted by their bare limbs! His account, with its strange

mixture of concrete detail and sentimental generalizations, offers an example of what Jonathan Freedman calls "the complicated rhetoric of fascination and contempt" deployed by post-Enlightenment poets such as Wordsworth and T. S. Eliot in their attempts to invoke the otherness of the common man or woman for the imaginative or social purposes of the poet and a "horrified fascination with the distasteful commonness those people insist on displaying" ("Autocanonization: Tropes of Self-Legitimation in 'Popular Culture,' " *Yale Journal of Criticism* [Fall 1987], 1(1):205–206.

12. See, for instance, poems such as "Guilt and Sorrow," "The Indian Woman's Complaint," "The Thorn," and "Her Eyes Are Wild."

13. A twentieth-century version of the songstress overheard by a male passerby appears in Wallace Stevens' "The Idea of Order at Key West." In Stevens' poem, the woman is a more elusive figure, a kind of platonic muse who personifies the "blessed rage for order" impelling all "makers" (poets). The exploitative element is missing.

14. In this remarkable poem, Wordsworth tells of a boyhood excursion in which he ravaged a grove of hazelnut trees ("a virgin scene!") with a nutting crook, leaving "the green and mossy bower,/Deformed and sullied . . ."

15. Notes to the MS. display copy of "The Solitary Reaper," William Wordsworth and the Age of English Romanticism, an exhibition at the New York Public Library, October 31, 1987–January 2, 1988.

16. Jane Ellen Harrison, *Prolegomena to the Study of Greek Religion*, 3d ed. (Cambridge: Harvard University Press, 1922), pp. 202–203.

17. Henry Alden Bunker, "The Voice as (Female) Phallus," *Psychoanalytic Quarterly* (1934), 3:427–428. For a rather different analysis of the relationship between the female voice and castration, see Kaja Silverman, *The Acoustic Mirror: The Female Voice in Psychoanalysis and Cinema* (Bloomington: Indiana University Press, 1988), pp. 72–87. Silverman's discussion of the trope of the maternal voice as a "blanket of sound" or "sonorous envelope" offers another perspective on the poem's castration drama. In its effect on Wordsworth, the reaper's voice resembles what Silverman calls the maternal voice in its fantasmic guise. The speaker's blissful tone, his rhetorical amplification of the reaper's voice, and his mystification of the song's content can be seen as elements of the utopian dream born out of the male subject's (inevitable) experience of division and loss. Unable to fully recover his (imaginary) union with the reaper's/mother's voice, Wordsworth can only produce a surrogate object, his poem. Possessed of a "copy" of her song, he can reexperience the infantile plenitude associated with her irrecoverable presence. From this theoretical viewpoint, "The Solitary Reaper" would originate from a fetishistic impulse. While I find Silverman's remarks about the female voice and castration convincing, my own reading of the poem stresses the hidden aggressive and appropriative elements in Wordsworth's response to the reaper's song.

18. If such an analysis of Wordsworth seems extreme, one might ask, by way of reply, whether the poet's earlier abandonment of his French mistress and their child does not haunt this poem. In any case, there is a striking

parallel between the youthful "adventure" in France with a woman of a different culture and language and the plot of the medieval pastourelle. Wordsworth was able to sow a few wild oats in France and then reap them poetically in Scotland! For a recent commentary on the William Wordsworth–Annette Vallon affair and a feminist analysis of the 1805 version of *The Prelude* as Wordsworth's need not only to "exorcise his illegitimate paternity" but also to "reestablish himself sexually in order to declare his imagination restored," see Gayatri Chakravorty Spivak, "Sex and History in *The Prelude* (1805): Books Nine to Thirteen," in *In Other Worlds: Essays in Cultural Politics* (New York: Methuen, 1987), pp. 46–76.

13

On Ravishing Urns:
Keats in His Tradition

FROMA I. ZEITLIN

Here is the old plague spot; the pestilence, the raw scrofula. I mean that there is nothing disgraces me in my own eyes so much as being one of a race of eyes nose and mouth beings in a planet call'd earth who all from Plato to Wesley have always mingled goatish winnyish lustful love w/abstract adoration of the deity. I don't understand Greek—is the love of God and the Love of women express'd by the same word in Greek? I hope my little mind is wrong. . . . Has Plato separated these loves? Ha! I see how they endeavor to divide but there appears to be a horrid relationship.

John Keats

> But my flag is not unfurl'd
> on the admiral staff—and to philosophize
> I dare not yet—oh never will the prize,
> high reason, and the lore of good and ill
> be my reward.

John Keats

The original version of Keats' "Ode on a Grecian Urn," published in the *Annals of the Fine Arts* in January 1820, presents an interesting textual variant from the later and now canonical transcript of the poem.[1] The conclusion to the first stanza that culminates in the violent interplay between masculine and feminine figures reads:

> What men or gods are these? What maidens loth?
> What mad pursuit? What struggle to escape?
> What pipes and timbrels? What wild ecstasy?

The first version, however, substitutes "what love? what dance?" for the single query, "what mad pursuit?"

Poetically, the revision is a substantial improvement. "What mad pursuit" is far more vivid than the colorless "what love? what dance?" The new division of the line into two phrases of four and six sylla-bles makes a fine chiasmus between "What mad pursuit? What struggle to escape?" (4/6) and the preceding verse ("What men or gods are these? What maidens loth?" 6/4). Taken as a couplet, the two shorter phrases ("What maidens loth?" "What mad pursuit?") follow one another and are framed by the more extended queries ("What men or gods are these? What struggle to escape?"). The strong initial alliteration (*m*en, *m*aidens, *m*ad) enhances the musical rhythm of the repetitive questions, while the double sounds of "*m*ad *p*ursuit" echo in reverse in the "*pi*pes and *ti*mbrels" of the last line.

As for the sense of the lines, "what mad pursuit?" more precisely defines what is happening on this first panel of the urn. Intervening between "what maidens loth" and "their struggle to escape," the phrase assigns the source of energy to the masculine passion that gives rise to the maidens' resistance and overcomes the seeming illogic of the original series: "love," "dance," and "struggle to es-cape."

Above all, "what mad pursuit" answers to the initial characteri-zation of the Grecian urn itself, addressed as "thou still unravish'd bride of quietness." How can there be ravishment (potential or oth-erwise) without a ravisher? How can there be struggle without a "mad pursuit"? And without this move, how is one to define the passionate intellectual quest of the poet himself to penetrate the mysterious silence of the urn, to learn, in fact, the identity of the very figures who are caught between pursuit and attempted flight? The opening of the poem announces an eroticized quest for knowledge[2]—and also suggests perhaps its inseparable converse: an allegorical displacement of the erotics of pursuit and conquest.

In the feminization of the urn—its swelling shape, its hollow interior—and the consequent virilization of the quester,[3] the sexual rhetoric of the poem organizes the relationship between the object and its viewer and implicates the reader/listener in the poet's own strategies of desire and the fluctuating rhythms of his "courtship." From the original imagining (the urn is a desirable female body), the poet (and the poem) are judged by the success or failure of the masculine drive to seize, possess, and consummate desire in the enterprise that is deemed the most potent sign of manliness.

Read within the thematics of art, life, and poetry, the ending of the poem, "beauty is truth, truth beauty," has disappointed (and shocked) many critics with its drastic shift from the poetic to the philosophical, the imagistic to the propositional—an anticlimax in its "sublime commonplace"[4] and a new and exasperating enigma instead of a solution. That disappointment, however, is also (and emotionally) predicated on the sexual expectations raised by the ambiguous phrase "still unravish'd" and by the overtly erotic scenes on the first two panels of the urn. "Friend to man" instead of "bride," a riddling motto instead of a kiss—or more—leave some readers with dissatisfactions not unlike the "burning forehead" and "parching tongue" that close the middle stanza of the poem and bespeak a sexual excitement that is never quite discharged in a gratifying lyric conclusion. The desires of both poetics and erotics are aroused by the language and rhythm of the poem, and these two aspects intersect throughout.

More specifically, the brilliance of the poem resides in the intersection (and interfusion) of two formal literary genres. As a description of a work of art, the poem is an ekphrasis, a rhetorical exercise in painting (or sculpting) images in words,[5] the genre characteristically concerned with the underlying tensions between the relative values of the visual and verbal arts. The address to the silent urn might even seem to literalize the famous dictum attributed to the ancient Greek poet Simonides, that "a picture" is "silent poetry" and "a poem is a speaking picture."[6] On the other hand, the poem also plays with the topos of the ekphrastic scene in which a viewer, enthralled at the sight of a work of art, seeks either to describe what is depicted or, if he (and occasionally she) does not recognize the subject, to find an interpreter who does.[7] The epigrammatic tradition is also recalled, that of an inscription upon a work of art, often a monument or votive offering, that invites the passerby to read it and, in doing so, to make it into a speaking object.[8] Keats' urn, then, invokes both the natural silence of the picture (for how can pictures speak?) and the utterance of the *objet parlant*, which is ventriloquized through the poet/reader's voice. Finally, the ekphrastic scene is designed to stimulate inquiry as to the identity of what is seen. Because all works of art are by their nature symbolic representations, the convention, even if it seems ornamental, instigates, in fact, the quest for deeper meanings and interpretation of the object's visual surface.[9]

The ode, however, can also be read against another set of conventions. In its address to the virginal bride, the object of desire, the poem initiates a familiar sequence of courtship, designed to overcome the reluctance of the mistress or beloved. The poet attempts to woo the maiden by invoking his desire, her beauty, and the supposed joys of sexuality, love, and romance and by resorting to other rhetorical means of gaining mastery over her. Such courtship poems from antiquity on trail along with them associations of death and mortality. Virginity is regarded as a temporal and temporary state, contrary to "nature" when the moment of generative ripeness arrives,[10] and the urgency to consummation is predicated on the short and feverish time of life. In this predictable scenario, the frustrated lover may finally reproach the unresponsive object of his affections for her unfeeling coldness (her marblelike disdain: "Cold Pastoral!"). Her virtues may no longer seem as compelling in his disillusioned eyes ("trodden weed"). Her seductiveness—her "ravishing" of him—may be just a tease, and he may resign himself and seek other sublimating consolations for his sorry state. These may be strategies of putting mind over body and involve those "higher" forms of contemplation such as religion ("what mysterious priest?) or even philosophy ("beauty is truth"). The articulation of the poem itself is in some sense its own cure, as the poet, having not succeeded in mastering the other, struggles through the poetic process to regain mastery over himself.

Keats' ode reorients these common elements in complex and cunning ways, beginning with the *glissement* from the metaphor of the urn-bride to the female figures actually represented on its surface (body). The "unravish'd bride" herself is not as yet ruined by the passage of time, but the first scene of attempted ravishment attests to the permanent precariousness of her position. Brides are "made for ravishing,"and as a quasi-oxymoron ("a bride and not yet a bride"), the figure already embodies the most prominent feature of the poem in its many conjoined contraries and its dramatization of a threshold or liminal state, poised especially between art and life, permanence and change, mortality and eternity.[11] At the same time, the virginal state—untouched, unravished—can, as many have observed, represent an exemption from time, a guarantee every lover seeks that the beauty of the beloved be immortal and unchanging (still "ravishing"?), forever the mysterious (and unobtainable) other who holds him in thrall.

It is this enchanting power, this enduring fascination, finally, that suggests the likeness between the woman and the work of art in the Western tradition that so appeals to the male subject. Both are beautiful, both are exposed to the poet-lover's worshipful gaze of desire and to his consequent craving for possèssion of her secrets—whether imaginatively or tactilely, intellectually or sensually—whether through violent enforcement or more guileful seduction. Her charms ravish him, we might say, and he, in response, is spurred on to take on the role of ravisher.

In representing the urn as a feminine figure, Keats makes the dramatic leap from simile to metaphor, from "as if" to identity, and as he both crosses and blends the two genres of ekphrastic and erotic poetry, he brings (or lets us bring) to the foreground some of the most important (and often unexamined) assumptions and associations of that rhetorical tradition in what these may imply about the female body and its place in masculine (un)consciousness whose subjectivity is the touchstone of the entire codified system. I understand this "system" not only in the light of the familiar Romantic ideology that lies behind Keats' ode but in what founds and perpetuates this system, the major historical antecedent that provides the content of the poem and also the prestigious staging ground for the concerns that the poet addresses. That is, the world of classical antiquity which the Romantics liked to call "Hellas," together with the forms that it bequeathed, as we shall see, of myth, poetry, rite, and philosophy, along with those equivocating relations between art and eros.

First, however, the semantics or ravishment itself. *Ravishment* is, of course, the pivotal term that describes both the acts of forcible seizure, ruination, and rape as well as emotional transports of pleasure and delight. As a term of force, the root meaning of *ravish* as "a taking by violence and carrying off" gives rise to both secondary meanings, that of rape in the technical sense of sexual violation and of the strength of a feeling that is synonymous with rapture and ecstasy. In the first instance, it is assumed that carrying off a woman will logically end in an illicit ravishment. In the second, the pleasurable sensation induced by a state of ravishment complicates the crude and unequivocal, but also etymologically related, term of *rape*. Indeed, the last line of the first stanza ends on the note of "wild ecstasy."

No longer a question but an exclamation, "what wild ecstasy!" is also a more evaluative summary of the entire scene. The phrase suggests passionate sexual intensity through a conventional image of pursuit and flight that either seems to avoid attaching any scandal to the underlying asymmetry between the one who is willing and the one who is not or possibly even presumes a mutual pleasure in the activity (women say "no" when they really mean "yes"). Earlier I pointed out the chiastic relationship between the preceding two lines in the counter rhythms of 6/4 and 4/6. But the last line resolves into an even balance of two phrases of five syllables each, as though equilibrating the relationship between male and female and leaving unclear the referent(s) of "wild ecstasy"—a move designed perhaps to include both men and maidens as well as the poet's subjective judgment of the scene.

"Ecstasy" also reaches back to embrace and qualify the "(un)ravish'd" of the first line, tugging the word away from its literal meaning of forcible seizure into its metaphorical connotation of rapturous transport under a joyous excess of emotion. "Ecstasy" in its Greek etymology of "standing outside oneself" also invokes a more formal notion of stylized ritual experience that endows the scene with a certain air of mystery, while the possibility that the males may be gods contributes to the same effect.

A romantic haze hovers around "ravishment," whose mitigating semantics may perhaps veil the crucial distinctions and be extended even to the case of licit sexuality, to the marital consummation implied in the first line (brides are ravished by bridegrooms). Yet more significantly, *ravishment* is the pivotal term in the interplay between aesthetics and erotics. The positive value of the pleasure produced by the aesthetic object that stirs desire in the beholder is compromised when taken in its sexual sense and its object is the unwilling maiden. The untouched virgin is simultaneously desirable and taboo. Ravishment is, after all, a physical violence directed toward the body of an other, and while the desire may attest to the virility of the pursuer and be heightened because she is a forbidden object, it is also shadowed with the more unfavorable taint of lust that does not accord well with socialized standards of masculinity. Rape, no; ravishment, maybe.

These standards are also those of the critics, and in the interests of what we might call a "politics of reading" it would be worth a detailed essay in its own right to chart the varieties of interpretation that this metaphor of ravishment has engendered. Briefly put, the range of response is remarkable. A few ignore the erotic element almost entirely[12] or explicitly deny its significance (" 'unravish'd' may have been prompted without much conscious thought by his 'maidens loth' and 'mad pursuit' ")[13] or, at the other extreme, may even judge the metaphor a dismal failure ("in retrospect 'unravish'd' will not do, but this is a retrospect created by his [Keats'] evoking of meanings which are not his to manage").[14]

Others, however, read the erotics with differing rhetorical attitudes. Some take for granted the presumption "of the Western reader" that "love and erotic satisfaction are identical"[15] and therefore praise the poet for presenting "the imagery of physical passion" with "relish and sympathy."[16] Others speak more metaphorically: "Like any work of art, the urn is . . . forever full of the wonder of young love and the promise of new and intimate discovery. The sexual metaphor . . . suggests that the vital penetration of the imagination is necessary to bring any object of regard into the fullness of aesthetic apprehension. In this sense, the ode is the expression of Keats's love for the urn; in the same way we are invited to enjoy the ode he composed upon it each time we take it up as readers."[17] Or more bluntly: "The figures on his Grecian Urn resist the explainer-ravisher. . . . We behold, as in a primal scene, the ravishments of truth, the identifying—and over-identifying—mind. . . . As the eye cannot choose but see, the soul cannot but desire truths; and art engages this lust for knowing or merging."[18]

Imagination, aesthetics, truth, knowledge: These are the concepts abstracted from the context of the poem and put at the service of the trope of desire. To these we may add the still more formal concerns of theory: the ode is a "drama of interpretation" and a questioning of language itself (e.g., "the syntax . . . diagrams his mad pursuit of his own maiden loth, the unravished what that might supply the absent meaning of the images he riddles").[19] Or it serves as an allegory of our own reading ("the as yet unravished bride is perhaps another maiden loth, struggling to escape her fate in the desire of the reader. . . ."[20]

Let us leave aside here the implications of the fact that this last critic, like most others, simply assumes that the reader is a male. In the case of the "Grecian Urn," this assumption is more than usually marked, in keeping with the notion (which the poem itself promotes) that the pursuit of meaning (like the quest of the poet himself) is a strictly masculine enterprise of *cherchez la femme*—no matter how the virile temperament of the narrator subject is judged. But to evaluate the force of the sexual metaphor, we should move back to the actual context of the poem and to its ostensible object of desire, which is named specifically as a *Grecian* urn.

Recently, the poem has been treated as an emblem of Keats' "romance with classical antiquity." "The representation of antiquity," as this critic claims, "involves a longing for presence, a desire to resituate sublime fictions of the past within the belated space of modernity." This "romance . . . can never be consummated, it can only ever be a liminal affair." The "fair youth" who cannot "leave/ Thy song," the "bold lover" who can never, never kiss is interpreted as "a virtual allegory of the poet's belatedness." "Has not the poet," the critic asks, "dared to approach the urn in the guise of a bold lover, bold to the extent of appearing a ravisher?" The fair youth cannot "leave" (abandon) his song; he also cannot "leave" it—that is, surround or decorate it with leaves, like the "leaf-fring'd legend" inscribed upon the urn.[21] To make his point about the "anxiety of influence," this critic must insist that "the poem, like the legend that it desires to recuperate, comprises a succession of discontinuous parts: the text is barely redeemable as a whole."[22]

Once the poem is interpreted as an exercise in radical futility, the failure of the poet's "romance with antiquity," it is perhaps inevitable that this critic should also stress the violence implied in the metaphor of ravishment: "It is the poet himself who assumes the role of the aggressive bridegroom-lover, as he tries to coax or indeed to violate the image out of quietness into significant discourse." But in "his recognition of the irreversible alterity of Greece, the inhumanity and (in)difference of the past," the poet finally "takes his revenge on the urn by moralizing it, by forcing it to speak" in highflown banalities.[23]

This negative, even savage, assessment of the poem's ambiguities represents an extreme position even among the ode's most uncompromising ironist readers. The poet's failure to "ravish" the urn in discovering the secrets it withholds seems to turn—ironically (and unwittingly)—into a successful "rape."[24] This reading does violence to the delicate structures of paradox and oxymoron that organize the poem; it does violence to the sexual metaphor itself, as it does to the import of this critic's own insight that highlights the Hellenic provenance of the urn.

It is true, of course, that the poet's unanswered questions as to the factual identity of figures and scenes suggest a distance from the past that cannot be recuperated—at least, not in the terms stated. It is true, too, as many have shown, that the "romance with antiquity" for Keats, as for other Romantic poets, was a complex affair and not only a matter of nostalgia for an age of perfection that had passed.[25] But the fragmentary quality attributed to the poem that denies it any coherent sequence is, in my opinion, misguided with regard to both its poetics and, above all, the Hellenic theme itself. After all, in addition to the two genres I have discussed above, the larger questions that are posed through the "courtship" of the urn's favors— the ambiguous relations between passion, love, art, reality, temporality, permanence, and finally truth and knowledge—can themselves be traced to their antecedents in "Hellas."

What the urn is made to represent, to be sure, is Keats' version of classical antiquity. He knew no Greek, although he several times expressed a desire to learn it. Homer for him was, after all, Chapman's Homer. Most of the information Keats absorbed came not from translations of classical texts available to him, but from popular accounts of antiquity and compendia of ancient art. Yet his self-education was obviously substantial enough to cause his friend Charles Cowden Clarke to observe that "his uncommon familiarity—almost consanguinity with the Greek mythology, I suspect to be traced to his reading."[26] Even so, it is perhaps paradoxical that one of the most traditional commonplaces about Keats is his close relationship to Hellenism. Although this was disputed by some in his own day and by others thereafter, Keats is considered the most "classical," the most "Greek" of all the Romantic poets, an affinity attributed to "a natural temper and sympathy" on his part rather than to a formal, even schoolbook training. What that "Greekness" might mean is also open to dispute, and one critic concludes that it "refers either to his choice of subjects from Greek mythology, fable, and history, or else to the notion that he looked at the world in the spirit of the Greeks."[27] A glance at Keats' choice of subject matter throughout his short but productive career makes the first alternative easy to justify. The second is more difficult to define (and indeed, the problem of definition was a recurrent concern of the late Enlightenment and early Romanticism)—but the very vagueness of the phrase is useful. It suggests an impression of the poet's outlook that corresponds to popular (if at times conflicting) ideas both then and now and confirms my point that the "Ode on a Grecian Urn" is pervaded with the "Grecian spirit," such as it was transmitted through the tradition that Keats inherited and that occupied such a central role in his work.

The urn is a prestigious icon from the past, an emblem of antiquity that condenses on its surface those elements of the classical world that persistently seized Keats' poetic imagination, starting from his fascination with the fine arts (especially sculpture). Each of the panels is a paradigm in miniature of these concerns: the repertory of myth with its gods or men, its typical motif of sexual pursuit and struggle to escape; the pastoral poetic decor with its lover, maiden, and poet; and finally, the priest and sacrifice as representative of pagan religious rite. If, for example, in the "Ode on Indolence" three feminine allegorical personifications pass before the poetic gaze and are compared to figures on an urn, we now confront an actual urn consisting of three scenes. Keats here incorporates the triad of individual female figures in his three panels and at the same time fixes his gaze on one single sculpted object, rhetoricized as feminine and identified as Greek. The result is that both form (urn) and content (scenes on the urn) continually reflect back upon one another. And it means that the poet's relation with this ornamented object is forever mediated through the feminine form that appears in various postures, guises, and disguises in each of these classical scenes as it is modulated throughout the poem.

I therefore want to take up the challenge of classical antiquity that the urn provides as not only informing the search for meaning upon which the poet embarks, but also itself implicitly (and even unconsciously) reproduced in the very strategies of the poem's discourse and the sequence of its narrative. Read as a progressive development of the poet's quest through a series of stanzas/stages that mirrors the spectator's progress from one panel to the next,[28] the ode's "romance with antiquity" links up to a quest for selfhood that is predicated on the "marriage" of the urn to its Grecian identity. The erotic metaphor, in this perspective, is not just a point of departure, an allegorical mode, or a troping of desire. Rather, the status of desire itself and the modes of its enactment itself are deeply implicated, even entwined, with what purports to be an intellectual pursuit in a classical context.

The ode in fact is a compact and especially revealing example of an evolutionary scheme that begins with mythos ("what leaf-fring'd legend") and ends with *logos* (the inscriptional "legend" on the urn and its words of wisdom). It is a process that depends on and is parallel with a concomitant shift in the treatment of the feminine object—from sexual maiden to abstract form ("O Attic shape! Fair attitude!"), from elemental passion to sublimation of instincts, and from "unravish'd bride" (erotically silent) to "friend to man" (oracularly speaking). The sequence in its entirety operates on two analogical planes and may be construed as a progress leading from lust/myth through love/poetry to religious rite/sacrifice until it arrives finally at philosophy and "truth." The personal and erotic are interlocked with the aesthetic (and cognitive/intellectual), and it is this symbiosis between the ekphrastic and courtship modes, this hesitation between the metaphor of urn as woman but also of woman as urn, that reproduces the very system that Keats claims to interrogate.

The fact that in the first stanza the poet insistently presses for more precise information in his repeated questioning of the urn's subject matter only to be met with no reply may suggest in context that academic exactitude is beside the point.[29] At the same time, the bride-urn's refusal to respond signifies that she does not acquiesce in the poet's desire or share the "wild ecstasy" he describes. The questions may not be suitable in the light of the poet's first attempt to understand the message of the urn as a series of mythological details, but the action represented on the urn—"mad pursuit" and "struggle to escape"—may thematically be equally improper. The poet must therefore abandon this line of inquiry together with his unseemly aggressive approach in favor of a tranquil pastoral scene involving a lover who courts more decorously and a piper who sings a higher form of song:

> Heard melodies are sweet, but those unheard
>   Are sweeter; therefore, ye soft pipes, play on;
> Not to the sensual ear, but, more endear'd,
>   Pipe to the spirit ditties of no tone.

This move is both a gain and a loss. The poet enters into the two roles (lover, piper) with which he can fully identify himself and through which he can expand his thoughts over the two stanzas that form the core of the ode. Yet he also loses the spontaneous energy that animated the first stanza and endowed the masculine actors with an active and confident power. The poet's reflections are deeper and more divided as they strike upon the paradox of a passion that, suspended in a sculpted relief on the vase, must forever remain unfulfilled ("bold Lover, never, never, canst thou kiss/ Though winning near the goal") but also equally undiminished ("yet, do not grieve;/ She cannot fade, though thou hast not thy bliss,/ Forever wilt thou love, and she be fair!"). The eternity of this passion ("more happy love! more happy, happy love!/ Forever warm and still to be enjoy'd,/ Forever panting, and forever young") is matched by a perpetual frustration "that leaves a heart high-sorrowful and cloy'd,/ A burning forehead, and a parching tongue."[30] Wild ecstasy has given way to the malady of love, but the poet's feverish crisis also indicates a step taken on the path to a higher wisdom.

In the failure of love's satisfactions, the poet now moves in a new direction with the third scene on the urn, and the heart "high-sorrowful" now succumbs to a greater melancholy in looking upon the depiction of a religious rite:

> Who are these coming to the sacrifice?
> To what green altar, O mysterious priest?

As the third stopping point in the poet's progress, the altar may be the destination to which the sequence was meant to lead, having moved up the scale from physical lust to a higher, more romantic form of love until it reaches the more purely spiritual domain of religion and pious celebration. That shift may also be construed, as some have pointed out, as moving from the personal and erotic to the communal and social and as relinquishing the idea of an uncomplicated happiness to accept the sorrow of sacrifice and the reality of time and loss.[31] On the other hand, considering the shape of the urn, this third scene rejoins the first and is also rhetorically linked to it by the poet's resort to the same device of mystified questioning and by the direct evocation of the first scene in the next stanza ("marble men and maidens").[32]

The essential point, however, is that the victim the priest is leading to the altar is a heifer, we are told, "lowing at the skies" and the poet brings her suddenly and dramatically to life with a vivid description: "And all her silken flanks with garlands drest." Unlike the reluctant figures of the first stanza, this feminine creature no longer struggles to escape, although her lowing might suggest a mild protest at her approaching fate. In marked contrast to the next two stanzas, where the maiden is simply the beautiful goal of the lover's kiss and not clearly locatable in the scene, the female body now appears in its most realized form. Its corporeal presence now bears the burden of the entire submerged feminine sensuousness of the poem in "her silken flanks." Yet as the most richly imagined female emblem in the poem, the heifer is at the same time its most ambiguous sign. The head "lowing to the skies" leads the eye (and thought) upward to spiritual realms, the "silken flanks" downward to the lower part of the body.[33] The sacrifice suggests the renunciation of the erotic in favor of a religious rite, but the image of the heifer, sensuously adorned, brings it back, thrusting it now into the foreground of consciousness. While the piety of ritual would seem furthest removed from the wild ecstasy of the first stanza and sacrificial death utterly antithetical to erotic passion, the heifer victim connects the two in an associative subliminal bond of potential violence to which the feminine body is perpetually subject.

This bond is strengthened by the fact that not only are virgins sacrificed as human victims, but the affinity between virgin and sacrifice is itself expressive of the links between the bloody violation of the sacrificial knife and that of defloration.[34] Poised at the moment when the pious priest leads in the heifer, the scene envisaged does not reveal (and thus represses) the killing act to come and the instrument it requires.[35]

We shall return to this technique of displacement that finds its fullest expression in this, the crucial stanza of the poem, and creates the powerful tension between what the poet wants and what he seems to renounce. On the overt level, however, the scene of sacrifice also belongs to the strategy of courtship and passionate appeal. Each of the poet's moves can therefore be construed as modulating efforts to win the urn, requiring that he abandon violent seizure for more sedate courtship and, next, that he try seduction of a different kind by appealing to her virginal sensibilities in the evocation of religious rite. Yet in so doing the poet seeks more than ever to possess the urn by seeking an entry into the world she represents. And this he does through his imaginative attempt to participate in the rite depicted on the urn and to embody more fully what belongs to her. As he seems to turn away from the urn itself to places outside and beyond its fictive space (the "little town"), he also imbues it with life by insisting on the reality of the figures who now crowd upon its surface and invoking the lived existence they once enjoyed, as though it were possible to cross the boundary that separates the actual from its representation:

> And little town, thy streets for evermore
> Will silent be; and not a soul to tell
> Why thou art desolate, can e'er return.

The poet, as disappointed spectator, was not able to induce the urn to answer his questions and thereby reveal its mysteries—above all, these religious mysteries. Now he sees the silence spread beyond the confines of the urn to an elsewhere that is co-temporal with it and whose sad fate he mourns. The displacement in the mind's eye to this other, more intensely imagined place provokes a desolate sense that the fullness of presence incarnated in the sculpted figures of the worshipers must also imply a corresponding loss. Held now in a suspended eternity on what might have been a morning's outing, they can never now return to dispel the silence and the emptiness of the place they once inhabited.

There are many ways to read these tantalizing lines, which broaden the poet's outlook by introducing new temporal and spatial notions of "whence" and "when." But viewed as the conclusion to his renewed effort at "courtship," we can take these lines as a failure that leads to a fuller and more absolute deflation. It fails, first of all, as we have seen, by the resurgence of the repressed that bodies forth in its most articulated feminine image, and it fails because the sexuality evoked by the "silken flanks" gives way to an emptiness that is displaced from the earlier "wild ecstasy" and the fever of the "burning forehead and parching tongue" to thoughts of the little town "emptied of its folk, this pious morn." It is this absent place (rather than his own condition) that he apostrophizes, and by evoking the little town, the association of death and the maiden in the image of the heifer is displaced finally upon the living poet himself.[36]

The urn cannot be seduced (or ravished) by any of the poet's strategies, and neither sacrificial renunciation nor melancholy appeal will suffice. The final stanza therefore marks the lover's acknowledgment of his defeat and even suggests his reproach of the desired object and a rereading of his own desire. The urn is now addressed abstractly as a thing: "O Attic shape! fair attitude" and as only a "silent form." Yet the poet's ambivalence toward this unresponsive object that he would bring to life is reflected in the marvelously punning line that has excited so much critical comment: "with brede / Of marble men and maidens overwrought." "Brede" (figured design) evokes its homonym "breed" (denied by the "unravish'd" urn); it shifts, by one syllable, from the "bride" herself, and through a partial assonance, it also recalls "breathe" ("all breathing human passion far above"). "Overwrought" is a still more significant word; it suggests there is something excessive now in both erotic and aesthetic spheres—the agitated excitement of the first stanza and the more general (over)elaboration of the vase's decorated surface.

The following line, "with forest branches and trodden weed" replaces the earlier exuberant flourishing of leaves and flowers ("leaf-fring'd legend," "flowery tale," "happy boughs that cannot shed your leaves") with a barer more disenchanted version, while the epithet "trodden" even hints perhaps that the pastoral scene is no longer quite 'virgin territory.'[37]

The rebuke is still more explicit in the poet's exclamation: "Cold Pastoral!" The erotic has reverted to its unfeeling marble substance. Instead, the poet might be thought to "win" the urn by calling her platonically a "friend to man" and to find his reward, if that is what it is, in her chaste message in which the erotic is sublimated into a purer, more unearthly guise: "Beauty is truth, truth beauty."

Yet at the very moment at which the urn is objectified, taxonomized, given its genre (pastoral), the name of its form ("Attic shape"), and its posture as an objet d'art ("fair attitude"),[38] at the very moment when it is viewed now as though at a distance, the description also paradoxically resonates with its tactile, palpable qualities. There is already a certain tension between reality and art in the phrase "silken flanks." "Silken" suggests the smooth surface of a "real" heifer; it also refers to the texture of marble itself whose sensuousness to the touch (and not just to the eye) summons up the idea of the object in its pure physical state.[39] Similarly, "marble men and maidens overwrought" reminds us that the figures are depicted in a high relief that may be best discerned by the probing hand. Above all, however, the reproach to the urn—"Cold Pastoral"—speaks not only of erotic disdain but also of the tactile quality of marble and its perennial coolness to the touch (cf. Endymion 2:265). Thus these apparently renunciatory moves also and at the same time reengage the urn in its paradoxes of real/not real, distance/proximity, eye/hand—and of course eros/art.

It has been observed that, despite the ekphrastic stance, the urn is shown in a more painterly rather than pictorial way.[40] In truth, no pictorial details are given until we reach the "lowing heifer" and the "marble men and maidens." The eye of the beholder is never mentioned. There are no words of vision or of the gaze for any figure on the urn, and the urn, for her part, has no returning look. She is, in fact, all body; she has no face, no eyes; her shape is headless—she is only a torso, a body personified. Yet she becomes a "friend to men," and at the last, she "speaks" to the poet ("thou sayest"). The virginal, by remaining virginal, acquires the power of speech, even more, a prophetic authority—like the Pythia of Delphi through whom the god utters his messages. The aphorism the poet reads is inscribed on the body of the urn, but the fruitful word that issues from the empty space within replies to the outcome of sublimated sexuality, replacing *eros* with *logos*—and "truth" that is at once both oracular and philosophical.

Here is the fitting conclusion to the classical evolutionary model. Myth gives way to philosophy, the body to the spirit, the sensuous to the intellect, and pursuit and struggle are translated into Platonic notions of beauty and truth. Sexuality is contrasted with and finally bested by chastity—under the name of the feminine. The eternally chaste urn-bride, reified into an immortality through her status as an ancient Greek artifact, grants the poet a glimpse of what might endure. She does so by compelling him to acknowledge his own mortality and to contemplate the process of generation—the very vocation rejected by the "unravish'd bride"—that now separates him definitively from her eternal virginity. This contrast between mortal and immortal status, mediated through the philosophical compromise of undying truths, may sum up the Keatsian dilemma between the permanent and the transitory. The contrast between myth and philosophy may represent the tug in Keats between imagination and reason. But these are dilemmas that inform much of Greek culture passed on into the mainstream of Western thought, which both places the highest priority on pure reason and identifies it with sublimated masculinity. The poet, in renouncing aspirations to immortality, also renounces the myth and the maiden. He has been socialized into his tradition by the terms of that tradition: philosophy has in effect almost "made a man" of him.

Yet the effort at violent seizure was the poet's ecstasy, truth and beauty his consolation prize. Does the poem imply that if one puts aside the desire to know the identity of the "leaf-fring'd legend," one also puts aside the desire to know the identity of the feminine other, the figure who remains as mysterious as the story she might tell?

Or is this really the case? Are matters so clear-cut? We have seen that they are not. Mythos itself and its substantive analogy in the poem—ravishment—remain as powerful points of departure and irresistible points of return. Moreover, Keats' poem also tells us that the discrete panels on the urn are not just separable domains of experience but are also mysteriously interrelated. Rape, love, marriage, sacrifice, and death are all implicated in one another through the feminine—whether as maiden, unfading beauty, or lowing heifer. This imaginative nexus partakes of a psychological intensity and a mythic significance that also belongs to this Greek system and cannot so easily be elided through Platonic idealism and its Romantic reinterpretation. In its outline, therefore, the "Ode on a Grecian Urn" faithfully reproduces the dual orientation of its heritage in both manifest and latent content and "saves," as it were, and condones the myth of ravishment—as Greek thought also does—through displacing the self's desire onto alien others ("what men or gods are these?") and by using it for "reading otherwise" in allegory and metaphor.

Yet in conclusion there is another displacement I would briefly like to address, one that entails the reversal of roles from feminine to masculine and puts back the role of violence into the idea of ravishment. Keats' own contradictory attitudes toward sexuality, women, and his own masculinity have been explored in recent criticism with important results, along with the charges of effeminacy leveled against him that had already begun with his own contemporaries.[41] I cannot take up these issues here, except to mention the degree to which, at times, he fully identifies with what he imagines is female sexual experience and especially with the situation of the maiden.[42] This cross-dressing is not surprising perhaps in view of his general principle, as expressed in his famous remarks on the "poetical character," that it "has no character. . . . It has as much delight in conceiving an Iago as an Imogen. What shocks the virtuous philosopher, delights the camelion poet." *(LK* 1.386–387). In his desire to take on different roles Keats seems to have wanted it both ways—to woo a woman and be a woman, to enter and be entered—savoring the freedom of his unlimited imagination and suffering the discomfort of compromising the masculine stance the world expected from him. Poetics and the politics of gender cannot be dissociated. This is even more the case if we consider what happens in the transference to the male of feminine experience. Is this a form of empathy or of appropriation, or is it both? And how are we to interpret the feminine as it passes through the male imagination, especially when it strives to incorporate or even imitate the feminine?

In this light, there is one text I wish to invoke that, true perhaps to the encircling experience of reading the urn, brings me back to the beginning of this essay: the question of an alternate (and suppressed) reading in a classical context—yet, as we shall see, in quite a contrary way.

The poem is the long epic fragment *Hyperion*, which Keats intended to treat, as he said, "in a more naked and Grecian manner" and which ends, unfinished, with the rebirth of the young god Apollo into his divine status through his confrontation with the goddess Mnemosyne, the incarnation of memory. Like the perplexed poet of the ode faced with a silent urn, Apollo also poses his questions to a mute female figure from the mythic past, but unlike the poet, the god "can read a wondrous lesson in [her] silent face." While the poet gets his lesson in the acceptance of his mortality, Apollo declares that "knowledge enormous makes a God of me." And instead of the "legend" the poet reads on the surface of the urn, Apollo's knowledge "pours into the wide hollows of his brain." This is finally the act that "deif[ies]" him. He has become immortal—or rather, perhaps, he has "earned" his immortality. What follows is a description of Apollo's violent rebirth:

> Soon wild commotions shook him, and made flush
> All the immortal fairness of his limbs;
> Most like the struggle at the gate of death;
> Or liker still to one who should take leave
> Of pale immortal death, and with a pang
> As hot as death's is chill, with fierce convulse
> Die into life. . . .
> During the pain Mnemosyne upheld
> Her arms as one who prophesied.—At length

> Apollo shriek'd—and lo! from all his limbs
> Celestial . . .

In this, the published version, Apollo is imagined as a parturient woman, giving birth with the assistance of the midwife Mnemosyne who, as a female, can attend to the physical side of life and yet still retain her spiritual oracular role. Yet, philosophically speaking, an inversion operates here in that it was Socrates who described himself as a midwife to bring men into the condition of self-knowledge so they might give birth to themselves, exactly as Mnemosyne does here and Apollo dramatically acts out. Keats returns the image of the midwife to its proper gender and yet keeps the Platonic idea of self-birth by which the male takes on both roles at the same time— the one who gives birth and the one who is born. But more interesting still is the manuscript reading of this dramatic apotheosis:

> Soon wild commotions shook him, and made flush
> All the immortal fairness of his limbs:
> ~~Roseate and pained as any ravished nymph~~
> Into a hue more roseate than sweet pain
> Gives to a ravish'd nymph ~~new~~ when her warm tears
> Gush luscious with no sob. . . .[43]

This first version compounds the identification with female experience, combining the images of both ravishment and parturition or, more accurately, using the violence and pain inflicted on the "roseate nymph" to describe the process of childbirth that the young Apollo undergoes by and for himself.

"Keats," as one critic remarks, "must have recognized the absurdity of a transformation which couples a nymph, ravished yet clinging to her adolescence, with the struggle at the gate of death," and this is the reason she thinks he omitted these lines. However, the image of the nymph, in her view, is a regression to the idealized world of pastoral that does not accord with the new Apollonian vision of the world.[44] It is true that there is a certain incongruence, as she says, between ravishment and death. At the same time, the nexus of forced sexual consummation, the pangs of giving birth, and images of death are all too consonant with one another—each a transitional state, each a physical experience of ravishment and enforcement visited upon the feminine body and hence often confused or merged with one another. "Wild commotions" and "fierce convulse" of the published version might pertain to female orgasm as well as to childbirth, and the pain of defloration can be equated with the pangs of labor. The continuity between "made flush" and "roseate and pained" associates the reddening blush with both experiences, with the aim of enhancing the oxymoron of death as life. But the graphic language of rape intensifies the sensation of suffering, although its erotic coloring allows the poet the further oxymoron of "sweet" and "pain," represented as a feminine response but interpreted by the male voice as a mingling of pleasure with pain. The ravished Apollo (Keats' favorite Hellenic god) glosses, we might say, the unravished urn. Although striving to soften its traumatic aspects, the ravished Apollo admits to the inherently brutal nature of ravishment so that the image, inverted and displaced, may be transferred from the female body to that of the male. In the ode the poet chooses the alternate reading of "mad pursuit" to give active force to his metaphor of potential rape but returns in the next line to reclaim ravishment as the pleasure of a "wild ecstasy." In *Hyperion*, Keats suppresses the "enormous knowledge" of what he had now fully imagined but did not, at this time of his life, feel free to print.[45]

NOTES

This essay was given as a lecture to the Interdisciplinary Seminar at Cambridge University, Fall 1989. A version was given at the joint seminar of the Classics Departments of Princeton University and the University of Athens on Mount Pelion in the summer of 1989. I dedicate this piece to Phyllis Furley, whose reading of the poem on that occasion ravished the ears of all her listeners. I acknowledge with gratitude the expert counsel of Susan Wolfson, who shared with me her remarkable knowledge of Keats and his work.

The first epigraph is from Keats' marginal comment (sometime in 1819) on a passage in Burton's *Anatomy of Melancholy* discussing the two-sided nature of erotic impulses, as represented by the two Aphrodites (or Venuses). *The Poetical Works and Other Writings of John Keats* (Hampstead Edition), ed. H. Buxton Forman; rev. Maurice Buxton Forman, 8 vols. (New York: Scribners, 1938–39), 5:309.

The second epigraph is from "Dear Reynolds," pp. 72–76, in H. E. Rollins, ed., *The Letters of John Keats*, 2 vols. (Cambridge: Harvard University Press, 1958), 1:261–262. It is dated March 25, 1818; hereafter abbreviated as *LK*.

1. The ode was published in *Lamia, Isabella, The Eve of St. Agnes, and Other Poems* (London: 1820). It is cited and reproduced here from *The Poems of John Keats*, ed. Jack Stillinger (London: Heinemann, 1978):

Ode on a Grecian Urn

1

Thou still unravish'd bride of quietness,
    Thou foster-child of silence and slow time,
Sylvan historian, who canst thus express
    A flowery tale more sweetly than our rhyme:
5   What leaf-fring'd legend haunts about thy shape
       Of deities or mortals, or of both,
         In Tempe or the dales of Arcady?
       What men or gods are these? What maidens loth?
    What mad pursuit? What struggle to escape?
10   What pipes and timbrels? What wild ecstasy?

2

Heard melodies are sweet, but those unheard
    Are sweeter; therefore, ye soft pipes, play on;
Not to the sensual ear, but, more endear'd,
    Pipe to the spirit ditties of no tone:
15   Fair youth, beneath the trees, thou canst not leave
       Thy song, nor ever can those trees be bare;
         Bold lover, never, never canst thou kiss,
       Though winning near the goal—yet, do not grieve;
         She cannot fade, though thou hast not thy bliss,
20   For ever wilt thou love, and she be fair!

3

Ah, happy, happy boughs! that cannot shed
    Your leaves, nor ever bid the spring adieu;
And, happy melodist, unwearied,
    For ever piping songs for ever new;
25   More happy love! more happy, happy love!
       For ever warm and still to be enjoy'd,
         For ever panting, and for ever young;
All breathing human passion far above,
       That leaves a heart high-sorrowful and cloy'd,
30   A burning forehead, and a parching tongue.

4

Who are these coming to the sacrifice?
    To what green altar, O mysterious priest,
Lead'st thou that heifer lowing at the skies,
    And all her silken flanks with garlands drest?
35   What little town by river or sea shore,

Or mountain-built with peaceful citadel,
    Is emptied of this folk, this pious morn?
And, little town, thy streets for evermore
    Will silent be; and not a soul to tell
40   Why thou art desolate, can e'er return.

                        5

O Attic shape! Fair attitude! with brede
    Of marble men and maidens overwrought,
With forest branches and the trodden weed;
    Thou, silent form, dost tease us out of thought
45 As doth eternity: Cold Pastoral!
    When old age shall this generation waste,
    Thou shalt remain, in midst of other woe
Than ours, a friend to man, to whom thou say'st,
    "Beauty is truth, truth beauty,"—that is all
50   Ye know on earth, and all ye need to know.

Ode on a Grecian Urn. Text (including heading) from *1820.* Variants from Brown's transcript (*CB*) and the version published in *Annals of the Fine Arts.*   Heading Ode on] On *Annals*   I still∧]~ , *Annals*   8 men or gods] Gods or Men *Annals*   9 mad pursuit] love? what dance *CB, Annals*   16 can . . . bare] bid the spring adieu *Annals*   18 yet] O *CB, Annals*   22 ever] never *Annals*   34 flanks] sides *CB*   40 e'er] ne'er *altered to e'er CB*   42 maidens∧ overwrought,] ~,~∧ *CB*   47 shalt] wilt *CB, Annals*   48 a] as *CB* "Beauty . . . that]   49 Beauty is Truth,—Truth Beauty,—that *CB;* Beauty is Truth, Truth Beauty.—That *Annals*

2. See, for example, Charles J. Rzepka, *The Self as Mind: Vision and Identity in Wordsworth, Coleridge, and Keats* (Cambridge: Harvard University Press, 1986), p. 187 (with bibliography in n. 22, pp. 274–275).

3. See, for example, Charles I. Patterson, "Passion and Permanence in Keats's 'Ode on a Grecian Urn,' " in Jack Stillinger, ed., *Twentieth-Century Interpretations of Keats's Odes: A Collection of Critical Essays* (Englewood Cliffs, N.J.: Prentice Hall, 1968), p. 50, note 4.

4. The phrase is Stuart M. Sperry's, *Keats the Poet* (Princeton: Princeton University Press, 1973), p. 278.

5. On the ekphrastic mode, see Jean Hagstrum, *The Sister Arts* (Chicago: Chicago University Press, 1958) and also Leo Spitzer, "The 'Ode on a Grecian Urn,' or Content vs. Metagrammar," *Comparative Literature* (1955), 7:206–207.

6. See also Ian Jack, *Keats and the Mirror of Art* (Oxford: Oxford University Press, 1967), p. 214.

7. For antiquity the important texts are Euripides, *Ion,* and the prose fictions of Petronius, Achilles Tatius, and Longus. I discuss this *topos* more fully in "The Poetics of Eros: Art, Nature, and Imitation in Longus' *Daphnis and Chloe,*" in D. Halperin, J. J. Winkler, and F. I. Zeitlin, eds., *Before Sexuality: The Construction of Erotic Experience in the Ancient Greek World,* (Princeton: Princeton University Press, 1990).

8. On the epigrammatic tradition and its transformations in Romantic poetry, see, in addition to Hagstrum, *The Sister Arts*, Geoffrey Hartman, "Wordsworth, Inscriptions, Romantic Nature Poetry," reprinted in *Beyond Formalism* (New Haven: Yale University Press, 1970).

9. See the useful discussion of M. Beaujour, "Some Paradoxes of Description," *Yale French Studies (Towards a Theory of Description)* (1981), 61:27–59.

10. Patterson ("Passion and Permanence," p. 50) conveniently gives the standard line in his discussion of the ode: "The richly ambivalent *unravished bride* . . . conveys, along with the inviolate, undisturbed sanctity of the urn-bride, a hint of disparagement: It is natural for brides to be possessed physically, to be 'ravished,' so to speak; it is unnatural for them not to be."

11. Most critics aim to elucidate these contraries, oxymora, and paradoxes.

12. e.g., Spitzer, "Content vs. Metagrammar."

13. E. C. Pettet, *On the Poetry of Keats* (1957; reprint, Cambridge: Cambridge University Press, 1970), p. 321.

14. John Jones, *John Keats's Dream of Truth* (London: Chatto, 1969), p. 223.

15. See the discussion in John Barnard, *John Keats* (Cambridge: Cambridge University Press, 1987), p. 74.

16. Patterson, "Passion and Permanence," p. 51.

17. Sperry, *Keats*, p. 269.

18. Geoffrey Hartman, "History Writing as an Answerable Style," in *The Fate of Reading and Other Essays* (Chicago: University of Chicago Press, 1975), p. 102.

19. Susan Wolfson, "The Language of Interpretation in Romantic Poetry: 'A Strong Working of the Mind,' " in Arden Reed, ed., *Romanticism and Language* (Ithaca: Cornell University Press, 1984), p. 40.

20. Peter Manning, "Reading Romantic Rhetoric: The 'Ode on a Grecian Urn,' " originally delivered as a talk at the MLA, forthcoming in an abridged version as "Reading and Ravishing: The 'Ode on a Grecian Urn,' " in Walter H. Evert and Jack W. Rohodes, eds., *Approaches to Teaching Keats's Poetry*, (New York: Modern Language Association, 1990).

21. Martin Aske, *Keats and Hellenism* (Cambridge: Cambridge University Press, 1985), p. 116.

22. Aske, *Hellenism*, p. 121.

23. Ibid., pp. 119, 126.

24. See also Sperry, *Keats*, p. 276: "In the jump from proposition to conclusion . . . it is as if the poet, frustrated by the silence of the urn in the face of his human questioning, had forced it to speak beyond the power of its means . . . almost as if he had attempted a kind of rape."

25. See, for example, the discussion in Aske, *Hellenism*; Barnard, *John Keats*; and Tilottama Rajan, *Dark Interpreter: The Discovery of Romanticism* (Ithaca: Cornell University Press, 1980). A standard work is Bernard Stern, *The Rise of Romantic Hellenism in English Literature 1732–1786*

(Menasha, Wis.: George Banta, 1940) and the collection of relevant sources in Timothy Webb, *English Romantic Hellenism 1700–1824* (Totowa, N.J.: Barnes & Noble, 1982).

26. H. E. Rollins, ed., *The Keats Circle: Letters and Papers, 1816–1879*, 2 vols. (Cambridge: Harvard University Press, 1965), 2:147–148. On Keats' education and reading, see, for example, Aske, *Hellenism*, pp. 33–35, and Stephen Larrabee, *English Bards and Grecian Marbles* (New York: Columbia University Press, 1943), p. 209.

27. Larrabee, *English Bards*, pp. 206–207.

28. Other critics also view the ode (like much of Keats' other poetry) as a developmental sequence and as consonant with Keats' own concerns, often expressed in his letters, about problems of identity and the issue of self- or soul-making. See especially Leon Waldoff, *Keats and the Silent Work of the Imagination* (Urbana: University of Illinois Press, 1985), pp. 87–88; Rzepka, *Self as Mind;* and Helen Vendler, *The Odes of John Keats* (Cambridge: Harvard University Press, 1983). We should beware, however, as Jerome McGann warns us, of "transform[ing] the critical illusions of poetry into the worshipped truths of culture . . . having absorbed the ideological commitments which these works themselves first made" ("Romanticism and its Ideologies," *Studies in Romanticism* [1982], 21:593, 592).

29. Spitzer, "Content vs. Metagrammar," 208.

30. Interestingly enough, some have read these lines as signs of sexual *consummation*, e.g., Vendler, *Odes*, p. 129, and Kenneth S. Calhoon, "The Urn and the Lamp: Disinterest and the Aesthetic Object in Mörike and Keats," *Studies in Romanticism* (1987), 26:13.

31. See, for example, Patterson, "Passion and Permanence," p. 52, and Vendler, *Odes*, pp. 142–143. Others also read this stanza as the beginning of a new intellectual stage: Waldoff, *Silent Work*, p. 140; Calhoon, "The Urn and the Lamp," p. 12; and Morris Dickstein, *Keats and His Poetry: A Study in Development* (Chicago: University of Chicago Press, 1971), p. 224.

32. Almost all critics point out the correspondence between the circularity of the poem and the urn, although in differing ways.

33. The original version read "sides" not "flanks." As with the substitution of "mad pursuit," this alteration also intensifies the sensualizing effect.

34. Note the association between heifer and the raped maiden in *Hyperion* 1:24–38:

> I saw an arbor, feast of summer fruits . . .
> Still was more plenty than the fabled horn
> Thrice emptied could pour forth, at banqueting
> For Proserpine return'd to her own fields,
> Where the white heifers low.

Keats knew also of the sacrifice of Iphigenia through Burton's *Anatomy of Melancholy*, 2:3.4.2.4, as he marked the end of the passage where she is mentioned. (*The Poetical Works and Other Writings of John Keats* [Hampstead ed.], ed. H. Buxton Forman; rev. Maurice Buxton Forman, 8 vols. [New York: Scribners, 1938–39].

35. Keats came closer to that moment in his verse epistle "Dear Reynolds," pp. 20–21, in *LK* 1:261–262:

> The sacrifice goes on; the pontiff knife
> Gleams in the sun, the milk-white heifer lows,
> The pipes go shrilly, the libation flows.

Even here he elides the actual sacrifice, stressing the knife instead. The cries of the heifer, again imagined as delicate and feminine ("milk-white"), are displaced onto the sounds of the shrill pipes, and libations flow instead of blood.

In *Endymion* in the great sacrificial scene, the vase, not the heifers, is milk-white (1.153; cf. 1.143), but consider also the description at the shrine:

> Soon the assembly, in a circle rang'd,
> Stood silent round the shrine: each look was chang'd
> To sudden veneration: women meek
> Beckon'd their sons to silence, while each cheek
> Of virgin bloom paled gently for slight fear. (1.185–189)

36. Or, as Vendler, *Odes*, puts it (p. 142); "Keats displaces his fear of death onto the abandoned town, which itself takes on the qualities of the life we shall have vacated when we die."

37. See also Calhoon, "The Urn and the Lamp," p. 12. The "trodden weed" also recalls the virginal "untrodden region of the mind" in the "Ode on Psyche."

38. See, for example, Vendler, *Odes*, p. 146.

39. See now Calhoon, "The Urn and the Lamp," p. 13.

40. Jones, *Dream of Truth*, p. 150.

41. See especially Christopher Ricks, *Keats and Embarrassment* (Oxford: Oxford University Press, 1974), and Barnard, *John Keats*, pp. 46–50, 73–75, 125–129; also Aske, *Hellenism*, pp. 69–72, Rzepka, *Self as Mind*, pp. 18–92, Waldoff, *Silent Work*, passim, Susan Wolfson, " 'Their She Condition': Cross-Dressing and the Politics of Gender in *Don Juan*," *ELH* (1987), 54:602–603 with note 29, and "Feminizing Keats," in Hermione de Alneda, ed., *New Approaches to Keats* (Boston: G. K. Hall, 1990).

42. In addition to his well-known expression, "the Chamber of Maiden-Thought," he speaks metaphorically of his "maidenhood" in various contexts in his letters: "I must endeavor to lose my Maidenhead with respect to money Matters as soon as possible" (to Bailey, 10 June 1817, *LK*, I:147–148 and "I have been on so many finer walks . . . so that not much touch'd with it, though I credit it for all the Surprise I should have felt if it had taken my cockney maidenhead . . ." (to Dilke, 31 July 1819, *LK* 2:135).

Lamia is the best poetic example and especially relevant here in that it pits philosophy against *eros*, also in a classical context. Based on a Greek legend about a young man's love for a beautiful woman who is really an incubus, philosophy is the proof against erotic enchantment ("Do not all charms fly at the mere touch of cold philosophy?", lines 229–230). Moreover, philosophy not only has the power to unmask the illusions of *eros*; it can accomplish metaphorically what the poet lover of the urn cannot: "The sophist's eye like a sharp spear, went through her [Lamia] utterly,/ Keen, cruel, perceant, stinging." In the contest between *eros* and truth, *Lamia* goes even further. Deprived of the phantasm he thought he loved, the lover, Lucius, undergoes a more literal version of the female's fate: at the end, his corpse is discovered "in its marriage robes," having suffered, it is said enigmatically, "a heavy body wound." Lucius has become the victim, the bride, as it were, of ravishment and death. Yet his end is perhaps his punishment, too, for his earlier "passion, cruel grown," that "took on a hue/ Fierce and sanguineous" (2:74–75), the only hint of physical sexual violence in Keats' work, which he seemed to endorse, however, if his friend Woodhouse's quotation is correct ("Women love to be forced to do a thing, by a fine fellow —*such as this . . .*" [*LK* 2:164]).

43. Ernest de Selincourt, ed., *Hyperion: A Facsimile of Keats' Autograph Manuscript* (Oxford: Oxford University Press, 1905).

44. Rajan, *Dark Interpreter*, pp. 162–163.

45. A parting shot. Keats' friend, Benjamin Bailey, reported Keats' reaction to a passage about Apollo in Wordsworth's *The Excursion:* "I remember to have been struck with this passage of *The Excursion* upon the Greek Mythology . . . 'Fancy fetched/ Even from the blazing Chariot of the Sun/ A beardless youth who touched a golden lute,/ *And filled the illuminated groves with ravishment.*' " Keats said: "This description of Apollo should have ended at the 'golden lute,' & have left it to the imagination to complete the picture—how he 'filled the illumined groves.' I think every man of taste will feel the justice of the remark" (Rollins, *Keats Circle*, 2:276).

14

Screen/Memory: Rape and Its Alibis in *Last Year at Marienbad*

LYNN A. HIGGINS

Although it enjoyed a *succès de scandale* when it was released in 1961 and quickly became a cult film, *Last Year at Marienbad*, directed by Alain Resnais from a script by Alain Robbe-Grillet, is still considered a difficult film. This is largely because its story remains stubbornly undecidable: both verbal narration and visual montage are systematically disjointed, preventing the viewer from piecing together any single coherent narrative. Many archetypal stories are suggested—Cinderella, Orpheus and Eurydice, a bargain with death—but none is complete, and each subverts the others. This indeterminacy is quite deliberate: Resnais has said about the film that it is "open to all myths," and one critic has likened the film to a Rorschach blot.[1] What *can* be said is that the film turns around a question: what, if anything, happened last year? The three principal characters are named in the script only as **A** (a woman, played by Delphine Seyrig), **M** (perhaps her husband or her doctor or . . . ?), and another man, **X**. The setting is an elegant spa or perhaps a sanatorium. **X** narrates almost the entire film, during which he attempts to convince **A** that the two of them had a love affair last year and that she had promised to go away with him. **A** does not consent to his amorous advances, however, and she also resists his story, claiming that they have never met before.

In spite of the film's many games and game structures, the critic's task is not simply to decide which of the competing plots "wins," any more than we are asked to judge which of the characters in Akira Kurosawa's *Rashomon* is telling the whole truth. Instead of weighing the relative merits of various understandings of the film, therefore, I want to *add* one significant meaning to those already proposed by *Marienbad*'s many interpreters. Then I will investigate why that interpretation has been overlooked, explained away, or denied by critics and even foreclosed by the film itself. More specifically, I plan to argue that one of the film's potential plots is that of a rape and a cover-up.

In his introduction to the script, Robbe-Grillet calls *Last Year at Marienbad* "the story of a persuasion."[2] Although, Robbe-Grillet, like Resnais, invites critical attention by claiming that the film is open to many readings, his word "persuasion" unobtrusively places a limiting frame around possible meanings. Accordingly, critics have seen the film as a fantasy, a memory (or a false memory), a game, a dream, an instance of hypnotic suggestion, or some combination of these. But what either took place or didn't is always a love affair. *Marienbad* remains a gentle and mannered story, and its hints of violence (aggression, fear, even pistol shots) either remain outside the frame of interpretation altogether or are locked into clichés of rivalry, adultery, and jealousy. While Robbe-Grillet's own statements have been this simplistic, I find the film itself much more subtle and challenging. Perhaps as a result of Robbe-Grillet's invitation, interpretations, while multiple, have not been infinite and in fact remain strictly circumscribed.[3]

Clearly, an approach that favors multiple over univocal reading can still exclude certain meanings, de-authorize some approaches. Moreover, within an ideology of polyvalence, criteria for limiting interpretation can remain invisible: a text can appear open-minded but still retain a frame of assumptions that excludes certain important meanings. When one considers that what might be excluded from *Last Year at Marienbad* is the possibility of rape, polyvalence itself begins to look less like an openness to interpretation than an extremely potent smokescreen. Such limitations on the proliferation of meaning are especially weighty in light of the fact that the same rhetorical maneuvers are used by **X** himself, by the film as a whole, and even beyond it, as I will show.

Viewers sympathetic both to feminism and to postmodernism must thread our way between the Scylla of univocal readings and the Charybdis of infinitely proliferating indeterminacy. The possibility of rape makes it especially urgent that we avoid both positions: a theocracy of a Single Truth is profoundly antidemocratic; on the other hand, real people (nearly always women) get raped, and they do not want to hear that rape is only one among an infinite number of possible meanings of their experience. When critics, a scriptwriter, and a character in a film want to persuade me not to pursue a reading, I can't help noting that the strategies used to keep viewers from seeing rape inside this text are those used outside it as well, which is why *Marienbad* is a particularly useful text for exploring the discursive binds into which anyone who wants to make rape visible is put. Examining the complex knot of images, themes, and narrative maneuvers that give rise to the possibility of rape in *Marienbad*, we will thus eventually be forced to confront the highly problematic intersection of postmodern narrativity with feminist interpretation.

But first, I want to show how *Last Year at Marienbad* dramatizes strategies used in fiction, in criticism, and in life to deny the existence of rape and to create more acceptable, alternative, and unfortunately often more readily believed "alibi" narratives. The film does not tell (indeed, film *cannot* tell, according to Robbe-Grillet and other film theorists) what "really" happened in the past, but it does show *how* discourses about the past are constructed, suppressed, and rewritten. We will also be able to discern how power comes into play in the construction of such discourses.

Is There a Rape in This Text?

The first part of my title—"Screen/Memory"—refers, then, to the split between what occurs on the screen, now, and what may have happened in the past. This is the apparent divergence between fiction and truth, between the verifiable present and the reconstructions of memory. As spectators, we receive the film as a conflict among various versions of something that may or may not have happened "last year." Even this understanding is invalidated by Robbe-Grillet's and other film theorists' observation that filmic images are always experienced as present and that the past can only be evoked through the use of narrative conventions. Such theories shift attention to the present: whatever event exists is happening right now before our eyes.[4] Similarly, except through arbitrary filmic conventions, internal mental or psychological states (such as intent, for example, or consent) cannot be portrayed. Since rape leaves no concrete, intersubjectively verifiable evidence to prevent the construction of multiple and contradictory narratives,[5] rape is a perfect crime for film. The specific difficulties of "proving" that what occurred was a rape, framed within the possibilities and limitations of filmic representation, add up to stage (even invite) the discursive disappearance of a crime.

Rewriting rape as another story is already part of the cultural discourses about rape and even in one of our most potent narratives for interpreting the past: psychoanalysis. In his controversial book, *The Assault on Truth*, Jeffrey Masson documents his discovery of Freud's abandonment, under pressure from the medical establishment and the public, of his "seduction theory" of hysteria.[6] Early in his career (e.g., "On the Aetiology of Hysteria," 1899), Freud expressed his shock at the number of his female patients who remembered, under analysis, having been "seduced" as small children. Over a period of time and working this time from his observations of infantile sexuality, Freud concluded that his patients fantasized these childhood seductions. Freud and the story of psychoanalysis thus provide a prototype of the sort of narrative reworking I am identifying in *Marienbad*. Freud too revised the narrative of rape to call it seduction (romance, "persuasion") and then fantasy. And Masson's book retraces the steps in the erasure of rape from the text of psychoanalysis, with the subsequent emergence of another developmental narrative, the Oedipus complex and the theory of infantile sexuality on which all subsequent psychoanalytic theory depends. Feminists today are examining the narratives of psychoanalysis as themselves a sort of hysterical discourse, seeking the feminine perspective that has been repressed. Its peculiar ambivalence about rape may help explain why feminists have found psychoanalysis useful for reinterpreting the past while at the same time maintaining a careful critical distance from its discourse.

Without the slash, my title refers to another sort of screen: that of the "Screen Memories" of Freud's 1899 essay.[7] In that essay, Freud problematizes the interpretation of memories using the image of a memory screen whereon are projected fragments, metaphors, even inversions of actual events. As in his study of dreams, here too Freud argues that the past may be repressed, censored or transformed by memory and that it is only through reading the metaphorical discourses of the present that we can have access to an event. So while in film theory the screen can represent a memory, in psychoanalysis memory can be a screen or metaphor. In both cases, past experience is accessible only as a metaphor, mediated by rhetorical conventions of representation. So we must contend, here and elsewhere, not with unproblematic representation of (a) rape, but with rape itself *as* representation.

The second part of my title, "Rape and Its Alibis," refers to my contention that *Last Year at Marienbad* can be seen as a rape story narrated by a rapist. According to such a reading, in the absence of any represented rape event, the film as a whole functions like an alibi. I am using the word "alibi" here in its etymological sense: as a claim to have been "elsewhere" at the time a crime was committed. Thus defined, alibi reveals its affinities with the metaphorical screens already mentioned. Like metaphor, alibi substitutes an image or narrative here and now that replaces and in some sense represents another virtual one elsewhere. I prefer the term "alibi," because it suggests that the substitution is *motivated* and that power (for our purposes the unequal distribution of power between men and women) is at issue.

What I am describing, then, is a pervasive phenomenon: in fiction and life, rape is a special kind of crime in relation to narrative. It differs from other violent crimes in the kind of alibis it permits. To prove his innocence, someone suspected of murder must show he himself was elsewhere or that the murder was committed by another person. He can rarely claim that no crime occurred. Murder is not a crime whose noncommission can be narrated. Rape, on the other hand, can be discursively transformed into another kind of story. This is exactly the sort of thing that happens when rape is rewritten retrospectively into "persuasion," "seduction," or even "romance." It happens, for example, in Jean Renoir's *A Day in the Country*, where we witness a rape and its subsequent reinterpretation by the young woman (and the film itself) into a nostalgically remembered romantic moment. A rape defense case can rest on the claim that what occurred was not a rape and so the question is not *who committed* the crime, but *whether a crime occurred at all*. It is thus not surprising that *Rashomon*—that prototypical examination of conflicting testimonies about a past event—is about a rape and not some other kind of crime.

Although no critic has taken seriously the possibility that rape is an issue in *Last Year at Marienbad* (in fact several have wound circuitous paths to avoid it),[8] ironically, Robbe-Grillet's script actually includes a silent and "rather swift and brutal rape scene" (p.

146), which he described elsewhere as "a rape, 'realistic' in the style of Punch and Judy, full of exaggeration and theatricality."[9] This scene was removed by Resnais during filming. Of course that excision makes it easier for me to argue that rape is an issue at all in a film where no actual rape occurs. But such a scene is not needed. Quite to the contrary, it is the way this absence/presence is orchestrated that gives *Marienbad* its postmodern resonance. And it is the absence of any rape *event* in the film that shifts the emphasis to *discursive processes*, furnishing a motive for **X**'s narration. It is in this sense that the entire film can be seen as an alibi: not as reference to a hidden past truth, but as the creation of a story in the present— a story that excludes another story while inscribing it nonetheless. Rape is thus not the "secret" of what happened last year. Rape in *Marienbad* is neither remembered nor forgotten; rather, it is shown. While not described, it is nevertheless inscribed, but rendered incomprehensible because fragmented and scattered about the film in inconsequential details, leaving a hole in the center.[10] We will thus do better to think of rape not as a past event but rather as a present threat, a possibility among others, a condition of meaning.[11]

In *Marienbad*, since **X** himself is present on the screen, narrating the film, it is the crime itself that is "alibi"; that is, it is not where we might expect to find it in the story, but rather it is fragmented, displaced, metaphorized, repressed from the narrative, and ultimately inscribed "elsewhere" (but still, on the screen, in the present). If rape as event has been suppressed from the story, it is present as discourse, dispersed in multiple thematic codes. It is represented symbolically by a series of broken things: a glass, **A**'s shoe, later a balustrade over which **X** escapes detection by **M**. It is present in a theme of penetration (into rooms, into thoughts). It can be seen in the fear **A**'s face reveals, suggesting inner experience and memory; it is present in her repeated and increasingly frantic refrain: "I beg of you, leave me alone." It is there in the various manifestations of **X**'s pursuit and **A**'s flight. It is visible in the actress' self-protective gesture (arm held diagonally across her torso) that becomes her character's signature.

Sexual violence is also implicit in one juxtaposition suggesting that **A** has been shot: scenes of **M** and other men with pistols engaging in a marksmanship game cut to a shot of **A** lying crumpled on the floor of her bedroom. As the camera moves closer, we see her opened eyes and her finger placed coyly on her mouth. The combined effect of the two scenes is that of a violent event transformed into an erotic one. Similarly, violence is suggested by **A**'s startling and otherwise inexplicable scream when, in a series of rapidly inter-cut shots, she drops a glass simultaneously in a bar and in her bedroom as she hears **X** approaching. The fact that the scream seems to come from nowhere and is explained away as a vague "malaise" is especially suggestive in light of Lacan's post-Freudian view that hysterical symptoms reveal themselves as signifiers for repressed traumas by their seemingly excessive or misplaced (displaced) affect. Ironically, it is **X**'s insistence on last year that serves as an alibi: his desperate and repeated efforts to turn the discussion to a "formerly" and an "elsewhere"—last year, perhaps in Frederiksbad or Baden-Salsa—avert attention from the discursive crime that is happening before our eyes: the reinscription of rape as a love story.

Eisenstein's theories of montage, with which New Wave film-makers experimented extensively, can help us understand how these examples work. According to Eisenstein, juxtaposition of images in montage permits dialectical emergence of meanings that are not present in any of the images alone.[12] So where *Marienbad*'s story is most visibly a "persuasion," the juxtaposition of its images (in the rapid montage and multiple jump cuts for which Resnais is famous) creates a space in which fragments of an obscured rape narrative can be glimpsed and, more important, in which we can unmask the narrative procedures whereby rape is reemplotted as persuasion. Thus in *Marienbad*, we are able to see the mechanisms whereby rape is always put elsewhere and made unrepresentable. It is always other to Truth, always alibi.

The most obvious moment of revision occurs when two alterna-tive versions of a scene are juxtaposed. Each of the sequences appar-ently follows from **X**'s ominously symbolic earlier statement: "I penetrate into your bedroom" (p. 110, my translation). In the first version, **X** advances along a corridor toward **A**'s bedroom. Hearing his approach, **A** retreats, seems trapped, makes self-protective ges-tures, is obviously frightened (see figure 1). Then—cut—the scene begins again. In a crescendo of desperation, **X** cries, "No, no, no! (violently:) That's wrong. . . . (calmer:) It wasn't by force" (p. 147).[13] This time, in a series of overexposed and rapidly cut shots, **A** ad-vances to meet **X**, whom she greets with a smile and opens arms (see figure 2). Fear is thus re-imaged as welcome, terror as joy, and rape as romance.

What is extraordinary here is not that the story is revised—that a brutal approach and metaphorical "penetration" into **A**'s room are recast as a warm welcome and that, even in the initial scene, resis-tance is depicted as erotic. (In everyday parlance, no means yes.)

What is extraordinary is that both versions coexist in the finished film. Instead of the product of revision, then, what we are given is the process itself. But of course the second scene does not replace the first. Watching the second version, we, as spectators, remember what happened last time. We are witnesses (accomplices?) to the construction of an alibi.

It can be and has been claimed that the idea of a rape in the film is controverted by the charm and seductiveness of **X**. Okay, maybe rape is a theme here, but does he rape her or does she rather desire or imagine it? The apparent absence of any motive for violence on **X**'s part can be invoked in support of this claim, as can **A**'s hysterical fear or her imputed guilt feelings at desiring or having sex with him. It has even been argued that we see the entire film through **A**'s point of view and that the story occurs inside her head, that the film is her "mindscreen."[14]

This is not a defensible interpretation. While we do occasionally enter into **A**'s visual mindscreen, it is crucial to notice, as critics have failed so far to do, that throughout the film both narrative and visual authority are clearly male. In the scenes described above, **X** is both the narrator and the angle of vision through which we know **A**. As can be seen in figure 1, the view from behind his head conflates the camera, the character, and the spectator, implicating all three in the revision of the scene and the production of an alibi narrative.[15] The film is narrated exclusively by **X**. **A** is an object of vision, of exchange, of desire, and of narrative. In one scene, for instance, **A** lies on her bed idly arranging photographs of herself in a configuration that repeats that of a game in which **X** and **M** engage throughout the film. She thus explicitly displays herself as the token in their game, thereby contributing to her own construction as object of exchange between men. She is never a subject of discourse except to voice her own rejection of the story **X** proposes. In treating her scream as a "malaise" and herself as an invalid, the characters and the film as a whole "invalidate" her subjectivity and her point of view.

A's desire for narration and interpretation—in short, her manner of reading or seeing—are also invalidated. Here again, the film thematizes the issue, inscribing its own viewers. A statue in the castle's garden portraying a man and a woman is an important *mise-en-abyme* (or interior duplication of the text's own functioning) because it is the excuse for a disagreement between **X** and **A** *about interpre-*

FIGURE ONE

FIGURE TWO

tation. Where absence of event highlighted discursive processes, absence of confirmable knowledge (of the statue, of the past) spotlights interpretation. **X** arouses and exploits **A**'s curiosity about the sculpted figures' identities because he knows that the goal of interpretation is to prolong itself: "To say something, I talked about the statue. I told you that . . ." he tells **A**, and then he proceeds to elaborate multiple alternative explanations of the statue. **A** is a different sort of reader; she wants to know whom the stone figures represent, and she makes several suggestions, as reported by **X**: "Then you asked me the names of the characters. I answered that it didn't matter.—You didn't agree with me, and you began giving them names, more or less at random, I think . . . Pyrrhus and Andromache, Helen and Agamemnon. . . . Then I said that it could just as well be you and I . . . (A silence.) Or anyone" (pp. 63–65). **X**'s response to **A**'s desire to know is his modus operandi: "Don't give them any name . . . They could have had so many other adventures," he says.

The statue's importance as an interior duplication or meta-commentary[16] derives from **X**'s desire for multiple meanings, an approach to interpretation that clearly applies to the whole film. Several points are worth noting about this important scene, because they open a distance between the film and the viewer's options for interpretation. First, there is the paradox, central to the film, that **X**'s discourse is double, even duplicitous. He is simultaneously telling **A** what supposedly happened last year and describing their conversation as it happens: his narration is simultaneously descriptive and performative. When **A** laughs, for example, **X** incorporates her laughter into the "remembered" scene, a maneuver that puts his past tense in doubt and suggests he is inventing the past from the materials of the present. It is thus also clear that **X**'s method of interpretation is not innocent. His (and the film's) continued existence and his project of persuasion depend on persevering in his dialogue with **A**. To determine a final meaning for the statue would put an end to the possibility of discussing it (as indeed **M** does, when he intervenes to "identify" the statue) and might even arrest meaning in an interpretation inimical to **X**'s motives and desires. **A**, who has less to lose from definitive interpretation, suggests two possible identities for the couple depicted by the statue: Pyrrhus and Andromache, Helen and Agamemnon. Her suggestions are not chosen "at random," as **X** testifies; each of the couples is a case of abduction and rape.

In addition to being a characteristic of the text as a whole, resistance to definitive interpretation is therefore also one of **X**'s most powerful strategies. This is where the text's polyvalence ceases to be neutral and starts to look like a cover-up. **X** doesn't care what the interpretations are, as long as they are multiple. He has much to gain from a method of reading that prefers (almost) infinite semiosis. Infinite minus one. Moreover, critics have colluded with **X** by assuming him to be a reliable narrator. Where *Marienbad* shows us how rape can be discursively deconstructed by the very character who has the most to gain from such a strategy and where the woman's perspective is systematically invalidated is where postmodern narrativity threatens to become problematic, even antithetical to feminist interpretation. *Last Year at Marienbad* constructs an incompatibility between feminine subjectivity and the plural text.[17]

Without sacrificing the openness and polyvalence of the text, we might begin to work our way out of that impasse by remembering to ask: plural for whom? and against whom? What has been consistently overlooked in discussions of *Marienbad* and what makes the film extremely useful for exploration of this problem is the fact that here interpretation is clearly gender-coded. **X**'s approach, the deconstructive one, the one the text itself prefers, is both positive and masculine. It takes the initiative in presenting itself as seductive and desirable. **A**'s approach, on the other hand, is both retrograde and coded feminine; it is what needs to be mastered or overcome in order to accede to modernity. Borrowing Roland Barthes' terminology, we could say that **X** sees the statue as a "writerly text," **A** sees it as a "readerly text."[18] In a conflict between two kinds of readers, what is important is not that **A** is a bad reader, but that bad reading is coded feminine. The woman's reading is thus easily invalidated. Rape, here, constitutes a kind of limit to postmodern interpretation, making it impossible for the feminist critic to say that these gender implications are coincidental.

Moreover, in an epistemological conflict about how the past can be known and indeed *what* can be known about it, the dispute between **A** and **X** about interpretive strategies must also be seen as a conflict between the text and its viewer. *Marienbad* thematizes its viewer via *mise-en-abyme* and filmic suture so that it becomes a thoroughly self-reflecting text. Thus questions of **X**'s authority are also questions of the film's (and Robbe-Grillet's and the New Novel's and New Wave's) relationship to its public. Critical arguments that erase rape from the film are exactly those used to invalidate real women's accounts of rape: It could have been many other things. Are you *sure?* Are you sure you're sure?[19] Rape becomes an interpretive "malaise": cared for by the authority of her doctor/husband, **A**, along with her experience and her point of view, are, as noted above, "invalidated."[20] **A**'s own lack of authority cancels out the possibility and invalidates the desire for definitive knowledge. The viewer is caught in a contradictory identification, thematically with **A** in her frustrated desire for understanding, but filmically with **X** as we see through his eyes and narrative. Viewers sympathetic both to feminist analysis and to postmodernism find themselves in a double bind. To read like (with) **X** is to collude with him in erasing the possibility of rape from the film. To read with (like) **A** is to reject postmodern textuality and interpretation.

Ultimately what is at stake for **X** and **A**, for the film as a whole, for (feminist) criticism, and even in rape cases outside the cinema is narrative authority and how it is engendered.[21] Discussions of narrative authority have rarely taken gender into account and just as often have bracketed questions of power. To take one of the most productive recent examples, Ross Chambers' *Story and Situation: Narrative Seduction and the Power of Fiction* describes "narrative seduction" as that which keeps the reader or viewer interested. In terms strikingly similar to Robbe-Grillet's, Chambers proposes that a text's seductive power

> is definable as the power to achieve authority and to produce involvement (the authority of the storyteller, the involvement of the narratee) within a situation from which power is itself absent. If such power can be called the power of seduction, it is because seduction is, by definition, a phenomenon of persuasion: it cannot rely on force or institutional authority ("power"), for it is, precisely, a means of achieving mastery in the absence of such means of control.[22]

The alternative to seduction is thus boredom: loss of interest on the part of the reader/viewer and loss of authority on the part of the narrative.

But it would seem somewhat dubious to posit, even hypothetically, an absence of power; neither in fiction nor in life do texts and narrators exist in a power vacuum (and power differences between the sexes is a form of "institutional authority"). Rather, it seems to me that the other mentioned alternative has to be reckoned with: authority ("persuasion," seduction) is an alternative to its lack, to be sure, but given the existence of power differences, failure of seduction can also lead to force. It is interesting that in a discussion of persuasion, authority, and seduction in and of narrative, Chambers never examines rape as a conceptual category. Again, we must ask: persuasion (seduction) for whom? The two polar alternatives to seduction are failure (impotence?), as Chambers argues, and also rape. And so like **X**, the filmmaker has to deny (or excise) the possibility of force—"No, no, no. That's wrong. It wasn't by force."—in order to maintain the film's authority as an interesting text.

But at another level, Chambers' approach is perfectly correct. The more a text has only itself to rely on (in Chambers' terminology, "narrational authority" and not simply the "narrative authority" of conveying information), in other words, the more it depends on fascination, seduction, and persuasion, the more rape is impossible to represent. Or the more rape comes itself to represent a failure of narrative authority and persuasion and seduction. (I will return shortly to the use of rape as metaphor.) Narrative and other seductions depend on the distancing of boredom, but *also* on the distancing of force. My essay has thus been about the consequences *and the necessity* of that absence of rape from narratives like *Last Year at Marienbad.* I am now compelled to argue that a text (or film) that wants to remain self-conscious and self-reflecting *cannot* portray rape; it *must* speak in terms of seduction and persuasion *because it is a text.* Such texts (and culture itself to the extent that culture is composed of self-conscious narratives) depend on denying or repressing any awareness of rape. This is why feminism must take postmodern textual self-awareness into account. As a first step, we must turn our attention from the text's power to represent to its power to *un*-represent. In this light, **A**'s desire for definitive interpretation and **X**'s multiplication of interpretations are ironic. Neither character favors truly polyvalent interpretation: **A** proposes only two identities for the statue (Pyrrhus and Andromache, Helen and Agamemnon), but **X** privileges a single reading *by excluding it.* ("No, no, no. That's wrong. It wasn't by force.")

If, as Craig Owens claims, postmodernism is primarily to be understood as "a crisis of cultural authority" and a loss of seductiveness and mastery,[23] *Marienbad*'s self-referential aspects and its deconstruction of all claims to authority foreground the postmodern character of the film. If we add to this list of metaphorical losses a loss of potency—both sexual and narrative—we can begin to understand why both rape and its absence become necessary elements in the struggle. We can then see another of *Marienbad*'s plots as being postmodernism's attempt to (re)establish authority (prove its masculinity). **X** wants to prove both that he *could* have raped **A** and that he *didn't,* just as someone who has an alibi could have committed a crime but didn't. Similarly, postmodern texts want to foreground not an *inability* but a *refusal* to master: "The story of a persuasion."

Postmodernism is also characterized by what I called hysterical discourse above, after Freud's explanation, in his analysis of Dora, that one of the defining characteristics of hysteria is "an inability to tell coherent stories" because of what has been repressed.[24] It is not by reducing such stories to readability, however, but only through reading their very incoherence that their particular rhetoric can be recognized. If, as some have claimed, *Last Year at Marienbad* is one of the earliest important examples of postmodernist fiction,[25] it is also another instance in which culture (in this case postmodern culture) is founded on the repression and rewriting of an act of rape.[26]

As I have just demonstrated, rape can easily become a floating signifier, available for the elaboration of metaphor. *Marienbad* has been seen through many metaphors: as the story of the film's seduction of its viewers, of the specificity of filmic narrative, of voice and its mastery over the image, even of the relationship between filmmaker and scenarist. In my turn, I am reading the film as a drama of narrative mastery and control, of postmodernism's mastery over modernism, and (as I am showing elsewhere) of France's identity crisis over Algerian independence. In all these scenarios, *Marienbad* is the story of a threatened *failure* of (narrative) authority and how easily it might become force. This accounts perhaps for an impression frequently held by readers/viewers of postmodernism that we are being assaulted by the text.

It is also possible that the ease with which such metaphorization occurs is one of the causes and consequences of the phenomenon I am describing. One of the most foolproof ways of hiding something, after all, is to call it something else, so that while rape metaphors can be used to illuminate *both* terms compared (as I hope I am doing here), if the metaphor is automatically and from the start a catachresis—that is, if rape is never seen as literal at all—rape metaphors themselves can serve, paradoxically, to cover up rape. Critics, busily constructing alibis along with the film itself, can thus all too easily buy into the claim that real meaning is elsewhere. In other words, in life, fiction, or criticism, rape can be rewritten by those who have the narrative authority to do so.

I want to conclude by asking whether, by ostentatiously pointing to what is absent and by its visible revisions, *Marienbad* can be called a liberating film, even a feminist film. I don't think so. The film's positioning of the spectator is consistently complicitous with **X**'s narrative perspective. The questions we are invited to ask about it resemble but fall short of moving beyond the ways we are encouraged to respond to rape in life: Is she leading him on? Was her door open? Is she denying a sexual encounter by calling it rape? If there was an event last year, all the film itself proposes was an encounter that **A** refuses to remember. In short, the film repeats the myths and representations of rape in nonliterary discourse, but does not demystify them. In fact, it offers the spectator the same old alibis.

The task of demystification is still left to the feminist viewer, who must first identify rape as rape (not simply and automatically as persuasion or seduction or metaphor), second begin to untangle the discourses that surround it and contribute to its disappearance, and third show how an interpretive strategy that valorizes multiple readings itself needs to be interpreted. We cannot claim that *Marienbad* is a rape story to the exclusion of other stories, but only how the other stories serve to cover up rape by rewriting it. And perhaps show how easy it is to hide rape, and thus how dangerous.

So then what of the dilemma of the critic caught between the postmodern text and feminist interpretation? Are the two, as Alice Jardine worries, oxymoronic?[27] If so and if keeping rape literal is our feminist goal (as it must be in nonliterary life), we have to be anti-postmodern. If, on the other hand, it is in our feminist interest (and I think it is) to understand how rape is metaphorized, becomes discourse, even a(nother) founding event of (postmodern) culture, then there are many serious questions we can ask of texts like *Marienbad*. We need to notice, for example, how mastery and authority are so often coded masculine and what is to be mastered (through authority, seduction, or violence) as feminine. We can imagine ways in which they could be coded feminine or not gender-coded at all. We might examine in what ways limiting frames can be imposed and meanings can be excluded even in texts acknowledged to be polyvalent or indeterminate. And if it is in our interest to know how rape can be un-represented, either through denying its existence entirely or through causing it itself to represent something else, then we had better take an interest in postmodern textuality.

NOTES

I am grateful to Carla Freccero, Marianne Hirsch, Lawrence Kritzman, Albert LaValley, Amy Lawrence, Neal Oxenhandler, Brenda Silver, and Steven Ungar, who read versions of this essay and offered valuable suggestions.

1. Andrew Sarris, *Interviews with Film Directors* (New York: Avon, 1967), p. 436; John J. Michalczyk, *The French Literary Filmmakers* (Philadelphia: Art Alliance Press, 1980), p. 111.

2. Alain Robbe-Grillet, *Last Year at Marienbad,* trans. Richard Howard (New York: Grove Press, 1962), p. 10. All quotations here are from the English translation, unless otherwise noted. The script of *L'Année dernière à Marienbad* was originally published as a *"ciné-roman"* (Paris: Editions de Minuit, 1961).

3. A few examples will give a sense of the astonishing variety of interpretations. Bruce Morrissette, *Les Romans de Robbe-Grillet* (Paris: Editions de Minuit, 1963), suggests that the principles of hypnosis provide one way to explain the characters' behavior. François Weyergans describes **A**'s internal conflict between the pleasure principle and the reality principle: "Dans le dédale," *Cahiers du Cinéma* 21(123):22–28. Claude Ollier, in "Ce Soir à Marienbad," *Nouvelle Revue Française* (October and November 1961), nos. 106/107, pp. 711–719 and 906–912, analyzes a similar struggle between reason (in the person of **M**) and irrational obsession (**X**). James Monaco decides that ultimately the film is "about storytelling. It is **X**'s job to convince, **A**'s job to resist: the primal relationship between storyteller and audience": *Alain Resnais: The Role of Imagination* (New York: Oxford University Press, 1978). Jean-Edern Hallier sees the film as a story about the desire for immortality, with **M** playing the role of Death: "Toute une vie à Marienbad," *Tel Quel* (1961), 7:49–52. These and other critics generally concede that the film invites multiple interpretations, of which their reading is only one. An exception is John Ward's *Alain Resnais, or the Theme of Time* (Garden City, N.Y.: Doubleday, 1968). Ward declares that "what exactly took place the year before" is that "**M** kills **A** and **X** is left alone to mourn" (p. 39).

4. Robbe-Grillet, *For A New Novel: Essays on Fiction,* trans. Richard Howard (New York: Grove Press, 1965), pp. 152–153. See also Roland Barthes, *Image, Music, Text,* trans. Stephen Heath (New York: Hill & Wang, 1977), pp. 15–51.

5. For a fuller discussion of this problem, see Frances Ferguson, "Rape and the Rise of the Novel," *Representations* (Fall 1987), 20: 88–112.

6. Jeffrey Moussaieff Masson, *The Assault on Truth: Freud's Suppression of the Seduction Theory* (New York: Farrar, Strauss & Giroux, 1984).

7. Sigmund Freud, "Screen Memories," *Collected Papers,* ed. James Strachey (London: Hogarth Press, 1950), 5:47–69.

8. For example, Allen Thiher, *The Cinematic Muse: Critical Studies in the History of French Cinema* (Columbia: University of Missouri Press, 1979), p. 174, identifies **A**'s room as "the locus upon which the narrative quest is centered, for it is here that the *full range* [my emphasis] of hypotheses are developed, ranging from rejection to death to joyous acceptance." Ward claims that **X** imagines several possible endings, including suicide, accident, and rape (p. 50). On the other hand, in his introduction to

the screenplay Robbe-Grillet speaks of "fantasies of tragedy in the heroine's mind: rape, murder, suicide . . ." (p. 11). In these and other examples, rape is mentioned briefly, if at all, and then never resurfaces. A second kind of circumvention is more interesting: rape appears just as fleetingly, but already metaphorized from the start. Gaston Bounoure's *Alain Resnaise* (Paris: Seghers, 1974), for example, cites Robbe-Grillet as saying that **X** introduces the past by force into a closed world ("quant au passé que le héros introduit de force dans ce monde clos. . . ," p. 75). And Thiher's entire analysis is based on an unexamined metaphor that would see the film as "a seduction . . . not only of the unknown woman whom the narrator pursues throughout the film, but also of our vision" (p. 166). Finally, Robbe-Grillet is reported to have said, enigmatically, "I would describe my relationship with Resnais as the rape of Resnais by Robbe-Grillet": Melinda Camber Porter, *Through Parisian Eyes: Reflections on Contemporary French Arts and Culture* (New York: Oxford University Press, 1986), p. 83.

9. André Gardies, *Alain Robbe-Grillet* (Paris: Seghers, 1972), p. 118 (my translation). Note that Robbe-Grillet's comment is already a first rewriting —of a "brutal" rape into a comical one.

10. Robbe-Grillet is well known for generating ambiguities by means of a gap in the story. For example, his 1955 novel *Le Voyeur* (Paris: Editions de Minuit) revolves around a brief lapse in the protagonist's memory and his fear that he has committed or will be accused of the rape and murder of a young girl. For an interesting discussion of alibis in *Le Voyeur*, see Jeffrey Kittay, "Alibi: On Handwriting, Rewriting and Writing Rhythms and *Le Voyeur*," *Romanic Review* (1980), 71(1): 57–74. About *Marienbad* Robbe-Grillet said in an interview: "What happened—if something did happen once upon a time—constantly produces sort of a gap in the story. . . . Everything, up to the 'hole,' is told—then told again after the hole—and we try to reconcile the two edges in order to make this annoying emptiness disappear. But what happens is the exact opposite: it's the emptiness that overruns, that fills everything" (Sarris, *Interviews*, p. 451).

11. Is it necessary to point out that this is how every woman is socially positioned? For a discussion of how rapability defines women, see Dianne Herman, "The Rape Culture," in Jo Freeman, ed., *Women: A Feminist Perspective* pp. 20–38 (Palo Alto: Mayfield, 1984), and Catherine A. MacKinnon, "Feminism, Marxism, Method, and the State: Toward Feminist Jurisprudence," *Signs: Journal of Women in Culture and Society* (1983), 8(4):635–658.

12. Sergei Eisenstein, *Film Form: Essays in Film Theory* (New York: Harcourt Brace Jovanovich, 1949), p. 49.

13. Earlier in the film, **X** calmly explains, ". . . finally . . . I took you, half by force," and then, "Oh no . . . probably it wasn't by force. [. . .] But you're the only one who knows that" (script, pp. 115–116).

14. The term is from Bruce Kawin, *Mindscreen: Bergman, Godard, and First-Person Film* (Princeton: Princeton University Press, 1978), p. 82.

15. In fact, the scene illustrates perfectly the way the cinema constructs

the viewer as male, as theorized by Laura Mulvey, "Visual Pleasure and Narrative Cinema," *Screen* (Autumn 1975), 16(3) and E. Ann Kaplan, "Is the Gaze Male?" in *Women and Film: Both Sides of the Camera,* pp. 23–35). (New York: Methuen, 1983).

16. Resnais has called the film a "documentary about a statue" (Sarris, *Interviews,* p. 451).

17. This is, of course, a problem that is frequently discussed by feminist critics: I am not the first to point out how feminism's construction of the female subject conflicts with postmodern deconstructions of the subject. See, for example, Alice Jardine, *Gynesis: Configurations of Woman and Modernity* (Ithaca: Cornell University Press, 1985). Craig Owens' view that feminism is part of postmodernism is helpful, as is his description of feminism's challenges to the reassuring stability of (male) mastery of meaning. See his "The Discourse of Others: Feminists and Postmodernism," in Hal Foster, ed., *The Anti-Aesthetic: Essays on Postmodern Culture,* pp. 57–82 (Port Townsend, Wash.: Bay Press, 1983).

18. Roland Barthes, *S/Z* (Paris: Editions du Seuil, 1970).

19. Ferguson, p. 89.

20. Think of Charlotte Perkins Gilman, *The Yellow Wallpaper* (Old Westbury, N.Y.: Feminist Press, 1973).

21. I use the term "engendered" to mean both "generated" and "given gendered meanings," following Teresa de Lauretis, *Technologies of Gender: Essays on Theory, Film, and Fiction* (Bloomington: Indiana University Press, 1987).

22. Ross Chambers, *Story and Situation: Narrative Seduction and the Power of Fiction* (Minneapolis: University of Minnesota Press, 1984), p. 212.

23. Owens, "The Discourse of Others," p. 57 and *passim.*

24. The specific narrative difficulties are relevant as well: in hysteria "communications run dry, leaving gaps unfilled." Sigmund Freud, *Dora: An Analysis of a Case of Hysteria* (New York: MacMillan, 1963), pp. 30–31. See also note 10 above.

25. Thiher, *The Cinematic Muse,* p. 170; Kawin, *Mindscreen,* p. 198.

26. Scholars in a wide variety of fields have explored other instances of founding rapes. For example, much feminist analysis has been devoted to rereading the rape of Lucrece as the founding event of the Roman Republic. See, for example: Coppélia Kahn, "Lucrece: The Sexual Politics of Subjectivity," in this volume; Nancy J. Vickers, "This Heraldry in Lucrece's Face," in Susan Rubin Suleiman, ed. *The Female Body in Western Culture: Contemporary Perspectives,* pp. 209–222 (1985; reprint, Cambridge: Harvard University Press, 1986); and Stephanie H. Jed, *Chaste Thinking: The Rape of Lucretia and the Birth of Humanism* (Bloomington: Indiana University Press, 1989).

27. Jardine, *Gynesis,* p. 22.

NOTES ON THE CONTRIBUTORS

CARLA FRECCERO is a leftist activist involved primarily in antiracist and feminist struggles. She is Associate Professor in the Department of French and Italian and in the Comparative Literature Program at Dartmouth College. She has published a book, *Father Figures: Genealogy and Narrative Structure in Rabelais* (forthcoming, Cornell University Press), as well as articles on early modern texts, feminist theory and contemporary cultural studies. She is currently completing a monograph on Marguerite de Navarre, *Subject to Representation: Contemporary Cultural Theory and Marguerite de Navarre*.

KATHRYN GRAVDAL is the author of *Vilain and Courtois: Transgressive Parody in French Literature of the 12th and 13th Centuries* (University of Nebraska Press, 1989) and *Ravishing Maidens: Writing Rape in Medieval French Literature and Law* (University of Pennsylvania Press, forthcoming 1991). She is Assistant Professor of French at Columbia University.

LYNN A. HIGGINS is Associate Professor of French and Comparative Literature at Dartmouth College. She specializes in literary criticism and theory and in postwar French novel and cinema. In addition to articles on Roland Barthes, Marguerite Duras, Jean-Luc Godard, Alain Robbe-Grillet, Christiane Rochefort, Claude Simon, Monique Wittig and others, she is the author of *Parables of Theory: Jean Ricardou's*

Metafiction (1984) and is completing a study of historical dimensions in the writings and films of the New Novel and New Wave Filmmakers.

NANCY A. JONES is Lecturer in Romance Languages and Literatures at Harvard University. She has taught at Baruch College-CUNY and Hobart and William Smith Colleges where she codirected the Women's Studies Program. She is currently at work on studies of the female voice in medieval song and the theme of embroidery in medieval French romance.

PATRICIA KLINDIENST JOPLIN is Assistant Professor of English at Yale University. Her study of Virginia Woolf, *The Mind's Natural Jungle: Re-Reading Virginia Woolf,* forthcoming. She is currently working on a study of shifting representations of rape in classical, biblical, and modern literature, the visual arts, and law, entitled *The Iconography of Rape.*

EILEEN JULIEN is from New Orleans, Louisiana, and teaches French, African, and Caribbean literatures at Boston University. She has been a Fellow at the Bunting Institute of Radcliffe College (1985–87) and has served as President of the African Literature Association (1990–91). She writes primarily on sub-Saharan literature of French expression and is the author of *Unknotting the Thread: Oral Narrative Genres and the Making of African Novels* (Indiana University Press, forthcoming).

COPPÉLIA KAHN is Professor of English at Brown University and the author of *Man's Estate: Masculine Identity in Shakespeare* (University of California Press, 1981). She has also written on Shakespeare, psychoanalysis, and feminist theory, and has coedited several anthologies, most recently *Making a Difference: Feminist Literary Criticism* (Methuen, 1985). She is currently writing a book on the sexual politics of Shakespeare's Roman works.

NELLIE Y. MCKAY is Professor of American and Afro-American Literature at the University of Wisconsin, Madison. Her publications include *Jean Toomer, Artist: A Study of His Literary Life and Work,* and an edited collection, *Critical Essays on Toni Morrison.* She is at work on a study of Afro-American women's autobiographies.

MARTA PEIXOTO is Associate Professor of Portuguese at Yale University. She has published several articles on nineteenth and twentieth-century Brazilian literature, in particular on gender and poetry, and a book on the contemporary poet Joao Cabral de Melo Neto, *Poesia com Coisas* (Rio: Perspectiva, 1983). She is now completing a book titled *Passionate Fiction: Gender, Narrative, and Violence in Clarice Lispector.*

ELLEN ROONEY is Associate Professor of English at Brown University and the author of *Seductive Reasoning: Pluralism as the Problematic of Contemporary Literary Theory* (Cornell University Press, 1989). She is currently at work on *Criticism and the Subject of Sexual Violence,* a study of representations of subjectivity in scenes of sexual violence.

BRENDA R. SILVER is Professor of English at Dartmouth College. She is the author of *Virginia Woolf's Reading Notebooks* (Princeton University Press, 1983), as well as essays on Woolf, Charlotte Brontë, John Le Carré, anger and authority, and the ideological implications of editing and critical reception. She is currently writing a book on feminist polemic and preparing a critical edition of Woolf's *Between the Acts.*

JOHN J. WINKLER (1943–1990) was Professor of Classics at Stanford University. He authored *Auctor and Actor: A Narratological Reading of Apuleius' Golden Ass* (University of California Press, 1985) and *Constraints of Desire: The Anthropology of Sex and Gender in Ancient Greece* (Routledge, 1989). He coedited *Nothing to Do with Dionysos? Athenian Drama in its Social Context* (Princeton University Press, 1990) and *Before Sexuality: The Construction of Erotic Desire in the Ancient Greek World* (Princeton University Press, 1990). His edition of *Ancient Greek Novels: The Fragments* (co-edited with Susan Stephens) and his Martin Lectures, *Rehearsals of Manhood,* are forthcoming from Princeton in 1991.

SUSAN WINNETT is Assistant Professor of English and Comparative Literature at Columbia University. She has completed a book on the novel of manners, *Terrible Sociability: The Text of Manners from Laclos to James,* and has published articles on gender and narrative theory.

FROMA I. ZEITLIN is Professor of Classics at Princeton University. She is the author of *Under the Sign of the Shield: Semiotics and*

Aeschylus' Seven Against Thebes (Rome: Ateneo, 1982). She is coeditor of *Nothing to Do with Dionysos? Athenian Drama in its Social Context* (Princeton University Press, 1990) and of *Before Sexuality: The Construction of the Erotic Desire in the Ancient Greek World* (Princeton University Press, 1990). She has edited *Mortals and Immortals: Selected Papers of Jean-Pierre Vernant* (forthcoming, Princeton), and additionally has written numerous articles on Greek myth and literature, among which is "Configurations of Rape in Greek Myth," in *Rape,* eds. S. Tomaselli and R. Porter (Blackwells, 1986).

GENDER AND CULTURE

A SERIES OF COLUMBIA UNIVERSITY PRESS

Edited by Carolyn C. Heilbrun and Nancy K. Miller